KNOW YOUR BIBLE

Commentary for our times on the Hebrew Prophets and Holy Writings (NaKh)

by

Rabbi Avraham Greenbaum

Edited by Nachum Shaw

Promised Land

JERUSALEM   LONDON   NEW YORK

For further information:

Promised Land Publishers

Apt. 8, 5 Gimmel Alroyi St.

Jerusalem 9210808

ISRAEL

or

Promised Land Publishers

8 Woodville Road

London NW11 9TN

ENGLAND

or

Promised Land Publishers

67 Wood Hollow Lane

New Rochelle

NY 10804

USA

Email: promisedland920@gmail.com

www.promisedlandpublishers.com

Volume Three

PROVERBS

JOB

FIVE SCROLLS

DANIEL

EZRA

NEHEMIAH

CHRONICLES

The first three books of Ketuvim (The Holy Writings), Psalms*, Proverbs and Job, poetic in form, are collectively known as Sifrei Emet (Books of Truth), an acronym of the initials of Job, Proverbs and Psalms (Emet = Aleph - Mem - Tav), in Hebrew איוב, משלי, תהלים– perfectly fitting for these works of such sublime and profound wisdom.

The Five Megillot (Scrolls) are in the order in which they are traditionally read over the course of the year, beginning with Song of Songs at Pesach – the Book of Ruth on Shavuot – Lamentations on the 9th of Av (the anniversary of the destruction of both Temples) – Ecclesiastes on Succot – and the Scroll of Esther on Purim.

The remaining books in Ketuvim - Daniel, Ezra-Nehemiah and Chronicles share a number of characteristics:

- Daniel and Ezra-Nehemiah are the only books in NaKh with significant portions in Aramaic.

- They also describe relatively recent events - the Babylonian captivity and the subsequent restoration of Zion.

- "Ezra wrote the Book of Chronicles with the help of the prophets Haggai, Zechariah and Malachi ..."Rashi.

*Please note that the Book of Psalms is not included in *Know Your Bible*.

CONTENTS

משלי

PROVERBS

CHAPTER 1

V 1: "Proverbs of Solomon, son of David king of Israel...." Unlike the prophets of Israel, King Solomon needs no biographical introduction, since the outer details of his life and times are described in full in I Kings chs 1-11 and II Chronicles chs 1-9. It is the inner soul and the unfathomable wisdom of Solomon that are revealed in his three works, contained in the Ketuvim or holy "writings" - Song of Songs, which he wrote in his youth, Proverbs (**Mishley**), which dates from his maturity, and Kohelet (Ecclesiastes), which he composed in his old age. The initial **Mem** of the opening word of **Mishley** is written large in the Hebrew text to indicate that Solomon fasted 40 days in order to attain Torah wisdom like Moses, who fasted 40 days and nights (Yalkut Shimoni).

The English word "proverb" is an attempt to render the Hebrew word **mashal**. The word "proverb" suggests a succinct, pithy and memorable saying that teaches deep wisdom. Much of **Mishley** is indeed made up of such sayings: Proverbs chs 1-9 are a lengthy prologue to the work, while almost all of the rest of the book from chapter 10 onwards is made up of such "proverbs" in the usual English sense of the word. However, the Hebrew word **mashal** does not only have the connotation of a "proverb" in this sense but also means a metaphor, graphic likeness or image that facilitates deeper understanding and insight into the **nimshal**, some subject or concept that is elucidated through being compared to or represented by the metaphoric image. "All his words are similes and metaphors: for example, he compares the Torah to a good wife while idolatry is compared to a harlot" (Rashi on Proverbs 1:1).

V 2: "To know wisdom (**Chochmah**) and instruction (**Mussar**) and to apprehend words of understanding (**Binah**)". The Spanish rabbi and moralist Rabbeinu Yonah of Gerona (d. 1263), author of the moralistic classic Shaarey Teshuvah, "The Gates of Repentance", explains in his commentary on Proverbs that **Chochmah**, "wisdom", is the defining trait of the righteous Tzaddikim who follow the way of truth, and it is this trait that will be explained in this work. **Mussar**, "instruction" or "reproof" (lit. chastisement) comes to castigate the wicked and explain the loss and damage they cause. **Binah**, "understanding", comes when one attains an understanding of the ultimate meaning or intention of something that is said and the thought that lies behind it.

V 3: "To receive the instruction of wisdom...." It is not enough to **know** wisdom. The point is to receive, accept and **apply** the lesson in practice (Rabbeinu Yonah). "...justice (**Tzedek**) and judgment (**Mishpat**) and equity (**Meisharim**)" - "**Tzedek** means going beyond the letter of the law; **Mishpat** means judging truthfully following the line of justice; **Meisharim** means knowing how to act rightly and intelligently in those areas where there is no clear legal decision or obligation" (Rabbeinu Yonah).

Vv 4-5: Application to the pursuit of wisdom will benefit even the simple and foolish, while the wise will gain ever greater wisdom.

V 6: "To understand **mashal** and **melitzah**..." - "When studying each verse, one must pay attention to understanding the two pathways of the **mashal** (here this means the object being elucidated through the metaphor), and the **melitzah** (= the rhetorical phraseology or stylistic device through which it is expressed). It is necessary to understand what it is that is being compared to the metaphorical image used, but one must also not disregard the stylistic device or metaphor itself - this too must be understood. Thus, when it says, 'to save you from the strange and alien woman' (Prov. 2:16) this is a metaphor for the idolatrous vanities of Egypt. One must also understand why he used the metaphor of a harlot" (Rashi).

V 7: "The fear of HaShem is the beginning of knowledge..." - "Until this point, Solomon explained his purpose in writing this work. Now the book proper begins" (Rashi). The very foundation of all wisdom and knowledge is to teach oneself to fear God.

V 8: "Hear, my son, the instruction of your father...." Rabbeinu Yonah explains that success in the service of God is founded on four prerequisites, which are explained one by one in the coming passages. (1) One must choose good guides and teachers and be willing to listen to their reproof (vv 8-9). (2) One must avoid all fellowship with evil people (vv 10-19). (3) One must understand that God requites evil and rewards righteousness and set oneself to fear God (vv 20-33). (4) One must toil and struggle to attain wisdom and avoid all extraneous, empty, alien "wisdom" (Prov. 2:1-22).

Vv 10-19 warn against joining those who seek to make great gains at others' expense because they do not understand that they are walking straight into a trap that will destroy them.

V 20: "Wisdom cries outside, she utters her voice in the streets...." Wisdom calls to us from everywhere, seeking to draw us near. We must understand that it would be a fatal error to reject the call of wisdom, for those who do "will eat the fruits of their way and be filled with their own devices" (v 31). This is the sage's answer to the very same doubts that the prophet Malachi (ch 3) addressed when he said that although God is long-suffering, He will eventually exact retribution from the wicked, showing that He is the God of true Justice.

CHAPTER 2

The moralistic philosophy of Proverbs is rooted in a worldview that sees man as a free agent living in a dangerously deceptive world from which God has purposely obscured the truth in order to make it necessary for man to strive to attain it through toil and effort, thereby earning his reward. Caught in a confusing maze in which the most likely-looking paths turn out to be blind alleys and worse, man desperately needs true guidance, which is precisely what Proverbs offers.

In verses 1-4 the voice of wisdom calls to the young, inexperienced "son", appealing to him to heed the message. He must dedicate all his faculties to the pursuit of the right and left columns of the kabbalistic tree - **Chochmah**-wisdom (v 2) and **Binah**-understanding (vv 2-3) - in order to attain the center-column attribute of **Da'at Elokim**, the "knowledge" of God (v 5). This is more than merely cognitive knowledge: **Da'at** has the connotation of deep attachment. It is necessary to seek out and cultivate these attributes with the same eagerness that people seek out wealth and treasure (v 4).

Verses 5ff set forth the benefits conferred by Godly wisdom. "For HaShem gives wisdom; from His mouth is knowledge and understanding" (v 5). The wisdom that King Solomon urges us to seek is great because it has been given from the mouth of God Himself, and this is why we should strive to acquire it (Rashi on v 5). This wisdom confers protection (v 8) and unlocks the secrets of God's justice (v 9).

V 12: Only the wisdom of the Torah can save us from the evil path of those who skillfully use language to turn everything around so that truth looks like falsehood and vice versa: "these are the **Apikorsim** who deceive Israel into abandoning their faith and turn the Torah into something evil" (Rashi ad loc.)

V 16: Likewise, the Torah saves from the "strange woman, the alien woman who makes her words smooth and slippery". This "strange woman" is the personification of heresy and atheism. "It would make no sense to say that he is merely talking about a literal adulteress, for what kind of praise of the Torah would it be to say here that it saves you from the strange woman but not from any other sin? This must refer to heresy, which causes people to cast off the yoke of all the commandments" (Rashi).

V 19: "None who go into her return again, they will not attain the paths of life". Rabbi Nachman explains that it is in the intrinsic nature of the conundrums of heretical philosophy that they can never be resolved, and those who try to unravel them simply get sucked in and sink without ever being able to reach any conclusion (Likutey Moharan Part 1 Torahs 62 & 64).

Vv 20-22: The wisdom of the Torah brings a person to keep to the ways of the righteous, who "will dwell in the **land**" (v 22) - "the world to come" (Rashi) - when the wicked are cut off and cast into hell.

CHAPTER 3

Until this point, King Solomon has explained the four preconditions for true service of God. As discussed in the commentary on Chapter 1, these are (1) choosing good teachers; (2) keeping one's distance from wicked people; (3) attaining fear of God through being aware of the reward for righteousness and the punishment for sin; (4) pursuing true wisdom while eschewing heresy as set forth in Chapter 2.

Now, in Chapter 3, King Solomon explains what serving God means and the great blessings of long life and peace that it brings.

V 3: "Kindness and truth will not abandon you..." - "He begins by emphasizing the qualities of kindness and truth... Kindness means setting oneself to make every effort to show kindness to people and to benefit them with one's possessions and through physical effort, to make them feel good and to seek out peace, goodness and honor for them while being careful not to harm them whether by deeds or words. With this trait one banishes cruelty, selfishness, hatred, jealousy and pride. Truth means not calling evil good or good evil, not using flattery to ingratiate oneself with people, giving honor to the righteous while despising the wicked and judging people fairly without favoritism." (Rabbeinu Yonah).

Vv 5ff: Perfect trust in God means that one does not put one's trust in man nor in one's own powers and intelligence. "In all your ways acknowledge Him and He will direct your paths" (v 6): this famous verse teaches that the essence of trust in God is to seek Him out in all the different aspects and details of our lives: it is through this interactive "partnership" with God that all our paths become blessed.

Vv 8-10: Service of God not only brings spiritual benefits but actual physical health and material blessings.

Vv 11ff: Even when one trusts in God, not everything goes well all the time! When seeking to attain wisdom and serve God, one must understand that suffering is an inevitable part of the pathway, "for HaShem reproves those that He loves…" (v 12).

V 14: "For its merchandise is better than merchandise of silver..." – "In every kind of exchange that people make in business, one person takes this and the other person takes that. But when a person says to his friend, 'You teach me your chapter and I will teach you my chapter, each one of them ends up with both chapters in hand!'" (Rashi).

Vv 17-18: These very beautiful evocations of the great benefits of Torah wisdom are recited in the synagogue after the public Torah reading as the scroll is returned to the ark.

Vv 19-20: "HaShem founded the earth with Wisdom and established the heavens with Understanding; with His Knowledge, the depths were split asunder and the clouds drop down the dew." These verses allude to deep kabbalistic secrets of the creation, showing that the wisdom we are exhorted to seek out is the inner wisdom of the Creator Himself.

Vv 21ff: "My son, let them not depart from your eyes...." The pursuit of this wisdom requires unremitting application, but this is worth it because of the perfect security and divine protection which it brings.

Vv 27ff set forth the principles with which one who would serve God must govern his conduct towards his fellows. "For the crooked person is an abomination to God, but His secret is with the righteous" (v 32). God deals with all **middah ke-neged middah**, "measure for measure".

CHAPTER 4

As mentioned in the commentary on Proverbs ch 1, the first nine chapters of the book are a kind of extended prologue consisting of a series of discourses that set forth the wise path in life and exhort us to follow it. Then from chapter 10 onwards, most of the rest of the book is a weave of "proverbs" in the usual English sense of the word - one-sentence sayings of wisdom each of which is a perfectly chiseled epigram. These proverbs are collected one after the other in verse after verse, chapter after chapter, with in many cases no discernible thematic relationship between them.

However, in these early chapters of the book, each discourse is a continuous whole in the sense that one verse leads into the next developing the overall theme of the discourse, while a logical thread can be discerned in the sequence of the discourses. These vary in length from a few verses to a whole chapter. They return again and again to the same underlying themes, exploring them in different ways and with different images. This is characteristic of **Mussar**, moralistic teaching, since its purpose is to drum home the message and to reinforce it with constantly renewed encouragement and exhortation.

The worldview and spiritual psychology of Proverbs are elaborated and explained at length in Kabbalistic literature as well as in the literature of Rabbinic **mussar** and **hashgachah** ("outlook", "worldview"). Proverbs has a unique style of its own, with a distinctive vocabulary and a system of cantillation (trope) that is different from all of the other books of the Bible except Psalms and Job. Even so, the fundamental structure of each verse is the same as it is throughout the Bible. Every verse divides into two parts, with a rest or pause in the middle (**etnachta**). The second part of the verse is normally an expansion or elaboration of the first, or sometimes its antithesis. This fundamental verse structure is an expression of the underlying thought pattern of the Torah, which proceeds from Chochmah (the start, initial statement or "thesis") to Binah (the explanation and elaboration, or sometimes the "antithesis"). Not only does every phrase and verse have its simple meaning, which Biblical translations strive to render; the Hebrew letters and words also carry multiple levels of overtones and allusions as well as mathematical equations and divine names and attributes that no translation can convey.

Chapter 4 vv 1-19 are a discourse on the theme of giving honor and devotion to the pursuit of Torah wisdom and keeping away from the path of the wicked which is its negation. This discourse is the third and last in the series that began in the previous chapter devoted to the overall theme of practical service of God, starting with faith and trust (Proverbs 3:1-20) and going on to practical fulfillment of the commandments of the Torah (3:21-35). These three discourses on the service of God came after earlier discourses explaining the four prerequisites for serving God: choosing good teachers (1:8-9), avoiding evil influences (1:10-18), being aware of the reward for righteousness and the punishment for evil (1:20-33) and pursuing wisdom (2:1-22). There the pursuit of wisdom was presented as the prerequisite for serving God, while in the discourse in our present text it is itself an act of service.

Ch 4 v 1: "Hear, you children, the instruction of a father...." The Torah commands each father to teach the Torah diligently to his children (Deut. 5:7) because the entire transmission of the Torah from generation to generation depends on this. Here, we are all the children, while King Solomon acts as the mouthpiece for the loving Father of all of us -- the Holy One, blessed be He (Rashi on Proverbs 4:1). "The prophet prophesies and speaks as the emissary of the Holy One blessed be He, and he acts as His mouth" (Rashi on v 2).

V 3: "For I was my father's son, tender and the only one in the sight of my mother" - "If you say that Solomon hated people because he warns against robbery and sexual immorality, things which people crave, he therefore says, 'I was my father's son, tender and the only one.' to show that his father loved him greatly yet still gave him this reproof, emphasizing that he is warning all of us only out of love" (Rashi on vv 3-4).

V 5-7: This loving father now urges us to acquire wisdom and understanding, which are the only truly enduring acquisitions we can gain from this world. Rashi (on v 7) explains that the acquisition of **Chochmah-**wisdom is the first stage: one must acquire, accept and internalize information from one's teacher. The next stage is then to apply one's own intelligence, **Binah-**understanding, in considering and analyzing this information in order to "understand one thing from another".

Vv 10ff encourage us to be mindful of the great benefits that accrue from gaining wisdom, including length of days. Wisdom is not a one-time acquisition: gaining wisdom is a pathway (vv 11-12). First and foremost, it requires persistence and constant application (v 13). One must therefore be constantly on guard against getting side-tracked onto the pathway of the wicked, which is antithetical to that of wisdom (vv 14-19).

Verses 20-27 make up a new section on the theme of **zehirut**, "caution". In the words of Rabbeinu Yonah: "Our sages said that study brings a person to practice (Kiddushin 40b) and practice brings one to caution. Therefore, Solomon started with a section speaking about the pursuit of wisdom, study (2:1-22) and afterwards arranged three sections dealing with practice: (1) faith and trust in God in all areas of life, Proverbs 3:1-20; (2) keeping the commandments of the Torah, 3:21-35; (3) honoring the Torah and those who teach it while distancing oneself from evil companions, 4:1-19. Now he turns to the subject of caution, arranging it in four sections. (1) Caution in keeping the commandments of the Torah, Proverbs 4:20-27; (2) Caution in preserving one's fear of heaven intact, 5:1-23; (3) Caution in avoiding monetary loss, 6:1-4; (4) avoiding the opposite of caution, which is laziness and lethargy, 6:5-11. His way in this book is to first teach about every desirable trait and every pathway to reverence, and then afterwards to speak disparagingly about the opposite of the trait in question in order to keep you well away from it."

The present section (4:20-27) exhorts us to caution in keeping the positive commandments of the Torah and avoiding infringement of its prohibitions. We are urged to devote all of our faculties to this mission: these verses mention the ears, the eyes, the heart, the mouth, the lips and the legs. Each limb of the body must be directed to the pursuit of the commandments.

CHAPTER 5

This chapter is a discourse in two parts (vv 1-6 & 7-23) on avoiding the "strange woman", who symbolizes the evil inclination in all aspects and in particular heretical beliefs, which provide a rationalization for everything that is contrary to the Torah. This "strange woman" is the very opposite of the archetypal God-fearing "Woman of Valor" whose traits are delineated in the closing chapter of Proverbs (ch 31).

The "strange woman" is seductive and alluring, holding out the promise of every kind of pleasure and satisfaction through the use of slick, tempting language. "But her end is bitter as wormwood..." (v 4). "Her feet go down to death…" (v 5). This verse teaches that those who fall victim to her seductions will lose the life of this world and the next. The verse is also adduced in the kabbalistic writings as alluding to the way in which lower levels ("feet") of the aspect of the attribute of **Malchut** are clothed in and sustain the realm of evil (**Sitra Achra** = death).

Vv 7ff explain the terrible consequences of falling prey to the allure of the "strange woman". Those who do so give all their strength to "others" (v 9) - these are the false gods to whom people devote their lives, while the "cruel one" to whom they give over their precious years is the angel appointed over hell, who punishes them for ever after for having spent their time in vain. All their energy is sapped by strangers and aliens, and all they are left with in the end is the terrible pain of regret and contrition (v 11), asking why they did not listen to their true guides and teachers (vv 12-14).

V 15: "Drink waters out of your own cistern...." Rather than turning aside to the "strange woman", one must remain faithful to the source of life that God has given as one's share - the Torah, which is "the wife of your youth" (v 18 see Rashi). This is the true antidote to the seductive heresies and temptations that surround us. The Torah is "a loving hind and a pleasant roe; let her breasts satisfy you at all times and be ravished always with her love" (v 19).

CHAPTER 6

Our chapter is made up of three sections each warning against a specific type of flaw or evil, followed by another section listing some of the worst offenses in God's eyes and then a discourse on the Torah as the general remedy against the "woman of evil" who tempts man to sin.

Vv 1-5: "My son, if you are guarantor for your friend, if you have struck your palms for the stranger...." On the simple level, this section gives advice to one who has already borrowed from someone or entered into some financial obligation, telling him not to rest until he has paid what he owes. On the allegorical level, Rashi explains that at Sinai every Israelite became a "guarantor" for the "friend" = God, and is therefore under an obligation to keep the Torah. After receiving the Torah, it is a most serious offence to have "struck your palms" (= shaken hands) with "the stranger", i.e. to backslide and turn from His ways and attach oneself to the heretics to go in their ways.

The advice is to humble oneself before Him like a doorstep (that everyone treads on) and to send many "friends" (advocates) to pray to and placate Him on our behalf. Just as one puts oneself in a dangerous position on the material plane if one fails to repay one's debts (in accordance with the **mashal**, simile/-metaphor of having borrowed), so one stands to lose greatly on the spiritual plane if one does not repent of one's sins after having been chosen by God to receive the Torah (this is the **nimshal**, the subject of the comparison).

In this case the evil has already been done - the situation is **bedi-avad**, "after the event" - but it is still possible to repair. One must do so swiftly. As to not shaking hands with and entering into a commit-ment to "the stranger", the Chassidim say that there is only one promise that it is permitted and indeed imperative to break, and that is a promise one has made to one's evil inclination to do something wrong!

Vv 6-11: "Go to the ant, you sluggard...." Here King Solomon develops the counsel of alacrity with which the previous section ended, preaching against another evil - that of laziness, inertia and apathy, which can cause a person to lose all the great riches he stands to gain from serving God in this world. The Midrash brings a beautiful story about how King Solomon went traveling with his entourage on a flying carpet and, on landing, squashed many ants. Bending down to listen to the queen of the ants' complaint, the king was deeply chastised on hearing that everything in creation has something to teach us, including even the humble little ant.

Vv 12-15: The concept of the "base" man –**Adam Belia'al** - is just about the worst in the moralistic vocabulary of the Torah (Deut. 13:14, I Samuel 25:25, I Kings 21:13 etc.). Here it is applied to the person who speaks evil, **Lashon Hara**, about others, both with his mouth and through the hints he makes with his eyes, feet, fingers, etc., thereby sowing discord among people. Rashi (on vv 13-14) explains that this section is also speaking about the heretics who seduce people into idolatry, thereby sowing discord between man and his Creator.

Vv 16-19: "There are six things which HaShem hates and seven which are an abomination to Him." Rashi (on v 16) explains that the "seven" is the seventh abomination. The written text (**ktiv**) says **to'avot** in the plural but the prescribed reading (**kri**) is **to'avat**, which is the singular possessive, the "abomination of His soul". This implies that the seventh is as bad as all the first six together. The six are (1) high eyes - pride; (2) a tongue of falsehood; (3) hands that shed innocent blood; (4) a heart that dwells on thoughts of criminality; (5) legs that run to do evil; (6) a false witness. The seventh, which is as bad as all of them put together, is one who sows discord between brothers through evil speech.

Vv 20-26: These verses teach that steadfast devotion to Torah and its commandments is the general remedy against all evil, and particularly against the "woman of evil", who is the worst enemy of the soul. Rashi (on v 24) emphasizes that this can only be interpreted allegorically as referring to heresy and idolatry.

Among these beautiful verses containing King Solomon's praises of the Torah are some that are very famous and widely quoted in Torah literature. V 22 is darshened in Pirkey Avot 6:10 as alluding to how the Torah protects one even in the grave and when one wakes up in the world to come.

Vv 27ff: "Can a man take fire in his bosom and his clothes not be burned?" The sin of going with the wife of a friend (v 28) is taken literally by Rashi and also as an allusion to going after idolatry, which is set apart for heathens and not for you (see Rashi ad loc.). Adultery/idolatry is much worse than stealing, which a person resorts to because he is hungry. Even so, he has to pay back heavily: how much more will the idolater/adulterer have to pay a heavy penalty for a sin which there was no need to commit.

CHAPTER 7

Again, King Solomon urges us to bind and attach ourselves to the Torah, and to make Torah **Chochmah**-wisdom and **Binah**-understanding integral parts of our lives, as familiar to us as our closest relatives and dearest friends. The Torah is the only true protection against the allurements of the "strange woman", which are the main subject of this chapter.

"For at the window of my house I looked out through my lattice." The wise Solomon looks out at the world and tells us what he sees:

"And I saw among the simple ones (**peta'im**), I discerned among the youths, a young man (**na'ar**) void of understanding." (v 7). It is mainly to the **peti**, "naïve, gullible" and the **na'ar**, lit. "youth" that Solomon's **mussar**, moralistic reproof, is addressed. This is because the villain (**eveel, kheseel, belia'al** etc.) and the scoffer (**leitz**) are normally so bent on their evil that their ears are closed to reproof. The **peti** and **na'ar** on the other hand are still innocent - too innocent, because they are inexperienced and easily seduced. They do not understand that the smiling face of evil is a deceptive front concealing its real essence and the long-term destruction it brings.

Vv 19-20: "For the man is not in his house, he has gone on a long journey; he has taken a bag of money with him…." Rashi says that the husband not being in the house alludes to how the Holy One blessed be He has withdrawn his Indwelling Presence (through the destruction of the Temple and Israel's exile) and has given all the good (of this world) to the nations. Rashi says that the "bag of money" he has taken refers to the good people whose lives He has taken. In the light of Rashi's explanations, we can understand better how the evil inclination needles the exiled Israelites to turn astray from the Torah when they see the great material success of the nations in a world where the Shechinah is concealed and where innocent people apparently suffer and die.

Vv 22f: Bitter is the end of anyone who goes after the "strange woman", and this is why the "children" should listen to the warnings of the loving Father not to go after her.

V 26: "For she has cast down many wounded, and many strong men have been slain by her." In case some women take offense because the evil inclination is repeatedly personified as a "strange **woman**", let it be noted that the Talmud clearly and explicitly darshens this verse as referring to **male** Torah scholars who are not fit to teach and rule yet still tell people what to do, thereby killing them spiritually (Sotah 22b). May the Almighty lovingly guide us to the true Tzaddik so that we will not go astray!

CHAPTER 8

Following the vivid depiction in Chapter 7 of the allurements of the "strange woman" and the long-term havoc and destruction she wreaks, Chapters 8 and 9 round off the long "prologue" of the Book of Proverbs with a progression of four sections in praise of Torah wisdom: Proverbs 8:1-21; 8:22-31; 8:32-36 and 9:1-18.

Chapter 8, v 1: "Does not wisdom call and understanding put forth her voice?" God has created this world of trial in which we live as a mixture of good and evil, and He has given us the freedom to choose between them. While the "strange woman" accosts us at every turn with her allurements, as we learned in the previous chapter, true Torah wisdom also "stands at the top of the high places by the way" and "cries out at the gates." If only we were to open our eyes, we would see that God's Torah also calls to us from every direction and out of every situation in which we find ourselves in life - except that most people are deceived by the superficial appearance of this world and fail to penetrate to the truth that underlies it.

V 4: "To you O men, I call…." The wisdom of the Torah beckons to each and every one of us to draw closer.

V 5: "O you simple (**peta'im**), understand prudence, and, you fools (**kheseelim**), be of an understanding heart". The **peti** is the simple gullible person who is open to the allure of evil because he is inexperienced and knows no better. The **kheseel** is one who has already succumbed to the desires of his heart. Wisdom calls out to both categories, because both can be redeemed - as opposed to the scoffer (**leitz**), on whom reproof is wasted (see below, 9:7-8).

Vv 10-11: "Receive My instruction and not silver, and knowledge rather than choice gold. For wisdom is better than rubies." Even those who have material wealth often do not enjoy it, and they certainly cannot take it with them when they leave this world. But Torah wisdom is a treasure of inestimable value since it not only benefits those who gain it in this world but also accompanies and sustains them in the world to come.

V 12: "I am wisdom, I dwell with prudence..." - "once a person has learned Torah, prudence enters into him in every matter" (Rashi).

V 15: "Through me kings reign and princes decree justice." Torah wisdom is the foundation of good government, if only the rulers would follow it!

V 17: "I love those who love me and those who seek me early shall find me". The Hebrew word for "shall find me" is **yimtza-oon'nee**. It is written with an extra letter Nun (which has the mathematical value of 50) to indicate that those who seek Torah wisdom can attain the 50 Gates of Understanding (Rashi).

V 21: "That I may cause those who love me to inherit substance...." The Hebrew word rendered as "substance" is **yesh**, meaning that which exists. **Yesh** consists of a Yud (=10) and a Shin (=300). Based on this verse, the sages teach that "God will give each and every Tzaddik 310 worlds" (Sanhedrin 100a). This verse concludes the discourse that began in 8:1 speaking about the benefits that Torah wisdom confers.

Verse 22 opens a new section (**Parshah Petuchah**) in which the Torah herself speaks to us directly in order to explain her position of supreme importance in the scheme of God's creation.

"HaShem created me as the beginning of His way...." Seven things were created before the world was created: the Torah, Teshuvah (Repentance), the Garden of Eden, Gehennom (Hell), the Throne of Glory, the Holy Temple and the name of Mashiach" (Pesachim 54a).

V 30: "Then I was by him as a nurseling (**amon**)...." The surface meaning is that even before creation, the Torah was, as it were, God's favorite child. The Hebrew text alludes to the level of **Keter**, the Crown, because the Hebrew for "I was" is **EKYEH**, the divine name associated with **Keter** (cf. Exodus 3:14). **amon** has exactly the same Hebrew letters as **ooman**, a "craftsman". Thus, the Midrash teaches: "The Torah here says, I was the craftsman's tool of the Holy One blessed be He. Normally in this world when a king of flesh and blood builds a palace, he does not build it out of his head but consults a craftsman (**ooman**), and even the craftsman does not build it out of his head. He uses plans and diagrams in order to know exactly how to make all the rooms and corridors. So too the Holy One blessed be He looked into the Torah and created the world." (Bereishit Rabbah 1). Based on our verse, this Midrash is the source of the idea that the Torah is the "blueprint" of creation.

V 32: "And now, children, listen to me, for happy are those who keep my ways". The logical conclusion arising out of the preceding sections explaining the benefits of Torah wisdom and its august place in the scheme of creation is that we should heed the call of wisdom and do everything in our power to acquire it.

V 34: "Happy is the man who listens to me, waiting daily at my gates...." The key to acquiring this most precious acquisition is to set aside regular study time every day. It is certainly worth it, "for he who finds me has found **life**!!!"

In parallel with the "strange woman", who has readied and bedecked her home and prepared a feast of love for those she seeks to entice (chapter 7 vv 14-18), Torah wisdom has also "built her house" and prepared a feast of "meat" and "wine" for those who have the good sense to go into her (chapter 9 vv 1ff).

V 1: "Wisdom has built her house; she has hewn out her seven pillars." The Talmud (Shabbat 115a) identifies these seven pillars with the 7 days of creation (= the seven lower sefirot, which all emanate from **Chochmah**-wisdom). The Talmud (ibid.) also identifies them with the seven books of the Torah (the book of Numbers is considered to consist of 3 books, because the two verses in Numbers 10:35-36 are considered as a whole book in itself dividing what proceeds from what follows).

Another interesting midrash from Yalkut Shimoni on this and the following verse darshens them as alluding to the War of Gog and Magog: "her house" is the Holy Temple; the "seven pillars" allude to the seven year duration of this war; the meat and the wine (v 2) allude to the "meat of the warriors and blood of the princes of the earth" that Israel will then consume (Ezekiel 39:18), while the "maiden" whom wisdom sends out to invite everyone to the feast (v 3) is Ezekiel, whose prophecy about the War of Gog and Magog is more detailed than those of the other prophets.

V 3: "She has sent forth her maidens..." - "Adam and Eve; another explanation: Moses and Aaron" (Rashi). Wisdom speaks to us in many ways, calling and appealing to us to heed her message.

Vv 4ff: "Whoever is simple (**peti**), let him turn in here...." As discussed earlier, the wisdom of the Torah is a lifeline for the innocent and gullible.

V 7-8: "He who reproves a scorner brings shame on himself.... Do not reprove a scorner lest he will hate you...." It is futile to try to reprove the wicked and the scoffers, because they are set in their ways and not only will they not listen; they are also likely to turn on the one offering the reproof and tell him that he too is blemished. "This is a warning that it is forbidden to speak to those who seduce others from the straight path, not even to reprove them or to try to bring them to the Torah" (Rashi).

Vv 13ff: The lengthy "prologue" to Solomon's collected one-verse proverbs (which begin in chapter 10) ends with a final warning about the Woman of Folly, who also sits in a most prominent position in town seeking to entice the same simple, innocent gullible passers-by to whom true Torah wisdom seeks to throw a lifeline. "Stolen waters are sweet and bread eaten in secret is pleasant" (v 17) - "the taste of relations with an unmarried girl is not the same as the taste of another man's wife" (Rashi). What the simple fool does not realize is that "the dead are there and that her guests are in the depths of hell" (v 18). May God help us to come to our senses and realize where we are in this world!

CHAPTERS 10-11

"The proverbs of Solomon...." (Chapter 10, v 1). From here until the end of the book, the greater part of the text consists of one-verse proverbs or at times short series of verses elaborating on a single idea. Sometimes an overall theme can be discerned in consecutive proverbs, yet often there is no specific relationship between one proverb and the next: each is a jewel in itself.

We have no information about how or why these proverbs were arranged as they are, but a very interesting clue as to how they have come down to us in their present form is contained much later in the book in Proverbs 25:1: "**These also** are the proverbs of Solomon which the men of Hezekiah king of Judah copied (**he-eteekoo**)." This verse introduces another seven chapters of proverbs.

Metzudat David comments on the above-quoted verse: "It would appear that the material from the beginning of the book until this point [i.e. until ch 25] was copied over and available in everyone's hands, whereas from this point until the end of the book the only copies were in the hands of Hezekiah's officers, who copied these words from scrolls of Solomon that were available to them. This is why the text says, 'these **also** are Solomon's proverbs' i.e. even though they were not available to everyone, nevertheless these too are his words which Hezekiah's officers copied, and they can be trusted as to the fact that these words came from the mouth of Solomon." [Hezekiah became king 13 generations or 235 years after the death of King Solomon.]

About a century and a half ago it became fashionable for a certain breed of Biblical "scholars" who in rebellion against traditional rabbinic explanations of the Bible to indulge in what they called "Biblical criticism" in which they tried to cast aspersions on the divine origins of the Bible (and, by implication, on its binding nature) by claiming that different parts of various books were written by different human authors and later redacted into their present form. However, nowhere in any of the classical rabbinic commentators is there the faintest hint that the authors of the Biblical books were anyone other than as stated in the text in each case or as handed down in rabbinic tradition, and there is no reason whatever to distort the literal meaning of the text or, for example, to take the above-quoted verse as explained by Metzudat David in any other way except literally.

Rashi on the above-quoted verse in Proverbs 25:1 comments that the word **he'eteekoo**, rendered as "copied", also has the connotation of "they **strengthened**", noting that when Hezekiah became king [after a lengthy period of rebellion against the Torah under previous kings] he established centers for students in every city until eventually a check was made from Dan to Beersheva and not a single ignoramus was found (Sanhedrin 94b). It would make perfect sense that a highly innovative revivalist Torah leader like Hezekiah would reveal new materials that had previously been handed down only among the inner circle of the House of David, in order to strengthen Torah observance in his kingdom.

We may infer that the redaction of Proverbs took place in two stages: the greater part of Solomon's proverbs were arranged in his lifetime, presumably at his behest, and copied by scribes for circulation among the people, while later on in the time of Hezekiah, supplementary materials were added from private royal manuscripts thereby giving the work the form in which we have it today.

How should we study this treasury of wise epigrams and aphorisms? In the absence of a continuous "story-line" it can be hard to take in, absorb and internalize verse after verse of such wisdom. It is somewhat like touring a vast museum of dazzling treasures: even with the best will in the world, one's eyes are likely to glaze over after a time. Moreover, practically every single verse is accompanied by an enormous wealth of rabbinic midrash, commentary and explanation dating from Mishnaic and Talmudic times until the present day. Each verse of Proverbs provides topics for lengthy consideration, discussion and debate, and may be susceptible to interpretations that go in radically different directions. Each of the four standard levels of Biblical interpretation (**PaRDeS**) can certainly be applied to Proverbs: (1) **p'shat**, the "simple" or "literal" meaning; (2) **remez**, the "allusions" to various Torah ideas, historical events, etc.; (3) **drash**, the teachings that are derived from the verse through the hermeneutical methods of Torah interpretation (such as the 13 Rules of R. Ishmael or the 32 Rules of Rabbi Eliezer son of R. Yose HaGlili as printed at the end of full editions of Talmud Bavli Berachot); (4) **sod**, the "secret", "mystical" or "esoteric" dimension of the words, which consist of divine names and numerical formulae, etc. - for the entire Bible was written through prophecy and holy spirit.

Rabbi Nachman of Breslov taught that in studying any part of the Torah, the essence of the mitzvah is simply to read the words in order one after the other trying to gain a general understanding without seeking to master every last detail. He also taught that wherever one is studying in the Torah, one's primary purpose should be to derive practical guidance in order to improve one's character and behavior. Thus, he taught that one should always try to find oneself in each text - to see how it relates to one's own issues and concerns.

Precisely because of the tremendous wealth of wisdom collected in Solomon's proverbs, one must expect that it cannot all be assimilated at one time. At different junctures in life, different sections, verses and phrases will become more meaningful. It often happens that a certain phrase or idea may seem very strange and incomprehensible, until life brings one to a certain point where suddenly its truth shines out in a flash of illumination. In order to prepare for such moments, we would do well to learn a lesson from the humble ant, who spends the entire summer working hard dragging heavy grains for storage until the winter, when she can relax, eat and enjoy the fruits of her labors (see Proverbs 6:8).

Almost all the proverbs in our present text, Chapters 10 and 11 consist of a single verse devoted to one idea, the first half of the verse stating a thesis and the second half its antithesis. The mode of thought is that of oscillation between holistic **Chochmah**-wisdom and analytic **Binah**-understanding. It is precisely the contrast between the thesis and antithesis that throws light on the meaning of each one, thereby generating the synthesis – **Da'at**, "knowledge", "comprehension".

The overall theme of the proverbs in chapters 10 and 11 is the contrast between the character, attitudes and behavior of the Tzaddik (the righteous person) and those of the Rasha (the wicked villain) and their respective destinies in God's order of Justice, where goodness is rewarded in the world to come while evil is punished in Gehennom. The mind of the Tzaddik is characterized by the qualities of **Chochmah** ("wisdom"), **Binah** and **Tevunah** (different aspects of "understanding") while the Rasha is **kheseel** and **eveel**, both of which mean "foolish", lacking in **Da'at**. The Tzaddik is generous and forgiving, while the Rasha is mean and selfish. The Tzaddik blesses; the Rasha curses, insults and disparages. The Tzaddik is straight and honest; the Rasha is deceptive and treacherous. The Tzaddik is pure and sincere, the Rasha stubborn and crooked. In accordance with their respective characters and behavior, the Tzaddik is rewarded with long life and wealth in the world of Truth, while the Rasha faces bitterness, disaster and death when the bubble bursts and the emptiness of his fantasies is revealed.

Ch 11 v 31: "Indeed, the Tzaddik is recompensed on earth…" - "even the Tzaddik pays the price in this world for a sin he commits" (Rashi) - "…how much more so the wicked and the sinner!" - "Then why should the wicked man trust that all will be well for him just because he is successful for the moment? If even the Tzaddik is punished, how much more so will the wicked man be punished either in his lifetime or when he dies" (Rashi).

CHAPTERS 12

Each of the proverbs in these chapters stands independently, with no single theme or progression of thought binding them all together. Each aphorism opens up a world of thought in itself. A full commentary would require a discussion of every verse in turn with an analysis in each case of the **mashal** (the metaphor or image) and the **nimshal** (the subject that is elucidated through the comparison). Such commentaries have already been provided by the classical Torah commentators (Targum Yonatan, Rashi, RaDaK, Ibn Ezra, RaLBaG, MaLBiM, etc.), but to give a digest of their discussions and of various comments by the rabbis of the Talmud and Midrashim on each verse would be well beyond the scope of this book, which will instead offer some brief comments on selected verses, leaving students to familiarize themselves with the actual Biblical text and to draw personal lessons and messages from those verses that speak to them particularly at this time.

Chapter 12 verse 1: One who loves true knowledge of God (**Da'at**) will love reproof because he has the humility to understand that he must constantly correct his own misconceptions, where as one who hates being criticized and corrected will not grow in wisdom and will therefore remain a **bo'ar**, a "fool", or more literally, an "animal" who lacks the exalted human faculty of **Da'at**.

As in the previous chapters, the main overall theme of most of the proverbs in our present text is the contrast between the thought patterns, ways of speech and deeds of the righteous **Tzaddik** and those of the wicked **Rasha**. The Tzaddik pursues justice while the Rasha is full of mischief and deceit (v 3). The wicked use words to trap and kill others, while the righteous seek to save them and promote peace (v 6). Since God rules the world with absolute justice, it is only fair that he should give endurance to the Tzaddikim and overthrow the wicked (vv 3, 7, etc.)

V 8: "A man should be commended according to his intelligence (**sechel**)...." The rendering of **sechel** as "intelligence" somewhat makes it seem as if high marks are given to those with high IQ, because in our highly-sophisticated society dominated by "experts", intelligence is associated in the minds of many with quick, sharp thinking whether for good or bad. But in the vocabulary of Torah literature, **sechel** refers to the triad of mental faculties known kabbalistically as holistic **Chochmah**-thinking, analytic **Binah**-thinking and their synthesis, **Da'at**, the knowledge of God. Since God Himself is totally beyond our intellects, the only way to "know" Him is with simplicity and sincerity, through faith. This is why "...he who is of a perverse heart shall be despised" - because one who allows himself to be dominated by the perversity of the evil inclination in his heart loses his holy good sense.

V 9: "The righteous man knows the soul (**Nefesh**) of his animal..." - Rashi (ad loc.) comments that "he knows what his animal and his family need". The Tzaddik's "animal" would allude to his physical body whose nature, requirements and purpose as the servant and agent of his own higher soul (**Neshamah**) the Tzaddik fully understands. He lives on the spiritual plane but understands the material plane.

"...but the kindnesses of the wicked are cruel". This can be understood on many levels. For example, "lovingly" plying one's family and children with candies and junk food can be extremely cruel in the long term. Also, those kindly "rabbis" of recent centuries who sought to "sweeten" Judaism for their congregations by "easing the burden" of Torah and changing or abandoning many of its most precious observances have proved in fact to be exceedingly cruel both to the lost souls of their congregants and to the entire people of Israel, whom they have left divided and largely bereft of a true, unifying tradition. Another form of "kindness" that is really extremely cruel is the failure to condemn and punish many crimes and acts of terror, or even to justify them on psychological or ideological grounds. It is this misplaced "kindness" of the wicked that has led to the rampant crime and terror in the world today.

V 11: "He that tills his land shall have plenty of bread...." Rashi comments that besides the obvious simple truth of this proverb, it also teaches that one who constantly reviews his Torah studies will not forget them.

V 14: "From the fruit of the mouth of a man shall he be satisfied with good..." - "From the reward for the work of the mouths of those who engage in Torah [repeating their studies orally out loud day by day] they eat the good in this world while the principal endures for them in the world to come" (Rashi). "...and the recompense of man's hands shall be handed to him" - the rewards God gives in the world of truth are strictly in accordance with our efforts in this world.

V 15: "The way of a fool is right in his own eyes, but the wise man listens to advice." The fool likes to decide everything for himself according to his own ideas, but in order to get through this mixed-up world we need guidance from a source of truth that stands beyond it - the Torah.

V 16: Fools vent their anger on the spot, but the wise are more prudent.

V 19: "The lip of truth shall be established forever...." Living as we do in a world of rampant falsehood, this should be very comforting to us.

V 21: "No evil shall befall the just...." God protects those who truly and sincerely follow the Torah, saving them from coming to sin even though this is all too easy in the complex, fast-moving world we live in.

V 23: "…the heart of fools declares their folly" - "they declare their folly in a loud voice" (Rashi). One who possesses **Da'at Torah**, "knowledge of the Torah", can rapidly discern the folly of those who do not understand the true nature of this world and its purpose: their words, their behavior and their very gait all cry out folly.

V 24: "The hand of the diligent shall **rule**..." - "shall become rich" (Rashi). The riches, of course, are spiritual. Everything depends on diligence and effort.

V 25: "Anxiety in a man's heart dejects it…" The Hebrew word rendered as "dejects it" is **yash'chenah**, the pi-el form of the root **shachah**, to come down low. The sages of the Talmud darshened this as (1) **ya-sichenah**, "he should put it out of his mind", or (2) **ya--sichenah**, "he should **talk about it** to others" (Yoma 75a). In fact, good talk therapy with an honest friend or true counselor helps remove anxiety from the heart.

CHAPTER 13

V 1: "A wise son hears his father's instruction…." Rashi comments that it is because the father gives instruction and reproof that the son becomes wise.

V 2: "A man shall eat good from the fruit of his mouth..." The first part of this verse is almost identical to Ch 12 v 14, "a man shall be **satisfied** with good from the fruit of his mouth", although the second part of the verse is different. There are also other cases where part or all of a verse recurs in more than one place in Proverbs.

V 3: "He who guards his lips keeps his life...." Guarding and sanctifying our faculty of speech is one of the most important keys to spiritual success in life.

V 4: "The soul of the sluggard desires and has nothing, but the soul of the diligent shall be richly supplied." Many people have dreams and wishes, but only through diligence can they be made actual and far-off goals turned into practical achievements.

V 7: "There is one who seems to be rich yet lacks everything, and one who seems to be poor yet has great wealth." Here is another verse pointing to the paradoxical nature of this world and God's way of running it: many things are very different from the way they seem on the surface.

V 13: "He who despises the word shall be punished, but he who fears the commandment shall be rewarded" - "When a person despises one of the teachings of the Torah, he ends up being snatched as a surety for it" (Rashi).

V 18: "Poverty and shame come to one who refuses instruction (**mussar**)...." Again and again, Solomon drives in the message that we must submit ourselves to the reproof and moralistic teachings of the Torah (cf. vv 20 & 24 etc.). Mussar literature, whether in the form of the moralistic classics ("Path of the Just", "Gates of Repentance" etc.) or Chassidut (Likutey Moharan, Tanya etc.) should be part of the regular diet of every Torah student.

CHAPTER 14

V 1: Only by employing the wisdom of Torah in one's life can one build a structure that will endure to eternity.

V 2: One who truly reveres God behaves correctly. Going crookedly is an affront to God.

V 3: The fool hits out at everyone with his stick of arrogance.

V 4: "Without oxen the crib is clean [i.e. the owner's house is empty of produce] but an abundance of produce comes through the strength of the ox" - "That is to say, in a place where there are no Torah sages, the teachings available are not in accord with the halachah" (Rashi).

V 6: "A scoffer seeks wisdom, but it is not there…" - "When he needs it, he does not find it in his heart" (Rashi).

V 7: Keep your distance from fools.

V 9: "Amends pleads for fools, but among the upright there is good will" - "The fools are the sinners: only by making amends and paying the penalty can they conciliate God. His will is to the upright" (Rashi).

V 10: "The heart knows its own bitterness, and with its joy no stranger can meddle" - "Each person knows the toil and effort with which he labors in the Torah, and therefore no stranger will have a share when he receives his future reward" (Rashi).

V 12: "There is a way that seems right to a man but its end are the ways of death" - The pathos of our condition in this benighted world is that we cannot see what the consequences of our choices will be, particularly in the very long term. This is why we require the guidance of God's Torah, since He sees to the end of everything.

V 13: The laughter of this world cannot last forever.

V 17: "He that is soon angry acts foolishly..." One of the most important virtues of the upright is patience and long-suffering, which can save us from much trouble.

V 19: "The evil bow before the good…" - "At the end. in time to come" (Rashi).

V 20: "Even by his own neighbor, the poor man is hated, but many are the friends of the rich man" - "The 'poor man' is someone who is ignorant of Torah, who does not know how to act in the proper way, and he is hated even by his close friends" (Rashi).

V 23: "In all labor there is profit, but the talk of the lips leads only to deficiency" - Work and action, not mere words!!!

V 24: The true "wealth" of the sages is their understanding of the Torah (Rashi).

V 26: Not only does one's fear of God give personal security; it also protects one's very children.

V 27: The reason why fear of God is the source of life is because it warns the person to avoid the snares of death - sins and transgressions (Metzudat David).

V 28: "In the multitude of the people is the king's glory..." - When many people carry out a mitzvah together, this brings God great glory (Talmud Yoma 70a).

V 29: More in praise of patience and forbearing, which save us from folly.

V 30: "A tranquil heart is the life of the flesh; but envy is the rottenness of the bones" - This verse is one of the foundations of the psychosomatic wisdom of the Torah, teaching that good, positive attitudes are conducive to physical health.

V 31: To oppress the weak is an insult to their Maker....

V 32: "...the upright has hope even in his death" - "When he dies he is assured that he will come to the Garden of Eden" (Rashi).

V 34: "Charity elevates a nation (= Israel, Rashi) but the kindness of the peoples is a sin" - "because they take from one to give to another" (Rashi).

CHAPTER 15

V 1: "A soft answer turns away wrath..." This is a lesson to imbibe.

V 3: God is watching everything; there is no escape.

V 4: "A soothing tongue is a tree of life…" The way we speak can have a decisive effect on our own health and that of those around us.

V 6: "In the **house** of the righteous is much treasure but in the **revenues** of the wicked is trouble." Rashi's comment on this verse illustrates the level of **remez**, "allusion", in the text. On the first half, Rashi writes: "The Temple [= the House] that was built by David, the righteous Tzaddik, is a great treasure and a tower of strength". On the second half, darshening the Hebrew word rendered as "revenues" - **tevooah** from the root "to **bring in**", Rashi writes: "…but through the **bringing in** of the idol that King Menasheh brought into the Temple, it was spoiled".

V 8: "The sacrifice of the wicked is an abomination to God..." - God does not want perfunctory outward expressions of service, He wants the devotion of the heart.

V 11: If everything in hell and destruction are revealed to God, how much more is it certain that He knows what is in people's hearts (Rashi).

V 13: "A joyous heart makes the face cheerful…" - Again, the soul and the mind influence the health of the body.

Vv 15-17: True happiness in life depends not on material prosperity or the lack of it, but on people's **attitudes**.

V 22: "For want of counsel purposes are frustrated; but in the multitude of counselors they are established" - the true counsel that all need is that of the Torah.

V 24: "The path of life (**orach chayim**) goes upward for the wise…." The authors of the Arba'a Turim / Shulchan Aruch chose the phrase **orach chayim** for the title of the first of the four sections of these foundational codes of Torah law as it applies in our times. **Orach Chayim** deals with the laws of the prayers and blessings of daily life and the laws of Shabbat and the festivals. Numerous other phrases from Proverbs were also chosen as the titles of famous Torah classics. Thus, in the present chapter, verse 7, **Siftey Chachamim**, "the lips of the wise", is the title of the most important super-commentary on Rashi, and verse 30, **Me'or Eynayim**, "the light of the eyes" is the title of an important Chassidic work by R. Menachem Nachum of Tchernoble.

V 25: "HaShem will pluck up the house of the proud; but He will establish the border of the widow". If a person sees an idolatrous temple, he should recite the first phrase of this verse; if one sees the houses of Israel in a state of habitation, he should recite the second part of the verse (Talmud Berachot 58b).

V 27: Unjust gains sully a person's house. One who hates free gifts and wants only what he works for shall live.

V 30: "The light of the eyes rejoices the heart; and a good report makes the bones fat." More on the mind-body connection!

CHAPTER 16

V 1: "The preparations of the heart are man's, but the answer of the tongue is from HaShem." When we arouse ourselves from below (**hit'orerut d'l'tata**) and strive to order and better ourselves, this evokes an arousal from Above (**hit'orerut d'l'eiyla**).

V 2: "All the ways of a man are clean in his own eyes; but HaShem weighs the spirits." It is very hard for a person to acknowledge that his attitudes and behavior may be wrong. But God knows the truth as to who is good and who is not (Rashi), for He is **inside** the spirit/soul of each person. The Hebrew word rendered as "weighs", **tokhein**, is from the root **tokh**, which means "within" (Metzudat David).

V 3: "Commit your works to God" - pray to Him about everything you need, and this will give a sound basis to all your thoughts, ideas and plans (Rashi).

V 4: God made everything to reveal His might and glory - even the evil day that befalls the villain reflects glory on God.

V 7: "When God is pleased with a man's ways, He makes even his enemies to be at peace with him" - including his own wife!!! (Bereishit Rabbah 54). If a person wants domestic harmony, the key is for him to put all his effort into serving God.

V 10: "There is a magic (**kessem**) on the lips of a king; in judgment, his mouth will not err." The "king" is the sage, when he sits in judgment. If he is a true sage, God gives him intuitive understanding of where the truth is to be found. **Kessem** here is a kind of power of divination, the ability to guess right.

V 11: "A just balance and scales are God's: all the weights of the bag are His work." The merchants of old, had bags containing a variety of weights in order to measure out different quantities. God has every kind of weight and measure, to pay each person exactly according to his behavior (Rashi; Metzudat David).

V 14: "The wrath of the King is like messengers of death, but a wise man will pacify it." Every Jew needs to be connected to a true sage, who through his great humility has the power to appease God and bring atonement (cf. Likutey Moharan I, 4).

V 17: "The highway of the upright (**mesillat yesharim**) is to depart from evil...." The phrase Mesillat Yesharim, "Path of the Just", was chosen by the outstanding sage Rabbi Moshe Chayim Luzzatto (1707-47) as the title of his outstanding moralistic classic on the path of ascent to true service of God.

V 18: "Pride goes before destruction...." This was so in the case of Haman in ancient Persia, and it will be so in the case of the latter-day Hamans now governing the same country.

V 20: "He who gives heed to the word will find good..." - "One who considers his words carefully and weighs his pathways will find good" (Rashi). "...and happy is the one who trusts in God" - "When he weighs his pathways and sees that he has the opportunity to perform a mitzvah that involves some danger or monetary loss, if he trusts in God and does good, he will succeed" (Rashi).

V 24: "Pleasant words (= words of Torah, Rashi) are like honeycomb, sweet to the soul and health to the bones" - We have the power to influence the health of our bodies through the very words we speak.

V 28: "A froward man sows strife, and a whisperer separates a leader (**alooph**)." When a person distorts the meaning of what was said, he stirs up strife among people (Metzudat David). Rashi interprets the "leader" as God: as a result of a person's complaints, he separates the Ruler of the world from himself.

V 31: The practice of charity lengthens one's days (Rashi).

V 33: "The lot is cast into the lap, but its whole disposition is from God" - Man may cast lots, but it is God who determines the outcome and the share that each will receive. Thus, when the Land of Israel was divided among the tribes, it was done through casting lots, and thus each tribe received their proper portion.

CHAPTER 17

V 1: Rashi comments on this verse: "It was better for the Holy One blessed be He to destroy His Temple and His city so as to be at peace from Israel's sins, because they used to offer the sacrifices of strife in His House."

V 2: "A servant that deals wisely shall have rule over a son that deals shamefully, and shall have part of the inheritance among the brothers." Rashi says that the "servant who deals wisely" is the **Ger Tzedek** ("righteous convert"). He is better than a home-born villain! And in time to come the converts will have a share of the inheritance among the Children of Israel (cf. Ezekiel 47:23).

V 3: "The refining pot is for silver and the furnace for gold, but God tries the hearts." The tests that God takes people through can be a refining through fire.

V 8: "When a person comes before God and placates Him with words and returns to Him, this is a precious stone and a pearl in His eyes, and in whatever the person asks of God, He will give him success" (Rashi).

V 9: It is better to overlook the bad things people may do to one and not to try to take vengeance, because by constantly harping on their evil he causes God - who commanded us not to nurse a grudge or take vengeance - to depart from him (Rashi).

V 15: "One who justifies the wicked, and one who condemns the righteous, are both an abomination to God." Both ills are also very prevalent in the public media today.

V 16: What use is it for a person to acquire the wisdom of the Torah if he does not intend to observe the Torah and studies only to acquire a name for himself? (Rashi).

V 17: Rashi's rendition of the verse is: Always show love to friends in order to acquire people who will love you, for in a time of trouble, your friend will be "born" and become a brother who will help you and take a share in your sorrow.

V 18: Agreeing to be a guarantor in some financial transaction is not considered wise. Rashi interprets the handshake as that of someone who "shakes hands" with the heretics in order to go in their ways when he has already made a guarantee to God (in the Sinaitic Covenant) to observe His commandments.

V 19: "…One who exalts his gate seeks destruction." "Exalting one's gate" means speaking arrogantly (Rashi).

V 22: "A merry heart is good medicine, but a broken spirit dries the bones." This is the Torah path of healing in a nutshell.

V 24: "Wisdom is before one who has understanding, but the eyes of a fool are in the ends of the earth." Rashi comments: The fool says, "Wisdom is not available near at hand, because it is very far from me. How will I ever be able to learn all thirty chapters of the Mishnaic order of Damages (the three Bavas), the thirty chapters of Tractate **Keilim** (the tractate on purity and impurity of vessels), the twenty-four chapters of Tractate Shabbat?" But for the wise man it is something easy. Today he studies two chapters and tomorrow another two, and says: This is what those who were before me always did.

V 26: "The Holy One blessed be He never said to wipe Israel from the Land, for it is not good in His eyes to punish all of them" (Rashi).

PROVERBS
CHAPTER 18

V 1: "He who is separated will seek his own desire; in all sound wisdom, he will be revealed." Rashi: "One who is separated from the Holy One blessed be He so as not to guard His commandments chases after the desire of his heart and his evil inclination. And in the end his shame will be revealed among the sages. Our rabbis darshened that this refers to Lot, who separated himself from Abraham, but in the end, his shame is revealed in the synagogues and study halls, for 'The Ammonite and Moabite [Lot's descendants] may not enter the assembly' (Deut. 24:4)".

V 2: The fool does not desire true understanding but only the fantasies produced by his own heart.

V 4: "The words of a **man**'s mouth are deep waters" - Rashi: Where the word **ish** (= man) is used in the Bible, it refers to a man of great might. "A flowing brook, a fountain of wisdom": Rabbi Nachman of Breslov took great pride in the fact that the initial letters of the last four Hebrew words of this verse are an acronym of the name Nachman: Nachal Nove'a Mekor Chokhmah!

V 5: "It is not good to respect the person of the wicked and to turn aside the righteous in judgment." Besides the plain meaning of the text, the sages darshened that it is not good for the wicked to be shown forbearance for their evil in this world since they are then punished for it in the next, while the righteous are punished for their sins in this world in order to attain the life of the world to come (Yoma 87a; Rashi).

V 6: "A fool's lips enter into contention and his mouth calls for strokes." A fool constantly accuses others but the effect is that his mouth calls out for suffering to be brought down upon himself (Rashi).

V 9: "Even one who is slack in his work is a brother to the destroyer." When a Torah student is slack in his studies, he comes to distort and forget the Torah.

V 10: "The Name of HaShem is a tower of strength; the righteous runs with it and is set on high." It is remarkable that a mere word or name could give such strength and protection. Even more remarkable is that one who takes refuge in a mighty physical tower is closed up in it and cannot go anywhere, but when the Tzaddik depends on the name of HaShem, he can run wherever he wants and still take strength there in God's name (Metzudat David).

Vv 11-12: Unlike the Tzaddik, who trusts in God, the rich man takes refuge in his wealth, but if he is haughty because of it, this can lead to his destruction (Rabbeinu Yonah).

V 13: "When one gives an answer about something before he has heard it out, this is folly and a disgrace to him." Unfortunately, this characterizes the level of much discussion of serious issues over wide areas of the contemporary media and education system, not to speak about most discussion in the "street".

V 14: "The spirit of a man will sustain his infirmity, but a broken spirit who can bear?" Man's soul has the power to strengthen him in face of the illnesses of the body, for the soul governs the body in health and even in illness, but if the soul is weak and broken because of sorrow and depression, the body is unable to strengthen it (Metzudat David). Mind over matter!

V 16: "A man's gift makes room for him...." Besides the simple meaning, this teaches that when one gives charity, it widens his share in the world to come (Rashi).

V 17: "He who pleads his cause first seems just, but his neighbor comes and searches him out." The first person to put his case often sounds right. The judge must be very careful not to allow himself to be influenced by his arguments without first balancing them with the arguments of the other side.

V 21: "Death and life are in the power of the tongue...." Every one of us should take this verse to heart and put a strong rein on our tongues.

V 22: "One who finds a wife finds a great good...." Besides the plain meaning of the verse, the "woman" also refers to the Torah (Rashi).

V 24: Rashi: "When a person acquires friends for himself, the day will yet come when he will need them and they will draw him near. And if you say, 'So what?' know that sometimes a friend is closer than a brother and reaches out to one more than one's relatives and brothers."

CHAPTER 19

V 2: "Also the soul that is without knowledge is not good..." - "It is not good for a man to be without Torah" (Rashi). "...And he who hastens with his feet is a sinner" - "The sinner tramples on sins underfoot saying, 'This is an insignificant matter and I can transgress'" (Rashi).

V 3: "A man's folly perverts his way and his heart frets against God" - "It is through his own sin that evil comes upon a person because in his folly he perverts his way and transgresses, with the result that he is punished. But when the trouble strikes, he frets against God, questioning His justice!" (Rashi).

V 4: One who is wealthy in Torah also gains many friends.

V 6: "This can be interpreted as referring to those who give charity, and it can also be interpreted as referring to those who teach and spread the Torah."

V 7: "All the brothers of the poor hate him; how much more do his friends go far from him. He that pursues words - they turn against him" - "He says, So-and-so and so-and-so are my relatives; so-and-so and so-and-so are my friends, but all his words are emptiness" (Rashi). Name-dropping does not help!

V 8: "He who acquires heart loves his own soul..." - "Because the knowledge of God is in the heart, the verse says that one who acquires heart loves his own soul" (Metzudat David).

V 12: "The king's wrath is like the roaring of a lion..." - "The 'king' is the Holy One blessed be He (Rashi).

V 16: "...One who despises his ways shall die" - "because he does not set his heart to weigh them" (Rashi).

V 17: "When a person is ill and near death, his charity pleads on his behalf before the attribute of Judgment, saying, 'That poor man's soul was about to leave his body because of hunger, but this man fed him and brought it back into his body; I too shall give him back his soul'" (Rashi).

V 19: "A man of great wrath shall suffer punishment, but if you save, you shall yet add" - "If you set aside your anger and save your enemy when you see that evil has come upon him, you shall yet add days and goodness to your life" (Rashi).

V 22: "The desire for a man is on account of his kindness..." - the main reason why people love a person is because of his kindness."...and a poor man is better than a man of deceit" - If a person promises but does not carry out his promise, a poor man is better than him (Rashi).

V 25: "When you strike the scorner, the simple will become prudent..." - "On seeing the plagues visited on Pharaoh and the war against Amalek, Jethro became wise and converted!" (Rashi).

CHAPTER 20

V 1: "Wine is a mocker..." because it gives the drinker the feeling that his mind is expanded, but this is deceptive.

V 2: Whoever provokes the king - God - endangers himself.

V 3: People often get into an argument because they feel affronted, but man's true dignity is to restrain himself and avoid being drawn into a quarrel.

V 4: Because of the cold, the lazy man avoids "plowing" - i.e. exerting himself in Torah study - and as a result, when his time of need arrives, he finds himself lacking (Rashi).

V 5: The way of the wise man is to conceal his counsel in the depths of his heart (deep beneath the surface of his words), making it hard for others to grasp it. His counsel is like waters that lie deep beneath the surface of the earth and are hard to draw out. But "a man of understanding will draw it out": he starts by drawing out the upper waters - seeking to understand the surface meaning - and this will bring him to what lies below (Metzudat David).

V 6: Most people like to give the impression that they are very kind and considerate, but who can find people who not only promise but actually deliver?

V 8: When God sits on His throne of judgment, all men's evil is "spread out" and visible in front of His eyes, even what they do in secrecy (Metzudat David).

V 9: "Who can say... 'I am pure from my sin' (**chatati**)?" The Hebrew word **chatati** can also mean, "I have sinned" - the opening word of the confession. Thus, the verse can be construed as saying, "Who can say. I am pure in the way I make my confession before God?" for even as we confess to God we may have ulterior motives. We have to repent not only over our actual sins but even over our inadequate confessions of sin (Rabbi Nachman, Likutey Moharan I:6).

V 10: "Diverse weights and measures are both an abomination of God." When a person uses one set of criteria to judge his friends and a different set to judge his enemies and opponents, this is an abominable distortion of judgment. This occurs almost daily in international condemnations of Israeli behavior, yet we also should not allow our disgust at the abominations of others to justify our turning a blind eye to our own imperfections.

V 12: The ear and the eye are God's work. What He wants is an ear that listens to reproof and an eye that sees what is likely to develop out of one's different possible choices in life (Rashi).

V 13: Wealth and satisfaction (= Torah, good deeds and the enjoyment of the reward they bring) do not come to those who are lazy and like to sleep away their days.

V 14: During the bargaining before a purchase, the buyer downgrades the article in order to push down the price, but after the purchase he is proud of his ability to strike a good deal. Similarly, when a person seeks to attain the wisdom of the Torah despite poverty and hardship, he complains, but afterwards he will be overjoyed over the great good that he has gained (Metzudat David).

V 15: Gold and jewels may be expensive yet they are quite abundant in this world. What is really precious and rare is a mouth that speaks true wisdom! (Metzudat David).

V 16: While it is forbidden to enter the house of a borrower to take a pledge, it is permitted to enter the house of the guarantor of the loan in order to do so, since he willfully agreed to be a guarantor (Bava Metzia 115a).

V 18: "If you come to fight against the Satan, come with wise stratagems - repentance, prayer and fasting" (Rashi).

V 19: Don't open your heart to those who are indiscreet.

V 21: "An estate may be gotten hastily at the beginning, but its end shall not be blessed" - Thus the tribes of Reuben, Gad and half Menasheh took their portion east of the River Jordan before all the other tribes - and they went into exile before all the other tribes! (Rashi).

V 24: Our very footsteps are governed by God although we do not know it. "A man does not hurt even his little finger here below unless it is decreed against him from above" (Chulin 7b).

V 25: "When a man stumbles into sin, he causes a flaw to his own holiness, and he must then offer sacrifices in order to plead for his soul" (Rashi).

V 27: Man's own soul bears witness against him on the Day of Judgment (Rashi).

CHAPTER 21

V 1: "The king's heart is in the hand of God: like watercourses, He turns it wherever He will." It should be comforting to know that the decisions made by the apparently self-willed rulers and leaders of this world are in fact all under God's complete control, and He will surely bring everything out right in the end!

V 2: People are naturally prejudiced in their own favor and rarely see their own guilt, but God knows the truth.

V 3: Even King Solomon, who built the Temple, the center for the offering of sacrifices, taught that what God really wants is not ritual atonement but charity and justice.

V 5: True gains come from toil and industry, while those who try to "get rich quick" are likely to end up lacking.

V 11: "Through witnessing the chastisements that befall the scoffers, the simple become wise and repent" (Rashi).

V 12: "The Righteous One considers the house of the wicked, overthrowing the wicked to their ruin." Metzudat David offers an interesting alternative p'shat (explanation): When a righteous person stands in the house of a wicked man, this righteous Tzaddik brings success to the house of the wicked man, who is blessed on account of the Tzaddik, and this itself causes the wicked man to continue doing evil, thinking that the blessing has been sent on his own account and that his behaviour is good in God's eyes. Metzudat's explanation would open a chink into the mysteries of God's providence, whereby the wicked are deceived into continuing their pursuit of evil in this world in order to cause them to lose everything in the world to come.

V 14: Rabbi Chanina Bar Papa used to distribute charity at night-time [when nobody could see him, thereby saving the recipients embarrassment]. One time the king of the demons approached him and said, "Have you not taught us, rabbi, that 'you shall not encroach on the boundary of your neighbor' (Deut. 19:14)? [I.e. why are you performing mitzvot at night, which is the time of the demons?] He replied, "Is it not written, 'A gift in secrecy pacifies anger'?" (Shekalim 15a).

V 15: "To do justly is joy to the righteous but ruin to the workers of iniquity" - "God's joy is to take retribution from the righteous in this world in order to give them merit for the life of the world to come, and the righteous rejoice when God chastises them in order for them to gain the life of the world to come. However, chastisements do not avail the wicked because they do not take note and repent, and instead they only complain" (Rashi).

V 18: "The wicked is a ransom for the righteous" - "The righteous is saved and the wicked comes in his stead, such as in the case of Mordechai and Haman" (Rashi).

V 22: "A wise man scales the city of the mighty..." - "This alludes to Moses, who ascended to heaven among the mighty angels, and brought down the Torah" (Rashi).

V 28: "A false witness shall perish, but the man that **obeys** shall speak unchallenged" - i.e. the man who **obeys** the Torah, which says, "You shall not bear false testimony against your neighbor" (Rashi).

V 31: Men may make their preparations for self-protection in the face of war, but ultimately salvation is from God alone.

CHAPTER 22

V 1: The "name" that should be chosen more than great wealth is one's own good name and reputation as keeper of God's Torah. It is also **the** "good name", God's holy Name that we should set before us at all times (Psalm 16:8; Shulchan Aruch, Orach Chayim 1:1). The "grace" (**chein**) that is better than silver and gold is the vessel one constructs through one's Torah study, prayers, good deeds and attributes in order to receive the light of God's presence in the form of awareness and knowledge of God (Likutey Moharan I:1).

V 2. The rich and the poor man meet when the poor man says to the rich man give me livelihood and the latter answers harshly. They meet again in the wheel of destiny, for "God makes them all" - He brings them to life again and makes the rich man poor and the poor man rich! (Rashi).

V 3: The prudent man sees evil - the punishment for sin - and hides away: he does not carry out the sin (Rashi).

V 4: English translations render: "The reward (**eikev**) of humility is fear of God," implying that fear of God comes as a result of, and is a higher level than humility. But literally **eikev** means a "heel" - i.e. implying that the main thing is humility, and its lowest level, the "heel", is fear of God (Rashi).

V 5: "Thorns (**tzeenim**) and snares are in the way of the stubborn...." From this the rabbis deduced that everything is in the hands of heaven (determined by God) except for chills and colds (the root **tzanan** means to be chilled), which a person allows to come upon him through his own obstinate negligence, while one who guards his life and soul will keep away from the things that cause them (Avodah Zarah 3b).

V 6: "According to what you teach a young child and how you educate him in different things whether for good or for bad, even when he is old he will not veer from that path" (Rashi). Early education in the good ways of God's Torah is vital.

V 7: "The rich man rules over the poor people..." - the ordinary people are always in need of a student of the Torah (Rashi).

V 8: As one sows, so one reaps - according to one's behavior in this life, so is the reward one receives afterwards. A person may rule over people with fierce anger, but eventually his straw stick of dominion is worn down because he uses up his own power (Rashi).

V 10: "Cast out the scorner and contention will go away...." The "scorner" is the evil urge (Rashi). By wholeheartedly embracing the good within us and dissociating ourselves from our bad impulses and negativity, we may free ourselves of inner conflict and attain harmony.

V 11: When one frees one's heart of impurity, and sanctifies his lips by speaking only words of grace - Torah and devotion - God loves him and favors him (Rashi).

V 13: "The lazy man says, 'There's a lion outside, I'll get slain in the streets'" – "He says, 'How can I go out to learn Torah?'" (Rashi).

V 14: The "strange woman" whose mouth is a "deep pit" is the preacher of heresy and idolatry.

V 15: King Solomon teaches us not to idealize children and imagine them to be perfect angels because "foolishness is bound up in the heart of a child". Children are subject to a natural folly, and they have to be trained with the "rod of correction". Likewise, in ch 23 v 13 King Solomon advises not to spare the child correction, "for if you strike him with the rod he will not die". The sages were opposed to cruel physical punishment but understood better than contemporary psychologists and "experts" in discipline that at times children are in need of wisely administered physical punishment in order to grow out of this natural folly.

V 16: If a person oppresses the poor for his own gain, he will eventually have to give away all his money to wealthy idolaters and the governments of the nations, so that all his efforts result only in his own loss (Rashi).

From the beginning of Proverbs Chapter 10 until this point the entire text has consisted of one-verse aphorisms that are often if not mostly unconnected thematically with those preceding and following them. However, from Chapter 22:17 onwards longer sequences of verses are often employed, making up short discourses, though not of the length of the discourses with which the book of Proverbs opens in Chs 1-9.

Vv 17ff: "Incline your ear and hear the words of the wise" - try to learn Torah from even the merest sage; "and apply your heart to **my** knowledge" - if your teacher is wicked, don't learn from his behaviour (Rashi). It is to the quest for the inner knowledge of God that Solomon is telling us to give our hearts - "In order that your trust may be in HaShem" (v 19): this is the very essence.

V 20: "Have I not written for you, excellent things (**shaleeshim**)". **Shaleeshim** literally means captains, honored leaders (cf. Ex. 16:4) - Solomon's proverbs are all important teachings. **Shaleeshim** also has the connotation of "threefold", alluding to the Torah, Nevi'im (Prophets) and Kesubim (Holy Writings). "If you say, 'How can I trust in God and turn my heart from all other activities so as to study the words of my teachers - maybe they are mistaken and there is no place to trust in God and expect to receive a reward?' - King Solomon answers this objection by saying that you can find words of true counsel and knowledge in the books of the Torah" (Metzudat David). Even if you feel you cannot fully trust the people who are teaching you Torah, if you are willing to delve into the Torah itself you will be able to find the truth.

Vv 22-29 is a short **Parshah Petuchah** ("open", free-standing section) containing several pieces of advice. (1) vv 22-23: Don't oppress the poor even though they are weak, because God will stand up for and avenge them. (2) vv 24-25: Don't befriend angry types, because you will learn from their bad ways, which will be a snare for you; (3) vv 26-27: Don't get involved in deals that leave you with commitments that you are unable to meet, to the point where your creditors take everything from you. (4) v 28: Don't encroach on others' territory, literally - and also, don't encroach on the boundaries set by the fathers: these are the ancestral customs of Israel, such as the three daily prayers, which should not be changed. (Yalkut Shimoni. (5) v 29: Be energetic and enthusiastic in your service of God.

CHAPTER 23

Vv 1-5: Ostensibly this short discourse advises against succumbing to the temptation to join the mighty and powerful in order to become wealthy because their tasty dainties are the bread of deception and any wealth one may gain will eventually fly off and disappear. However, the sages darshened this discourse as advice to a student sitting before his teacher seeking to gain the wealth of Torah: "Consider well he that is before you" - "If you know that he will give you an answer to anything that you ask him, be careful to ask him whatever you need to know. But if not, keep quiet (v 2 - "put a knife in your throat") and (v 3) separate yourself from him in order to go to a worthy teacher. Vv 4-5: Don't try to "get rich" in your studies by learning heaps of unrelated details which you will only forget - try to understand how the various details fit logically together (Chulin 6a).

Vv 6-8: Don't eat the bread of the mean-eyed.

V 9: Don't waste wise words on a fool who will despise their wisdom.

V 10: Don't encroach on others' rights, such as that of poor orphans to the agricultural gifts that must be given to the poor: **Leket**, the gleanings, **Shich'chah**, the forgotten sheaf and **Pe'ah**, the corner of the field that must be left unharvested (Rashi).

Vv 12-14: Submit yourself to correction and chastisement and do not withhold it from those whom it is your responsibility to educate - correction **does not kill!**

Vv 15-16: God's greatest delight is when His children follow the path of wisdom and speak the truth.

Vv 17ff: The perennial temptation is to want to follow the sinning herd because of their apparent success. Don't give in.

V 20-21: Don't give into the desire to quaff wine and eat much meat in this world, for those drunk with and gluttonous for the pleasures of this world will end up poor in Torah and they will have nothing but tattered rags with which to clothe their souls in the world of truth.

V 23: It is forbidden to "sell" the Torah by charging a fee for teaching. Yet if you see that the only way to acquire the truth is by paying, "Acquire the truth…." (See Bechorot 29a).

Vv 26-28: Again and again, Solomon reiterates the importance of following the path of Torah wisdom and distancing oneself from the "harlot" and "alien woman" = heresy.

Vv 29-35 give a vivid depiction of the cries, complaints and self-caused injuries of the red-eyed drunkards who sit up late drinking, always in search of good liquor. One should not so much as look at wine when it is red (v 31), despite the fact that it is so lusciously tempting and high quality (on the basis of this verse, red wine is considered the best and choicest for Kiddush and the Four Cups of Pesach). The redness alludes to **Gevurah**, the very might that contracts and conceals Godliness. Thus, the drunkenness depicted in this section comes from the "wine" of alien wisdom offered by the strange woman. In the end, it bites like a serpent (v 32) making the eye see strange things and turning the heart into confusion (v 33). The person ends up completely addicted (v 35).

CHAPTER 24

Vv 1-14: Having warned against associating with the "strange woman" (23:27ff) and falling into drunkenness (23:29-35), King Solomon now warns against following in the ways of those who seek to build their fortunes through robbery and mischief (24:2). Rather, one should seek out wisdom and understanding, for these bring true and enduring wealth, the wealth of the spirit. "For a house is built through wisdom and established through understanding. And with knowledge the rooms will be filled." (vv 3-4). These verses are the foundation for important kabbalistic teachings about the Sefirot of Chochmah, Binah and Da'at.

V 6: "Make your war with wise stratagems (**tachboolot**)...." The war in question is that against our evil urge. It is often impossible to engage the evil urge directly in order to overwhelm it, because its power is very great. It is better to use wise stratagems in order **circumvent** and get around it. For example, when a person rises early in the morning to pray and follows his prayers immediately with a session of Torah study, this takes the wind out of the sails of the evil urge before it even has a chance to attack. "Who do you find fighting the war of the Torah? The person who has in hand bundles (**chavilot**) of mishnahs!" (Sanhedrin 42a).

Vv 8-9: When a person does not devote his intellectual faculties to the pursuit of wisdom but instead uses them to plot evil, he will get a reputation as a man of mischief and his evil thoughts and scoffing are a sin and an abomination.

Vv 10-12: "If you are weak on the day of adversity, your strength is small indeed." On the simple level, these verses are teaching that one should not abandon his friends on their day of trouble because he will then be too weak to help himself when trouble strikes him. The rabbis darshened that if a person allows himself to become lax in studying the Torah, he will not have the strength to stand on his day of trouble (Rashi on v 10; Berachot 63a).

Vv 13-14: A person should pursue wisdom with the same if not more enthusiasm than that with which people like to eat sweet honey!

V 15ff: Solomon cautions the wicked not to lie in wait to take advantage when they see a righteous man tottering, because even if the Tzaddik falls repeatedly he will still rise up in the end. The final letters of the four Hebrew words **shevA yipoL TzaddiK va-kaM** ("the Tzaddik may fall seven times but rises") are an anagram of AMaLeK, the archetypal evil. When the wicked fall, they do not rise up again.

Vv 17-18: Even a righteous person should not exult triumphantly when his enemy falls. For this reason, on the festival of Pesach, with the exception of the first day it is customary not to recite the complete **Hallel** (Psalms 113-118) so as not to show undue glee at the time of the overthrow of the Egyptians and their drowning in the Red Sea (Yalkut Shimoni).

V 21: "My son, fear God and the king..." - "One should show respect to the ruler on condition that he does not turn you away from fear of God: the fear of God always takes priority" (Rashi). "...and do not meddle with those who are given to change (**shonim**)" - "These are the heretics who say there are two (**shnayim**) domains" (Rashi).

V 23: "These also are sayings for the wise..." - "All the teachings below are directed particularly to the sages who sit in judgment - they must have no respect for persons when judging" (Rashi).

Vv 24-25: "One who says to a wicked person, 'You are righteous', will be cursed. But to those who offer reproof, it will be pleasant." Metzudat David (on v 25) explains the connection between these verses: If one tells a wicked person that he is righteous, this will merely encourage him to go further in his wickedness. However, in the case of those who seek to reprove the wicked, it can be advantageous to say to a wicked person, 'In truth you really are a Tzaddik, but you have gone astray in certain particulars and these you should correct'. If they were to openly call him wicked, it could cause him to counter-react and stubbornly protest his innocence, whereas this way they can draw his heart to them and induce him to listen to their words. Metzudat's comment can help us better understand Rabbi Nachman's teaching to search for the good even in bad people in order to elevate them.

V 27: "Prepare your work outside and establish it for yourself in the field, and afterwards build your house." The rabbis interpreted this verse literally as advising that one should first get a place to live, then work on establishing a livelihood (with fields and vineyards) and only afterwards build his house = marry. They also interpreted the verse homiletically as teaching that one should first study Bible, then master the Mishnah, and only afterwards try to darshen and fathom the depths of the Torah (Sotah 44a).

V 30: "I passed by the field of the sluggard..." - "This is the person who fails to review what he has studied. First, he starts forgetting some of the main principles, and in the end, he twists the words of the sages ruling that which is pure to be impure and that which is impure to be pure, and he destroys the world" (Rashi). The Talmud darshens: "I passed by the field of the sluggard" - this alludes to King Ahaz; "...and by the vineyard of a man lacking heart" - this is Menasheh. "...and lo, it was all grown over with thistles" - this is Ammon; "...its face was covered with nettles" - this is Yeho'akim; "...and its stone wall was broken down" - this is Tzedekiah, in whose time the Temple was destroyed (Sanhedrin 103a).

CHAPTER 25

V 1: "These too are the proverbs of Solomon, which the men of Hezekiah king of Judah copied out." Metzudat David writes on this verse: "It would appear that the proverbs from the beginning of the book up until this point were copied over and available in everyone's hands, but the proverbs from here until the end of the book were only available to the staff of King Hezekiah, who copied these teachings from scrolls of King Solomon that they discovered. This is why it says that **these too** are the proverbs of

Solomon despite the fact that they were not available to everyone. Nevertheless, these too are his teachings, which were copied over by Hezekiah's men, and they are reliably attributed to Solomon."

V 2: "The glory of God is a matter that must be concealed, but the glory of kings is a matter that may be investigated." The "glory of God" refers to the esoteric wisdom of **Ma'aseh Merkhavah**, the "Work of the Chariot" and **Ma'aseh Bereishit**, the "Work of Creation", as well as to those statutes of the Torah that are beyond the grasp of human reason (such as the ashes of the Red Heifer and the prohibition against wearing mixtures of wool and linen etc.). It is forbidden to investigate these matters too deeply or to search for reasons. On the other hand, the "glory of kings" alludes to the rulings and enactments which the sages made as a "fence" around the Torah: here it is permitted to investigate and ask for reasons (Rashi).

Vv 4-5: Just as the removal of impure admixtures from silver leads to the production of a good vessel, so the removal of the wicked from the kingdom establishes the throne of the ruler.

Vv 6-7: It is inadvisable to flaunt oneself before those who are greater than oneself; it is better to wait modestly to be called to greatness rather than to push oneself forward only to be cast down.

V 11: "Like apples of gold in settings of silver is a word spoken fitly (**al ophnav**)." The phrase **al ophnav** literally means either "on its foundation" or "on its wheel". Just as golden knobs set on a background of silver are most beautiful, so is a word - a **mashal** or "metaphor" - that sits and fits perfectly on its basis, which is the **nimshal** or subject of the comparison. A good **mashal** should perfectly reflect and constantly return to its **nimshal** just as a wheel revolves and always goes back to its place (cf. Metzudat David).

V 14: When someone boastfully gets up in the synagogue and promises a large gift of charity but then fails to deliver, it is like clouds and vapors but no rain: the poor are desperately longing for his help, and it does not materialize (Rashi).

V 15: While God is still showing patience before exacting retribution, this is when the sinners should set themselves to conciliate Him with repentance and prayer, for a "soft tongue" - prayer and supplication - have the power to break the harsh decree (Rashi).

Vv 21f: "If your enemy is hungry, give him bread to eat...." The rabbis darshened: If your enemy, the evil urge, is "hungry" and tells you to satisfy him with sins, then you should take yourself off to the study hall and feed him with the bread and water of Torah, for this way you rake burning coals onto his head, and God will deliver you from him so that he will not get the better of you (Succah 52a).

V 27: "Eating too much honey is not good, but the investigation of their glory is glory." Eating too much honey, refers to delving too deeply into the esoteric wisdom of the Work of Creation and the Work of the Chariot. One should not reveal these secrets in public as it causes the ignorant to ridicule them and to enquire "what is above" and "what is below". Where then should one focus one's investigations? Upon the words of the sages, "whose glory is glory": it is permitted to ask the reasons for their various enactments and for the "fences" they erected around the Torah (Rashi).

V 28: A person who cannot control his own temper makes himself vulnerable to danger just like a city whose defenses have been torn down.

PROVERBS
CHAPTER 26

Verses 1-12 speak out in various ways against the "fool" - **kheseel**. The **kheseelim** are defined by Rabbeinu Yonah (on Proverbs 1:22) as those who have acquired a stock of bad deeds, transgressing in order to satisfy the demands of their eyes for pleasures and delights. He explains that when a person pursues worldly pleasures, he becomes ever more distant from the spiritual and intellectual levels of his soul.

V 1: "Like snow in summer and like rain at harvest time, so honor is not seemly for a fool." Snow in the summer fruit-drying season is disastrous, as is rain during the harvest. Likewise, honor - meaning not only worldly prestige but also knowledge of the Torah, particularly its esoteric dimension, as in 25:2 above - is not fitting for one who is not in control of his evil urge.

V 2: Such a person is liable to lash out at others with harsh judgments and curses. One need not worry when abused by a fool: he may scatter gratuitous curses like darting birds, but if they go anywhere it is only upon himself.

V 3: Chastisement is the only medicine for the **kheseel**, who is like a stubborn animal.

Vv 4-5: These two verses teach us when to avoid an argument with a **kheseel** and when it is necessary to answer him. If the **kheseel** tries to draw one into a quarrel, one should give no answer in order not to lower oneself to his level (v 4). However, if the **kheseel** makes an assertion which, if unanswered, will cause him to be wise in his own eyes, it is necessary to counter it explicitly and not to leave him unanswered (Rashi).

V 6: It is not worth appointing a **kheseel** as one's representative or envoy because this will involve one in much extra work trying to undo the damage he is liable to cause.

V 7: A person limps when one thigh is higher than the other. Likewise, when the fool employs a **mashal** to express himself, it is not even with - it does not **fit** - the **nimshal**, and his thoughts merely "limp".

V 8: The **margema** is a sling: a stone placed in it does not stay there long, and likewise the honor - Torah knowledge - transmitted to a fool does not stay with him. From this verse, the sages deduced that teaching an unworthy student is like practicing the idolatrous ritual of throwing stones towards **Markulis** (Chulin 133a).

Vv 9-10: Rashi interprets these two verses as connected. The **mashal** or parable touted by the fools (v 9), is that expressed in v 10: God created everything (= **rav meholel kol**) and evidently employs both fools and idlers for His purposes. Since He seemingly judges everyone equally, whether wise or foolish, there is no need to pursue wisdom! This false proverb provides the fool with justification for continuing on his own path of folly.

Vv 13-16 speak out against the sluggard, who finds endless excuses for avoiding doing what he has to do, turning from side to side on his bed in order to avoid getting up.

Vv 17ff preach against various kinds of evil-intentioned, quarrelsome and argumentative types.

V 17 cautions not to get involved in other people's strife as this is like taking a dog by the ears, only to get bitten.

Vv 18-19: "As a madman who casts firebrands, arrows and death, so is the man that deceives his neighbor and says, 'Am I not in sport?'" - these verses are taken to typify **Ishmael**, whom Sarah saw "playing" with Isaac (Gen. 21:9; see Rashi on Gen. 29:10).

V 20: Contention is caused by somebody: there is always someone who instigates it.

Vv 23ff: Burning lips and a wicked heart are the hallmarks of those dissimulators who speak smooth, seductive words as if they love their listeners when in fact they are their enemies and harbor evil intentions.

V 27: The archetypal case of one who dug a pit only to fall into it was Bilaam, who advised Balak to seduce Israel with the Midianite women but when he went to Midian to demand his reward, he was killed there. The archetypal case of one who rolled a stone that later killed him was Avimelech: he killed his seventy brothers on one stone, but in the end, was killed by a millstone that crushed his head (Judges 9:53; see Rashi on Proverbs 26:27).

CHAPTER 27

V 1: "Man proposes but God disposes": When making plans for the future, those who fear God and know His great power qualify themselves by saying, **im yirtzeh HaShem** - "if God wills".

V 5: Even if a person is subject to an open rebuke that causes him shame and embarrassment, this is good if it stems from true love hidden in the heart of the one delivering the rebuke.

V 7: When a Torah student feels he has already learned sufficient and does not yearn for more wisdom, he comes to loathe even "honeycomb" - he is not interested even in sound Torah reason. But for a person who craves Torah wisdom, even the things that come to him with bitterness and effort are sweet to him (cf. Rashi).

V 8: Just as it is hard for a bird to be away from her nest, so it is hard for a person to be away from his true place. This alludes to the soul, whose true place is in the world to come and which is like a wanderer in this world (Zohar Devarim 278a).

V 9: Offering sweet words of wise counsel to our friends is the surest way to uplift them.

V 10: "Do not forsake your own friend..." (=God) "...and your father's friend..." (God favored your fathers, and if you forsake Him you will suffer.) "…neither go into your brother's house in the day of your calamity…" (do not trust that the children of Esau and Ishmael will show you favor). "Better is a neighbor that is near..." (this is God, who is **near** to those who call Him) "…than a distant brother" (this is Esau; Rashi).

V 14: "He that blesses his friend in a loud voice early in the morning, it shall be counted a curse to him." The Midrash gives examples of people who loudly praised the great wealth and success of certain individuals, only to cause government officials to confiscate their possessions or thieves to steal them (Avot d'Rabbi Nathan 22b).

V 17: Torah students sharpen each other mentally through their discussions (Rashi).

V 19: The feelings we radiate to others have a decisive influence over the feelings they radiate back. The more we open our hearts and show kindness to those to whom we seek to reach out, the easier they will find it to open their hearts to us.

V 21: "...and a man is tried by his praise" - "In virtue of the way people praise a person for his good deeds, he is tested as to whether he is good or bad" (Rashi).

Vv 23-27 are ostensibly addressed to the shepherd or owner of flocks cautioning him to consider constantly what they need, for the investment will be well worth it. Wealth and power are evanescent, but even when there is no more pasture left for the flocks, the flock-owner will still benefit from their wool, their skins and meat and cheese etc. Homiletically, these verses are darshened as advising the Rabbi appointed over the community to take his "flock" under his wing and lead them gently, so that he will eat the fruits of his endeavors while the principal will remain. As his teachings spread, these "lambs" will provide him with "garments", for his students will give him a name and a garb of splendor and glory (Rashi).

CHAPTER 28

V 1: "The wicked flee when no-one pursues [they will be easily routed on their day of doom, Rashi], but the righteous are as secure as a young lion [the Tzaddik strengthens his heart in God, Rashi]." While the English translation renders the main sense of the verse, it misses an interesting nuance in the original, where the Hebrew word for "wicked" is a singular form (**Rasha**) while the verb "flee" (**nasoo**) is a plural form, and conversely the Hebrew word for "righteous" is a plural (**Tzaddikim**) while the verb rendered as "are... secure" (**yivtach**) is in fact singular. This seems to imply that each wicked person is alone unto himself but collectively they will all flee, while the Tzaddikim are together and united, but each one has the strength and confidence of a young lion!

V 2: "For the transgression of the land, many are its princes..." - "This is the punishment of the land, when its officers are many and they pursue only their own gain" (Rashi). This applies directly to the present-day government of Israel, where prime ministers patch together their shaky coalitions by creating ever more ministries to provide "jobs for the boys". It may also be safely assumed that the many grotesque publicized cases of corruption at the highest levels of government represent only the tip of the iceberg of the corruption that actually exists.

V 3: The "poor man" who oppresses the weak is the judge who is an **am ha-aretz** (=Torah ignoramus). This would be a fair description of the great majority of the judges of the Israeli High Court ("**BaGaTz**"), who have been notorious for trampling on the laws of the Torah since the inception of the state.

V 4: "Those who have abandoned the Torah praise the wicked, but those who observe the Torah contend with them." It would be interesting to use this proposition to analyze the heroes of secular Israel and those who have forced the Torah observant to contend with them.

V 5: Even when punishments befall the wicked, they do not understand that this is to requite their evil because they think everything comes by chance. But the righteous understand that everything comes from Heaven, and they are able to understand why and for what reason, because they do not attribute anything to chance (Metzudat David).

V 8: Profiting from taking interest on loans to fellow Israelites is considered one of the most serious transgressions of the Torah. The verse says that the profits will go to "him that is gracious to the poor".

Midrash Tanchuma interprets this as the government, which on hearing of someone's great wealth confiscates his profits and uses them to build bridges and repair the roads to benefit the public. It will indeed be a great comfort when our governments really do take the exorbitant profits of the bankers and lenders and use them for the genuine benefit of the poorer sectors of society.

V 9: One who willfully flouts the Torah cannot expect his prayers to be heard.

V 11: "This verse is speaking about a teacher and a student: when the student scrutinizes what the teacher says, this makes the teacher wise!" (Rashi).

V 12: "At a time when the righteous rejoice because they enjoy great success, and everything is done according to their instructions, great is the beauty and harmony of the place because the voice of the oppressor is not heard. But when the wicked rise to rule, it is then that 'a man is sought out,' because these wicked people seek them out to steal their possessions" (Metzudat David). Another way in which many smaller players tend to be "sought out" in the corrupt political life of our times is through being submitted to grueling trials by the public media over often tiny misdemeanors while the big fish are left to get away with murder.

V 13: It is best to own up and confess to one's wrong-doing and to let go of it: this is what elicits God's compassion.

V 14: When a person is fearful of the punishment for sin, this keeps him away from sin (Rashi).

V 17 refers to a person who leads another astray, causing him to lose his soul: the person who caused him to stumble may flee for help and atonement until the day of his death, but Heaven will not allow him to repent so that he should not sit in the Garden of Eden while his student is in hell (Yoma 87a).

V 20: The "faithful man who abounds with blessings" is the person who gives his tithes to the poor "in faith" - i.e. he gives what he is obliged to give even though there is no witness to see exactly how much he gives. But God sees and multiplies his blessings (Rashi).

V 21 is addressed to the judge, cautioning him to have no respect for person and not to take bribes - for how can a person twist judgment for a mere morsel of bread???

V 23: "One who rebukes a man shall in the end find more favor than one who flatters with the tongue" - "Anyone who rebukes his neighbor for the sake of heaven attains a share in God, and not only that, but a thread of kindness is drawn down upon him" (Tamid 28a).

V 24: "One who robs his father and his mother and says, 'There is no transgression', is a companion of the destroyer" - "...his father..." is the Holy One blessed be He; "...his mother..." is the Assembly of Israel. One who causes the public to sin robs God, separating His children from Him, and robs them of goodness. The "destroyer" is Jeraboam (Rashi). This verse is also applied to a person who eats or has some other enjoyment from the world without making the appropriate **brachah** (blessing) (Berachot 35a).

V 27: One does not lose from giving a poor man help.

V 4: "With justice does the king establish the land, but he that exacts gifts overthrows it" - "If the judge is like someone who does not need to buy lovers and take bribes, he will establish the land, but if he is like a priest going around to all the barns to ask for tithes, he will destroy it" (Ketubot 105b).

V 7: "The righteous knows the cause (**Din**) of the poor..." - he knows the suffering of the poor and what they require, and he gives his heart to them" (Rashi).

V 8: The way of the scoffers is to foment strife, setting everywhere on fire, while the way of the righteous is to mediate peace and turn away people's wrath against their brothers.

V 11: "A fool spends all his spirit, but the wise man stills it afterwards." When having to argue with a fool, it is often best to let him pour out everything he has to pour out before answering wisely in order to still him.

V 12: "If a ruler listens to falsehood, all his servants are wicked" - "When the ruler listens to falsehood or accepts slanderous reports, all his attendants then turn into villains because in order to find favor in his eyes they give him slanderous reports and sin with their very souls" (Metzudat David). Parents, teachers, managers and leaders etc. who must constantly listen to what their children/students/workforce etc. have to say about each other should take careful note of Solomon's wisdom here.

V 13: "The poor man and the oppressor (**ish techamim**) meet together; HaShem enlightens the eyes of both of them." Metzudat David interprets the word rendered "oppressor" as someone that has been beaten down and broken, explaining that whether a person was born poor or was originally born rich but afterwards lost his wealth and was broken by the "illness" of poverty, this is not by chance. Everything comes from heaven through God's decree, and likewise if they afterwards become wealthy, this too is God's decree. Rashi interprets the **ish techamim** as a master of Torah, while the "poor man" is his student. When the student asks the teacher to teach him a chapter and the teacher does so, "God enlightens the eyes of both of them.

Vv 15 & 17: "The rod and reproof give wisdom..." "Correct your son and he will give you rest..." - "If you do so, you will not get angry on his account and you will yet rejoice over his deeds" (Metzudat David). King Solomon taught the opposite of the widespread present-day philosophy of leaving children without moral direction.

V 18: "When there is no vision, the people cast off restraint..." - "When Israel cause prophecy to depart from them through insulting the prophets, they breach holes in the walls and go astray" (Rashi). Part of the medicine is for us to study the prophets!!!

V 21: "When a person spoils his servant from youth, in the end he will be a ruler" - The "servant" is the evil urge (Rashi).

V 25: Is it the snare that causes man's fear, or his fear that causes a snare? The Hebrew can be read both ways, but Rashi's preferred interpretation is that the snare of a sin causes fear in man, i.e. if a person has sinned, this causes him to fear. This can be the key to many of people's phobias.

V 26: Many people try to accomplish their goals by trying to "pull strings" and use the influence of those in positions of power, but in truth, whatever a person attains is decreed by God and instead of appealing for help from flesh and blood it would be better to start by appealing to the true Judge.

CHAPTER 30

V 1: "The words of Agur Bin Yakeh...." After the very lengthy series of profoundly wise proverbs stretching all the way from Chapter 10 until this point, the present abrupt introduction to the closing discourses of Proverbs is very surprising. No names are in the TaNaKh by chance. Each has its own meaning, overtones and midrashim. Agur is none other than Shlomo himself, who here calls himself **Agur** from the Hebrew root **agar**, "he gathered" - for Solomon gathered and acquired Torah and understanding. **Bin-Yakeh**, the child that **vomits**! For he "vomited it out": The Torah writes "...and he shall not multiply wives for himself that his heart shall not go astray" –**ve-oochal**, "and I shall be able": Solomon said, "I shall multiply but I shall not go astray" (Tanchuma).

"The burden, says the man, unto Iti-el, unto Iti-el and I shall be able." The "man" = Shlomo, utters this burden = prophecy about himself, concerning Iti-el (= "God is with me"), because he depended upon his wisdom in multiplying gold, horses and wives, which the king is warned against, and he said "**Iti-Kel**, God is with me, and I shall be able: I shall multiply wives and they will not turn my heart astray, I shall multiply gold and not go astray, I will multiply horses and not return the people to Egypt" (Rashi).

V 2: "Surely I am brutish, unlike a man, and I do not have the understanding of a man" - Here Solomon expresses contrition, deploring his having relied on his own wisdom in a matter over which God warned him in case he would sin (Rashi).

V 3: "And I have not learned wisdom that I should have the knowledge of the Holy One" - "because I subtracted from or added to the words of the Torah" (Rashi).

Having spent the entire book of Proverbs urging us to seek wisdom, in these verses of contrition, Solomon is warning us not to depend on our own wisdom and reason but only upon the letter of the Torah, without seeking to change it or add or subtract in any way.

V 4: Solomon's rhetorical questions in this verse are darshened in various ways as referring to God Himself, who gave the Torah, and to Moses, who ascended to Heaven and brought the Torah down to earth (Yalkut Shimoni, cf. Rashi, Metzudat). "What is his name and what is the name of his son?" This is part of Solomon's self-reproof. As Rashi puts it: "If you say there was already someone else like him, tell me what his son's name is, from which family he came forth so that we may know who he is. "...if you know" - "if you know who he is; then how is it that you were not afraid to transgress His words?"

Vv 7-9: Now Solomon prays to God, making two requests: (1) Keep me away from falsehood. (2) Provide my needs so I will be neither poor nor rich, lest I become haughty and deny God or so poor that I steal, lie and take His name in vain.

V 10: This verse teaches that one should not cry to God asking Him to carry out judgment on someone, even if he is evil, not even if he and his generation carry out all the abominations enumerated in this and the ensuing verses (11-14). The proof is from the prophet Hoshea, who suggested that God should exchange Israel for another people, only to be commanded by God to take an adulterous woman as his wife (Rashi).

Vv 15-17: "The leech has two daughters..." - "The two daughters are the Garden of Eden and Gehennom. The one says, 'Give me the Tzaddikim' while the other says, 'Give me the wicked'" (Rashi). King Solomon is teaching us his conclusion after having erred through relying on his own wisdom. "There is no wisdom and no understanding before God" - the Torah has decreed what is righteous and what is wicked, and this cannot be changed. One who mocks this wisdom will suffer.

Vv 18ff: "There are three things that are too wonderful for me, yea four that I do not know" - "What this means is that just as there are three things that are concealed from me so that I do not know the path along which they went, so in the case of the fourth I do not know how to recognize the matter after it occurs" (Metzudat David). The fourth matter is expressed in v 20 - the way of an adulterous woman. For since she is married and no longer a virgin, if she has an adulterous relationship she can clean her "mouth" (down below) and no-one will be any the wiser. Solomon is deploring the adulterer and adulteress for believing that just as they can hide their act from men because of the speed and secrecy with which may be performed, so they think they can hide it from God.

The third of the four things that were "too wonderful" for Shlomo was "the way of a man with a young woman" (v 19). It is particularly important for those who have suffered from exposure to non-Jewish distortions of the meaning of the Biblical texts to note that the Hebrew term for "young woman" in this verse is **alma**, and it is perfectly clear from the context - the **way** of a man - that this verse is referring to physical relations. In the words of Metzudat Tzion (= Metzudat David when he defines the meanings of words) commenting on v 19: "A woman tender in years is called an **alma** even if she has had intercourse, as in 'Behold the young woman (**alma**) has conceived' (Isaiah 7:14)". Careful contemplation of the meaning of these verses together with Metzudat's comment shows that the translation of **alma** in Isaiah 7:14 as a "virgin" is preposterous.

V 21-3: The very earth quakes and rages over the upside-down human world in which slaves and maidservants rule - these are the empires of the Sitra Achra which rule during Israel's long exile.

V 24ff: We should learn from the industriousness of the ants, the patience of the rabbits who labor despite their weakness until they succeed in boring holes even in the rocks, from the discipline of the locusts who unify even without a leader and from the self-sufficient spider, who even in the chambers of kings prefers to eat from the own labors of her own hands.

CHAPTER 31

V 1: "The words of King Lemu-el, the burden with which his mother corrected him." Like the first verse of the previous chapter, the king in this verse is interpreted in rabbinic midrash (Bereshit Rabbah 10, Sanhedrin 70b) as referring to Solomon himself. He is **lemo-Kel**, facing or turned to God. He here recounts his mother's rebuke to him as if it is a prophecy received from God (Metzudat David). In the early sections of Proverbs, Solomon spoke of his father's chastisements to lead him on the path of wisdom. Now he speaks of those of his mother after the death of King David, after which he launches into a praise of the Wise Woman built as an acrostic on the letters of the Aleph Beit in vv 10-31 (Ibn Ezra). The rabbis tell that when King Solomon married the daughter of Pharaoh, on the day of the inauguration of the Temple she brought into him various kinds of musical instruments and he was awake for the whole night. The next morning, he slept until the end of the fourth hour of the day, and because the keys of the Temple courtyard were under his pillow they were unable to offer the daily perpetual offering, and his mother entered and rebuked him in the words that follow" (Metzudat David).

Batsheva's rebuke to Solomon consists of invaluable advice to the king not to dissipate his strength on women and not to drink, because wine is not for kings. "Open your mouth for the dumb..." (v 8) - "This means that if someone comes before you in judgment and is like a dumb person lacking the knowledge to order his claims and pleas, you should open your mouth for his sake to put his claims and pleas in order" (Metzudat David). The final advice to the king is that he must rule with justice (v 9).

Vv 10-31, **Eishet Chayil**, "A woman of valor," is well known to those who observe and love the holy Shabbat since this passage is recited weekly at the Friday night Shabbat table after greeting the angels prior to making the Kiddush. The evocation of the righteous, God-fearing woman makes a fitting conclusion to Solomon's Book of Proverbs, which has taken us along all the highways and byways of wisdom. Having warned repeatedly against succumbing to the allurements of the "strange woman" and her wares of heresy and sin, Solomon seals his book with the praises of "the woman that fears God" (v 30).

On one level **Eishet Chayil** is Solomon's praise of his own wise mother Batsheva (Metzudat). Midrashically, the passage is interpreted as a praise of the ideal woman of Israel as embodied in Sarah, the founding matriarch of the nation (Tanchuma). Rashi also interprets the Woman of Valor as referring to the Torah itself, and offers a detailed commentary on the entire passage from this perspective. Metzudat David more specifically relates the Woman of Valor to man's intelligent soul, which may dwell with him to a greater or lesser extent depending upon his deeds. "Who is it that can attain the intelligent soul to perfection so as to know and understand by himself every word of wisdom and intelligence???" (Metzudat David).

"The Woman of Valor is the Torah: happy is he who is worthy of finding her! He eats the fruits in this world and the world to come. To those who study her, she brings blessing and sustenance. From the fruits of her works she planted a vineyard - Israel - to sustain them for the life of the world to come. She is not afraid of the snow - of Gehennom - for her household. They are clothed in scarlet - the blood of circumcision. She laughs on the last day - they do not have to be depressed about God's attribute of Judgment because they will be saved from it. She looks to the ways of her household - the Torah teaches the good pathway so as to separate oneself from sin. Her children - the students - rise up and call her blessed, and her husband - the Holy One blessed be He. Grace is deceitful - this refers to all the nations and the vanity of their greatness and beauty. Give her - in time to come - of the fruit of her hands - beauty, greatness, strength, glory and rulership" (Rashi).

אִיּוֹב

JOB

CHAPTER 1

The book of Job is unique in the entire Bible canon as being a complete work devoted to one question: Why do good people suffer? This question has proved to be a most difficult and, at times, insuperable challenge to many people's faith in the God of justice.

The identity of Job himself and that of the author of the book bearing his name are both obscure in the extreme. The Talmud in Bava Batra (15b) brings no fewer than eight different opinions as to the period of time in which Job lived: at the time of the Exodus / in the time of the spies / in the time of Ezra / in the days of the Judges / in the time of Ahasuerus / during the ascendancy of Sheba / during the ascendancy of the Chaldeans / in the time of Jacob. The same passage in the Talmud also brings another opinion - that Job never existed at all but is a purely allegorical figure. Perhaps this opinion comes to emphasize that it hardly matters when Job actually lived or, because in truth he is a universal figure and the lessons to be learned from his book apply in all ages.

They apply not only to the people of Israel, to whom most of the books of the Bible are primarily addressed, but to all humanity. Thus although, according to some of the rabbinic opinions cited in the Talmud, Job could have been an Israelite, the most widely accepted opinion is that he was a righteous gentile, and it is precisely this that gives the book its universality. Job's own testimony about his upright path (chapter 29) provides a shining ideal to which all mankind should aspire.

When Job's companions came to comfort him in his suffering, they argued that suffering is sent to man because of his sins and that Job could therefore not have been completely righteous. Yet Job himself was unwavering in his protestations of his own innocence, and most of the rabbis agreed that Job did not sin. It is his very innocence that makes him the exemplar of the suffering Tzaddik, whereas had he sinned, it would have detracted from his quest to unravel the mystery of why the righteous suffer.

Many of the rabbis were of the opinion that the book of Job was written prophetically by Moses.

V 1: "There was a man in the land of **Ootz**...." The commentators associate this land with Aram Naharayim, where Nahor the brother of Abraham lived (Gen. 24:10) - Ootz was Nahor's firstborn (ibid. v 22). Targum on Lamentations 4:21 identifies "the land of **Ootz**" with Armenia, stating that this was inhabited by Edomites. Ibn Ezra and Ramban (on Job 1:1) concur in identifying Ootz as a land inhabited by Edomites. Ramban suggests that Job was a descendant of Abraham through Esau and that he knew his Creator and served him through fulfilling all the **Mitzvot** dictated by human reason and commonsense, in particular the **Mitzvot** of the heart, the root of all of which is the fear of God. Ramban argues that Job's companions were also Edomites, and in his introduction to the book of Job he suggests that it is appropriate that the lengthy dialogs it contains about human suffering are attributed to the descendants of Esau, the archetype of the sword-wielding warrior, symbolizing the Accuser who brings punishment into the world.

"And this man was pure and righteous, and he feared God and turned aside from evil." This description is to be taken at face value since these are not the words of Job himself but those of the author of the book.

Vv 2ff: Job attained the very summit of material success, possessing abundant livestock - the main wealth in antiquity - as well as being blessed with seven sons and three daughters, who lived in the lap of luxury, feasting every single day.

For fear that his children may have become arrogant and denied God, Job regularly offered **Olah** (whole burnt) offerings on their behalf. Verse 5 is adduced by the Talmud as proof that out of all the different kinds of Temple sacrifices, the **Olah** offering specifically came to atone for untoward thoughts (Yerushalmi Yoma 42a).

V 6: "And the day came when all the sons of God came to stand before HaShem..." - "This whole matter could have been known only by way of prophecy" (Ramban ad loc.). The prophet who wrote the book of Job depicts the heavenly scene on "**the day**" - "this was Rosh HaShanah, the Day of Judgment" (Rashi) - when all the angels gathered in the **Beit Din shel Ma'alah**, the "heavenly court". Although God is perfect unity and encompasses and includes all His angels, they are depicted as being "separate" from Him and "standing before Him" because each of the different angels depicts a different aspect or quality.

"...and the Satan too came in their midst." Again, God is perfect unity, but there is an aspect that comes to test and try men, and this aspect is embodied in the figure of the "Satan". The Hebrew word Satan relates to the word **sitnah** (Gen. 26:21 and Ezra 4:6) meaning strife and accusation. Commenting on our verse, the sages of the Talmud stated that the Satan has three roles. (1) He is the Tempter or **Yetzer Ra**, man's evil inclination. (2) Having tempted man and caused him to stumble, he then stands up as the Accuser, pointing to man's sins and demanding retribution. (3) Having indicted man, he comes to punish him in his third role, as the Angel of Death (Bava Batra 16a).

Vv 8-9: God Himself attests that in spite of Job's outstanding material success, he had not sinned in the way that so many of the wealthy and powerful sin, with arrogance and the denial of God. Yet the Satan argues that Job's righteousness had not yet been genuinely tested since he had been insulated from poverty and other harsh aspects of life.

Vv 11ff: The Satan demands that Job be tested to see if he will not blaspheme when he has a taste of suffering. God gives Satan authority to destroy Job's wealth and kill all his children - yet even in the face of these terrible calamities, Job does not complain that God has been unjust. Instead he stoically states in his immortal words: "Naked I came forth from my mother's belly and naked shall I return there. HaShem gave and HaShem took away - let the name of HaShem be blessed (v 21).

CHAPTER 2

"Health, children and livelihood are not dependent on merit but upon **Mazal**" (='fortune'?)" (Mo'ed Katan 28a). So far, the Satan had struck at two of the three fundamental pillars of Job's life - his livelihood (wealth) and children. But even this was not enough of a test.

V 4: "Skin covers skin…." If a person sees a blow coming to the skin of his face, he instinctively raises his hand to protect himself, preferring to suffer the blow on the skin of his hand in order to protect his head (see Rashi and Metzudat David on this verse). The Satan argues that Job had been content to suffer the loss of his wealth and children in order to protect himself from the loss of his life, but claims that as soon as the blow will come to Job's very skin and bones, he will break down and curse God because of his suffering. God now authorizes the Satan to submit Job to the worst of all tests, physical illness and pain, as long as he does not actually kill him.

Job's wife sees his terrible suffering and asks him what point there is in continuing to serve God now that he has lost everything: he might as well curse his bad fortune and die since he has nothing to live for. Job answers her with another immortal line (v 11): "Shall we accept the good from God but not accept the bad?"

In verse 11 our text testifies that even in the face of this terrible physical suffering, Job did not sin with his lips. The Talmud infers that "with his lips he did not sin, but he sinned in his heart! What did he say? 'The earth is given into the hand of the wicked, He covers the face of its judges' (Job 9:24)" (Bava Batra 16a). This implies that in his heart Job wondered if there is really a God. Since most of us have such thoughts at one time or another, it is somewhat comforting that even the righteous Job could not avoid them. Had he never had any doubts at all, he would have been a plastic Tzaddik. The fact that he did have them makes him all the more real.

V 11: "And three friends of Job heard…." Given that they all lived at great distances from one another in the days before emails, phones and faxes, how did they know that their friend was in trouble? "Some say that they each had a crown on which were modeled the faces of each one of them, and when suffering befell one of them, his face changed. Others say that they each had a tree and because it withered, they knew" (Bava Batra 16b).

When Job's friends arrived, they could not even recognize him because of his abject suffering. Nobody could bring himself to speak for seven days until at last Job opened his mouth and "cursed his day", as we will see in the following chapter. From the description of how Job's friends sat down on the ground to empathize with him and did not speak until he spoke first, the rabbis learned several important laws of conduct for those coming to comfort mourners (Moed Katan 18a).

CHAPTER 3

STRUCTURE OF THE BOOK OF JOB

Chapter 3 consists of Job's opening speech wishing that he had never been born rather than having to suffer in life, apparently for no just or intelligible reason. In chapters 4-5, Eliphaz HaTeimani, the leader of the three companions, answers Job, after which the latter speaks again in chapters 6-7. Job is then answered in chapter 8 by the second of his three companions, Bildad HaShoohi, and Job answers back in chapters 9-10. Next, in chapter 11, the third companion, Tzophar HaNa'amati, answers Job, who replies in chapters 12-14.

The cycle repeats itself in exactly the same way in chapters 15-21, where the three companions successively answer Job, who answers them back after each of their speeches. There is then a third cycle of speeches in chapters 22-31, in which Eliphaz and Bildad (but not Tzophar) again address and are answered by Job. Job's answer to Bildad is contained in chapters 26-31, in which Job gives a lengthy defense of himself, finally silencing his three companions, who despair of persuading him to change his view of his situation in any way.

A new interlocutor - Eli-hoo ben Barach-el - then enters and embarks on a lengthy address to Job in chapters 32-37. After this, God Himself addresses Job in chapters 38-41 in what is surely one of the most beautiful passages in all of Biblical literature. Finally, in chapter 42, God "adjudicates" in the debate between Job and his companions, and at last restores the chastened Job to a life of prosperity, wellbeing and honor.

Chapter 3 vv1-2: "And Job spoke and said, 'O that the day on which I was born had perished….'"

An invaluable insight into Job's stance is provided by the outstanding Talmudic scholar and Biblical commentator RaMBaN (Rabbi Moshe ben Nachman, or Nachmanides 1194-1270) in his comment on how Job "cursed his day": "We find the prophets cursing in this way, for Jeremiah also said, 'cursed be the day on which I was born' (Jer. 20:14) but in Job's case the intention was bad, and his companions understood what he was thinking from what he said. When Job saw the many terrible troubles and evil that came upon him - and he himself knew his own righteousness - he thought that perhaps God is neither aware of nor makes a reckoning of men's deeds and that there is no watchful providence over them. He started by saying that it is the influence of the planets and stars on the day and hour of people's birth that determine the good and evil that will befall them. He inclined to the view of the astrologers and therefore opened by cursing the day on which he was born, thinking that this was what caused him this evil. He argued that because of man's inferiority and God's exaltedness, He pays him no attention. Thus, man is under the rule of chance according to what the stars determine and how they rule on earth. Thus, Job believed that the same applies to man as we believe applies to animals - that there is no supreme guardianship over them except to keep their species in existence, but that no individual member of the species receives either punishment or reward. In the case of animals, we do not say they sinned when they get slaughtered or that they must have been meritorious if they have a long life, and we see that their livelihood is available in plenty [and not governed by a higher Providence]. This is his meaning in this first speech" (Ramban on Job 3:2).

The Biblical commentator Metzudat David, who provides a brief summary after each of the speeches of Job and his companions, takes a line similar to that of Ramban in his summary of Job's opening speech: "Job was perplexed and fell into doubt, thinking that everything that happens to man is determined by the heavenly order of the stars and planets in accordance with the way they rule at the moment of conception and birth. This is why Job cursed his day of birth and not the night when he was conceived. He also complains against God, who laid down this governmental order, asking why He did not so arrange things that someone who was born under the order that ruled when he was born should not die either in his mother's womb or at the moment of birth so as not to suffer such evil, for it would be better for him to die" (Metzudat David on Job 3:25).

From the fact that Job curses the **day** on which he was born but not the **night** on which he was conceived, the Rabbis learned that it is not fitting for man and wife to come together by day (Niddah 16b).

Verses 1-8 elaborate on Job's curse of his day of birth and night of conception, while in verses 9ff he explains **why** he was cursing them - because it would have been better for him to have died in the womb or immediately after being born rather than having to endure his present suffering. In verses 12-18 Job explains that death would have been better because - according to his understanding - death is a "sleep" and a "rest" (v 12). In verses 12-18 Job expresses how death is the great equalizer, because death comes to all, great and small.

In verses 19-25 Job asks why God gives life to those who are suffering when in fact they are longing to die.

V 24: "For the thing that I had feared has come upon me...." We are all uncomfortably aware that but for the grace of God, we could also be in the same terrible position as Job, and indeed many of those suffering from illness and other troubles and afflictions are only too familiar with Job's frustration at having been born and his longing to die.

CHAPTER 4

Eliphaz of Teiman's reply to Job is contained in chapters 4 and 5.

Rashi (on Job 4:1) states that Eliphaz is identical with Eliphaz, the firstborn son of Esau (Genesis 36:4) and that because he was raised on Isaac's lap he merited that the Shechinah rested upon him. Rashi states that Teiman (=Yemen/Aden) was part of the land belonging to Esau.

Vv 2-6: Eliphaz chastises Job for complaining against God's government of the world. Job had chastised others and given them support in their suffering, but now that his turn came to suffer he was already "exhausted" and unable to come to terms with it and accept that it was just. In verse 6 Eliphaz says that this showed retroactively that the "fear" of God Job had displayed in better times was not based on pure love but rather on the expectation of reward.

Vv 7-11: Eliphaz argues that calamity and suffering come upon men because of their sins and evil.

V 12: "Now a word came stealthily to me...." Having chastised Job for complaining about his suffering, Eliphaz now states that on Job's account a prophecy has been sent to him. Verses 12-16 evoke the way in which he experienced the prophecy. Rashi (on v 12) comments that the prophecy came in this stolen manner "because holy spirit is not revealed to the prophets of the heathens in a manifest way [as in the case of the prophets of Israel, who say, "Thus said HaShem."]. This can be compared to the case of a king who has a wife and a concubine. When he comes into his wife he comes openly, but when he comes into his concubine he does so secretly and with stealth. This is how the Holy One blessed be He comes to the prophets of the heathens. 'And God came to Avimelech in a dream of the night' (Gen. 20:3), and this was how He came to Laban (Gen. 31:24). Likewise, Bilaam was 'fallen and with open eyes' (Numbers 24:4). But in the case of the prophets of Israel, it is written: 'Mouth to mouth shall I speak in him, in a vision and not in riddles' (Numbers 12:5).

Verses 17-24 express the content of Eliphaz's prophetic message for Job. This is that it is not possible that man could be more pure and righteous than God who made him. It is inconceivable that a fully-rounded and mature man who had to establish some system for governing people would arrange things such that good and bad people would be treated in one and the same way. If so, how could anyone imagine that God would have given over everything into the hands of the heavenly order of stars and planets - for in that case the righteous and the wicked would be treated in exactly the same way, and then man (who would not arrange things in such a way) would be more righteous than God (see Metzudat David on Job 4:17).

CHAPTER 5

Job Chapter 5 is the continuation of the speech of Eliphaz which began in the previous chapter. In the Masoretic Hebrew text there is no break of any kind between the two chapters.

The previous chapter had ended with the prophetic message that Eliphaz had received for Job - that man is not more righteous than God and that His order of government must be just. Rashi (on Job 5:1) explains that Eliphaz' prophecy ended at the end of the previous chapter and now he returns to his rebuke.

Ch 5 V 1: "Call now - is there anyone that will answer you...?" - Metzudat David explains that Eliphaz is rebuking Job, saying that he has become a disgrace in God's eyes for kicking in protest against his suffering, so that now neither God nor any interceding angel ("the holy ones") will answer him.

V 2: "For anger kills the foolish man…" - "For the anger of a fool like you kills him, because if you had kept silent God's attribute of compassion might have been restored to you" (Rashi). When we become angry in the face of suffering, we make it impossible for ourselves to come to terms with it, and our life is simply consumed through our own folly.

Vv 3-5: Eliphaz returns to his theme that Job must have sinned, because wickedness may succeed temporarily but cannot endure forever. Eventually someone who oppressed and exploited others is punished by having his children become helpless orphans while his illicitly acquired wealth is returned to the poor from whom it was taken.

V 6: "For affliction does not come out of the dust..." - "A blow that comes to a man does not come for nothing and does not simply spring out of the dust" (Rashi).

V 7: "For man is born to trouble" - "for it is not possible that he will not sin and as a result receive trouble in order to receive his punishment. Man is not like the 'sparks that fly upwards' - these are the angels and spirits, who fly upwards and are not from the lower realms such that the Satan and the evil inclination could rule over them" (Rashi).

Ramban (on vv 7-8) writes that the two verses are connected together: Man is born to a life of exertion and anger and he cannot be saved from this, because God Himself brings this upon him just as He has made it the nature of the 'sparks' to fly upwards. "But I would seek to God..." (v 8): It is impossible to ascribe this governmental system to any planet or constellation but only to HaShem alone, for He deals with men's sins justly.

In vv 9ff Eliphaz begins recounting the praises of God, who governs even the rains with Providence. V 10 is cited in Ta'anit 10a as proof that God Himself sends the rains in the Land, i.e. of Israel, while the **chootzot**, the outside lands, are sent rains through His agents. These are aspects of His Providence. God lowers and raises up, frustrating the thoughts of the crafty (v 12) who wrongly believe that they can succeed in their devices. But God knows that the frustration of their plans and the suffering He sends them is for their own ultimate good (Ramban).

V 16: "So the poor person has hope, and iniquity stops up her mouth" - everything works out justly in the end.

V 17: The moral of Eliphaz' entire speech is that if a person suffers, it is for his own good, and he must not reject God's rebuke. It is God alone who sends suffering (v 18) and He too has the power to heal, saving the person from many evils. The seven evils from which He saves are: hunger, war, slander, robbers, famine causing unaffordable prices, wild animals and stumbling blocks (Metzudat David).

Vv 24ff: If only Job will accept his suffering with patience and humility, Eliphaz promises him that all will be well, his offspring will multiply and flourish and he will die satisfied.

Metzudat David summarizes Eliphaz' answer to Job as follows: "Eliphaz asserts definitively that everything comes through Providence, bringing proof from the way the wicked fall and cannot rise up, whereas the righteous are not destroyed in this way. Eliphaz refutes Job's view that everything is entrusted to the mechanistic order of the stars and planets and that the righteous and wicked both suffer one and the same fate. If a human were to devise such a system, it would be considered to be abominable even though man is imperfect and cannot even be compared to the angels let alone to the Holy One. It is inconceivable that there could be any injustice in God's way of governing the world. If there are things that seem to come in an arbitrary way as a result of the mechanistic order of the heavens, the truth is that everything comes about through Providence and it is only because of the limitations of human understanding that we are unable to know their real meaning.

As we follow the successive arguments and counter-arguments of Job and his companions, it will be wise to bear in mind that we are not expected to determine which side is right and which is wrong. The purpose of the complex weave of arguments and counter-arguments in this sacred text is to explore and help us understand the many different and often contradictory aspects of the profoundly difficult question of why people suffer.

CHAPTER 6

Job's reply to Eliphaz begins in chapter 6 and continues to the end of chapter 7. Eliphaz had criticized Job's fool's anger (5:2). Now Job answers that his pain and anger simply cannot be measured, and this is why he has been driven to distraction (ch 6 vv 2-3) because of God's terrible chastisement.

V 5: "Does the wild ass bray when he has grass…? - "Am I crying out for nothing? Even a foolish animal doesn't bray when it has food" (Rashi).

V 6: "Can that which is unsavory be eaten without salt...?" - "Do you really believe that Eliphaz' arguments can be accepted when they contain no substance?" (Rashi).

V 7: According to the commentators (Rashi, Metzudat David), Job expresses now the disgust of his soul at his repulsive affliction of boils.

Vv 8f: This is why he begs and hopes for death, and he is not afraid of this because he knows that he has not denied the words of the Holy One - he has not committed any sin.

V 11ff: "What is my strength that I should hope…?" Eliphaz had advised Job that if he would only accept his suffering stoically all would be well in the end, but Job (who was actually going through the suffering rather than merely observing it from the outside like his companions) explains that he has no strength to wait for the end because the suffering is so intolerable.

Vv 15-21: Job feels betrayed by his friends, comparing them to a river that flows abundantly when the snows melt but which disappears in the heat of summer precisely when people need it, causing them only disappointment.

Vv 22-23: Job tells his companions that he has not asked them for any gift of money, or to do anything themselves to save him from his adversary.

V 24: All he is asking them is to teach and show him the meaning of his suffering.

Vv 25f: What are all their words of reproof worth if they cannot show him this?

Vv 28: Job pleads with his companions to hear him out carefully and see his innocence.

CHAPTER 7

Chapter 7 continues Job's reply to Eliphaz, which started at the beginning of Chapter 6. At the end of Chapter 6 Job had protested his innocence of any sin that could be accounted as the cause of his suffering, asking his companions to examine carefully and see that he had committed no wrong. Now in

Chapter 7, Job counters Eliphaz' argument that if he would only submit to his suffering and accept its purgative power, God would in the end "settle" with him, protect him from trouble and evil and show him goodness.

Vv 1-2: "Is there not a limit to man's service on earth...." Man's life has an end: he is like a hired laborer whose contract is for a limited period and who longs for it to come to an end. Job is unable to wait for the good end promised by Eliphaz because his suffering is so great that his only hope is to die.

In vv 3-4 Job depicts the terrible suffering caused by his illness. His pain keeps him awake all night hoping for relief in the morning, and when the relief does not come he tosses and turns on his bed all day hoping for relief in the evening.

In v 5 Job depicts the horrible effects of the boils with which he is afflicted, which are full of maggots, while his skin is cracked and disintegrating.

Vv 6-10: Job feels that his life is "slipping through his fingers" at a rate faster than that of the weaver's shuttle, and there is therefore no hope of a better future.

Vv 7-9: "My eye shall no more see good.... As a cloud is consumed and vanishes away, so he who goes down to the grave shall come up no more." From here the Rabbis learned that Job denied the resurrection of the dead (Rashi and Metzudat David ad loc.; Bava Batra 16a). If death is but a sleep (Job 3:12) and there is no afterlife, what hope is there of a better future for Job if his life in this world is slipping away consumed by his suffering?

V 11: "I **also** shall not restrain my mouth...." Job is saying that if God will not leave him alone and refrain from hurting him, he too will not restrain himself from crying out over His way of dealing with him. If he complains, it is because of the terrible bitterness of his soul.

V 12: "Am I a sea or a sea monster that You set a watch against me?" The sea is limited by the shore, and the sea monster cannot move beyond the depths of the sea. Similarly, Job feels God has set a watch against him from which he cannot escape, because of the Satan, who has been charged to ensure that despite his suffering the soul will not go out of him, so that there is no refuge for him in death (see Rashi).

Vv 13-16: Job is sick of this life of suffering, in which he finds no relief or comfort but only anguish. He would much prefer to die.

Vv 17-18: Job now challenges Eliphaz' argument that everything is under God's Providence, asking how it could be fitting that God would constantly watch over man and pay attention to his deeds when man is so lowly and despicable.

V 18: "That You should remember him every morning and try him at every moment." From this verse, the Rabbis learned that man is judged every day and at every moment (Rosh HaShanah 16a).

V 19 is the desperate cry of the suffering invalid: How long before You will leave me alone? You do not even give me a moment to swallow!

Vv 20-21: Job now asks how it could affect or harm God even if he had sinned. If God knew from the very outset of Job's creation that this is how it would be, why did He create him simply in order to take vengeance from him like the target of an arrow? Why can He not simply take away his sin since his life will soon be over?

CHAPTER 8

The second of Job's three companions, Bildad HaShoohi, now makes his contribution to the first cycle of arguments and counter-arguments, answering Job by asking how it could be possible that God would corrupt justice (v 3).

V 4: If Job's children died, this must have been because of their sinful life of constant banqueting (Metzudat David).

Vv 5-7: If, as Job claims, he is innocent, then God will surely "settle" with him in the end so that although he is suffering now, he will enjoy relief later on.

Vv 8-10: Bildad adduces the wisdom handed down from the earliest generations based on their experience and investigations.

Vv 11ff: Bildad explains this received wisdom through the metaphor of the reed grass and rushes, which expresses the evanescence of the success of the wicked. As long as the reeds and rushes have an abundant supply of water they flourish, but as soon as the water disappears they dry up and wither. Similarly, the wicked flourish as long as the hour "laughs" at them, but as soon as their measure is complete, the success in which they trusted turns out to be as flimsy as a spider's web.

There is a difference in the way vv 16-19 are explained by Rashi and Ramban on the one hand as opposed to the way they are explained by Metzudat David on the other.

Rashi and Ramban explain vv 16-19 as a continuation of the metaphor of the reed grass and rushes. No matter how extensively their roots may spread, as soon as they are consumed they disappear forever and it is as if they had never been in the place where they grew.

However according to Metzudat David's interpretation, vv 16-19 contain a second metaphor expressing how the righteous endure and are regenerated, as opposed to the wicked who were compared to the reed grass that quickly dries up and disappears. Thus, Metzudat David interprets v 16 as referring to a mighty tree that remains moist even when it stands in the sun, and its branches spread over the whole garden where it is planted. Its extensive roots reach down to deep deposits of water. Metzudat David explains vv 17-18 as saying that such a tree is so strong that even if it is transplanted so that it is as if it never existed in its first place, even so, it has the power to regenerate itself and grow even better in the new place to which it is transplanted. According to Metzudat David, the metaphor comes to teach that even the trouble that strikes the righteous, who are compared to a mighty tree with extensive roots, is actually for their benefit because since the tree is intrinsically strong. Even when it is transplanted elsewhere, it still has the power to grow and flourish. Likewise, even when the Tzaddikim are "transplanted" into a life of suffering, it can still be turned to their advantage even though we cannot know how this is so because of the limitations of human understanding.

Vv 20: Bildad's inference from this received wisdom of the early generations is that if Job is truly pure and innocent, God will not reject him and eventually the tables will be turned on his adversaries.

CHAPTER 9

In his speech in the previous chapter, Bildad, like Eliphaz before him, had argued that everything is under God's direct providence and that if the wicked enjoy goodness, it will turn out to be to their detriment, while the evil that befalls the righteous will turn out to be for their good.

In answering Bildad in this and the following chapter, Job's main complaint is that he is pure and righteous, and that suffering has come upon him despite his innocence. Job agrees with Bildad that God cuts off the wicked, but argues that the righteous also do not escape from His hand and that He deals in the same way with the pure and with the wicked.

V 2: "...but how should a man be just before God?" - Metzudat David explains: "My entire complaint is: What kind of reward is this if a person acts justly before God and goes in His ways yet is also left to the government of the heavenly system of stars and planets and suffers the same fate of the wicked?"

V 3: But if the righteous man wants to argue with God over the loss of his reward, God will not even answer one out of a thousand of his questions.

V 4: God is wise to perfection and supremely powerful, and it is therefore impossible for a lowly mortal to argue against Him.

Vv 5-10 evoke the supreme power of God. He makes earthquakes (vv 5-6) and nobody really knows why they are sent. "He commands the sun and it does not rise" (v 7) - "The darkening of the sun through God's decree is a metaphor for the destruction of one empire and the rise of another" (Ramban). God's wondrous ways are beyond the comprehension of the human mind.

V 11: "Even though He is constantly passing before me and the whole world is full of His glory, I cannot see Him and even though He passes before me I am unable to understand his form or likeness" (Metzudat David).

V 12: He can snatch away a man with great power and speed and nobody can challenge Him and ask why He does this.

Vv 13-15: Even the celestial angels could not come to the help of proud Egypt (=Rahab). How much less so can a weak human like Job challenge God. Metzudat David notes that at times Job asserts that he does want to argue with God, while at other times he says he is unable to argue with Him: this is the way of a person who is wracked with pain and one time says one thing and another time something else.

V 16: "If I called and He answered me, I would not believe that he had listened to my voice" - Job is saying that it seems so inconceivable to him that God would listen to him that even if it happened, he would not believe it. Job could not believe that everything he was suffering was under God's detailed providence, as he goes on to explain:

V 17: "For he crushes me with a storm and multiplies my wounds without cause." If a storm wind comes, it causes suffering to all and does not discriminate between the righteous and the wicked - Job felt that all his suffering was for nothing.

V 19: "If the suffering that he has brought upon me is because of His great power and might, I know that He is all-powerful and nothing is held back from Him. But if my suffering has been sent through the attribute of justice, if only someone would appoint a day when we can come together to judge and determine who is in the right" (Metzudat David).

Vv 20-21: Job holds resolutely that he is innocent, but feels unable to stand up to God and assert his innocence because in his human weakness and lowliness he will never be able to make his point.

V 22: ".....Therefore I said, 'It is all one: he destroys the innocent and the wicked.'" This is Job's argument against Bildad, who said that the suffering of the righteous is for their good, which is not so in the case of the wicked. Job asserts that suffering afflicts the righteous and the wicked equally and does not discriminate between them. The "scourge" (Heb. **shot**) that strikes suddenly and laughs at the innocent (v 23) is the **Sat**an (Rashi).

V 24: "The earth is given into the hands of the wicked. He covers the face of its judges. If this is not so, who will get up and deny it?" - "As long as the wicked man lives, the earth is his to do as he desires, to rob and oppress, and because of his great power, even the judges of the earth hide their eyes from him so as not to look upon his deeds" (Metzudat David).

Vv 25-31: Job is haunted by the speed with which his life is slipping away. He is convinced that even if he holds his peace and stops complaining about his unjust suffering, God will still not send him relief, because even if he were to repent and chastise himself to cleanse himself of any sin, God will still send him down to the grave and never restore him to his former self. If he cries out and tries to justify himself, he will still come out as if a wicked man, while if he remains silent he will gain nothing. "Woe to me if I speak, and woe to me if I don't" (Ramban).

Vv 32ff: Job yearns for an impartial arbitrator before whom he can argue against God without feeling fear of God's overweening power and might.

CHAPTER 10

One cannot but admire Job's unflinching boldness in refusing to accept his companions' view that he must have sinned and insisting on his own innocence. Only Job himself knew what was truly in his heart and whether or not he had sinned. For this reason, whenever he wants to press the question of why the righteous suffer, he complains about his own suffering rather than about that of anyone else, because he could never know from the outside if that other person was truly righteous or not (see Ramban on Job 9:25).

V 2: "I say to God, 'Do not condemn me, let me know for what reason You are contending with me'" - Job is complaining that although he is righteous, he is suffering in the same way as the wicked deserve to suffer. This is why he wants God to explain to him the reason for his own suffering in order not to be equated with the wicked.

V 3: Why does God oppress the righteous - the work of His hands - yet gives success to the wicked?

V 4: Surely God sees into the heart of each one - if so why does He treat the righteous no differently from the wicked?

V 9: God formed Job like a potter makes a vessel out of clay: why does He now want to return him to the dust?

Vv 10ff: After having formed Job's body so wondrously, why is He now destroying him?

V 15: "If I am wicked, woe is me, and if I am righteous, I cannot lift up my head." Job again emphasizes that he sees no difference between the fate of the wicked and that of the righteous.

Vv 16ff: Again, Job wishes that he had never been born or that he had died at birth and gone straight to the grave instead of having his present life of futile suffering.

CHAPTER 11

The third of Job's companions, Tzophar the Na'amatite, now answers him. Ramban (on Job 11:2) explains that "Tzophar's intention was to give support to the argument of his companions that Job had sinned and this was why all this evil had come upon him. The new idea that he introduces is that some of God's deeds are revealed while some are concealed. For God overlooks the sins of the wicked and although He sees their evil, He does not at first pay attention in case they will repent. All this is because of His mercy over His works. If He benefits the wicked and shows them mercy, how much more so will He not harm the righteous. The only reason why suffering has come upon Job is to prompt him to direct his heart to repentance and to stretch out his hands to God in prayer, and in the end, he will attain tranquility. For the tranquility of the wicked turns into calamity in the end if they do not repent. Thus, Job's problem over the cases of the wicked people who enjoy a good life turns into a proof of God's mercy over His creations - for He does not reject the work of His hands. All the more so will He not harm the righteous."

Vv 5-6: But O that God would speak… and He would tell you the secrets of wisdom, for wisdom is manifold!" The Hebrew phrase for "wisdom is manifold" is **kiphlayim** (= "there is double"). **Le-tooshiyah** (= "…to wisdom"). The Hebrew word **tooshiyah** is from the root **yesh**, "it exists", because God's wisdom is forever and never returns to nothingness in the way everything else does (Metzudat Tzion). In the words of Ramban (on v 6), "All that visibly exists in the world is double and contains both revealed wisdom and hidden wisdom. That is to say, God's Providence over the creations is good both on the revealed and concealed level." Tzophar tells Job that God has exacted less of a payment for his iniquity than is warranted, and this is proof that He will not exact any more than is warranted.

Vv 7-10: God's wisdom is unfathomable, and nobody can call Him to account for what He does.

V 11: God sees men's iniquity and if He appears to pay no attention, it is because He shows patience in case they will repent (see Rashi).

V 12: Even an empty, foolish man can gain himself a heart and subject himself self-reckoning and return to his Creator. Man starts life as a wild ass's colt, but he has the power to teach himself to be a new man and follow a good path (see Rashi, Metzudat David).

Vv 20: If Job will come to his senses and distance himself from any sins he may have committed, his suffering will pass, and he will have a good end.

CHAPTER 12

Job's answer to Tzophar occupies the whole of Chapters 12-14. Job's opening words can be construed as if he is denigrating his companions for thinking that they alone have wisdom. However, Ramban prefers to interpret that Job shows respect for his companions, who were the choicest sages of their generation and could fittingly be called a "nation" since other people were animals compared to them. Nevertheless, Job protests that he is no less than them, and he also knows that God is exalted and concealed from the understanding of His creations, who cannot fathom His ways (Ramban on Job 12: 2-3).

Job complains that he has become a laughing stock to his friends, who maintain that he must have been wicked when in fact he knows he is innocent.

Vv 5ff: Job suggests that his friends, smugly satisfied with their own success, show contempt for him because he has stumbled. He implies that as they sit back, unscathed and complacent, they are like the wicked who enjoy tranquility and prosperity.

Vv 7ff: "But ask now the beasts and they shall teach you...." Tzophar and his companions had spoken as if they had a monopoly of wisdom, but Job retorts that the unfathomable depth of God's wisdom can be inferred by all from the animals, birds and fish of the sea in all their manifold variety.

V 11: "Does not the ear try words as the palate tastes food?" Many things can be understood from experience or through reason.

V 12: "With aged men is wisdom...." Through many years of experience men can become wise: wisdom is not exclusively in the hands of Job's companions.

Vv 14ff: Job is no less aware than Tzophar of the paradoxical nature of God's ways. These beautiful verses in which Job depicts how the high and mighty are brought down and the wise are shown to be ignorant serves as an introduction to the next part of Job's answer to Tzophar, which comes in the following chapters, because he wants to break out of simple explanations and conventional categories in seeking an answer to his question about why the innocent suffer.

CHAPTER 13

Chapters 13 and 14 are the continuation of Job's answer to Tzophar, which began at the start of chapter 12. Tzophar had been the third of Job's companions to address him, and his was the last of the first cycle of speeches. Having heard the arguments of all three of his companions, Job now addresses his answer to all three collectively.

In the opening section of his reply in the previous chapter, Job had denied Tzophar's view that he had attained little wisdom and that Tzophar and his companions were wiser, Now Job castigates the three of them for "flattering" God and finding justifications for His chastisements, as if Job was a great sinner when in fact he was not. Job refutes Tzophar's opinion that his suffering had come upon him because he was not as wise as he should have been on his level. Job argues that, being born in and through impurity, it is impossible for any man to be completely pure and it would not make sense that God would punish him because of this (Metzudat David on Job 14:22).

Chapter 13 v 1: "Lo, my eye has seen all this...." Job protests that he is no less wise than his companions.

V 3: "Yet I would speak to the Almighty...." Job wants to get to the real truth and not accept his companions' glib answers.

V 4: "But you are forgers of lies...." Granted that the wicked suffer because of their sins, Job maintains that his companions' answers still fail to explain why the innocent suffer, and therefore their answers are lies.

V 7: "Will you speak wickedly for God…?" It is wickedness to condemn an innocent man in order to justify God (Metzudat David).

V 8: "Will you show Him partiality…?" If the companions show favor to God in this debate and satisfy themselves with easy answers in order not to impugn His honor, this is an affront to truth and justice.

V 13: "Hold your peace, let me alone, that I may speak and let come on me what will." With extraordinary boldness and courage, Job is determined to press his question without compromise.

V 15: "Though He slay me, yet will I trust in Him; but I will maintain my own ways before Him…." Job will prove himself innocent, no matter what he may have to endure to do so.

V 20: "Only do not do two things to me…." The two things Job asks God not to do to him are enumerated in v 21: (1) Not to deal him any blow during their "debate" so as not to throw him into confusion. (2) Not to frighten him so that he will not shrivel into silence out of fear (cf. Metzudat David).

Vv 23f: Job returns to his fundamental challenge to God to make known to him what sin or transgression he has committed to deserve such suffering, because he is not aware of any (Metzudat David).

V 28: "And he is consumed like rottenness, like a garment eaten by moths" - "This body that you are persecuting will be consumed like rottenness: it does not befit Your glory to persecute me!" (Rashi).

CHAPTER 14

Vv 1-3: "Man that is born of a woman is of few days and full of trouble…. And do you open Your eyes on such a one and bring me into judgment with You?" Since man is so fragile and evanescent, Job questions why God watches over and judges a creature as lowly as this.

V 4: "Who can bring a clean thing out of an unclean? Not one!" Man comes from a putrid, impure drop - how is it possible for man to be pure? There is not a single man who is entirely pure: even the righteous are conceived in sin (cf. Psalms 51:7; Metzudat David, Ramban).

V 6: Again, Job appeals to God to take away his suffering and let him live out the remainder of his short life in peace before he is ready to die.

V 7: "For a tree has hope…." Even after a tree is cut down, the stump can still put forth new shoots and regenerate, but this is not so in the case of a man:

V 10: "But man dies and is laid low; yes, man perishes, and where is he?"

V 14: "If a man dies, shall he live again?" If man could come back to life after death this might provide the basis for an answer to Job's question about the meaning and purpose of the suffering of the innocent. However, while reincarnation and the resurrection of the dead are articles of our faith, in this life we see no clear and indisputable proof of them, leaving us in our existential anguish about the futility of our lives.

V 19: Just as stones are worn away by water until nothing is left, so man's life is wasted away.

V 22: "Only when his flesh is on him does he feel pain, and while his soul is within him does he mourn." Since man is condemned to this life of pain and futility, Job pleads with God to let him alone. The Talmud interprets this verse very differently from the way it is rendered in English, learning that after a person's burial the soul hovers over the body, weeping and mourning and feeling the very bites of the maggots (Shabbat 152a-b).

May God have mercy upon us!

CHAPTER 15

Job's lengthy speech in Chapters 12-14 brought to an end the first cycle of arguments and counter-arguments by Job and his three companions. Eliphaz' answer to Job in our present chapter begins the second of the three cycles of speeches, in which each of the companions successively addresses and is answered by Job.

Metzudat David in his comment on Job 15:35, explains that in his present speech Eliphaz is challenging Job for having said he had not sinned when in fact these very words cause others to sin even more because they plant in people's hearts the idea that no-one watches over men or judges them for their actions. As to Job's complaints about his suffering after all the good he had done, Eliphaz answers that he had already received his reward for his good deeds whereas he still had sins and transgressions in hand for which he was now paying the penalty. Eliphaz brings proof of God's providence over man from the way that the wicked eventually fall without being able to rise up, and even when times are good for them, they are filled with anxiety and apprehension about the evil that is destined to come upon them, which is not so in the case of the righteous.

Ramban in his comment on Job 15:2 points out that in his previous speech (in chapter 4), Eliphaz had not explicitly condemned Job but had simply urged him to bear God's reproof without chafing. However, now that Job had sought to justify himself and debate with God, Eliphaz argues that Job's very words show that he was wicked and lacked the proper fear of God.

V 1: "Should a wise man utter windy knowledge…." In Job's answer to Tzophar he had chastised his companions, telling them that they had no monopoly of wisdom (Job 12:2ff). Now Eliphaz retorts that Job's words do not befit a wise man.

V 4: "Indeed, you cast off fear and you slight the prayer that is made before God." Eliphaz is saying that despite his great wisdom, Job is undermining people's fear of God (which ought to make them afraid to sin) in saying that everything that befalls people is determined mechanistically by the heavenly order of stars and planets, implying that there is no such thing as any reward for righteousness or punishment for sin. In addition, Eliphaz accuses Job of discouraging people from praying to God, because if everything is determined mechanistically there is no place for prayer since it has no power to change anything, and doing such a thing is in itself a great sin (Metzudat David).

V 5: "For your mouth utters your iniquity..." - "The very words of your mouth teach others to sin, because by saying it is futile to serve God you encourage other people to hold by the same opinion and to sin just like you" (Metzudat David).

V 6: "Your own mouth condemns you…." Job's companions do not need to condemn him because his sin is glaringly obvious from his own words.

Vv 7-10: Job had accused his companions of speaking as if they had a monopoly of wisdom, but Eliphaz retorts that Job was the one who had spoken as if he had a monopoly of wisdom, and this is manifestly untrue.

V 11: "Are the consolations of God too small for you when a matter is hidden within you?" Metzudat David explains this verse as follows: "Why should you complain over your suffering just because you practiced goodness and righteousness to some extent. Is it a small thing to you that God has already given you consolation over the pain of your suffering through the goodness and success that you enjoyed previously, whereby you received sufficient reward for the good you did. But you still have sin hidden and concealed within you and now you must receive the punishment for your evil just as you previously received a reward for your goodness. Indeed, that previous reward should itself be your consolation for the suffering that has now come upon you."

V 14: "...and how can one born of a woman be righteous?" - "How can any man claim that he is so righteous that God has perverted justice so as to punish him for nothing?" (Metzudat David).

V 17: "I will tell you: hear me...." The lesson that Eliphaz wants to teach Job is contained in v 20ff: "All the days of the wicked man, he is in travail..." The apparent success of the wicked is illusory, because even during their time of good fortune they are filled with fear and anxiety, and eventually calamity is bound to strike.

V 27: "Because he has covered his face with his fat and has put collops of fat on his flanks." It is noteworthy that obesity is the leading health problem in all of today's advanced societies.

Vv 29ff: Eliphaz concludes his speech by emphasizing that the wicked cannot succeed forever and that calamity always comes in the end.

CHAPTER 16

Ramban on Job 16:2 states that Job's answer to Eliphaz in Chapters 16-17 does not contain any new ideas. Job only says to his companions that their words are vain and empty and that in order to offer him comfort they are resorting to falsehood in arguing that the destruction of the wicked is intentional in order to carry out justice. Job complains over his pains and sickness, which he considers to have come upon him for nothing, and this is his proof that there is no providence. He complains against his companions for denying his innocence, for in his own eyes he is righteous.

V 4: If you were in my place, would I speak to you in the same way?

V 6: "Though I speak, my pain is not assuaged, and even if I forebear, will any of my suffering go away?" Job is saying that it is not true that his words of complaint are undermining people's fear of God and are themselves responsible for bringing suffering upon him. For just as if he speaks, his pain is not assuaged, so if he will refrain from speaking it will not reduce his suffering. This is because, being innocent, his suffering has come upon him for no reason and it cannot be expected to disappear merely through not complaining about it (see Metzudat David).

Vv 7ff: Job complains that not only is he suffering because of the afflictions that were sent to him, but also because his enemy (=the Satan, Rashi on v 9) is persecuting him by sending his companions to abuse and denigrate him.

Vv 12ff: Job further depicts his terrible suffering, all of which in his opinion has come upon him for no reason (v 17).

V 19: Job's companions may think he is a sinner, but Job himself is confident that God in heaven will testify to his innocence.

CHAPTER 17

Our present chapter completes Job's answer to Eliphaz' second speech, which began in Chapter 16. Job continues to bemoan his lot, the pain of which is exacerbated by what he perceives as the mockery of his companions.

V 3: "Give now a pledge...." Job turns from his companions to address the Creator directly (Rashi), appealing to Him to give him a guarantee that he will be able to pursue his disputation to the very end and arrive at the truth.

V 4: Job complains that his companions' hearts are closed to true wisdom and that God's glory will not be enhanced through their arguments (Rashi).

V 5: His companions have used slippery talk in their debates with him and they will be punished as a result, because their children will languish (Rashi).

V 6: "He has made me also a byword of the nations and I shall be a horror to every face." Job has indeed become the proverbial archetype of human suffering. By simply switching around the order of the middle two Hebrew letters of Job's name, **Eeyov** turns into **oiyev**, "an enemy" - as if God has turned him into His enemy and is persecuting him.

V 8: "Upright men are astonished at this, and the innocent stirs himself up against the godless." Job asserts that if truly righteous people were to hear the mockery of his companions, they would be shocked.

V 9: "Yet the righteous will hold on his way, and he that has clean hands will grow stronger." Eliphaz had accused Job of undermining people's fear of God through implying that there is no reward for righteousness and no retribution for sin (Job 15:4). Now Job retorts that the opposite is true. "The righteous man will not abandon his pathway thinking that it is futile to serve God, because he knows that he will receive goodness - the delights of the soul. One whose hands are clean of robbery and exploitation will become even more resolute in his path when he sees how easily worldly acquisitions and success can be totally lost. This will make him despise them and place his hope only in the attainment of success in his spiritual endeavors, keeping well away from engaging in the oppression of his fellow man" (Metzudat David).

V 10: Job is certain that eventually his friends will come to realize that the truth is with him.

Vv 11ff: Again, Job complains how all his hopes in life have been dashed, and how his companions' mockery turns his nights into day - because the pain it causes him drives away his sleep - while the light of day is short because of his troubles, which are dark as night (Rashi on v 12).

Vv 13-16: Contrary to his companions' promises that if he will repent, God will give him a good end, Job complains that his only hope is to die in order to find relief from his pain. "And where, then, is my hope?"

CHAPTER 18

Bildad HaShoohi, the second of the three companions in order of seniority, now gives his answer to Job in this second cycle of their speeches. Metzudat David (on Job 18:21) summarizes Bildad's argument as follows: "He answers Job by saying that he cannot agree to his claim that God does not watch over the world providentially, despite Job's cries that he is suffering despite having committed no crime such as to deserve it. Bildad brings proof from the way the fall of the wicked comes about through their very own counsels and stratagems to the point that their name is forgotten. This does not happen in the case of the righteous. As to the evil that has come upon Job, it is likely that it has come to him because he fell short in the service of God and attained less wisdom than was befitting to a man of such abundant understanding as he had. In this respect he was equivalent to a sinner."

V 2: The commentators differ as to whether Bildad is addressing Job, telling him to stop interrupting the companions but to hear them out in order to understand what they are saying (Rashi) or addressing his companions, asking why they put an end to their words in order to give Job the opportunity to answer each one in turn, since there is nothing to what he is saying, and it is worthless to hear him out (Ramban).

V 3: Bildad asks rhetorically why Job looks on his companions as if they are on the level of animals, without wisdom?

V 4: Bildad castigates Job for tearing himself to shreds through his rage and anger over his suffering. "...Shall the earth be abandoned because of you or shall the Rock be removed from His place?" - "Just because you are crying out that you are righteous and that you are suffering for no crime, why should we therefore conclude that the earth has been abandoned to the rule of the heavenly order of stars and planets and that the Creator has withdrawn from the world and does not watch over it providentially?" (Metzudat David).

Vv 5ff: In returning again to the theme of the inevitable downfall of the wicked, Bildad once again implies that Job is guilty of some sin even though he will not admit it. "Indeed, the light of the wicked shall be put out...." The apparent success of the wicked (="light") will be put out and turn into darkness.

Vv 8ff: "For he is cast into a net by his own feet...." The very counsels and stratagems employed by the wicked contain hidden traps that bring about their downfall.

Vv 13-14: The children of the wicked shall be consumed by "the firstborn of death" - this is the angel of death (Rashi). "He shall be cut off from the tent of his security" - this is the sinner's wife (Metzudat David). "And shall be brought to the king of terrors" - this is the king of the demons (Metzudat David).

Vv 16-21: In the end, the wicked face total extirpation of themselves and their seed for ever.

CHAPTER 19

This chapter contains the whole of Job's answer to Bildad HaShoohi in this second round of his exchanges with his three companions.

Ramban (on Job 19:2) comments: "In this answer Job does not innovate any new idea but complains at length about his pains and the evils that have come upon him. Again, he protests that they have come upon him for no reason and that they are a perversion of justice. His intention is to negate the opinion of his companions that his suffering has been sent as a rebuke, and to weep and mourn over his soul in the way that people do when in pain. He takes his terrible illness as proof of his opinion that man is not under God's watchful providence. Job ends up by saying to his companions that they will be punished for not having wept with him over the harsh time that has struck him and for not having been shaken over the great evils he is suffering and the strange blows to which he is being subjected."

V 3: "These ten times you have put me to shame..." - "Up until this point in the book Job has made five speeches and his companions have answered him reprovingly five times. They have shamed him not only in their answers but also in not accepting what he has had to say" (Metzudat David).

V 4: "And if indeed I have erred, my error remains with me" - "Even if I have made some unintentional error and done something wrong, it remains with me alone for you have never seen me commit any wrong. While it could be that I have done some wrong privately, what claim does that give you against me - for how could you know my hidden secrets?" (Metzudat David).

V 6: "Know therefore that God has overthrown me…." The Hebrew word rendered in the English translations as "has overthrown me" - **eevtanee**, is from the root **le-aveit**, to twist, pervert or corrupt. "God has twisted my case, and the very net He has surrounded me with in order to trap me is a perversion of justice" (Metzudat David).

Vv 7-11: Job complains how God is persecuting him as if he is His enemy, as if **Eeyov** (Job) is His **oiyev** (="enemy").

V 12: "His troops come together... they are encamped around my tent". These are the troops of pains that Job is suffering (Metzudat David). The "troops" also seems to allude to his "companions", who came initially to comfort him but have been castigating him ever more strongly.

Vv 13-19: Here Job expresses how all those that used to be close to him and show him respect have become alienated from him because of the horrific nature of his suffering. Unfortunately, the great majority of people do indeed back away from those going through very severe and extreme forms of suffering, especially when their bodies have become seriously misshapen and repulsive. While the reaction is very natural, it leaves the suffering person with a terrible sense of isolation and shame. [Franz Kafka's story of "Metamorphosis" in which the central character has turned into a huge beetle, much to the horror of his family, is a study in the psychology of repulsion.]

V 20: "My bone clings to my skin and my flesh, and I have been saved by the **skin of my teeth**". Rashi explains that all Job's flesh was afflicted with boils and worms except for the gums of his teeth.

Vv 21ff: "Have pity on me, have pity on me, O my friends…." Job's plaintive appeal cries out until today from the ancient text.

Vv 23ff: "O that my words were now written…." It is from this verse that the Talmud (Bava Batra 15a) infers that Job lived in the time of Moses and that the latter wrote this book.

V 25: "But I know that my Redeemer lives…." Rashi explains that this phrase harks back to v 22: "You, the companions, are persecuting me, but I know that my Redeemer lives and will exact retribution from you".

V 26: "...and from my flesh I see God." Like so many verses in the Hebrew text of Job, this verse is darshened to produce very important teachings, in particular the idea that man can attain perceptions of

God through contemplation on the form and structure of his own physical body. At the same time, no verse ever departs from its **p'shat** (the simple meaning of the text). Rashi notes that the Hebrew name of God in this verse is **Eloah**, having the connotation of "Judgment" and punishment. Job is facing God's harsh judgments on his own flesh. Metzudat David explains this verse as part of Job's lament that he is going through terrible suffering despite the fact that he had attained such an apprehension of God that he saw and perceived Him more than he saw and perceived his own flesh.

V 29: Job concludes his answer to Bildad HaShoohi by warning his companions that their lack of willingness to understand the meaning of his suffering would elicit God's retribution.

CHAPTER 20

Tzophar HaNa'amati, the third of the companions, now takes his turn to answer Job in this second cycle of speeches.

Ramban (on Job 20:2) comments that in this speech Tzophar teaches only about the calamity that awaits the wicked, which he greatly emphasizes. Ramban refers students back to his comment on Job 11:2 where he explained that the companions do not address Job's essential issue - why the righteous suffer - because this problem is not very evident to the wider world since whenever someone is destroyed it can always be said that he must have done something to make himself liable. The suffering of the righteous is only a question to one who knows within himself that he is genuinely righteous and guilty of no sin and that he does not deserve the evil that has come upon him. This is why from chapter 11 onwards the companions dwell only on the destruction of the wicked and the extirpation of their seed, because this is the problem that was most evident to them, as it was to the prophets, such as Jeremiah and Habakuk, who asked why the wicked prosper. And each time the companions emphasize the retribution exacted from the wicked in the end, Job goes back to protest his innocence, and argues further that there are many wicked people who die in tranquility (see Ramban loc. cit.)

V 3: "I have heard the censure which insults me...." In his previous answer, Job had complained of how deeply his companions had insulted him. Tzophar now turns this back against him, asserting that on the contrary, it is Job who has insulted his companions.

Vv 4ff: Tzophar emphasizes that no matter how high the wicked may ascend, they will eventually be cast down and thrown away like excrement.

V 10: The descendants of the wicked man will have to conciliate the very poor people whom he oppressed: he will have to return everything he took unjustly.

Vv 12-13: The wicked person may secretly nurse his sinister plans, keeping them to himself so that nobody will be able to thwart them. But on the day of his destruction, "his food will be turned in his bowels" (v 14). He will have to vomit out all that he swallowed (v 15).

V 27: The very heavens will reveal the iniquity of the villain. "This is the portion of a wicked man from God" (v 29).

CHAPTER 21

Job's answer to Tzophar, contained in our present chapter, is his last speech in the second cycle of arguments and counter-arguments between Job and his companions, which began with Eliphaz' second speech contained in Chapter 15.

Ramban (on Job 21:2) explains: In his present speech in answer to Tzophar, Job emphasizes that there are wicked people who have it good in this world because of their wealth and possessions, status, children and peace of mind. Job mocks his companions for arguing that the seed of the wicked is cut off after them, seeking to demolish their claims with undeniable proofs. Earlier, he had argued with all three of his companions that he was innocent of wrongdoing, but they would not accept this on account of the fact that the suffering of the righteous is not a self-evident philosophical problem. This is because any time a person goes to ruin, it can always be said that he sinned and rebelled. The companions also argued that if one sees a wicked person who has it good, it can always be said that he will be destroyed in the end and likewise his seed after one or more generations. The companions had accused Job of hidden sins in order to establish his guilt and they warned him that the seed of the wicked will eventually be cut off.

Ramban continues: For this reason, Job now answers that he has seen with his own eyes how the wicked are successful and how their offspring and houses are tranquil in their lifetimes. If the companions argue that their descendants will be cut off after hundreds of years, how will that harm the wicked themselves and what pain will they suffer as a result? The companions must admit that the judgment is perverted and for this reason it is impossible to believe their claim that the seed of the wicked will be cut off on account of their sins. Likewise, even if a righteous person like Job is destroyed today, the companions should not condemn him, because judgment is not in God's hands but is a matter of chance (see Ramban loc. cit.).

Vv 2-3: If Job's companions really want to comfort him they should have the patience to hear him out before mocking him.

V 4: "As for me, is my complaint to man? Why should I not be impatient?" - "A mortal man may not have the wisdom to answer me, but my challenge is to God, who knows everything. If He will not answer me, how could I not be impatient?" (Metzudat David).

Vv 5-6: In these verses, Job warns his companions that he is about to mention something that is truly shocking - that in fact the wicked enjoy every kind of success, as he goes on to show in vv 7ff.

V 7: "Why do the wicked live, become old, and indeed grow mighty in power?" The Talmud (Sanhedrin 108a), Midrash (Yalkut) and commentators (Rashi on Job 21:6 etc.) all see the coming verses as alluding to the generation of the Flood, who enjoyed legendary prosperity and tranquility until their destruction. Similarly, the rabbis relate sections of Eliphaz' answer to Job in the chapter that follows to the generation of the Flood and the overthrow of Sodom. While to us these may seem like far-off events that took place in the remote past and which may appear irrelevant to the present, for Job and his companions, living in the time of Moses or not long afterwards, they were relatively recent cataclysms of enormous magnitude that cried out with moral lessons for future generations.

V 13: "They spend their days in wealth and in a moment, descend to She'ol (=the grave)" - "After enjoying such a good life, when his day of death arrives, the wicked man dies peacefully without pain and suffering" (Rashi).

Vv 14f: "Therefore they said to God, 'Depart from us for we do not desire the knowledge of Your ways.'" If this was the motto of the generation of the Flood and the people of Sodom, it would seem also to be the motto of many of the prosperous, contented exponents of freedom and license in our time.

V 17: "How often is the candle of the wicked put out...?" Job denies his companions' argument that in the end the wicked are always destroyed, because there are numerous cases where this is manifestly not so.

Vv 19-21: Even if the offspring and house of the wicked are eventually destroyed, what does he care when he is no longer in the world?

V 22: "Shall anyone teach God knowledge, seeing that He judges those who are high?" Rashi (ad loc.) offers two interpretations of this verse: (1) Job is telling his companions that not one of them is able to explain the manifest success of the wicked or the suffering and retribution exacted from the righteous. (2) Does Job need to teach God wisdom so as to judge the world in truth when He Himself knows that this is so? But in His exalted height and greatness He passes lofty judgments without taking care to be exact. [That is to say, God is so exalted that He does not pay attention to this world with the result that the judgment comes out crooked.]

Vv 23-26: The wicked die prosperous and tranquil, while the righteous die with a bitter soul having tasted no goodness - and in the end both lie in the ground and are eaten by the worms! Where is the justice???

V 27: "Behold, I know your thoughts and the devices you wrongfully imagine against me." Metzudat David renders the end of this verse somewhat differently, "the devices you **withhold** from me". He explains that Job is saying that he knows not only the arguments his companions will bring against him in support of their claims but also the counter-arguments that refute their views and which they seek to withhold from him and conceal.

Vv 28ff: The companions have argued that the houses of the wicked are eventually destroyed, but it is common knowledge that even when a major calamity comes to the world the wicked are often saved (Metzudat David).

CHAPTER 22

Eliphaz' third and final address to Job contained in Chapter 22 begins the third and last cycle of arguments and counter-arguments between Job and the companions who came to "comfort" him in his misery. However, in this third cycle Tzophar does not speak: only Eliphaz (ch 22) and Bildad (ch 25) address Job, whose lengthy response to the latter (chs 26-31) finally silences the three companions, prior to the entry of a fourth interlocutor in Chapter 32, Elee-hu son of Barach-el.

Ramban (on Job 22:2) explains Eliphaz' intent in his present speech, stating that of the three companions, he was the greatest in wisdom, which is why the text gives him precedence. Eliphaz had inferred from Job's opening speech that he did not believe in God's watchful providence over this world. Ramban writes that the most reasonable way to understand Job's standpoint is that he did not deny God's justice in the world of the souls (after death), because if so he would have rebelled even more, yet he said, "Even if He kills me, I will hope in Him" (Job 13:15). What Job could not accept was that the Tzaddik only receives his reward in the world of the souls - for why should God send harm in this world to those who perform His will, and conversely, why should He benefit those who rebel against Him? Job's main complaint thus related to the seeming lack of justice in the world of the bodies (this material world), for in Job's view the human body was no different from the body of an animal which is born under the dominion of the planets and stars and which is subject to chance, while only the soul is from God who gave it.

Ramban explains that in Eliphaz' present speech he introduces a new idea, saying that God wants man to do what is good and righteous in the eyes of God and man and to turn aside from evil only for the benefit of the created beings, and this is his proof that God wants to deal righteously with His creations and to show mercy on the work of His hands. This is why He gives them commandments and watches over them providentially. If so, Job's troubles have come upon him either because of his evil deeds - as Eliphaz specifies in his speech - or because of his denial of God's providence and his rebellion against God's testing and reproving him. Eliphaz concludes by saying that if Job will repent, God will return and benefit more in the end than at the beginning (see Ramban loc. cit.).

Vv 2-3: God gains nothing from man's service: it is man himself who benefits.

Vv 4-5: It is not through any fear of Job that God is chastising him but because of his own evil deeds. Eliphaz is not suggesting that Job was some kind of common villain. Metzudat David (ad loc.) explains that for a man on Job's great level even apparently minor deviations were very serious because others would learn from and follow him.

Vv 6-9: Metzudat David explains each of Eliphaz' accusations against Job in these verses as specifying how he must have perverted justice through abusing his own position of authority as an elder, leader and judge in his community: "For you have taken a pledge from your brother for nothing" (v 6) - "you imposed monetary fines and took pledges even when people owed you nothing…" "…and you stripped off the clothes of the naked" (ibid.) - "from those who had nothing to pay as a fine, you took their garments as a pledge." "You did not give water to the weary to drink and you withheld bread from the hungry" (v 7) - "for if you had someone put in prison, he was denied bread and water." "The land belongs to the man with a strong arm" (v 8) - "while you acted cruelly to the poor, you gave honor to the wealthy and powerful", oppressing widows and orphans.

V 10f: It is because of these subtle crimes that Job's troubles have come upon him.

V 12: "Is not God in the height of the heavens?...." - "If indeed you committed all these crimes and yet you deny them and say that you were righteous, this is only because you think that God is so high and exalted above everything that He is remote from the earth" (Metzudat David).

Vv 13-14: Eliphaz argues that Job considers that God knows nothing of the deeds of men, as if He is separated from the world by a dark fog.

V 15: "Have you marked the old way which wicked men have trodden?" As in the case of Job's speech in the previous chapter, the rabbis of the Talmud and Midrash and the later commentators saw in Eliphaz' depiction of atheistic power and pleasure-hungry villains in the following verses allusions to the generation of the Flood and the wicked men of Sodom, who were destroyed by rivers of water and fire respectively.

Vv 21ff: Eliphaz draws his discourse to a close by appealing to Job to make his peace with God so that good can come to him in the end.

Vv 27f: If Job will repent, his prayers will be answered, and "You shall decree a thing and it shall be established for you" (v 28). The true Tzaddik has the power to decree what will be through the power of his prayers (see Ta'anit 23a on this verse).

Vv29-30: God delivers the humble and innocent. Eliphaz' conclusion is that in order to be saved from his suffering, Job must repent.

CHAPTER 23

In his reply to Eliphaz in this and the following chapter, Job - angered by his companions' suspicions that he had been evil towards God and men - does not answer them directly. Rather, he wants to argue with God alone over the fact that despite his innocence he was plagued with suffering, while the wicked sin yet enjoy success and die quickly without pain (Ramban on Job 23:2).

In the words of Metzudat David: "Job denies Eliphaz' accusations against him, insisting that he had followed the ways of God and practiced justice in all that he did. Job fulminates over the fact that God shows patience to the wicked and does not destroy them despite the fact that they themselves destroy many souls. What sense does it make that He has mercy on them but not on the people they destroy? Success accompanies the wicked not only in their lifetimes but even when they die, because they die quickly without the pain of protracted illness. This is because their success is determined at the time of conception and birth by the heavenly apparatus of stars and planets. Job asks why God does not bend the heavenly order so as to rule justly since He established it (Metzudat David on Job 24:25).

V 2: "Today also my complaint is bitter; the blow to me is heavier than my groaning" - Despite all the "consolations" offered by his companions, Job has found no comfort, and his actual suffering is greater than the groans of pain he emits.

Vv 3-7: "O that I knew and could find Him…." Job yearns to fathom the answer to the mystery of why he has to suffer despite his innocence. He is convinced that if he could argue his case before God, he would be able to prove his innocence.

V 8: "But if I go east, He is not there, and if I go west I cannot perceive Him. I go to the left hand [=north] where He works, but I cannot behold Him; He hides Himself on the right side [=south] but cannot see Him." Job is scouring for answers in all directions of the universe, but God remains invisible and inscrutable.

Vv 10-12: The reason why Job wants to argue with God and not with his companions is because he knows in his own heart - and he knows that God knows - that he acted justly and followed His commandments, treasuring His teachings more than his own food.

V 13: "But He is unchangeable [Heb. **be-echad**] and who can turn Him?..." The literal meaning of the verse is that despite the fact that Job's innocence was known to God, He remained with one and the same intention and did not desire to remove his suffering. The Hebrew rendered as "unchangeable" – **be-echad** - literally means "in one". This alludes to the secret of God's transcendence beyond the world simultaneously with His immanence within it - "for Job was a sage and a **mekubal** who knew the secret of Godliness and of His unity" (Ramban ad loc.)

Vv 14ff: "For He will complete what is appointed for me...." The decree seems to be irreversible and the Judge implacable, despite Job's innocence - and "**therefore** I am shaken by His presence" (v 15) - Job is shaken by contemplating the fact that God apparently does not treat a person according to his ways (Rashi).

CHAPTER 24

Chapter 24 consists of the continuation of Job's answer to Eliphaz, in which he now turns in a new direction. In the previous chapter Job complained that he could not find an answer to the question of the suffering of the righteous, while in the present chapter he complains about the success of the wicked.

V 1: "Why are the times not hidden away from the Almighty, and why do those who know Him never see His days?" - "Since Job erroneously held that everything depends upon the influence of the heavenly order of stars and planets at the time of conception and birth, he now asks why the rulings made at those moments were not put away in the sense of being made subject to the superior power of God who created that order. All who know God know that He is timeless - no limit can be set to His days - and therefore He surely has the power to bend the influence of the heavenly order so as to do justice (see Metzudat David ad loc.).

In verses 2-11 Job catalogues the crimes of the wicked: They take other people's land; they take away the livestock of widows and orphans who cannot pay their debts; they push aside the poor, forcing them to flee. They are like wild donkeys, plundering in the plains. They steal people's crops but leave the vineyards of the wicked untouched. They strip poor people of their clothes, leaving them freezing in the cold.

V 12: "Men groan from out of the city, and the soul of the wounded cries out, **yet God lays no blame on them**." Here is the very essence of Job's question about why the wicked cause such suffering to others, yet God does not appear to exact retribution from them.

Vv 13-17: "They were of those who rebelled against the light…." In these verses Job poetically evokes how the wicked pervert God's order of light and darkness, day and night. By day, they blatantly defy Him by committing daylight murder, while they take advantage of night-time, when people are asleep, to steal (v 14). The adulterer goes about in the twilight hours, thinking that in the semi-darkness he is concealed from God.

V 18: The Hebrew in this verse can be construed in various ways: the simplest **p'shat** is that these wicked people are swift in making their getaway and succeed in escaping being caught (Metzudat David, Ramban).

V19: "Dryness and heat steal the waters of snow, and so does She'ol [=the grave] steal those that sinned" - "When their time comes, they die with a quick, easy death, just as dryness and heat quickly and easily "steal" and evaporate the waters that drip from snow. For She'ol quickly destroys the wicked, who despite their sins do not suffer the pain of illness" (Metzudat David).

V 20: The very womb that gave birth to the sinner quickly forgets him: the worms eat him up leaving no trace, and he is broken quickly like a chopped down tree - all without the protracted pains of illness and suffering (Metzudat David).

Vv 21-22: Despite the fact that the wicked prey on the barren woman and show no favor to the widow, God shows great patience - until He draws the mighty away with His power quickly, on one day, without causing them great suffering.

V 23: "All the days of his life God allows him to dwell securely - it is as if His eyes are upon the wicked to ensure that they will not stumble" (Metzudat David).

V 24: Job concludes his bitter speech with a challenge to anyone to prove him wrong.

CHAPTER 25

In this brief chapter Bildad HaShoohi, second in seniority out of the three companions who had come to "comfort" Job in his misery, gives what turns out to be their final answer to him - after Job's speeches in the chapters that follow, the companions could find no more to say to him to try to change his attitude. As we end this third cycle of the interchanges between Job and the three companions, we note that the third companion, Tzophar HaNa'amati, does not even attempt to answer Job.

Job had said, "I shall set forth my case before Him!" (ch 23 v 4). Bildad's short reply to Job is in the form of a **kal va-chomer** (an argument from a light to a serious case, or vice versa). So great is God, with His countless armies of angels, that the very heavens are impure in His eyes - how much less can a putrid mortal, destined to be eaten by the worms, justify himself before God?

V 2: "Dominion and fear are with Him...." - "'Dominion' is the archangel Michael (**Chessed**); 'Fear' is the archangel Gabriel (**Gevurah**) - you are quite incapable of answering even one of them!" (Rashi). This is Bildad's answer to Job's saying he would put his case before God. In the words of Metzudat David (ad loc.): "Great is the dominion and the fear that are with HaShem. Each one of them makes peace in the celestial order of the stars and planets so as not to work contrary to the other in running the lower world [=earth] and so as not to change their mission. It is not as you [Job] say - that the celestial order is not subject to God. For they do indeed bow to Him, whether through awe at His exaltedness or fear of punishment."

This verse contains the phrase "He makes peace in His high places," which is recited daily numerous times, at the conclusion of Birchat HaMazon (the Blessing after Bread), the Shmonah Esray prayer and the full Kaddish.

The Midrash comments on this verse: "Rabbi Yaakov said: Even the celestial beings need peace. The constellations ascend, and Taurus says, 'I am first' - and does not see what came before him. Gemini says, 'I am first' and does not see what came before him, and likewise each one says, 'I am first'. They complement one another, and they do not harm each other. See how the celestial beings need peace. Rabbi Shimon bar Yochai said: The firmament is made of water and the angels are made of fire and they live with each other. It is not only a matter of the relationship between one angel and another. Even within one angel himself, half is fire and half is water, and He makes peace within him! Great is peace, for the celestial beings need peace. Is it not a case of **kal va-chomer**: if peace is necessary in a place where there is no hatred, no enmity and no contentiousness, how much more so in a place where all of these exist - on earth!" (Tanchuma).

V 5 alludes to the mystery of the diminution of the moon because of her jealousy of the sun (Chulin 60b; see Metzudat David on this verse). Even though her rebellion was very minor, and her status was very great, she is nothing in comparison to God and even her small rebellion is considered very great. Similarly, even the stars are not pure in God's eyes -

V 6: How much more contemptible is man - destined to be eaten by the worms - and even a minor rebellion on his part against God is considered very great. Where then is Job's "righteousness"?

CHAPTER 26

Job now replies to Bildad, saying that his words cannot help or avail either Job or other men seeking to investigate the question of apparently meaningless suffering, and they do not have the power to penetrate the secret. For when a person says that the judgment meted out to man is subject to chance, he says so because of the very greatness of God - for man is too insignificant for Him to pay him any attention (Ramban on v 2).

Metzudat David explains: Job mocks Bildad for having stated what everybody knows while speaking very minimally about the wonders of God. Job describes His wonders at even greater length and says that nevertheless, he too has not come to tell of more than a small portion of His wonders. It is as if he is saying to Bildad: What does it matter if considering God's greatness and man's lowliness, even a small rebellion is considered to be very great. In that case the rebellion of the wicked must be considered even greater - why then does God apparently not exact retribution from them? (Metzudat David on Job 26:14).

Vv 2-4 Job mocks Bildad for failing to provide any help. "To whom have you uttered words" (v 4) - "Who is there who does not already know what you have said?" "...and the soul of whom came forth from you?" (ibid.) - "Whose spirit was speaking through you - who did you hear these words from: Job is speaking scornfully" (Metzudat David).

V 5: Job begins to speak about the mysteries of the **repha-im**, the "shades" - i.e. the dead, who go down to Gehennom, which weakens (**me-rapeh**) the creations, and which consists of seven chambers beneath the sea and those that dwell in it (see Rashi and Metzudat Tzion). Job is saying to Bildad: If you have come to tell of the greatness of God, I know even more than this and I too will speak of it (Metzudat David).

V 6: "She'ol is naked before Him" - "Even though it is in the depths of the earth beneath the waters, God still knows all that is in it, as if it is naked before Him without a covering" (Metzudat David).

V 7: "He stretches out the north over the empty place...." Metzudat David explains that he is referring to the earth, because the main inhabited areas are in the north. The wonder is that the earth stands with nothing holding it up.

V 8: "He binds up the waters in His thick clouds and the cloud is not rent under them" - "He binds the rain-waters in the clouds to be stored up so as to send them down only drop by drop, and the cloud is never rent apart under the water so as to pour it all down in one moment" (Metzudat David).

V 9: "He closes in the face of the throne...." The "throne" is the heaven, for "the heaven is My throne" (Isaiah 66:1). God sets the boundaries of the heaven as one encloses a house with walls (cf. I Kings 6:10; see Ramban on our verse).

V 10: God sets boundaries for the sea forever.

Vv 11-12: His rebuke causes the very heavens to tremble, and He stirs up the sea with His power. He smites Rahab - this is Egypt, which was overthrown in the Red Sea.

V 13: "...His hand slew the slant serpent" - This is Pharaoh. The "slant serpent" is also considered to be an allusion to the mystery of the **Teli** mentioned in Sefer Yetzirah 6. Some identify this with the constellation of Draco. For an extensive discussion of this concept, see the commentary on Sefer Yetzirah by Rabbi Aryeh Kaplan pp. 231ff.

V 14: Job concludes his answer to Bildad by saying that he has only described a small portion of the wondrous ways of God.

JOB
CHAPTER 27

V 1: "And Job **added**, bearing his parable, and he said...." When Job saw that his companions had stopped answering him (for which Eli-hu later castigated them, Job 32:16), he added further arguments, raising his voice and speaking in similes, metaphors and parables. The following chapters are replete with such parables (e.g. in Job 28:16, where wisdom is said to be incomparable with finest gold; see Rashi, Metzudat David and Ramban on our verse).

V 2: "By the living God - who has turned away my just cause, and the Almighty has embittered my soul". With these words Job takes a solemn oath that God has caused him evil despite his being innocent, for in turning Job over to the forces of nature He has not fairly requited his righteousness. The Midrash comments that the fact that Job swore in the name of God shows that his service was the service of love and did not derive from fear of punishment, "for no man swears by the life of the king unless he loves the king" (Tosefta Sotah on this verse). Out of love of God, seeking to justify His ways without flattery, Job was seeking a true answer to the problem of why the righteous suffer in this world.

Vv 4-6: "My lips shall not speak wickedness nor my tongue utter deceit...." Protesting his complete innocence of any of the evil of which his companions had accused him, Job declares that he cannot say that the truth is with them, because this would be untrue and then he would be a hypocrite and a villain - either through flattering them by saying they were telling the truth when they were not, or through flattering God by giving a glib answer to the question of why the righteous suffer - because they are not righteous - which does not solve the problem at all (see Ramban). The problem of why the righteous suffer remains - because Job knows in his heart that he never departed from his righteousness.

V 7: "Let my enemy be as the wicked...." So detestable to Job is any trace of wickedness that he would curse his enemy that he should be wicked (Metzudat David).

V 8: "For what is the hope of the hypocrite...." Job is asking why he would want to be a villain and a robber - for what happens to the villain and the robber in the end (Rashi). Metzudat David explains Job to be saying that although in his view everything that happens in this material world is given over to the implacable government of the heavenly order of the stars and planets so that there is no difference between the lot of the righteous and that of the wicked, nevertheless he would still not choose the path of evil. For what hope will the villain and the robber have when God takes his soul from him. Even though the righteous may have suffered in this world, they can still hope for spiritual delight in the world of the souls. But what hope have the wicked? (Metzudat David ad loc.). The above-quoted explanation by Metzudat David fits with Ramban's explanation (on Job ch 22, see our commentary thereon) that while Job could see no justice in the dispensation of health, children and wealth in this material world, which he saw to be governed by fate as determined by the astrological signs, he did believe in justice in the non-physical world of the souls.

V 11: "I shall teach you concerning the hand of God; that which is with the Almighty I will not conceal." Metzudat David explains that Job is saying it is not his intention to incite people to choose wickedness. He only wants to teach his companions the true nature of the government that comes from God's hand, and he will not refrain from speaking in order that people should not attribute the apparent injustice of the suffering of the righteous and the wellbeing of the wicked to any imperfection in God since everything comes down through the heavenly order of stars and planets (Metzudat David ad loc.).

V 12: "Behold, all you yourselves have seen it - why then do you thus altogether breathe emptiness?" Job is saying that the destruction of the wicked which the companions had so emphasized is a well-known, regular phenomenon to which everyone can bear witness, and he will not deny it - so why should the companions suspect that Job had chosen the path of wickedness? (Metzudat David).

Vv 13-23: In these verses Job acknowledges that no matter how great the success of the wicked, their wealth will eventually be taken from them and given over to others and retribution will come to their descendants. Ramban (on v 13) explains Job to be saying that even if all the troubles in the world come to the descendants of the wicked man while his glory flies away when he dies, this still does not resolve the problem of the success of the wicked because he has no interest in his house after his death. In addition, there is the problem of the righteous who suffer, over which he complained from the outset and his main outcry is against this.

CHAPTER 28

There is no break in the Hebrew text between the end of Chapter 27 and the beginning of Chapter 28. They are one continuous discourse until Ch 28 v 12, which starts a new section.

V 1: "Surely silver has its source...." Rashi on this verse explains the connection of thought between the opening of Chapter 28 and the earlier part of Job's discourse in the previous chapter. "Surely silver has its source" - "This too provides another argument in support of what he said earlier, 'I have held by my righteousness' (27:6). For why should I be wicked? If it would be for the sake of silver and gold - everything has its origin and its end. But 'from where does wisdom come?' (ch 28 v 20) - wisdom is more precious than everything, and for that reason I set my heart all my days to learn" (Rashi on v 1).

Vv 1-11: Job lists some of the wondrous, paradoxical ways in which natural phenomena come into being, each from its own unique source. Four different metals - silver, gold, iron and copper - each have their own source (vv 1-2). God has set a fixed time for darkness to rule - there is a "stone (**evven**) of darkness and the shadow of death", a kind of black hole from which punishments come forth, and it is called a "stone" after the way in which a man stumbles on a stone and gets hurt (Rashi). The literal meaning of verses 4ff is explained by Ramban to refer to the hidden source of water-courses, which come up from under the ground, while the source of bread is from the ground, yet paradoxically, if one digs deep beneath the surface of the ground, one finds the element of fire in the form of sulfur and salt. The ensuing verses speak about other mysterious sources of natural phenomenon.

Verses 4ff were also darshened by the sages as referring to the calamity that overtook Sodom, when rivers of fire and sulfur burst out over them. A most lovely habitation that had wealth in plenty and was never subject to marauders, foreign spies and hostile enemies was turned into a barren, uninhabitable waste (Sanhedrin 109a).

Verses 12ff: Having expressed how material wealth and resources have their source and also come to an end because they are finite, Job now contrasts this with the inestimable wealth of true wisdom. "But where shall wisdom be found?" The Hebrew text can also be construed as, "Wisdom comes forth out of nothingness". "Rabbi Yochanan said, 'From this verse we learn that Torah wisdom endures only in one who makes himself as nothing'" (Sotah 21b). Wisdom comes from humility. And Kabbalistically, the Sefirah of Chochmah, Wisdom, emanates out of **Ayin**, referring to Keter which is beyond any form of conceptualization.

V 14: "The depth says, It is not in me..." - "If you ask those who go down to the depths to find pearls or to the sources of gold and silver in the depths of the earth, they will tell you, It is not in me - because they are not proficient in Torah law! The people who go across the seas to trade will tell you wisdom is not with them, because they cannot purchase it for money like other merchandise" (Rashi).

Vv 20: Job continues in this most beautiful discourse, asking where Wisdom and Understanding can be found - because they are hidden from all the living.

V 23: "God understands its way..." - "He knows where wisdom dwells, and thus they praise wisdom, saying of it that 'God understands its way' - He looked into the Torah and created the world through its letters: according to their order and their values He formed all the creations as is written in the secret Sefer Yetzirah" (Rashi on v 23).

V 25: "He makes a weight for the winds and he weighs the waters by measure" - Everything in the world is precisely measured (see Rashi on this verse).

Vv 27-28: "Then He saw it, and declared it, he established it and indeed He searched it out. And to man he said, Behold the fear of Hashem - that is wisdom, and to depart from evil is understanding." True wisdom is known only to God, who "looked into the Torah and made the creation" as alluded to in verse 27, which kabbalistically refers to the four worlds. However, to man God says: Since your mind is insufficient to attain the depths of the hidden secrets of wisdom, know that fear of HaShem is the entry into wisdom while turning aside from evil is the way to attain understanding. This means that through fear of God one may attain hidden secrets that cannot be understood through natural means, for then God will put wisdom into the person's heart (see Metzudat David on v 28).

Metzudat David summarizes the intent of Job's argument in chapters 27-8 along the following lines: Job is arguing that wisdom is better than all possessions, and it is impossible to acquire it except through fear of God. For this reason, even though there is no distinction between the righteous and the wicked in the accidents of fate that befall them in the material world, one should still follow the path of righteousness in order to attain wisdom, which is worth more than anything, for it provides spiritual delight. If so, who would choose wickedness and lose the beauty of wisdom because of it? This is part of Job's self-vindication from his companions' accusations that he was wicked (see Metzudat David on v 28).

Ramban on verse 28 elaborates on the esoteric interpretation of Chapter 28 beginning from verse 1, explaining that the passage alludes to the four elements (bound up with the mystery of the four metals), the ten Sefirot and the 22 letters of the Aleph Beit. 10 plus 22 = 32: These are the 32 Pathways of Wisdom known to the sages. (The 50 Gates of Understanding are alluded to later on in Job ch's 38ff, as discussed in detail by Raavad, Introduction to Sefer Yetzirah.)

CHAPTER 29

V 1: "And Job **added**, bearing his parable, and he said:" After the conclusion of his sublime praise of Wisdom in the previous section, Job saw that none of his three companions had any answer to give him. Accordingly- he continued speaking further, again with the use of **mashal** - the metaphors and parables with which the following poetic passages are replete.

Until this point in the book, we have largely seen Job only in his suffering and misery - a man crushed and broken physically (though not in his spirit). Even if we have had references to what Job was in his time of glory, they have been only fleeting and indirect. Despite his protestations of innocence and righteousness, we have seen little of the actual content of this righteousness. On the contrary, from the castigations of his companions, we may have come to wonder whether Job was not seriously flawed. In order for us to see who the real Job was in all his true righteousness and purity - he was compared in greatness to Abraham (see Rashi on Job 30:19 and Tanchuma Ki Teitzei 5) - he now gives us his own supremely eloquent and moving self-vindication in the present chapter and the two chapters that follow it, which in the Hebrew text are one continuous parshah (section).

V 2: "O that I were as in months past, as in the days when God preserved me" - "If only I could be now as I was in earlier times" (Metzudat David).

V 3: "When His candle shone upon my head…." In the simple sense, this verse refers to the time when Job was at the height of his greatness as a most respected sage, elder, leader and protector of his people, guiding them through darkness with the light of God's Torah. A well-known Midrash explains the **remez** (allusion) in the verse as being to the time when the embryo is in the womb and the soul - His "candle" - can see from one end of the universe to the other, prior to the moment of birth, when an angel comes and taps the baby on the mouth and makes him forget the entire Torah (Niddah 30b).

Vv 4ff: Job now begins to evoke the days of his youth, as a prophetic figure with whom God dwelled, making him a fountain of wise counsel and leadership.

Vv 7-10: When Job used to come out to the "gate of the city", the gathering place of the elders, young and old would show him the deepest respect and reverence. The leaders would remain silent, awaiting his words.

Vv 12-13: Job imitated his Creator in saving the poor, the orphans and the widows. "He used to steal a field from orphans, invest in it and improve it, and then return it to them. Wherever there was a widow that nobody wanted to marry, he would go and attach his name to her, saying he was her relative, and then people came wanting to marry her" (Bava Batra 16a).

V 14: "I put on righteousness and it clothed me…" - "I pursued justice and it was to be found with me like a beautiful ornamental cloak and a turban" (Rashi).

V 16: "...and the cause which I knew not I searched out." Job was not one of those complacent judges who did not trouble to dig deeper to find the real truth. If something did not make sense to him, he made it his business to investigate and discover the truth.

V 17: Job was a fearless champion of the poor against those who oppressed them.

V 18: At the peak of his glory, Job could not imagine that it could all be taken from him.

V 19: "[I thought] my root would remain spread out to the waters and the dew would lie all night upon my branch" - "Job said, Because the doors of my house were always wide open for all, everyone else used to harvest dry ears of corn but I would harvest fat ones. Because I used to engage in Torah, which is compared to water, I merited to be blessed with dew" (Bereishit Rabbah 68).

Vv 21-23: Again, Job describes the profound respect and deference that he was accorded.

V 24: If Job smiled at the people, they could not believe that he would act so informally with them because of his great importance in their eyes, and they were still afraid to come closer and act casually with him (see Rashi).

V 25: Job was not too proud to visit those in mourning. He had the majesty and graciousness of a king. This verse is the source of some laws relating to comforting mourners (Mo'ed Katan 28b).

CHAPTER 30

V 1: "But now they that are younger than me laugh at me...." In contrast to his one-time position of prestige and honor, Job now describes how he has become the laughing stock of low-down people. While ostensibly Job is talking about all the common people who now mock him in his pathetic state, the Midrash implies that he is actually complaining against his companions for abusively having claimed he was a villain. "...whose fathers I would have disdained to have set with the dogs of my flock" - "Job said to Eliphaz, Are you not the son of Esau. If your father had stood begging me to give him food with my dogs I would have disqualified him!" (Tanchuma).

V 2-8: Job describes the utter lowliness and worthlessness of the people who now mock him.

V 4: "They cut off mallows from upon some bush (si'ach) and their bread is the root of broom-plants" - "Anyone who abandons Torah wisdom and engages in idle conversation (si'ach) is fed with coals of the broom-plant" (Chagigah 12b). Those who mock Job are ignoramuses.

V 9: "But now I have become their song...." Job's enemies - such as wrong-doers whom he punished - now triumph over him. In the words of Ramban (on Job 30:1): "Job complains about people's mockery of him even more than over his illness and the loss of his children and possessions. He speaks emphatically and at length about his pain over his enemies' joy over his trouble. For this reason, an ancient book of parables says that when they asked Job what was the worst of all his troubles, he replied that it was the joy of his enemies over the evil that struck him." Shame and humiliation can be the worst torment of all.

V 15: "Terrors are turned upon me, my **dignity** (Heb. **nedivati**, lit. 'my generous one') is pursued as by the wind" - "This refers to the soul" (Metzudat Tzion).

Vv 16ff: Job now again elaborates on the excruciating physical suffering caused by his illness.

V 18: "By the great force of my illness, my garb is changed...." Job's clothes were filthy with sweat and the morbid discharges from the boils in which he was covered.

V 19: "He has cast me into the **mud**, and I am become like dust and ashes" - Job had to sit in mud to try to cool the burning inflammation of his boils. "Rabbi Berachiah said, 'In my righteousness, I [Job] am compared to Abraham, who called himself 'dust and ashes' (Gen. 18:27), yet God has judged me like the villains of the generation of the dispersal, who rebelled against him with the building of the Tower of Babel, of whom it is written that 'the **mud** was cement for them' (ibid. 11:3)" (Rashi; Tanchuma, Ki Teitzei 5).

Vv 20f: "I cry to You, but You do not answer me." All Job's cry and complaint is addressed not to his companions but to God alone.

V 25ff: Again, Job complains that he acted righteously and with profound sensitivity for those suffering, yet now he is sunk in affliction. Why do the righteous suffer???

CHAPTER 31

In the Hebrew text of Job, Chapter 31 is the direct continuation and climax of the final section of Job's last discourse in answer to his three companions, contrasting his former glory with his present abject state and protesting his complete innocence of any sin that could be accounted its just cause. (The discourse began in Chapter 26, and the final section started at the beginning of Chapter 29.)

V 1: "I have made a covenant with my eyes…." In the last verses at the end of the previous chapter, Job had detailed the enormity of the physical suffering that has come upon him in spite of his righteousness. Now he is saying, 'Why has all this suffering come upon me? Did I not strike a covenant with my eyes not to look at anything that it is forbidden to look at?!?' (Metzudat David). "Come and see Job's righteousness. Every man is permitted to look at a virgin to see if he wants to marry her or marry her to his son or one of his relatives. If Job did not even look at what was permitted, how much less did he ever look at another man's wife, at whom it is forbidden to look. This is why the sages said that a woman should not go out in public in all her ornaments even on a weekday [let alone on Shabbat] because people would look at her. For God gave ornaments to the woman only in order that she might adorn herself with them in the privacy of her own home, for one does not present even someone who is pure with a breach in the wall [a grave temptation], let alone a thief" (Tanchuma). [I have quoted this Midrash at length not only because of the light it throws on Job but also because it contains the answer as to why modest married women do not go with uncovered hair etc. in public when they could say that men who don't want to should simply not look at them.]

And after all Job's righteousness, he continues in verse 2: "And see now what is the share that has been given to me from God above in payment for my deeds! Surely destruction is due to the wicked."

In vv 4-6 Job asserts that God, who sees and knows everything, will testify to his innocence.

Verse 5 begins a series of seventeen oaths and affirmations by Job continuing to the conclusion of his speech at the end of this chapter, in each of which he swears himself to be innocent of the crime specified in each case. Each of the oaths or affirmations begins with the Hebrew word **eem**, "if". Seventeen is the gematria of **tov**, "good".

Vv 7ff: Job invokes upon him the severest sanctions if it be true that he strayed from the path. If he ever stole anything, he curses himself that his seed should be cut off; if he committed any kind of adultery even by merely passing by his neighbor's door to look at his wife, he curses himself that his own wife should be taken by others, for adultery is the most terrible abomination.

Vv17ff: Written thousands of years before the "emancipation of slaves" (which simply heralded new kinds of human enslavement to the powers that be), Job's timeless declaration in these verses of the proper Torah way to treat slaves and servants rings out as an affirmation of the ultimate, existential equality of all men, for "Did not He who made me in the belly make him?"

Vv 16-20: Job never withheld support from the poor or the orphan, the hungry and the naked. "For from my youth he (=the attribute of charitableness) raised me like a father, and I have practiced it from the belly of my mother" (v 18, see Rashi and Metzudat David).

Vv 21-22: Job curses himself that his very arm should fall out of his shoulder and be broken if he had ever oppressed a helpless orphan.

V 23: Job abstains from sin out of terror of God's retribution.

Vv 24-25: Job never turned wealth into an idol.

Vv 26-28: He never entertained a thought of idolatrous worship of the sun or moon worship, which was prevalent throughout antiquity and vestiges of which remain until today.

V 29f: Job never showed vengefulness or rejoiced in the downfall of his enemies.

V 31: The people of Job's household hated him and wanted to eat him up because he was always burdening them with the many people to whom he provided hospitality.

V 33: Job never tried to hide his sins as most people do.

V 34: In the time of his greatness, Job showed no fear of anyone, reproving even the mightiest. But now that he has fallen, the most contemptible of people frighten him and he dare not venture out of his house (Metzudat David).

V 35: "Oh that someone would hear me! Here is my mark [or 'my desire'] - let the Almighty answer me and let my adversary write a book" Job's poignant cry is that **someone** should hear what he is saying. Let God testify for Job in his case. According to the simple meaning of the verse, Job is ready for his very adversary to write the book about him, as even the adversary will find nothing with which to damn him. On the level of allusion, the adversary is He who sent Job his suffering. And indeed, in answer to Job, God's testimony about him is written in chapter 1 verse 8 in His words to the Satan: "...there is none like him in the land, pure, righteous and God-fearing." Moreover, Moses, who wrote his own book and that of Job, came to testify for Job (see Rashi on this verse).

V 38-40: "If my land cry against me, or its furrows complain together...." Job's very gravesite - which is all that he can ultimately call "my land" - will attest to his righteousness (see Yalkut Shimoni). Rashi comments that Job's field could never cry out that he had failed to give away the gifts of the corner of the field, the gleanings, forgotten sheaves and tithes to the poor: he was correct and orderly in all of his affairs and never ate at anyone else's expense - and if not, let his fields sprout weeds!!!

"The words of Job are ended." The commentators take this not as an editorial gloss marking the end of Job's speeches - because we see that Job does speak again briefly later on in answer to God (ch 40 vv 3ff and ch 42 vv 1ff). Rather Metzudat David explains that Job is saying, I have already set forth the innocence of my ways and the enormous suffering that has come upon me after the utmost greatness and success, and if so what more can I add?

CHAPTER 32

ENTER ELI-HU BEN BARACH-EL

The three companions who came to "comfort" Job had been reduced to silence because their essential answer to the question of why he was suffering was that he must have committed some sin, yet Job protested his absolute innocence to the very end. The companions had tried to resolve the question of why the righteous suffer by saying they must have done something wrong. But while this may have "let God off the hook", as it were, for sending apparently meaningless suffering to a Tzaddik, it did not satisfy Job, who knew in his heart of hearts that he was innocent. Indeed, their answer was outrageous in his eyes because it covered over a seeming perversion of justice on the part of the Creator by smearing Job.

It is at this moment of impasse - with the companions silenced and Job still finding no answer to his question of why the righteous suffer - that Eli-hu ben Barach-el, a fourth sage enters. Although younger than the first three companions (he waited respectfully for them to finish before intervening), Eli-hu turns out to have attained greater wisdom than them. At the conclusion of the book, after God has spoken to Job, He tells Eliphaz that He was angered by him and his **two** companions (Bildad and Tzophar) and that they must bring sacrifices of atonement (ch 42:7ff). However, no criticism whatever is voiced over the lengthy discourses of Eli-hu, which occupy a total of six chapters (Job 32-37).

As we shall see in the ensuing chapters, Eli-hu patiently and systematically explains the flaws in the answers of the first three companions in trying to resolve Job's problem over the suffering of the righteous, and he offers a different answer. Eli-hu's discourses are a further ascent in unlocking the mystery of human suffering, in preparation for the very climax of the book, when God finally answers Job out of the whirlwind (chs 38ff).

Eli-hu ben Barach-el was enumerated by the Talmud as one of the seven prophets who prophesied to the nations, together with Eliphaz, Bildad, Tzophar and Job himself, and Bila'am and his father (Bava Batra 15b). The same Talmudic passage implies that Eli-hu was an Israelite, because he is described as coming from the family of Ram (i.e. of Avraham), and that he is called a prophet to the nations because his prophecies are directed to all the nations as opposed to being directed to Israel specifically. A different opinion is brought down by Metzudat David, who learns from his being called the Buzite that he was from the family of Buz, the second son of Nachor, brother of Avraham (Gen. 22:1). Talmud Yerushalmi Sotah 5 records a discussion in which Rabbi Akiva darshens that Eli-hu is Bila'am, while Rabbi Eliezer objects that this is not so and darshens that Eli-hu is Isaac.

V 2ff: Eli-hu is angry with Job and he is angry with his companions. He is angry with Job "because [Job] justified himself **more than God**" - i.e. **not** because Job claimed innocence - this Eli-hu does not dispute - but because he reproved God, as it were, for abandoning him to blind fate ("the heavenly order of the stars and planets") and the accidents of the flesh in spite of his great righteousness, which made it seem as if God is not just. Next Eli-hu is angry with Job's companions, because they had not found an adequate answer to his basic question about why the righteous suffer, and as long as his question was unanswered, this too made it seem as if God is not just.

V 6: "I am young and you are very old" (cf. Rabbi Nachman's story of the Blind Beggar).

V 7: "I said, 'Days should speak and a multitude of years should teach wisdom'". Initially Eli-hu had believed that just as after a given period of time a child develops the ability to speak, so years of experience and investigation should develop wisdom in people (see Metzudat David).

V 8: "But there is a spirit in man and the breath of the Almighty gives them understanding" - Having heard the first three companions, his seniors in years, speak, Eli-hu now knows that there is an intelligent spirit in man that can teach him wisdom regardless of whether he is old or young.

Vv 11ff: Eli-hu explains that he has patiently waited to hear out his elders but that when he carefully considers what they have said it is clear that they have failed to give Job an adequate answer.

V 13: "Beware lest you say, 'We have found out wisdom, God has thrust him down, not man'". Metzudat David renders: "Lest you would think to say that you have found an intelligent and sophisticated answer in telling Job that he must have committed a great sin seeing that God Himself has turned against him and not a mere mortal like me, because the Holy One is not suspected of practicing injustice. Eli-hu is saying that the companions had not spoken with wisdom because this is not an answer fit to silence the turmoil in Job's heart since he himself knows that he was not guilty of great sin" (Metzudat David on v 13).

V 14: "Now that he has not directed his words against me, so that I will not answer him with your speeches." Despite the failure of the companions to answer him, Eli-hu is saying that Job should not think he is right, because all the arguments that he had advanced against his companions, protesting his innocence, would not stand up to the explanations that Eli-hu has in mind to give in the coming chapters. Eli-hu is not going to advance the same arguments that the companions had already advanced: he is going to say something new.

Vv 18ff: Eli-hu is bursting to speak, and he will not soften his blows in order to give respect to any man, because if he were to try to cover over anything it would be such an offense that he feels he would be burned up by God (see Rashi, Metzudat David).

CHAPTER 33

Having completed his prologue (Chapter 32) explaining why he had not intervened earlier in the discussion, Eli-hu ben Barach-el now begins to set forth his arguments against Job, quoting point by point things that the latter had said and answering them one by one. From the fact that Job does not answer Eli-hu or dispute what he says, we may infer that he accepted his arguments.

Verses 6-7: "Behold I am just like you before God, I too am formed out of clay. Behold my terror shall not make you afraid, nor shall my pressure be heavy upon you." Job had earlier complained that God is not like a man on his own level whom he could challenge to come with him to an independent arbitrator to determine who was right - one who would not throw Job into fear, terror and confusion so as to prevent him putting his case (see Job 9:32-5). Eli-hu is now reassuring Job by saying that although he will, as it were, speak on behalf of God, he is still only a man, just like Job, and he will not cast him into fear and prevent him from answering back if he has any question that is not fully resolved.

Vv 8ff: Before King Solomon would pass judgment, he would first repeat the claims of the parties to the case to show that he understood them correctly (see I Kings 3:23). Likewise, Eli-hu first restates succinctly each of the various points Job had made in his arguments with his three companions before going on to answer them one by one. Job had said that he was innocent of any sin, yet God had treated him like an **enemy**, **Eeyov** (=Job) had become like an **oiyev** (="enemy") - and was seeking pretexts against him.

V 12: "Behold in this you are not right. I will answer you - for God is greater than man." Metzudat David explains Eli-hu to be saying that God's level is far higher than that of man. If a mature man would not seek out pretexts to needlessly persecute someone, all the more so that God would not do such a thing. "I will not answer you as your companions did - that you are not innocent but are full of sin - because it could well be that you are righteous, yet you are still not justified in fulminating, because God is certainly just - this will be explained in ch 35 v 2 ff (see Metzudat David on v 12).

V 13: "Why do you strive against Him [saying] that He will not answer all a man's words?" Metzudat explains: "Why do you claim that He does not inform a person in what respect he has sinned or transgressed in order that he may cease from his sins and repent quickly?" (cf. Job 13:23, "make known to me my transgressions and my sins").

Vv 14ff: Eli-hu now explains to Job that God has his own unique ways of communicating with man. God speaks once to a person, and if the person does not understand, He speaks to him again.

Vv 15-16: The first way God communicates with man is through dreams, showing him through dream images of what has been decreed against him, measure for measure, because of his deeds (Metzudat David).

V 17: "...that He may withdraw man from his purpose and hide pride from man": The purpose of God's communications to man is **preventative**. He sends people messages to deter them from committing acts they have been intending to do. This is in order to save man's soul from destruction. Eli-hu here introduces a new dimension in the understanding of pain and suffering that was not present in the discourses of Job's first three companions.

Vv 19ff: If the person ignores the message sent in his dreams, the "preventive medicine" becomes steadily stronger, and he is afflicted with the pains of illness and disease in order to stir him to repent.

Vv 22-24: Man veers ever closer to death and the grave. But "If there is an angel over him, a defender, one among a thousand, to declare to man his righteousness, then He is gracious to him and says, 'Deliver him from going down the pit; I have found a ransom.'" In the words of Metzudat David: "When the person will be judged then in the heavenly court, if even a single angel will be found arguing in his merit and telling the righteousness of some deed that he performed, even if this angel is the only one arguing in his favor against 999 accusing angels, God will be gracious to him and tell the defending angel that he has redeemed him from destruction, because his righteous deed outweighs everything else."

V 27: Even after having been saved, the true penitent continues publicly admitting his earlier sins.

V 29: "Behold, God does all these things twice or three times with a man." Even if a person reverts to sin, God will again send him dreams or "communicate" with him through the "language" of the illness He sends him in order to stir him to repent. "Rabbi Yosse bar Yehudah says, 'When a person sins for the first time, he is forgiven, and likewise when he sins a second time, he is forgiven, and likewise when he sins a third time, he is forgiven. But if he sins a fourth time, he is not forgiven, as it is written, Behold, God does all these things twice and three times with a man'" (Yoma 86b).

V 32: "If you have anything to say, answer me; speak - for I desire to justify you" - "It is best for you to speak out everything that is in your heart, and I will answer you about everything in order to guide you on the true path. For if you stop speaking and keep your words stored up in your belly you will remain with a false view and you will not be innocent any more" (Metzudat David). It is better to speak things out than to keep everything bottled up inside one.

CHAPTER 34

Vv 5-6: "For Job has said, 'I am righteous and God has taken away my proper reward. Despite my right I am counted a liar; my wound is incurable though I am without transgression.'" Prior to answering Job, Eli-hu again repeats his claims, which were that: (1) God had not given him his reward for his righteousness, and (2) even worse, He had sent him terrible suffering instead.

V 7: "What man is like Job, who drinks up scorning like water?" Eli-hu is particularly angry with Job for these claims, because, as he explains in verse 8, this way of thinking is likely to encourage sinners.

V 9: "For he has said that man does not profit even if he is willing to be with God [and follow His ways]." The perverse view that man gains nothing from serving God is the logical corollary of Job's attitude that he is suffering terribly despite being innocent of any sin, and that everything happens purely by chance without any divine providence.

Vv 10ff: "Far be it from God that He should do wickedness...." Not only does Eli-hu emphasize that God deals with men measure for measure (v 11). He also argues that it is inconceivable that God would needlessly cause His creatures suffering since if He wanted to he could sweep away the entire creation in a moment, so why should we imagine he comes against His creatures with pretexts? (see Metzudat David on v 14).

Vv 16ff: Eli-hu now adds a further argument. Job had complained that the government of the world had been handed over to the implacable heavenly order of stars and planets and that one and the same fate strikes the righteous and the wicked indiscriminately and without justice. But Eli-hu asks how it is possible that the righteous God would have entrusted the government of the world to an unjust system (v 17, see Metzudat David).

Vv 19ff: The Almighty has no need to show partiality to any of His creatures whether in the higher realms or the lower - for He created them all. He knows everything and deals with each individual strictly according to his ways.

V 23: "For He will not lay upon man anything more that he should enter into judgment with God" - "It is not His way to give a person a punishment greater than befits him such that he should say he will take Him to court for giving him a greater punishment than he deserves" (Metzudat David). In the following verses (24-30) Eli-hu describes the punishment of the wicked, measure for measure.

V 31: "For surely it is fitting to say to God, I suffer, I will no more offend" - "That is to say, since it is evident that He does what He does with justice, it is proper to say to God that I will bear my pain and not behave wrongly from now on" (Metzudat David).

V 32: It is fitting for the person enduring suffering to pray to God asking Him to show him what he does not see himself in order that if he has sinned in the past he will not do so any more.

V 33: "Eli-hu asks Job: 'Was the Holy One blessed be He required to consult you as to how to exact payment from you, such that you say you are sick of living? Do you imagine that He must exact retribution according to the way you choose?'" (Rashi).

V 36: Eli-hu would prefer Job to be tested continuously with suffering to see if he will regret what he has said and then discover that the suffering will leave him only after he repents – this, in order to teach other sinners to repent when they see that nothing helps except repentance (Metzudat David).

CHAPTER 35

V 1: "And Eli-hu answered and said:" (v 1). In Eli-hu's second discourse, contained in the previous chapter, he had answered Job regarding the question of reward and punishment, whereas now he is going to discuss the suffering that came upon Job himself. For this reason, he paused between one subject and the other in order to gather his thoughts. (Metzudat David ad loc.)

V 2: "Do you think this to be right, that you say, 'My righteousness is more than God's'...? "Ramban (ad loc.) explains that Eli-hu will repeatedly blame Job for having said he was more righteous than God. For Job was convinced that he was righteous and that the terrible calamities that befell him were not because of any crime. He gave expression to this in different ways, sometimes arguing that God considered him His enemy, sometimes that He does not watch over the creatures of the lower world providentially. In addition, Job had complained that man's sin does not harm God nor does his merit benefit Him and if so, He does not need or want man to repent - for Job had wanted to fear God but suffering came upon him anyway, so what more could he do to conciliate Him? This is another argument against providence. Eli-hu now addresses this in the coming section of his discourse (ch 35 vv 3-16).

V 3: "For you say, what advantage it will be to you? 'What profit shall I have more than if I had sinned…?'" - Eli-hu reviews Job's argument prior to answering him: "You say that if everything comes through fate as decreed by the heavenly order of the stars and planets, what benefit do you have from serving God and refraining from sin: (Metzudat David).

V 4: "I will answer you and your companions with you." Ramban (on v 2) explains that the reason why Eli-hu included Job's companions with him in this verse is because their leader, Eliphaz, had also implied that man's merits are of no benefit to God (see Job 22:2-3). Eli-hu will answer that it is true that sin neither harms nor benefits God, but nevertheless He commanded man to act righteously and warned him against sin for the good of His creatures. For this reason, He sends punishment and does not accept the prayers of one who cries to Him and wants to fear God - on account of his acts of oppression against others, of which he may not even be aware. Thus, Job is exonerated from the charge of having been a liar in his claims about his righteousness, yet God is shown to be the righteous one (see Ramban at length on v 2).

V 5: "Look to the heavens..." - "Since He is exalted and you are lowly, and He has no benefit whether you are wicked or righteous, why should you boast to Him about your righteousness?" (Rashi).

V 8: "Your wickedness may hurt a man as you are, and your righteousness may profit the son of man" - "He is saying that evil is only called wickedness on account of the harm it does to a man on Job's level, while righteousness and charity are only called good on account of the fact that they benefit another man - for God commanded his creations to practice justice and righteousness for their own benefit" (Ramban).

Vv 9-11: The oppressed cry out because of the strong arm of their oppressors, and no one asks, "Where is God my Maker…?" The simple meaning of the verse is that the oppressors do not stop to think about and heed God's law forbidding oppression, despite the fact that they themselves are His creatures. Metzudat David construes the phrase "he gives songs in the night" as referring to the righteous man, who may offer his prayers to God yet is nevertheless accounted responsible for the sins of the wicked if he does not stand up to protest against them. According to Metzudat David, Eli-hu is implying in this and the following verses that Job's suffering came to him not because he was not righteous but because he did not protest against the wicked for their oppression. [This fits with the Midrash telling that when Pharaoh consulted Bilaam, Job and Jethro as to whether to enslave Israel, Bilaam agreed and was later killed, Jethro disagreed and was rewarded, while Job failed to protest and had to suffer.]

V 12: "There when they cry He does not answer…." At times God may not answer the cries of the righteous - this, according to Metzudat David, because they have not protested against the wicked.

V 13: Metzudat David construes: "But it is false to say that God does not hear and that the Eternal does not see it" - God may appear hidden at times, but this does not mean He does not hear and know everything that is going on.

V 14: "Even though you say, 'You do not see it', nevertheless, there is law before Him - and you must have hope in Him" - God watches over everything, and therefore there is a place for prayer to Him (Metzudat David).

CHAPTER 36

V 1: "And Eli-hu **added**" - "Until now, Eli-hu has given three discourses (chapters 33, 34 & 35 - chapter 32 was merely introductory) corresponding to Job's three companions. What follows is a fourth, and this is why it is called **additional**" (Rashi).

Ramban comments: "In this discourse Eli-hu does not attack Job, for he had already blamed him enough in each of his first three discourses. Now Eli-hu comes like the companions to speak the praise of God, telling how He watches over the world. Since God watches over His world constantly despite His loftiness and exaltedness, it is impossible to believe that He has entirely removed His providence from the beings of the lower worlds on account of His exaltedness and the lowliness of man. For the lower worlds were created for the sake of man, for none besides him recognizes his Creator. If so, all God's providence over the varieties of lower creatures is for the sake of man - so how could it be that He pays no attention to him? Moreover, we must attribute Justice to the Creator of all when we see Him to be a great King and a righteous Judge who watches over everything providentially (Ramban on v 1).

V 2: "Wait for me a little…" - "Eli-hu did not want Job to think that he had finished everything he had to say in case he would interrupt, therefore he asked him to wait a little longer" (Metzudat David).

V 5: "Behold God is mighty and will not despise anyone…." This verse is cited in the Talmud as proof that when many people pray together God does not reject their prayers, and for this reason one should try to worship with a congregation, or at least - if this is not possible - at the time the congregation are praying (Berachot 8a).

Vv 6-7: It is not true that God is indifferent whether people are righteous or not, for He will not give life to the wicked, whereas He will eventually vindicate the poor.

Vv 8-12: Poverty and other forms of suffering are a test. "Then He declares to them their work" (v 9) - "For through this suffering He informs them that they have sinned before Him" (Rashi) - suffering is a message sent to man from God. If man heeds the message, he will end his days well, but if not he will pass from the world and die without ever having attained true understanding.

V 13: Those who flatter their hearts - giving way to all the desires of their evil inclination - chaff against suffering and do not cry out to God when they suffer despite the fact that it is He who sends them the suffering.

V 15: "He delivers the poor by means of his affliction and opens their ears through oppression" - "On account of their having been afflicted, He delivers them from Gehennom, and through the oppression He brings upon them He opens their ears to hear Him when He says, Return to Me" (Rashi).

V 17: Metzudat David explains: "Even if you have been filled up with the judgment of suffering that would be fit for the wicked, so what - because it must really be considered a benefit since the judgment and suffering that have come upon you will sustain you and save you from the punishment of hell so that you will delight in the world to come."

Vv 18-21: Eli-hu warns Job not to prefer the success of the wicked to his own suffering, for their success leads only to ultimate destruction.

Vv 22-26: God is exalted above all, and no one can accuse Him of any miscarriage of justice.

Vv 27ff: The detailed way in which God watches over the world providentially is exemplified in the way He sends the rains - sometimes in abundance, sometimes very sparingly. "For through them He judges the peoples..." (v 31) - It is through sending abundant rain or withholding it that God sends each nation its deserts. He also judged the generation of the flood with excessive rain, and rained down fire and sulfur on the wicked inhabitants of Sodom (Rashi, Metzudat David).

CHAPTER 37

CONCLUSION OF ELI-HU'S SPEECH

The concluding section of Eli-hu's answer to Job, which occupies the whole of our present chapter, is a direct continuation from the previous chapter. In the Hebrew text there is no section break between the two chapters. Moreover, the chapter break in the printed Bible texts actually violates the thematic continuity of Eli-hu's speech. This is because in the closing verses of chapter 36 vv 26-33, he had begun to give expression to God's unfathomable power and His detailed providence over the universe through depicting specifically the wonders of rainfall, which is the foundation of human prosperity and which is responsive to men's behavior and their prayers. Now in the conclusion of his speech in Chapter 37, Eli-hu expands on the theme of the wonders of thunder and lightning, storms and rain clouds, lifting our eyes and our inner thoughts steadily higher, level by level, to the heavens and beyond, to the inscrutable Ruler of all, who knows man's thoughts before he even speaks.: "Hear this, Job, stand and contemplate the wonders of God!" (v 14).

After Eli-hu concludes his speech, Job does not answer him - he had no answer because apparently, he accepted Eli-hu's arguments. This enabled him to rise to the level of prophecy (see our commentary on the next chapter), and immediately after the end of Eli-hu's speech, HaShem Himself answers Job out of the storm-wind (chapters 38ff).

Eli-hu's speech thus marks a transition from what might be seen as the lower level of wisdom on which Job and his three companions conducted their debate about the problem of suffering, to a higher level where new hints and suggestions are offered as to how to approach this inscrutable mystery. Eli-hu's repeated challenges to Job in our present chapter to acknowledge that the mysteries of creation are beyond us constitute a preparation for God's own direct challenges to Job to acknowledge the inscrutability of His ways.

Before discussing comment on individual verses in the present chapter, let us see the chapter as a whole in the context of Eli-hu's entire discourse, as summarized by Metzudat David (on Job 37:24): "Eli-hu affirms that God indeed watches providentially over the very details of creation, and separates the wicked from the goodness that comes into the world while also separating the righteous from the evil in it. If at times evil befalls a Tzaddik, it comes providentially to open his ear to rebuke when he turns somewhat from the straight path. Eli-hu answers Job that in his case too, suffering has come to open his ear to rebuke so that he will repent and return to God, and this way he will be saved from the judgment of hell and will delight in spiritual lushness. For if he had had a life of constant tranquility he would have rebelled against God because of the abundance of everything, and he would have been lost eternally like the generation of the Flood. Eli-hu also reproves Job for not humbling himself before God since everything is in His hand and there is none like Him. Eli-hu proves God's providence: He formed the eye, so how could it be that He does not see? Eli-hu adduces the wonders of God that are known to us and those that are concealed. Thus, he answers Job by saying, 'Surely, you know something of the natural phenomena of this world, why do you not understand more? You must admit that everything comes from God and is under His providence and we cannot understand it all. For this reason, we may not question His deeds, for man's intelligence is too limited to be able to understand God's work and how He governs the world'" (Metzudat David on Job 37:24).

Vv 1-5: Eli-hu's heart shudders at the thought of the flashes of lightning and roaring thunder that God sends as part of the water cycle.

V 6: "For He says to the snow, be [on] the earth...." The simple meaning of the verse refers to the ecological phenomenon of snow as part of the water cycle. On the esoteric level, this verse is quoted in the Midrash (Pirkey d'Rabbi Eliezer 3 etc.) and in [some but not all editions of] Sefer Yetzirah 1:11 as referring to the mystery of the "congealment" (Tzimtzum) of the "fluid" spiritual levels of Creation - i.e. the letters of the Hebrew alphabet - so as to form the "solid" material world (see R. Aryeh Kaplan's edition of Sefer Yetzirah loc. cit.).

V 7: Metzudat David offers a simple **p'shat** on this verse relating it to the preceding verses explaining that knowledge of coming weather developments is hidden from men, whereas the animals (next verse) exhibit behavior patterns showing their intuitive knowledge of coming rains and storms etc. However, on the level of Drash, this verse is famous as teaching that "at the time when a man leaves this world for his eternal home, all his deeds go before him and they say, 'You did such and such in a certain place on a certain day', and he replies, 'Yes'. They say to him, 'Sign', and he signs, as it is written, "In the hand of each man will he put a seal, and moreover, he accepts the justice of the verdict and says to them, 'You have judged me beautifully!'" (Ta'anit 11a).

V 12: "...and it is turned about through His counsels." The infinitely complex tapestry of interconnected causes and factors in blowing the clouds, each one exactly where He wants it in order to bring about His desired effects, is evidence of His absolute providence over everything. The Talmud darshens from here that if Israel's repentance on Rosh Hashanah warrants a judgment of abundant rainfall but later in the year they sin, He does not revoke the decree but rather makes the rains fall where they are not needed, while sometimes it is the other way round (Rosh Hashanah 17b see Rashi on our verse).

Vv 18-19: Did you stretch out the heavens with Him...? Tell me what arguments can we bring against Him? We cannot argue against Him because of the darkness and concealment that surround Him (see Rashi).

Vv 20f: God knows man's thoughts before he even speaks.

V 21: Metzudat David explains: "As Eli-hu comes to complete his speech, he says, 'And now I say to you in general terms: sometimes people do not see the light of the sun because the clouds cover it - yet even so, it is bright in its place in the heavens and shines very greatly. But when a wind passes and "cleanses" the skies of the clouds, the sun becomes visible.'" As if to say, 'God's light shines all the time whether man sees it or not - His providence is constant.'

V 22: "Gold comes out of the north (tzaphon=hidden)..." -- "The good 'gold' is hidden away for those who bring themselves to fulfill the commandments of the Holy One blessed be He and who believe in God, who is most awesome" (Rashi).

V 23: "The Almighty (we cannot find Him out) He is excellent in power and in judgment, and with plenty of justice, He will not oppress" - "God does not send judgments against His creations according to His own great power but rather with mercy, accepting their atonement according to their limited ability. He does not oppress anyone to excess and He does not oppress the righteous man more than is necessary" (Rashi).

V 24: The bottom line is: Fear of God. God does not regard the "wise of heart" - those who come against Him with sophistry - for their wisdom is nothing in His eyes (see Rashi).

CHAPTER 38

V 1: "Then HaShem answered Job out of the storm wind (**se'arah**)…."

Ramban explains: "Job now attained the level of prophecy because he was 'innocent and righteous, God-fearing and one that turned away from evil' and he had been proven through being tested. And even though he had sinned in doubting God's justice on account of a lack of wisdom, the test helped to bring him close to God, for he accepted Eli-hu's arguments and saw that they were a sufficient answer to his question, and he was now God-fearing and an innocent Tzaddik. God speaks to him 'out of the storm wind', because his prophecy was not on the level where the heavens were opened up to him so that he saw clear visions of God as in the case of Isaiah, Ezekiel and Daniel etc. He attained the level that the prophets reach first at the beginning of their vision, as in the case of Ezekiel, who first saw a "**storm wind** coming out of the south" (Ezekiel 1:4; cf. Elijah's vision I Kings 19:11). Out of the storm wind came a voice to Job answering him with tremendous power.

"The purpose of His answer is to let Job know that He is perfect in knowledge in general and in particular over all the created entities in their entirety and He watches providentially over all of them, while man is too brutish to understand even the phenomena of nature, let alone to understand God's justice and its foundations. He also hints to him that Eli-hu's answers were based on the truth, for so far Job only accepted that he **might** be correct and that accordingly even the phenomena of the suffering Tzaddik and the wicked man who has it good might be based on justice. However, Eli-hu had no decisive proof and man cannot know this except through received tradition. Now God tells Job that this is true." (Ramban on Job 38:1).

In Ramban's Introduction to the Book of Job, he notes that only in the opening two chapters of the book and in this final section of the work does the "essential name of God", **HaShem**, the Tetragrammaton, appear, while throughout the main body of the work, in all the speeches of Job and his companions including Eli-hu, He is called by other names such as **E-l**, **El-oah** and **Sha-dai**. (Out of respect, these are pronounced respectively as **Keil**, **Elokah** and **Shakkai** except when used in prayer or when reciting as opposed to merely quoting of the Hebrew Biblical text). The work begins and ends with the absolute unity of God, who rules over all with complete justice, but in the quest of Job and his companions for answers in the main body of the text, they invoke the different attributes of God as expressed in His various other names.

The Talmud teaches: "Rabbah said, Job blasphemed with a storm wind (see Job 9:17) and He answered him with a storm wind. Job said to Him, 'Perhaps a storm wind passed before you and you mixed up **Eeyov** (Job) and **oiyev** ("enemy")'. And He answered him with a storm wind (**se'arah**). He said to him, I have created many hairs (**se'arah**="hair") in man and for each hair I created its own follicle so that no two hairs should suck energy from one and the same follicle, because if two were to draw from one follicle they would darken the light of man's eyes. I do not mix up one follicle with another - how much less would I mix up **Eeyov** and **oiyev**!" (Bava Batra 16a).

In the words of the Midrash: "A gentile asked Rabbi Meir how it could be since He fills the heaven and earth that He could speak to Moses from between the two poles of the Ark. Rabbi Meir asked him to bring a mirror that enlarges the reflected object and told him to look at his face in it. He then had him bring a mirror that diminishes the reflected object and likewise told him to look at his face in it. He told him: 'If you are flesh and blood yet you can change the way you appear at will, how much more so can He that spoke and brought the world into being. Sometimes the entire world cannot contain His glory, and at times he speaks to a man from between the hairs of his head!!!'" (Bereishit Rabbah 4).

God's answer to Job is one of the most sublime passages in the Bible, evoking the inscrutable mysteries of creation, the elements, the constellations, stars and planets, the manifold forms of animal, bird and fish life on land, in the air and in the sea, as well as so much more. As mentioned in our commentary on Job ch 28, embedded allusively in the present passage (chapters 38-41) are the Fifty Gates of Understanding (**Binah**), as explained in detail by Raavad (Rabbi Avraham ben David of Posquieres, Provence, c. 1128-1198) in his lengthy Introduction to Sefer Yetzirah. Thus, verse after verse in God's series of challenging questions to Job opens with the word **Mi**...? (Who...?), alluding to the Fifty Gates of Understanding (**Mem**, 40 + **Yod**, 10 = 50).

Let us have the humility to know the limits of our own understanding and start our quest for wisdom with the cultivation of true fear of Heaven.

CHAPTER 39

Our present chapter is the continuation of God's first answer to Job out of the storm wind, which began in chapter 38 v 1 and runs until the end of chapter 39. In the Hebrew text there is no pause or break between the end of chapter 38 and the beginning of chapter 39.

Metzudat David (on Job 39:30) summarizes the main import of this first answer to Job as follows: "God rebukes Job asking how he had the temerity to question His ways - Do you understand all My works? He relates wonders that cannot conceivably be thought of as deriving from the forces of blind fate working through the heavenly system of stars and planets, but which are clearly providential. For this reason, it is impossible to deny the resurrection of the dead even though it may seem contrary to nature. There is thus no room for Job's complaint about reward and punishment, because after the resurrection of the dead, each one will receive according to his works. God relates His awesome works at length as if to say, 'If so, why were you not afraid to have doubts about Me?' In addition, He answers Job that he was not right in deciding that God does not watch over the lowly creatures providentially, for it is not so: I watch over everything, including even the animals, and He relates some of the ways in which He watches over them."

The reference to the resurrection of the dead mentioned by Metzudat David is contained in the earlier part of God's first answer to Job, in chapter 38 vv 13-17. Having first spoken about the wonders of the creation of the world, it says in v 13 - "To take hold the corners of the earth and the wicked shall be shaken off it": this clearly refers to the judgment of the wicked. The specific allusion to the resurrection of the dead comes in the following verse (38:14), "It is changed like clay under the seal and they stand as a garment" - "Even though the seal of the form of a man changes at the time of his death to be like clay and mud, nevertheless they will stand at the resurrection and be as they were at first, just like a garment, which may be folded up but when afterwards it is unfolded, it is just as it was at first. This comes to answer Job's denial of the resurrection of the dead (see Job 7:9) on account of his view that everything comes about through blind fate and nature, while the resurrection of the dead defies nature. God's answer is that since He watches over all, there is no need to wonder at the resurrection of the dead" (Metzudat David on Job 38:14). In the same passage in v 17 God challenged Job as to whether the "gates of death were revealed to him" - for if not, how could he know that the dead will not be revived?

The ensuing passage in chapter 38 went on to give example after example of the unfathomable mysteries of creation - light and darkness, snow, hail, rains, ice, the stars and constellations and the livelihood of lions and ravens.

Our present chapter (Job 39) now continues with further examples of the mysteries of the behavior of different species of wildlife - the mountain goats, the wild donkey, the buffalo, the ostrich, the stork, the horse, the hawk and the vulture. In each case it is God alone who gives each one its unique powers and traits, provides for them and watches over them to ensure their survival - so how can Job claim that God does not watch over the lower realms providentially?

CHAPTER 40

In the Hebrew text, there was a pause at the end of the previous chapter, indicating that God wanted to give Job an opportunity to answer Him but that since he remained silent and gave no answer, God spoke to him again (Metzudat David): "And HaShem answered Job and said..." (v 1). God pressed Job to speak: "Shall a reprover contend with the Almighty? Let he who reproaches God answer it!" (v 2).

Forced to answer, Job admits that he is truly humbled. In the words of Metzudat David on v 4: "Behold, I recognize in myself that I am very insignificant and I have not learned sufficient wisdom to understand that everything comes under providence. What can I answer you? There is no answer in my mouth and for this reason I have put my hand to my mouth and I said nothing when You stopped speaking."

V 5: "Once I have spoken but I will not answer, yea, twice, but I will proceed no further" - "The first thing I said at the beginning of my speeches was in complaint over Your having entrusted everything into the hands of blind fate. I spoke then, but now I will not say any more in answer to Your words in order to strengthen what I said, for now I see that You have not entrusted anything to fate, but everything is in Your hands. As to my other question as to why - if all is under providence - does evil befall the righteous while good comes to the wicked, even though I still do not know the answer, nevertheless I shall not proceed any further and ask more questions, for I am afraid to entertain doubts about You" (Metzudat David).

In order to answer the latter question, God now gives His second answer to Job, challenging him:

V 8: "Will you also negate My justice, will you condemn Me in order that you may be in the right?" - "It is as if He is saying, 'Is not your asking this question a more serious offense than the first - if you think My justice is nothing because it appears that I do not pay a person back according to his deeds, and if you condemn my justice because you consider yourself a Tzaddik? For the question as to why the wicked have it good is not such a wonder since nobody knows whether deep inside another person is righteous or wicked.' Job's main question was over the Tzaddik who suffers because he considered himself a Tzaddik and he was asking about himself since he suffered terribly. God said to him, 'Just because of what you **thought**, will you condemn My justice?'" (Metzudat David).

V 9: "Do you have an arm like God or can you thunder with a voice like Him?" Metzudat David explains that man is made in the image of God and when he perfects himself and does not turn aside even slightly from the path of God, his strength is very great and he has power over everything, including even the hosts of heaven, as in the case of Joshua, who caused the sun to stop (Joshua 10:12f).

God is here asking Job how he can hold himself to be so righteous - does he have the power in his arm like God to rule over everything? Can he thunder like Him and give commands to the hosts of heaven as would a truly perfect Tzaddik?

Vv 10-14: If Job is so perfect, God challenges him to cast down the wicked as would be befitting for a perfect Tzaddik, and if he can do it, God will concede that he is indeed a complete Tzaddik (Metzudat David).

Vv 15-24 speak about **Behemoth**, while vv 25-32 speak about **Leviathan**. Having previously challenged Job to take on the wicked, God now asks him if he could take on these two wonders of His creation. Ramban (on v 15) comments: "**Behemoth** is a generic term for all large animals and beasts, while **Leviathan** is a generic term for enormous fish. However, our rabbis of blessed memory had a tradition that **Behemoth** and **Leviathan** mentioned here are two unique creatures bearing these names." The aggadic traditions about them are contained in Talmud Bava Batra 74bf, while deep kabbalistic teachings relating particularly to **Leviathan** are contained in the writings of the Vilna Gaon.

"Rabbah said in the name of Rabbi Yochanan: In time to come the Holy One blessed be He will make a feast for the righteous from the flesh of Leviathan, as it says, 'The companions (a drush on the Heb. **chabarim**) will heap up payment for him, they shall divide him among the traders' (Job 40:30) - the 'companions' are the Tzaddikim while the 'traders' are those who will portion out the flesh and sell it in the streets of Jerusalem. And Rabbah also said in the name of Rabbi Yochanan: In the future, God is destined to make a **Succah** for the Tzaddikim out of the skin of Leviathan, as it written, 'Can you fill his skin with barbed irons (**Succot**)?' (ibid. v 31). If someone is worthy, they will make him a Succah. If he is less worthy, they will make him a belt; if he is less worthy, they will make him an ornament; if he is less worthy, they will make him an amulet. There are different groups (**Chaburot**) of companions. Some are masters of the Bible, others are masters of the Mishnah, others are masters of Gemara, some are masters of Aggadah, some are masters of many Mitzvot, some possess good deeds. and each group will come and take their share."

"Rabbi Levi said, 'Everyone who fulfills the mitzvah of Succah in this world will be seated in the Succah of Leviathan in time to come. And if you say that the skin of Leviathan is not so remarkable, our rabbis have taught that the different colors it contains make the sun look dark!'" (P'sikta).

CHAPTER 41

In the original Hebrew text, chapter 41 is the direct continuation of God's second answer to Job, which began in ch 40 v 6. The conventional chapter break between chapters 40 and 41 is quite arbitrary as it falls in the middle of the description of Leviathan. The last verse of the previous chapter contained God's challenge to Job to try to fight against Leviathan - "Lay your hand upon him - you will no more think of fighting" (Job 40:32). The first verse in our present chapter then goes on to say that the hope of anyone who does try to fight him will be disappointed since it is enough just to look at him to make a person backtrack in fear.

The powerful evocation of Leviathan's awesomeness and might in this part of God's answer to Job provides the foundation for the **kal va-chomer** (argument from a light to a serious case) in verse 2: If nobody dares to arouse Leviathan (who in all his awesome might is the "light" case), then "Who is able to stand before Me?" (this is the "serious" case). Who can protest over what God does? This continues the rebuke to Job implicit in the previous chapter that however righteous he may have been, he was still not on the level of the perfect Tzaddik who could "raise his hand and stop the sun" (see our commentary on Job 40:9). It is as if God is telling Job: "If you had been a true Tzaddik in the proper way, I would have rewarded you, because no one can protest or stop Me doing anything" (Metzudat David).

V 3: "Who has a claim on Me from before that I should repay him?" - "This means that there is no one who has ever taken the initiative to perform some act of righteousness before God first did him some favor" (Metzudat David). "Who gave praises before Me before I first gave him a soul? Whoever stepped forward to circumcise his son unless I first gave him a son? Who made Tzitzit before I gave him a Tallit? Who made a parapet unless I gave him a roof? Who made a Succah before I gave him a place? Who separated **Pe'ah** (the corner) before I gave him a field? Who separated the Terumah and Ma'aser tithes before I gave him a granary? Who separated firstborn animals and animal tithes before I gave him a flock?" (Tanchuma).

The Hebrew words of verse 4 are susceptible to a number of different interpretations. Rashi (ad loc.) explains them as an affirmation that if there is indeed a truly righteous Tzaddik, God will protect and reward his offspring on account of his constant determination to do only goodness and righteousness. Metzudat David, on the other hand, connects this verse to the coming passage which continues to evoke the great might of Leviathan, explaining: "There is enough in what I have told you already to answer your arguments, but nevertheless I will not refrain from telling you more of the might of Leviathan and his limbs and his majestic greatness compared to the other creatures, in order that you should gain deeper understanding of My supreme exaltedness" (Metzudat David on v 4).

From verse 5 until the end of the present chapter is all a further description of Leviathan. It starts with his fearful lips and mouth (vv 5-6), his armor of scales (vv 7-9), the bolts of flashing light emerging from his sneezes, eyes, mouth, nostrils and his very soul (vv 10-13), the power of his neck and his solid flesh and heart. (14-16). The mightiest warriors are in terror of him, because he is impregnable to human weapons of any kind (vv 17-22). He plows through the sea leaving a trail of gleaming foam (vv 23-4).

After all this, it is interesting to find that the sages determined that Leviathan is kosher! "Rabbi Yosse ben Dourmaskis says, 'Leviathan is a pure species of fish, as it says, 'his **scales** are his pride' (Job 41:7) and 'his underparts are like sharp potsherds' (ibid. v 22) - these are the **fins** with which he swims'" (Chulin 67b; see Leviticus 11:9). Let us hope that we too will be worthy of a taste of the kosher flesh of Leviathan together with the true Tzaddikim!

"None on earth can be compared to him: he is made without fear. He beholds all high things; he is a king over all the children of pride" (vv 25-6). Metzudat David (on v 26) comments: "Even though he is in the water beneath the earth, he sees all who are high and mighty upon the earth and knows of all kinds of amazing creatures, and he is not afraid of anyone. He is the king and head over all men of pride, for he is prouder than all of them. As if to say: 'I have told you about the wonders of a creature made by My hands - understand from this the greatness of My exaltedness!'"

Metzudat David continues with a summary of God's answer to Job: "This is an answer to his complaint about his terrible suffering after all the good he had done. God answers that a true Tzaddik has a power in his arm like that of God to rule below and above. See now if you can punish the sinners with the words of your mouth and then I too will acknowledge that you are a perfect Tzaddik. So, what if you praise yourself as having been a Tzaddik if it was not the case? For if you had been a true Tzaddik My hand would not have been short in repaying you, because none can protest against Me. He relates the wonders of the wild ox and the wonders of the whale in order to know something of God's greatness through them - for no-one can prevent Him from paying someone their reward, even though He has no obligation to pay a reward because He already did the person a favor before he performed the mitzvah.

Nevertheless, He will yet pay a reward out of His loving kindness and likewise He would have paid Job a good reward if he had been a complete, perfect Tzaddik."

CHAPTER 42

Deeply humbled, Job admits his error in having thought that God had put men's destinies in the hands of blind fate, confessing that this was because he had been "without **Da'at**, knowledge" (v 3) because he did not understand the wonders of His watchful providence. For all that God had related about His great providence was previously hidden from him, whereas now, after he had been told, he admitted that it is true that He watches providentially over everything (see Metzudat David on v 3).

V 4: "Hear, please, and I will speak: I will ask You and You inform me" - "For I cannot know anything of Your wonders unless You Yourself in Your loving kindness make it known to me" (Ramban).

V 5: Rashi explains: "Many times I heard reports but now my eyes have seen Your Shechinah (Indwelling Presence), and because I have been worthy to see Your Shechinah, I despise my life and I will be content to dwell in the grave and return to the dust and ashes from which I was taken."

On vv 5 and 6, Ramban explains: "I had a tradition (**kabbalah**) about Your Godliness, but now I have attained prophecy and I know the truth of Your existence, and that You exist and know and watch over all providentially, and that You are a righteous Judge and full of loving kindness and truth. Therefore, I despise what I always wanted until now - the life of this world and the tranquility that I desired and over whose loss I complained. I repent over my having favored the body - which is dust and ashes - thinking that having the life of the body is kindness while death to the Tzaddik is an outrage. Now I repent over having desired the body and I want only to be attached to You and to live in the light of Your face and that my soul should be bound with You in the bond of life."

V 7: "...and HaShem said to Eliphaz the Teimanite, My anger burns against you and your two companions [Bildad the Shoohite and Tzophar the Na'amatite] - because you have not spoken of Me the thing that is right - like My servant Job." Metzudat David explains that Eliphaz and his two companions had failed to give a correct and true answer to Job although supposedly arguing on God's behalf. For they had said that his suffering came upon him because of his many sins, yet this was not so, because he had not sinned greatly even though he may not have attained the ultimate perfection of saintliness, which was why he was not fit to receive God's kindness, since the reward for a person's deeds is because of kindness. "...like **My** servant Job" - for Job too did not speak correctly when he said that everything comes about through blind fate as governed by the heavenly system. Yet even though Job had not spoken correctly, He calls him "My servant", and from this the rabbis learned that a person cannot be faulted for what he says when in pain, for it was only because of his harsh suffering that Job had said what he said (Bava Batra 16b; Metzudat David on v 7).

V 8: "Take for yourselves seven cows..." - "Their sin had been unwitting, and could be atoned for through a sacrifice in the same way as the Torah provides for the atonement of unwitting sins through sacrifices" (Ramban). The companions had to go to Job and appease him, and he would then be the Cohen-priest who would offer their sacrifices and pray for them. The rabbis compared Job's prayer for his companions to that of Abraham for Avimelech after he was afflicted with illness on account of having kidnapped Sarah (Genesis 20:7; Tosefta of Bava Kama ch 8). The rabbis also learned out from Job 42:10 - "And HaShem restored the fortunes of Job when he prayed for his friends" - that "Whoever begs for mercy for his friend when he himself is in need of that same thing is answered first" (Bava Kama 92a).

V 11: All Job's siblings and friends from before his tribulations now came to comfort him - for during his suffering they all kept away from him, as he said: "and my friends have become estranged from me" (Job 19:13; Metzudat David).

V 12: The numbers of Job's flocks, camels, teams of oxen and donkeys were all exactly doubled (see Job 1:3).

V 13: "He also had **shiv'anah** sons": Rashi explains the unusual Hebrew grammatical form **shiv'anah** (in place of **shiv'ah**=seven) as a dual form, implying that Job now had two sets of seven sons. [Likewise, the seven Hebrew letters – BeGeD KaPoReT - are doubled, since they can be either "hard" or "soft".] Although Job's daughters were not doubled in number, they were doubled in beauty. **Yamimah** was as radiant as the daylight; **Ketziah** was as fragrant as frankincense, while **Keren Hapooch** was as graceful as a garden crocus (Bava Batra 16b).

With the death of Job, "old and satisfied of days" (v 17), we complete a work that might be called **Masechet Yissurim**, "Tractate Suffering" - inasmuch as the sublime heights of Biblical poetry are combined with the thoroughness of incisive Talmudic examination and analysis of all of the different answers and approaches to this most inscrutable subject, until we finally arrive at God's truth, if we have the humility to accept it.

Blessed be God for ever and ever!!! Amen!!!

חמש מגילות
FIVE SCROLLS

SONG OF SONGS
RUTH
LAMENTATIONS
ECCLESIASTES
ESTHER

שיר השירים

SONG OF SONGS

Rabbi Akiva said: "The world was never so worthy as on the day on which the Song of Songs was given to Israel, for all the Biblical writings are holy, but Song of Songs is Holy of Holies!" (Yadayim 3:5). The rabbis taught: "When a person reads a verse from Song of Songs and makes it into a kind of song lyric, he brings evil into the world, because the Torah swathes herself in sackcloth and says before the Holy One blessed be He, 'Master of the World, your children have turned me into a kind of guitar played by jokers'" (Sanhedrin 101a).

Taking the form of a dialogue between a youthful lover and his beloved, Song of Songs is particularly susceptible to gross misinterpretation by those who are so sunk in the material that they are unable to conceive of the love between male and female as anything but physically erotic. But Song of Songs is "holy of holies" precisely because the relationship is purely and completely spiritual. Thus the work can be understood on many different levels, in particular as a dialogue of spiritual love between God and the Soul or between God and His chosen people of Israel. Besides the simple meaning of the verses, every single word and letter is laden with a multiplicity of allusions on all the levels of **Pardes**, **P**'shat (the plain meaning), **R**emez (allusion), **D**rash (homiletic lessons) and **S**od (the mystical, esoteric and kabbalistic "secret" level).

Rashi writes in the introduction to his commentary on Song of Songs: "'God spoke one thing; I heard two' (Psalms 62:12). A single verse may be susceptible of numerous explanations, but in the end no verse ever departs from its plain meaning. And even though the prophets spoke all their words metaphorically, it is necessary to explain the metaphor according to its own internal logic as it develops verse by verse. I have seen many aggadic midrashim on this book, but they do not always fit with the language and order of the verses. I say that Solomon saw with holy spirit that Israel were destined to go into exile after exile and suffer destruction after destruction, and that in exile they would grieve over their first glory and remember God's first love when they were His treasure above all the nations. They would say, Let me go and return to my first Husband, for it was better for me then than now (Hosea 2:9) and they would remember His kindnesses and their wrongdoing and all the goodness He promised to do to them at the end of days. Solomon therefore wrote this work with holy spirit, using the metaphor of a woman bound up as a widow while her husband is still alive. She longs for him and remembers her youthful love for him, acknowledging her wrongdoings. Likewise, her lover is pained over her pain and remembers the kindnesses of her youth and her beauty and good deeds, in virtue of which he is bound with her with strong love, in order to let her know that he is not tormenting her intentionally and that her divorce is no divorce, for she is still his wife and he is still her husband and he is destined to return to her."

These study notes will be mainly based on the explanations contained in the **Targum** (ancient Aramaic interpretation attributed to R. Yonatan ben Uziel) and the commentary of Rashi.

V 1: "Song of songs...." This is the ninth of ten great songs. (1) The song of Adam when he was forgiven his sin and sang the song of the Shabbat day, Psalm 92. (2) The song of Moses and Israel after crossing the Red Sea, Ex. 15:2. (3) Israel's song over the well given in the wilderness, Numbers 21:17ff. (4) Moses' song before leaving the world, Deut. ch 32. (5) Joshua's song after the battle at Giv'on, Josh. 10:12. (6) The song of Deborah, Judges ch 5. (7) Hannah's song on the birth of Samuel, I Sam. ch 2. (8) David's song, Psalms 18, II Sam.ch 22. (9) **Song of Songs**. (10) Israel's future song on going out of exile, Isaiah 30:29.

"Song of songs of **Solomon (Shlomo)**." - "Every time the name **Shlomo** appears in Song of Songs, it is a holy name of God, who is the King of Peace" (Talmud Shevuot 35b).

V 2: The "kisses of His mouth" are the teachings of His Torah, which are better than "wine" = YaYiN = 70, the seventy nations.

V 3: "Therefore the maidens love You" - these are the righteous proselytes.

V 4: "The King has brought me to His chambers" - "even today I still have joy and delight because I have attached myself to You" (Rashi).

V 5: "...daughters of Jerusalem...." The nations of the world are called "daughters of Jerusalem" because Jerusalem is destined to become the capital city of all of them, as prophesied by Ezekiel 16:61, "And I shall give them to you as daughters".

V 6: Do not look down upon me if I appear blackened with sin, because I was not so from birth but only because the mixed multitude that came up with me from Egypt (the "children of my mother") caused me to go after idols (Rashi).

V 7: Knesset Israel speaks to God like a flock asking how she can escape the seductions of the "wolves" = the nations.

V 8: "The Shepherd answers, 'Go in the pathways of the righteous, teach your children to go to the synagogue and the study hall, and this is how you will survive the exile'" (Targum).

V 9: When God destroyed the Egyptians at the Red Sea, He almost destroyed Israel because of the scoffers among them (Targum).

V 10: The "circlets" and "beads" with which God adorned Israel are the teachings of Torah He gave them in the wilderness (Targum).

V 12: "While the king still sat at his table" - at Sinai - "my spikenard (which smells foul) gave forth its fragrance" - Israel sinned with the Golden Calf.

V 13: Even so, God forgave Israel, commanding them to build the Sanctuary in order to atone. The "bag of myrrh" alludes to Mount Moriah, the Temple Mount.

V 14: Henna, **kopher**, alludes to atonement, **Kaparah**.

V 15: Despite Israel's sin and shame, God encourages her with praise of her true, essential beauty.

V 16: Israel replies that the beauty is not hers for it all comes from God (Rashi).

V 17 speaks in praise of the wilderness Sanctuary and the Future Temple (Targum; Rashi).

CHAPTER 2

V 1: "Knesset Israel says: 'When the Master of the Universe causes His presence to dwell with me, I am compared to a lily and a rose that are moist from the Garden of Eden'" (Targum).

V 2: Even though the nations seek to entice Israel to whore after their idols, she remains faithful to God (Rashi).

V 3: Israel compares God to the **tapuach** (=Etrog, Targum), whose fruit is excellent in taste and fragrance.

V 4: "He brought me to the house of wine" - this refers to the giving of the Torah at Sinai (Targum). "And his banner (**diglo**) over me is love" - "When an ignoramus or a little child mispronounces words when trying to study Torah, God says, 'And his stammering (**liglugo**) over Me is **love**'" (Midrash Shir HaShirim).

V 5: Even in exile, Israel is love-sick for God and craves His dainties.

V 7: "I adjure you, O nations, that you will be abandoned and consumed like the gazelles and hinds of the field if you try to spoil the love between me and God and try to entice me to go after you" (Rashi).

V 8: God "leaps over the mountains" and "skips over the hills" in redeeming Israel even before the appointed time (Targum).

V 9: When the Israelites sat in their houses in Egypt eating the Pesach sacrifice with Matzah and bitter herbs, God was looking in through the windows and protected them from the destroying angel that came to overthrow the Egyptians.

V 10: The following morning He told Israel to get up and leave Egypt.

V 11: For the time of exile had passed.

V 12: "The flowers appear on the earth…" - these are Moses and Aaron, who appeared in Egypt and performed the miracles of the redemption.

V 14: "O My dove, you are in the clefts of the rock…" - "This refers to when Pharaoh chased after them and caught up with them encamped at the Sea, and they had nowhere to turn. At that moment they were like a dove fleeing from a hawk. The dove tries to enter a cleft in the rocks only to find a serpent hissing there. How can she escape? But God said to them, Let Me hear your voice - 'And the Children of Israel cried out to God' (Ex. 14:10)" (Rashi).

V 15: The "foxes" allude to the Amalekites, who attacked Israel after the crossing of the Red Sea (Targum).

V 16: "My beloved is mine and I am His" - "Everything He requires He demands only from me: celebrate Pesach, sanctify the first-born, build a sanctuary, offer sacrifices. He did not demand this of any other nation" (Rashi).

V 17: Owing to the sin of the Golden Calf, the protective shadows fled, but God did not destroy Israel on account of His covenant with the patriarchs, who were swift as a gazelle and a young hart in serving Him (Targum).

V 1-2: When Israel sinned, the Divine Presence departed. In her distress in the night-time of exile, Israel - the soul - seeks out God but cannot find Him, "for I shall not go up in your midst" (Exodus 32:11).

V 3: "The watchmen that go around the city found me...." The watchmen or guards are the Tzaddikim, such as Moses and Aaron, who entreat God on behalf of Israel.

V 4: "Only a little after I passed on from them...." After 38 years in the wilderness, just after Aaron and Moses departed the world, Israel "found" God when Joshua brought them into the Land of Israel, miraculously defeating the 31 kings of Canaan. "I held him and would not let him go until I had brought him into my mother's house and into the chamber of her that conceived me" - After entry into the Land, Israel built the Sanctuary at Shilo.

V 5: "I adjure you, O daughters of Jerusalem...." Israel tells the nations not to spoil God's love for her by enticing her to abandon Him and go after their idols (Rashi).

V 6: "Who is this that comes out of the wilderness…?" When the nations saw Israel miraculously cross the River Jordan and enter the Land, they could not but wonder at the greatness of this upright nation advancing in the merit of the patriarchs (Targum).

V 7: The ultimate purpose of the entry into the Land was to build the Temple, which is the "bed" upon which the King of Peace causes His presence to rest (cf. II Kings 11:2). The "sixty mighty warriors" allude to the 600,000 souls of Israel ordered around the Sanctuary (in Hebrew, 600,000 is expressed as 60 **reebo**, where each **reebo** is 10,000). The "sixty warriors" also allude to the sixty Hebrew letters that make up the Priestly Blessing (Numbers 6:24-26) recited daily in the Temple.

V 8: "They all handle the sword and are expert in war..." - "The priests and Levites and Israelites are all expert in the Torah which is compared to a sword" (Targum). "Every man has his sword on his thigh" - This alludes to the sign of the Covenant cut into the flesh by the thighs: this gives protection against all the forces of evil (Targum).

V 9: "King Solomon made himself a palanquin...." This alludes to Solomon's Temple, built from the precious timbers of Lebanon.

V 10: Having completed the Temple, Solomon brought in the Ark of the Covenant, and the Divine Presence dwelled between the cherubs on its cover. "...the seat of it of purple (**argaman**)" - this alludes to the woven Parochet-screen that was hung in front of the Ark. As an example of the deep allusions contained in every word and letter of Song of Songs, it may be noted that **argaman** is an acronym of the initial letters of the names of the archangels, Oori-el, Repha-el, Gavri-el, Micha-el and Noori-el, who are the "seat" or "chariot" upon which the Divine Presence "rides".

V 11: "Go forth and gaze, O daughters of Zion, upon the King of Peace, upon the crown with which His **mother** crowned Him on the day of His wedding and on the day of the joy of His heart". "Rabbi Elazar the son of Rabbi Yosse said, This is like a king who had an only daughter whom he loved very greatly. He had such great affection for her that he called her 'my daughter' (Psalms 45:11); so great was his affection for her that he did not move until he called her 'my sister' (Songs 5:2). So great was his affection for her that he did not move until he called her 'my mother' (cf. Isaiah 51:4 where the Hebrew text reads 'My mother')" - (Rashi on Songs 3:11).

CHAPTER 4

Chapter 4 vv 1-7 is the Lover's description of the beautiful features of his Beloved. Kabbalistically, this description alludes to the **Partzuf** of the Shechinah, Malchut (kingship), the Nukva (female), for with the completion of Solomon's Temple, the attribute of Malchut was fully revealed.

V 1: The "eyes" are the leaders of the assembly and the sages of the Sanhedrin. The "hair" alludes to the rest of the people: even the merest of the "people of the land" (**am ha-aretz**) are righteous like the sons of Jacob, who heaped up stones on Mount Gilead, Gen. 31:46 (Targum).

V 2: The "teeth" are the priests and Levites, who eat the meat of the sacrifices and the Terumah and Maaser tithes of the people. They are compared to flocks that are clean after having been washed since they are guiltless of any theft or robbery (Targum).

V 3: The "lips" are those of the High Priest, whose prayers on the Day of Atonement whitened the "scarlet" sins of the people (Targum).

V 4: The "neck" alludes to the **Nasi**, President of the Sanhedrin, whose merit is a tower of strength to the nation, who thereby win all their wars as if holding every kind of weapon in their hands (Targum).

V 5: "Your two breasts are like two fawns..." The two breasts allude to Mashiach ben David and Mashiach ben Yosef (who nurture and redeem Israel): they are compared to two fawns = Moses and Aaron, who "feed among the lilies" - during their 40 year leadership of the people in the wilderness, they provided them with Manna, fat quails and Miriam's well (Targum).

Rashi interprets the two breasts as alluding to the Two Tablets of Stone. They are called "twins" because the five commandments on one are intrinsically bound up with the five commandments on the other. "I am HaShem..." - "Do not murder": a murderer destroys the divine form, since man is created in God's image. "You shall have no other gods" - "Do not commit adultery": idolatry is like marital disloyalty. "Do not bear God's name in vain" - "Do not steal": a thief ends up swearing falsely. "Remember the Sabbath" - "Do not bear false testimony": Desecration of Shabbat is like bearing false testimony against the Creator. "Honor your father and mother" - "Do not covet": One who covets another man's wife ends up bearing a son who despises him and honors one who is not his father.

V 6: "As long as the House of Israel practiced the craft of their saintly forefathers, all the destructive forces fled from them, just like they fled from the incense offered in the Temple built on Mount Moriah" (Targum).

V 8: "With Me from Lebanon, my bride, come with Me from Lebanon…" - "When you go into exile from this Lebanon (= the Temple), you will go into exile with Me, for I will be in exile with you. And when you return from the exile, I will return with you. And through all the days of the exile, I shall share in your sorrow" (Rashi). "Look from the top of Mount Amanah". Mount Amanah is the northern boundary of the Holy Land (=Hor HaHar, Numbers 34:7). Amanah = Emunah, Faith. "When I gather in your dispersed exiles, examine and contemplate what is your reward for your achievements, from the beginning of the Emunah with which you believed in Me when you went after Me into the wilderness." (Rashi).

V 9: "You have ravished My heart... with one bead of your necklace" - even your smallest is righteous as one of the rabbis of the Sanhedrin! (Targum).

V 12 praises the great modesty of the women of Israel.

V 13: "Your offshoots are an orchard of pomegranates..." - "Even the smallest of Israel are moist in good deeds like an orchard of pomegranates" (Rashi).

V 16: "Awake, O north wind..." "God says, 'Since your fragrance is so sweet to me, I command the north and south winds to blow, gathering in all your exiles, and bringing them as an offering to Jerusalem.' Then Israel answers, 'Let my Beloved come to His garden - if You are there, everything is there!'" (Rashi).

CHAPTER 5

V 1: "I have come into my garden, my sister, my bride..." - With the completion of the Temple, God's presence enters, accepting the incense offerings and wine libations, and He invites the priests to eat their share of the sacrificial offerings.

V 2: "I am asleep...." With the passage of time, even having the Temple, Israel became lax in God's service and began to sin. "...but my heart is awake..." - The "heart" is the Holy One blessed be He, who is called "the rock of my heart" (Psalms 73:26). "...the voice of my Beloved is knocking..." - God repeatedly sent His prophets to warn the people, asking His "bride" to open up and admit Him into her house just as a lover seeks to steal in to visit his beloved even at night despite getting wet from the rain or dew (Rashi).

V 3: The beloved bride replies like a faithless wife making excuses why she cannot admit her husband. "I have taken off my coat..." - "I have already fallen into other habits (idolatry) and I can no longer return to You" (Rashi).

V 4: "My beloved put in his hand through the hole of the door..." - God began to strike Israel, first sending the tribes of Reuven, Gad and half of Menasheh into exile some generations before the destruction of the Temple (Targum). This caused a stir of repentance among those who remained.

Vv 5-6: However, even this arousal of repentance in the last generations before the destruction was insufficient to revoke the decree and restore the divine Presence to the Temple (Rashi on v 7).

V 7: "The watchmen that go about the city found me...." These are the Babylonians, who slaughtered and exiled Judah (Targum). "They took away my mantle from me" - the mantle alludes to Tzedekiah, the last king of Judah, whom Nebuchadnezzar killed (Targum).

V 8: "I adjure you, O daughters of Jerusalem, if you find my beloved, what will you tell him? That I am love-sick" - Israel adjures the Babylonians to bear witness on the future day of judgment how even in exile, she remained faithful, with Tzaddikim like Daniel, Chananiyah, Misha'el and Azariah being willing to sacrifice their lives to sanctify God's name (Rashi).

V 9: The nations ask Israel how God is different from their gods such that she is willing to be burned and hanged for His sake.

This question of the nations, elicits Israel's praiseful description of God's attributes, which is in parallel with God's description of the attributes of Israel in ch 4 vv 1-5. Just as that description kabbalistically refers to the Partzuf of Malchut/Nukva/Shechinah, similarly the description here in chapter 5 vv 10-16 alludes kabbalistically to the Partzuf of Zeir Anpin/Kudsha Berich Hu. The commentary on the coming verses is mainly based on Rashi's lengthy comment on Ch 5 v 16 where he discusses the entire passage.

V 10: "My beloved is white and ruddy...." God "whitens" and cleanses sins out of loving kindness (Chessed). He is "ruddy" in punishing His enemies (Gevurah). He is "pre-eminent above ten thousand" - many "troops"=angels surround Him.

V 11: "His head is like the finest gold…" - the "head" is the first of the Ten Commandments, in which He asserts His kingship. Having done so, He then proceeds to make His decrees: "His locks are curled..." - this alludes to the multitude of laws of the Torah. "...and black as a raven" - the primordial Torah was written with black fire on white fire.

V 12: "His eyes are like doves...." Just as doves look to their cotes, so God's eyes are upon the synagogues and study halls, where the Torah, which is compared to water, is found. "...washed with milk...." When God's eyes look in judgment, they clarify the true verdict, justifying the righteous and condemning the wicked, requiting each according to his ways.

V 13: "His cheeks..." refers to His revelation at Sinai; "...his lips…" refers to the Torah portions that He revealed out of the Tent of Meeting (the laws of sacrifices in Leviticus).

V 14: "His hands…" refers to the Tablets of Stone. "His body...", lit. the torso, refers to the book of Leviticus, which is in the middle of the Five Books of Moses just as the torso is in the middle of the body.

V 15: "...his aspect is like Lebanon..." - one who studies and contemplates His words (in the Torah) finds them like a forest that is constantly in blossom, because they are always fresh.

V 16: "His mouth is most sweet...." Could anything be sweeter than the Torah code, which even gives us a reward for fulfilling a mitzvah such as not causing ourselves injury (Leviticus 19:28) and which guarantees that if a wicked man repents his very sins are turned into merits? (Rashi).

CHAPTER 6

V 1: "Where is your beloved gone...?" The nations taunt Israel, asking why He has left her as an abandoned widow. "Let us seek him with you!" When God restored Judah from exile to Jerusalem and they began to build the Second Temple, the surrounding nations asked to participate in the building in order to try to stall it.

V 3: "I am my beloved's and my beloved is mine...." Israel replies to the nations that they have no share in the building of Jerusalem (cf. Ezra 4:3; Nehemiah 2:20).

V 4: "You are beautiful, O my love...." God praises Israel for this reply to the nations. "...comely as Jerusalem..." - With the rebuilding of the Temple, Israel was restored to her former glory. "...terrible as an army with banners." God struck fear into the heart of the adversaries so that they were unable to stop the rebuilding.

V 5: "Turn away your eyes from me, for they have overcome me...." God speaks to Israel like a lover so overwhelmed by his beloved that he has to ask her to turn her eyes away from him. This alludes to the fact that the Second Temple lacked the Ark of the Covenant etc. which in the First Temple caused such overwhelming passion that this in itself led Israel into betrayal (Rashi).

V 6: "Your teeth are like a flock of lambs...." Every part of the lamb can be used for holy purposes: its wool is dyed **techeilet** (sky blue) for Tzitzit, its flesh is offered as a sacrifice, its horns are used for shofars, its leg-bones for flutes, its innards for stringed instruments and its skin for drums, while the nations are compared to dogs (Psalms 22:17 etc.), no part of which is used for holy service (Rashi).

V 8: "Sixty are the queens and eighty are the concubines...." The sixty queens allude to Abraham and his descendants as listed in Genesis, while the eighty concubines allude to Noah and all his other descendants as listed there. (See Rashi on this verse for the complete listings.) "...and maidens without number" - these are all the families into which the primordial souls later became divided (Rashi).

V 9: "My dove, my undefiled, is but one...." Out of all of them, only one is God's choicest. Israel is compared to a dove because the dove is completely loyal to her spouse.

V 10: "Who is she that looks forth as the dawn...?" Israel in the time of the Second Temple are compared to the dawn, which little by little becomes lighter and lighter, in that initially they were subject to Persia and Greece but under the Hasmoneans became an independent kingdom.

V 11: "I went down into the garden of nuts...." God sent His presence to dwell in the Second Temple. Israel is compared to a garden of nuts, because from the outside a nut appears to be all wood but when you crack it you find it to be full of compartments of edible food. Also, even when a nut falls into the mud (= exile), its contents are not spoiled.

V 12: "And since it is revealed before God that they are righteous and occupied with the Torah, God says, I shall strike them no more, nor shall I destroy them, but I shall set myself to show them beneficence" (Targum).

CHAPTER 7

These notes on the final chapters of Song of Songs consist of a translation of the Aramaic Targum, which is exceptionally beautiful and inspiring. While the Targum may appear far-fetched and distant from the surface meaning of the text as rendered in the standard English translations, those who have some understanding of the Hebrew original and of the methods of Midrash will be able to see that every word and idea in the Targum is soundly based on the actual Hebrew text.

Chapter 7 v 1: Return to Me, O Assembly of Israel, return to Jerusalem, return to the Torah study hall, return to the prophets who prophesy in the Name of HaShem - why should the false prophets seek to lead the people of Jerusalem astray with prophecies that are contrary to God's word in order to defile the camp of Israel and Judah?

V 2: King Solomon said with prophetic spirit from God: How beautiful are the feet of Israel when they go up to appear before God three times in the year and bring their sacrifices, and their children are beautiful as the gems in the crown that the craftsman Betzalel made for Aaron the Priest.

V 3: The head of the Academy, in whose merit the entire world is sustained like an embryo is sustained in the womb of its mother, shines in Torah like the crescent of the moon when he comes to rule pure or impure, innocent or guilty. Words of Torah are never lacking from his mouth, just like waters are never lacking from the great river that goes forth out of Eden. Seventy sages surround him like a round threshing floor, with their store-houses full of the holy tithes that Ezra the Priest and the Men of the Great Assembly - who are like roses - assigned to them in order that they should have strength to engage in Torah day and night.

V 4: The two redeemers that are destined to redeem you, Mashiach son of David and Mashiach son of Ephraim, will be like Moses and Aaron, who are compared to two fawns, twins of a gazelle.

V 5: The father of the court of law that judges your cases takes pity on the people, disciplining them, giving lashes to those who deserve it, as did King Solomon, who built a tower of elephant's tusk and mastered the people of Israel, restoring them to the Ruler of the Universe. Your sages are full of wisdom like fountains of water, and they know how to calculate the months and leap years, fixing the new moons and new years in the gates of the great Sanhedrin, while the leader of the House of Judah is like King David, who built the Fortress of Zion, which is called the Tower of Lebanon, all who stand on which can count all the towers of Damascus.

V 6: The king appointed as head over you is righteous like Elijah, who was zealous for the King of Heaven and killed the false prophets on Mount Carmel, restoring the House of Israel to the fear of God. Even the lowliest of the people who go with their head bowed down are destined to wear purple, as did Daniel in Babylon and Mordechai in Shushan, in the merit of the patriarchs.

V 7: Said King Solomon: How beautiful are you O Assembly of Israel when you bear upon you the yoke of my kingship when I chastise you over your sins and you accept this with love.

V 8: At the moment when your priests stretch out their hands in prayer and bless their brothers the House of Israel, their fingers are spread like the branches of a palm and their stature is like the date palm, and your assembly stand face to face with the priests, their heads bent over to the ground like bunches of grapes.

V 9: God says: I will go and test Daniel and see if he can withstand one test just as Abraham, who was straight like the Lulav, withstood ten tests, and I will also test Chananiyah, Misha'el and Azariah, and if they stand firm I will in their merit redeem the people of Israel, who are like a bunch of grapes, and the fame of those Tzaddikim will be known throughout the earth and their fragrance will spread like the fragrance of the apple trees of the Garden of Eden.

V 10: Daniel and his companions said, Let us accept God's decree as did Abraham, who is compared to old wine, and let us go in His paths like Elijah and Elisha, in whose merit the dead - who are like a man asleep - came to life, and like Ezekiel, through the prophecy of whose mouth the dead were revived in the valley of Doura.

V 11: Jerusalem says: As long as I go in the ways of the Master of the Universe, He rests His Presence upon me and His desire is upon me, while if I stray from His paths, He withdraws His Presence and makes me wander among the nations and they rule over me as a man rules over his wife.

V 12: When the House of Israel sinned, God sent them into exile in the land of Edom. Then the Assembly of Israel said: Master of the Universe, please accept my prayer, which I offer to you from the cities of my exile and the provinces of the nations.

V 13: The Children of Israel say to one another, Let us rise early in the morning and go to the synagogues and the study halls and study the scroll of the Torah and see if the time has arrived for the redemption of Israel, who are compared to the vine, and let us ask the sages - since it is revealed before God that the righteous are full of merits like the pomegranate - if the end has come so that we may go up to Jerusalem to give praise there to the God of Heaven and to offer holy sacrifices and libations.

V 14: And when God's desire will be to redeem His people from exile, King Mashiach will be told: The time of the exile has reached its end, and the merits of the righteous are fragrant as the scent of balsam, and the sages of the generation are constantly by the gates of the study hall engaging in the teachings of the scribes and the words of the Torah. Arise now and receive the kingship that I have stored up for you.

CHAPTER 8

V 1: At that time King Mashiach will be revealed to the Assembly of Israel, and the Children of Israel will say to him, Come and go with us like a brother and we will go up to Jerusalem, and we will feed upon the deep wisdom of the Torah just as a baby suckles at his mother's chest. For all the time that I was wandering about outside my land, when I remembered the Name of the great God and sacrificed myself for His sake, even the nations of the land did not despise me.

V 2: I will take you, King Mashiach, and bring you up to my Temple, and you will teach me to fear God and go in His ways, and there we will partake of the feast of Leviatan and drink the old wine that has been hidden away since the day the world was created and partake of the pomegranate fruits destined for the Tzaddikim in the Garden of Eden.

V 3: The Assembly of Israel says: I am the choicest of all the nations, for I bind the Tefilin on my left arm and upon my head, and I fix the Mezuzah on the right-hand door post, so that no destructive spirits have the power to harm me.

V 4: King Mashiach will say: I adjure you, my people the House of Israel, why do you provoke the nations of the earth in trying to go out of exile, and why do you rebel against the forces of Gog and Magog. Tarry here a little while until the nations that go up to make war against Jerusalem will be destroyed, and afterwards God will remember in your favor the kindnesses of the Tzaddikim, and it will be His will to redeem you.

V 5: Solomon the prophet said: When the dead will come to life, the Mount of Olives will be split and all the dead of Israel will come up from beneath it, and even the righteous who died in exile will go through tunnels under the earth and come out from under the Mount of Olives, while the wicked who died and were buried in the Land of Israel will be cast out as a man casts a stone. Then all the inhabitants of the earth will say: What is the merit of this people who go up from the land in their multiple thousands upon thousands as on the day when they went up from the wilderness to the land of Israel, delighting in the kindnesses of their Master as on the day when they surrounded Mount Sinai to receive the Torah? At that hour Zion, who is the mother of Israel, will give birth to her children and Jerusalem will receive the children of the exile.

V 6: On that day, the Children of Israel will say to their Master: Please place us like the seal of a ring upon Your heart, like the seal of a ring upon Your arm, so that we will be exiles no more. For the love of Your Godliness is strong as death, and the people's jealousy of us is fierce as hell, and the hatred they bear against us is like the coals of fire of Gehennom, which God created on the second day of creation in order to burn up the idolaters.

V 7: The Master of the Universe says to His people the House of Israel: Even if all the nations, who are compared to the many waters of the sea, were to gather together, they cannot drown My love and make it depart from you. And even if all the kings of the earth, who are compared to the waters of a mighty river, gather together, they will not be able to obliterate you from the world. And if a man pays all the money of his house to acquire wisdom while in exile, I will return him double in the world to come, and all the spoils of the camp of Gog will not be enough to compare with this reward.

V 8: At that time the angels of heaven will say one to another: We have one nation on earth whose merits are slender and she has no kings or rulers to go out to do battle with the camp of Gog. What shall we do for our sister on the day that the nations say they will go up against her in war?

V 9: Michael the guardian angel of Israel will say: If she stands like a wall among the nations and pays money to unify the Name of the Master of the Universe, then, I and you, together with their scribes, shall surround her like walls of silver and the nations will have no power to rule over her, just like worms have no power to destroy silver. And even if she is poor in merits, let us entreat God for mercy upon her and remember the merit of the Torah written on the tablets of the heart which the children study, and she will stand against the nations like a cedar.

V 10: The Assembly of Israel answers and says: I am firm as a wall in following the teachings of the Torah, and the children are strong as a tower. At that time the Assembly of Israel will find favor in the eyes of her Master, and they will seek the peace of all the inhabitants of earth.

V 11: One nation went up as the share of the Master of the Universe to whom peace belongs. She is compared to a vineyard. He settled her in Jerusalem and entrusted her into the hand of the kings of the House of David to guard her, just as a tenant tends a vineyard. After Solomon king of Israel died, they were left in the hands of his son Rehaboam. Jeraboam came and divided the kingdom with him and took ten tribes from him in accordance with the words of Achiyah of Shilo.

V 12: When King Solomon heard the prophecy of Achiyah, he sought to kill him, and Jeraboam fled from Solomon and went to Egypt. At that hour King Solomon was told in a prophecy that he would rule over the Ten Tribes all his days, but that after his death Jeraboam son of Nevat would rule over them, while the two tribes of Judah and Benjamin would be under the rule of Rehaboam, son of Solomon.

V 13: Said King Solomon at the end of his prophecy: At the end of days, the Master of the Universe will say to the Assembly of Israel: You, O Assembly of Israel, that is compared to a small garden among the nations, and you sit in the study hall with the members of the Sanhedrin while the rest of the people listen to the voice of the head of the Assembly and learn from the words of his mouth. Let Me hear the sound of your words of Torah when you sit in judgment, whether to vindicate or condemn, and I will agree with everything you do.

V 14: At that hour the elders of the Assembly of Israel will say: Run, my Beloved, Master of the Universe, from this impure land and let Your Presence dwell in the heavens above. And in times of trouble, when we pray to You, be like a gazelle, which when it sleeps keeps one eye closed and one eye open, or like a young hart, which when it flees looks behind it. So too may You look upon us and see our pain and suffering from the heavens above, until the time when You will show favor and redeem us and bring us up on the mountain of Jerusalem, and there the priests will offer the incense spices before You.

רות

RUTH

CHAPTER 1

The book of Ruth - an enchanting agricultural allegory replete with some of the deepest Torah mysteries - centers on the theme of embrace of the Torah itself through conversion and the practice of the Kindness it teaches, which is the very pillar of the Universe. It is the union of Torah and Kindness that leads to redemption. Ruth is the archetypal convert who accepts the Torah. Her need to benefit from the agricultural gifts to the poor, an integral part of the pathway of kindness it teaches, leads her to the field of Boaz. And out of their encounter springs the line that leads to David, the Messianic king and redeemer of Israel (Ruth 4:13-22).

It is customary to read the book of Ruth in the synagogue on the morning of the festival of Shavuot, the summertime harvest festival celebrating the Receiving of the Torah at Sinai. Ruth is read prior to the Torah reading, which describes the revelation at Sinai, where all those who accepted the yoke of the Torah were "converts". Shavuot is also by tradition the anniversary of the birth and death of King David.

"Why was she called Ruth? Because she merited that out of her came David, who delighted (**reevah**) the Holy One blessed be He with songs and praises" (Berachot 7b). Ruth herself was a royal princess, daughter of Eglon king of Moab, who merited such a righteous descendant as David because he rose from his throne in honor of God when Ehud called him (Judges 3:20). Yet Ruth gave up her royal status and its luxuries in order to follow Naomi into a life of abject poverty. She was willing to do this in order to attain the greatest wealth of all, the life of Torah. She was prepared to descend to the very bottom of the social ladder and play the role of '**Ani**, the poor man, who is needed by the **Ba'al HaBayit**, the rich householder,in order to fulfill the mitzvot involved in the practice of kindness and charity. First and foremost, among these in a simple agricultural society are the gifts to the poor of **Pe'ah**, the unharvested corner of the field, **Leket**, the gleanings of fallen ears of corn, and **Shich'hah**, the forgotten sheaf.

Ruth starts off as the receiver of kindness, but "More than the rich householder does for the poor man, the poor man does for the rich householder" (Midrash Ruth 4), because in the merit of the householder's kindness to the poor man, he receives a blessing that he could not have attained without the poor man serving as the recipient of his gift. In the merit of Boaz' kindness to Ruth, she becomes attached to him and bears him a son who fathers the father of Mashiach.

V 1: "And it was in the days when the judges judged..." This was prior to Samuel, some say in the time of Barak and Deborah, others say in the time of Shamgar and Ehud (Yalkut Shimoni). The Hebrew phrase "the judges judged" can also be construed as meaning that people used to judge the judges. "Woe to the generation that judged their judges and whose judges needed to be judged!" (Introduction to Midrash Ruth). **Vayehi**, "and it was", is an expression of woe (Megillah 10b).

"...And there was a famine in the land..." Targum on this verse enumerates ten major famines - in the times of Adam, Lemech, Abraham, Isaac, Jacob, Boaz, David, Elijah and Elisha, "...and the tenth famine will be in time to come, not a famine to eat bread and not a thirst to drink water, but to hear words of prophecy from HaShem."

R. Ovadiah of Bartenurah (author of the standard commentary on the Mishnah) wrote a kabbalistic commentary on Ruth. He states that "in the days when the judges judged" means it was a time when the Attribute of Judgment was judging Israel, and the blessing was taken from her. "There was a famine in the land" means that the Shechinah left the throne and ascended on high, and correspondingly down below, the kings of Israel (Elimelech and family) left their "thrones" and went out into exile.

"…And a man (**ish**) went out from Bethlehem…" The word **ish** teaches that he was very wealthy and the leader of the generation (Rashi). "**Ish** alludes to the Holy One blessed be He, cf. Exodus 15:3" (Bartenurah).

"…to dwell in the fields of Moab, he and his wife..." - "The Holy One blessed be He is the 'man', Israel are His wife, and when the wife is among the nations of the world, represented by the fields of Moab, the "man" is also with them, as the Rabbis taught: wherever Israel were exiled, the Shechinah went with them" (Bartenurah).

V 2: "And the name of the man was Elimelech..." - **Eli** is the name of the Holy One, blessed be He, and to Him alone is the kingship (**Melec**h) fitting" (Bartenurah).

The ten Hebrew letters of the names of Elimelech's two sons, **Machlon** and **Chilyon** (which have the connotations of Forgiveness and Destruction respectively), correspond to the Ten Sefirot.

V 4: "And they took for themselves Moabite wives..." Bartenurah explains: **Machlon** and **Chilyon** are the places from which influence flows into the world, and now, because of our sins, they send blessing to the wicked, while Israel receive troubles and evils through them because they are weak in performance of the commandments and turn the back (**oreph**) of their heads to God instead of their faces, and for this reason they are saturated (**ravvim**) with troubles and evils, and this is alluded to in the names of **Orpah** and **Ruth**.

V 5: "And the two of them died also, Machlon and Chilyon..." Bartenurah explains: "The text says 'also' to suggest that this was not literal death but rather it is a metaphor for the absence of the Shechinah, so that even though there is blessing in the world, it cannot be compared to the blessing that flows when Israel are meritorious, and the blessing that comes down to Israel is not as it was in the days of old when they received it from the hand of the Holy One blessed be He. But when they are in exile they receive it through the angels, who are alluded to in the "lads of Boaz". For Boaz alludes to the Holy One blessed by He, who is destined to rule over Israel with might (**'oz**) and power when He will be aroused from His "sleep", but in the meantime, He hides His power and might from them and does not fight their wars.

V 8: "…Let HaShem perform kindness to you just as you have done kindness with the dead and with me." The "kindness" of the two daughters-in-law to the dead was that they made them shrouds (Yalkut Shimoni). Giving honor to the dead is **Chessed shel Emet**, **True** Kindness since one can expect no recompense whatever from the recipient. The theme of the practice of Kindness recurs repeatedly in Ruth because this is one of the three pillars on which the universe stands (Avot 1:2).

Vv 7ff: Orpah and Ruth accompany Naomi on her way home to the Land of Israel, but Naomi seeks to dissuade them from going with her. Three times she tells them, "Return!" (vv 8, 11 & 12) teaching that the would-be convert is rejected three times, and only if he makes an exceptional effort is he received (Yalkut Shimoni).

V 14: Orpah eventually turned her back on Naomi and ended up giving birth to four sons who became formidable adversaries of David, including Goliath (II Samuel 21:22).

However, Ruth persisted. Her beautiful words to Naomi in vv 16-17, "wherever you go I will go", were darshened by the rabbis as stating her complete acceptance of the Torah (her "conversion"). "Wherever you go, I will go" - I will only walk within the Sabbath limits. "Wherever you lie down to rest, I will lie down to rest" - I will not go into forbidden seclusion with a male. "Your people is my people" - I accept the 613 commandments by which your people are distinguished from all others. "And your God is my God" - I will not worship idols. "Where you die, I will die" - I accept on myself the Four Death Penalties of the Court (stoning, burning, decapitation and strangulation). ".and there I will be buried" - I accept that there are separate areas in the cemetery for executed sinners (see Rashi on vv 16-17).

V 21: "I went out full but HaShem has brought me back empty..." Having returned to Israel, Naomi is now the very epitome of poverty, lowliness and humility, and with her is Ruth, the former princess, who must now go out into the field to gather fallen gleanings in order to survive. Poverty and humility are the attributes that God chose as the most fitting vessel through which to receive His Torah!

CHAPTER 2

V 1: "Now there was a relative of Naomi's husband…" The rabbis taught that Elimelech and Sal'mon (the father of Boaz, Ruth 4:21), Ploni Almoni (Ruth 4:1) and Naomi's father were all brothers, the sons of Nachshon ben Aminadav, Prince of Judah.

"And his name was Boaz." Bartenurah explains: "The allusive meaning is that the name of the Holy One blessed be He has the power and might to restore the captivity of Israel.

V 3: "…and she happened to come..." A higher Hand was guiding Ruth to her destiny. Of the Hebrew words, **va-yeeker meeker-ha**, Rabbi Yochanan said, "Everyone who saw her had a **keri**" (Yalkut Shimoni) - Ruth was exceptionally beautiful.

V 4: "…and he said to the reapers, HaShem be with you…" From here we learn that HaShem's name may be invoked in blessing others (Berachot).

V 5: "…And Boaz said. Whose maiden is this?" - "Could it be that Boaz was in the habit of asking after women? No! Rather, he saw in her the ways of modesty and wisdom. Two fallen ears she would take, but if three had fallen together, she would not take them [as prescribed by the halachah]. Ears that were standing up she picked while standing; those lying on the ground she sat down to pick in order not to bend over." (Rashi).

Vv 8-9: "And Boaz said to Ruth..." The deep allegory contained in this verse is darshened at length by Rabbi Nachman (Likutey Moharan I, 65, see "Rabbi Nachman on Suffering" translated by R. Avraham Greenbaum, pub. Breslov Research Institute).

Vv 10-11: Why did Boaz show Ruth exceptional kindness going beyond the letter of his obligations under the laws of **Leket**? Because of Ruth's exceptional kindness to Naomi and her having left her parents, homeland and native culture in order to join a people she had not known before. Kindness begets kindness.

CHAPTER 3

V 1: "And Naomi her mother-in-law said to her…" Having seen how God's guiding hand had brought Ruth to reap in Boaz' field and how generously Boaz had responded, Naomi now seized the initiative, priming her widowed daughter-in-law to throw herself before him in the hope that he would marry her. (It is a sad reality that the convert is not generally perceived as having a high value in the marriage market, particularly not a Moabitess for the reason that will be discussed in the commentary on Chapter 4.) The dramatic initiative whereby Ruth at the bidding of her mother-in-law went into Boaz to plead with him directly is somewhat reminiscent of Esther's dramatic appeal to Ahasuerus at the bidding of Mordechai.

V 2: "And now, is not Boaz our relative…" Naomi was not merely trying to make a good match for Ruth. From the ensuing narrative we learn that Naomi wanted Boaz to fulfill the Biblically-ordained role of the "redeemer" of an impoverished relative's field, as laid down in Leviticus 25:25. Naomi and Ruth had been reduced to complete poverty, and they were forced to sell the field that had been the ancestral portion of Ruth's late husband Machlon. In order not only to retain the family property but also to keep the name of Machlon alive, Naomi wanted Boaz to buy the field **and** marry Ruth so that Machlon's name would live on when people would see her going in and out of the field and say, "She was Machlon's wife" (see Rashi on Ruth 3:8).

What Naomi wanted to accomplish was **not** exactly identical with **Yibum**, the "levirate" marriage in which the widow of a man who dies childless is married by her dead husband's surviving brother in order that the child she will hopefully bear him will perpetuate the dead brother's name (Deuteronomy 25:5-6). Nevertheless, the mystery of **Yibum** lies at the very center of the story of Ruth and Boaz, just as it lies at the heart of that of Boaz' illustrious ancestors, Judah and Tamar (Genesis ch 38). Thus, the ceremony described in Ruth ch 4 whereby Boaz in the presence of the elders at the gate "purchased" the field, and Ruth with it, from the other candidate for "redeemer", including the taking off of the shoe as a mark of the transaction, is conceptually bound up with the ceremony of **Chalitzah** in Deut. 25:7-10.

V 3: "Wash yourself and anoint yourself and put your dress on…" - "Wash yourself from the filth of idolatry, and anoint yourself with mitzvot" (Rashi). Was Ruth naked so that Naomi had to tell her to put a dress on? No! She was telling her to change her clothes and put on her Shabbat dress! (Yalkut Shimoni). Ruth, symbolizing repentant Israel, was about to go to seek out her Redeemer, and she had to prepare herself.

V 6: "And she went down to the threshing floor and did according to all that her mother-in-law had instructed her." In fact Ruth reversed the order, because Naomi had told her to get ready first and then go to the threshing floor. Wisely, Ruth understood that if she were to go through the streets adorned and bedecked people could get a very bad impression, which is why she adorned herself only after arriving at the threshing floor. All of this took place at **night-time**, signifying the darkness of exile, whereas the redemption of Ruth by Boaz, symbolizing God's redemption of Israel, takes place in the full light of the morning.

V 8: "And it came to pass at midnight." These are exactly the same words as in Exodus 12:29 when Israel was redeemed from Egypt.

"…the **man** was startled. and behold there was a **woman** lying at his feet." - "The **man** alludes to the Holy One blessed be He, while the **woman** lying at his feet alludes to Israel, as in the Talmudic phrase '[the sign of the 3rd watch of the night is] a **woman** talking to her **husband**' (Berachot 3a; Bartenurah on Ruth 3:8).

V 9: "…And she said. spread your garment over your handmaiden, for you are the redeemer." Rashi (ad loc.) explains that the spreading of his garment over her is a euphemism for marriage. On the esoteric level, Bartenurah explains that Ruth was requesting that God Himself should redeem Israel rather than a mortal hero like one of the ancient judges such as Samson or Gideon, for He is their true Redeemer.

V 10: "And he said, blessed are you to HaShem…" - "Reish Lakish said, A man should never hold himself back from going to an elder to bless him, for Ruth was forty years old and she had never had children [the rabbis said she was congenitally barren, Yalkut on Ruth 4:13 'And HaShem **gave** her conception'], but after that Tzaddik prayed for her she was granted a child" (Yalkut Shimoni).

V 12: "...and also there is a redeemer who is closer than me". The other candidate to fulfill the Biblical precept of redeeming Ruth's field was a relative "closer" than Boaz, because, as the rabbis explained, this **Ploni Almoni**, "Mister Someone" (Ruth 4:1), who was also called **Tov** (in our present chapter in the very next verse if we construe the Hebrew text literally) was the surviving **brother** of Elimelech and Sal'mon (who had also died already), whereas Boaz was Sal'mon's **son** and therefore not as close (see Rashi on our present verse).

Bartenurah, discussing the mystery of the other candidate for redeemer, explains that the redemption of Israel can take place in one of two ways. Either Israel repents and they are redeemed immediately, or they fail to repent and have to be redeemed by God Himself. The first way in which redemption takes place is "closer", and indeed there were times in the history of Israel when they merited redemption in virtue of their repentance, as in the time of Hezekiah. (This explains the opinion of R. Hillel in Sanhedrin 99a that Israel will not have any further Mashiach, because they already "ate" him in the days of Hezekiah.) The second way in which redemption takes place is "further off" because it will only happen at the end of days.

Bartenurah explains that esoterically, Boaz' praise of Ruth for "not going after the young men, whether poor or rich" (Ruth 3:10) indicates that even though redeemers like Samson and Gideon etc. had great power and strength, Israel prefers that the redemption should come from God Himself. "You have shown more loyalty at the end than at the beginning" - because Israel wants the final redemption to come from God, as opposed to the earlier redemptions, which came about through human leaders, the earlier redemptions were followed by further exile while God's redemption will be final and everlasting.

V 13: "Stay this night and it shall be in the morning..." If Israel waits for God to redeem them, they may have to stay longer in the darkness of exile, but in the end the morning will arrive and then God will redeem them (Bartenurah). The rabbis taught that the oath that Boaz took in this verse was that despite being sorely tempted, he would not lie with Ruth without first formally marrying her (see Rashi ad loc.)

V 15: "…And he measured **six** measures of barley…" - "He hinted to her that a son would come forth from her who would be blessed with **six** blessings, 'a spirit of wisdom and understanding, a spirit of counsel and strength, a spirit of knowledge and the fear of God' (Isaiah 11:18; Rashi on our verse).

CHAPTER 4

V 1: "Then Boaz went up to the gate..." Boaz' intended marriage with Ruth was fraught with halachic complications since Ruth was a convert from Moab, and the Torah clearly states that "an Ammonite and a Moabite shall not enter the assembly of HaShem even in the tenth generation (=forever)" (Deuteronomy 23:4). According to the oral tradition, the use specifically of the masculine form of **Ammoni** and **Moavi** in the verse teaches that the prohibition does **not** apply to Ammonite or Moabite **women**. However, this halachah flies in the face of the apparent simple meaning of the text to the point that it was frequently forgotten. This happened in the generation of David after he killed Goliath, when Saul's counsellor Do'eg argued that David was not even eligible to enter the assembly, being descended from a Moabitess (see Rashi on I Samuel 17:55 and Yevamot 77b). And according to our commentators, the same forgetfulness was also present in the time of Bo'az, because the even closer relative who was the other candidate for redeeming Ruth thought that the Biblical prohibition applied to Moabite women as well as men, and he was afraid of marrying her for fear of putting an inerasable blemish on his issue.

"…And [Bo'az] said, 'Turn aside, wait here Mister so-and-so [**Ploni Almoni**]…' " The Hebrew word **ploni** is from the root **pele** meaning something hidden (cf. Deut. 17:8) - Rashi explains that his actual name is not written in the text because he did not want to redeem Ruth. Rashi explains **almoni** (from the root **eelem**, "speechless", "dumb") as meaning that he is "without a name", and also that he was dumb and a "widower" (**alman**), bereft of Torah, because he did not know that the halachah forbids only a **Moavi** from entering the assembly but not a **Moaviah**!!!

V 2: "And he took ten men from the elders of the city…" Boaz intentionally assembled a **Minyan** (quorum) of men of stature in order to publicly teach the correct halachah that a **Moaviah** is indeed **permitted** to enter the assembly (Ketubot 7b). We also learn from this verse that the marriage ceremony must be performed in the presence of a **Minyan** of ten men (ibid.).

Vv 3ff: When Boaz began to explain to **Ploni Almoni**, the other candidate for redeemer, that he was being asked to buy Elimelech's field, initially he was willing to do so (v 4, "…I shall redeem it"), until Boaz started to explain that there were some "strings attached" as he would also have to marry Ruth. At this point **Ploni Almoni** baulked "…lest I harm my own inheritance…" (v 6), because he thought Ruth's children would not be Israelites.

V 7: "Now this was the custom in former time..." The removal of the shoe is parallel to the present-day custom of formalizing an act of **kinyan**, "acquisition", through the parties lifting up a **soodar** ("scarf" or other garment or vessel, often a "gartel") whereby through the law of **Chalifin** the acquisition comes about (**Kinyan Soodar**). As discussed in the commentary on the previous chapter, the taking of the shoe also relates to the mystery of **Yibum** and **Chalitzah**. In this way Bo'az formally acquired Ruth.

V 11: "And all the people that were in the gate said with the elders as witnesses, Let HaShem grant that the woman coming to your house shall be like Rachel and like Leah..." Boaz and the people of Bethlehem were from the tribe of Judah, Leah's fourth son, yet they gave primacy to Rachel as Jacob's principal wife (Rashi).

V 13: "And Boaz took Ruth and she was his wife…" The rabbis taught that on the very night that Boaz came into her, he died (Yalkut Shimoni). This is why the child was raised by Naomi.

Vv 18-22: "And these are the generations of Peretz... and Yishai begat David". The whole purpose of this remarkable story of Ruth is to trace the origins of Melech HaMashiach.

איכה
LAMENTATIONS

CHAPTER 1

The original Hebrew name of Lamentations is **Kinot**, "Mourning Dirges" (see II Chronicles 35:25), but the work is more generally known by the name of **Eichah** after the Hebrew word with which chapters 1, 2 and 4 all open, meaning "How???"

The book of **Eichah** was written in stages by the prophet Jeremiah. He wrote Chapter 4 as a mourning elegy over King Josiah, the last righteous king of Judah, who was slain in battle at the height of his efforts to cleanse Israel, and whose death signified that the sun had gone down for the House of David (Ta'anit 22b). "And Jeremiah lamented for Josiah, and all the singing men and singing women spoke of Josiah in their laments to this day, and he made them an ordinance in Israel, and behold they are written in the laments (**Kinot**)" (II Chron. 35:25). Rashi writes on this verse: "When they are struck by some trouble or occasion for weeping and they mourn and cry over what happened, they recall this trouble with it, as for example on the Fast of Tisha b'Av, when mourning dirges are recited over those who died in the decrees that have occurred in our days, and likewise they weep over the death of Josiah" (Rashi ad loc.).

The other chapters of **Eichah** were written prophetically by Jeremiah not many years after the death of Josiah, in the fourth year of the reign of his son, the wicked King Yeho-yakim, as a warning of the disaster that was to strike Judah and Jerusalem if the people did not repent. The full account of how Jeremiah composed Eichah and how it came to be read before Yeho-yakim, who cut the scroll to shreds and burned it in the fire, is contained in Jeremiah ch 36. Jeremiah had previously prophesied to the women of Judah: "Teach your daughters wailing and each one her neighbor lamentation" (Jer. 9:19). Now in the scroll that he composed as a graphic warning to the people of the coming doom, he depicted the relentless destruction of Jerusalem as if it had already happened, penning words of mourning and lamentation that the people would have to repeat from generation to generation in order to make amends for having failed to repent in time to avert it.

The Mishnah in Mo'ed Katan 3:9, discussing mourning practices, explains that a **kinah** dirge (e.g. at a funeral) would be recited responsively: "One woman speaks a verse and all the others answer, as it is written, '…and each one her neighbor lamentation'". Chapters 1-4 of **Eichah** are written in the form of alphabetical acrostics. Chapters 1, 2 and 4 each consist of 22 verses starting with successive letters of the Aleph-Beit, while Chapter 3 consists of 66 verses, the first three of which begin with Aleph, the second three with Beit and so on. Prior to the availability of printed texts for everyone, alphabetical acrostics were a useful mnemonic device. Moreover, "Rabbi Yochanan said, 'Why were Israel punished with troubles depicted in verses beginning with the letters of the Aleph Beit? Because they violated the Torah, which was given with the letters of the Aleph-Beit!'" (Sanhedrin 104a).

"Rabbi Abahu began expounding on the scroll of **Eichah** quoting the verse, 'And they, like the man (**ke-adam**), have violated the Covenant' (Hosea 6:7). What does 'like the man' mean? The verse is comparing the people to Adam, the first man. The Holy One blessed be He said: I brought Adam into the Garden of Eden and gave him a commandment, but he violated My commandment, so I drove him out and banished him and mourned over him with the phrase, 'Where are you?' (=**Ayekah**, Genesis 3:9, consisting of the same Hebrew letters as **Eichah**). Likewise, I brought his children to the Land of Israel and gave them commandments, but they violated My commandments and I banished them, and I mourned over them with the word **Eichah**!!!" (Introduction to Eichah Rabbah).

This Midrash is teaching us that the disaster which befell Judah and Jerusalem must be seen as part of the greater cycle of human sin and consequent suffering and chastisement that began with Adam and continues until today. Just as God's call to Adam, "Where are you???" (Gen. 3:9) was a call to repentance, so is the scroll of **Eichah**, a call to repentance, challenging us to see the meaning and purpose of the suffering with which Israel has been afflicted. There are many ways in which humans react to terrible reverses and suffering. Sometimes they fall into the depths of helpless grief, despair and depression. In other cases, they react with rage and anger, kicking and rebelling against God or "fate" for sending them such troubles. But in putting the laments of **Eichah** onto the lips of Israel, the prophet Jeremiah was providing them with words and images by means of which they could not only give expression to their pain and grief but also come to terms with their suffering by understanding its meaning and purpose through the recognition that it was divinely sent to chasten and purify them from their sins. The prophet (**Navee**) draws his words from the level of **Binah**, "understanding", sweetening the bitter pill of suffering by justifying the ways of God. "For great as the sea is your breach: Who (**mee**) can heal you?" (Lam. 2:13). Kabbalistically, the word **mee** alludes to **Binah**, which lies at the root of God's judgments and through which they are "sweetened" when we gain deeper understanding of their meaning and purpose.

Not only is **Eichah** full of allusions to the historical disasters that struck Israel with the destruction of the Temple and the exile. The multi-layered text is also replete with allusions to the metaphysical roots of Israel's fall, which lie in the "Breaking of the Vessels" as explained in the Kabbalistic writings. For "He cast from heaven to earth the glory (**Tiferet**) of Israel and did not remember the stool of His feet (=**Malchut**) on the day of His anger. The Lord has swallowed up (**beela**) and has not shown pity" (Eichah 2:1-2). **Beela** has the same Hebrew letters as Bela son of Be'or, first of the Seven Kings of Edom, who correspond to the shattered vessels of the Sefirot.

Rabbi Chayim ben Attar, author of the commentary **Ohr Ha-Chayim** on the Five Books of Moses, explains in his commentary **Rishon Le-Tzion** on **Eichah** that the way the Elegist accomplishes his purpose, which is to arouse weeping in his listeners, is by crafting each and every verse as "a lamb's tail with a thorn caught in it". Without digressing to give expansive explanations and background, each verse is designed to pierce the listener in the heart with a sharp evocation of some detail of the calamity.

The opening verses of **Eichah** chapter 1 contrast the lost greatness, power and prestige of Jerusalem with her present abject state of subjection, isolated like a leper, having been betrayed by those she thought were her friends.

"She weeps sore in the night..." (v 2). The doubled Hebrew verb for weeping alludes to the weeping over the destruction of the two Temples, which came about because of the needless weeping of the Children of Israel in the wilderness on the night after they received the Ten Spies' negative report about the Land (Numbers 14:1). This was on the 9th day of the month of Av, which was thereafter marked out as a day of weeping for all the generations (Ta'anit 29a; see Rashi on Lam. 1:2).

Already in verse 5 the Elegist weaves into his depiction of the overthrow of Israel at the hands of their enemies the understanding that it came about "because HaShem has afflicted her for the multitude of her transgressions" (Lam. 1:5) - for "Jerusalem has sinned a sin..." (ibid. v 8).

Israel is depicted as a widow (v 1), an unclean Niddah-woman (v 8) and a raped virgin (v 15). The pathos of Israel is increased by the fact that there is none to comfort her. This leads the Elegist to call upon God Himself to look on her in her wretchedness (verse 9), thereby drawing into us the understanding that everything is under His watchful providence. The Elegist depicts the full horror of the calamity, evoking the fire that burned in the people's very bones, their sense of being helplessly trapped in a snare (v 13), the destruction and devastation of the youth (vv 15-16) etc. Yet after all this he says, "HaShem is righteous, for I have rebelled against His mouth..." (v 18).

Israel's pain over her suffering at the hands of the nations, brings her to call for vengeance against them, but this is because they are truly guilty. For if Israel must suffer because of her sins, so should they (vv 21-22).

CHAPTER 2

The first nine verses of Chapter 2 depict the calamity that struck Zion in such a way as to emphasize that it was God who sent it. As the text states explicitly later on in the chapter: "HaShem has done that which He devised: He has fulfilled His word that He commanded in the days of old..." (Lam. 2:17). The cycle of sin and consequent suffering that culminated with the destruction of Jerusalem is deeply rooted in God's plan for the world, which is laid down in the Torah: "If you will not listen to me, then I will punish you seven times more for your sins" (Lev. 26:18, see Rashi on Lam. 2:17).

The Elegist makes no attempt to "sweeten" the suffering by trying to minimize how terrible it was. On the contrary, he heightens our sense of the horror by repeatedly emphasizing the way in which the kind, merciful God became like an enemy in the fury with which He brought death and destruction upon the people and their land (vv 1-8). All who were pleasant to the eye were slaughtered (v 4). The precious Temple was ravaged (v 6). The rejoicing of the Sabbath and the festivals became forgotten. Without respect for person, the king and the princes were sent into a humiliating exile, the prophets were bereft of vision, and all that was left for the people to do was to mourn as children fainted in the streets and little babies starved (vv 7-12).

It is precisely through articulating the full intensity of the horror and showing how the soothsaying false prophets had betrayed the people while their mocking enemies gloated triumphantly over their plight that the Elegist leads his listeners to the understanding that they have no recourse except to cry out to God (vv 18ff). The moral of **Eichah** is: "Rise, cry out in the night at the head of the watches, pour out your heart like water before the face of the Lord..." (v 19).

CHAPTER 3

Like Chapters 1, 2 and 4 of **Eichah**, Chapter 3 takes the form of an acrostic built upon the Aleph-Beit, except that in this case each of the letters of the Aleph-Beit is used in succession as the initial letter of three short verses or triplets.

"I am the man who has seen affliction by the rod of His wrath" (v 1). Starting with this verse, the first six triplets in this elegy (vv 1-18) all pour forth from the heart of the Elegist himself - a righteous prophet - complaining that God has set him up as His target: "He is to me like a bear lying in wait and like a lion in secret places" (v 10). The entire passage is somewhat reminiscent of Job's complaints that God was tormenting him for no reason, and the rabbis of the Midrash point to a **Gezerah Shavah** (identical phrase in two disparate texts indicating a midrashic connection between the two) between the first verse of our present chapter, "I am the man (**gever**)…", and a verse in Job where his interlocutor Eli-hoo criticizes him, saying "Which man (**gever**) is like Job, who drinks up scorning like water?" (Job 34:7). "Rabbi Yehoshua ben Levi commented: 'I am the man...' - I am the same as Job, of whom it is written, 'Which man is like Job, who drinks up scorning like water?' Everything You brought upon Job, You have brought upon me!" (Eichah Rabbah). The Elegist is simultaneously pouring out his own pain and giving expression to the national pain. Rashi on v 1 explains the pain of Jeremiah himself: Jeremiah was complaining that he "witnessed greater affliction than all the other prophets who prophesied about the destruction of the Temple, because it was not destroyed in their days but in mine!"

In Job's case it was Eli-hoo who brought him to understand that although he may have been righteous, he had perhaps not been righteous enough and that was why he suffered. But in the case of the present elegy here in **Eichah**, it is Jeremiah himself who is in dialog with the thoughts in his own heart, and simultaneously with those in the hearts of his people, who felt that the cruelty of their plight meant that God had become their enemy. [Many have felt similarly about the Holocaust.] "And I said, 'My strength and my hope are perished from HaShem'" (v 18). But immediately after this expression of despair, there is a change in the tone of the elegy in the seventh triplet (vv 19-21). Having given expression to the real feelings of despair in his heart, Jeremiah begins to pray to God to remember his suffering even as his soul is bowed down within him, and he discovers how to reply to that inner voice of despair: "With this shall I give an answer to my heart, therefore I have hope" (v 21).

The ensuing message of hope begins in the beautiful passage in vv 22ff: God's kindnesses and mercies are truly unending. They are renewed every morning! It is this that gives the Elegist the courage to address God directly: "Great is Your faithfulness!" (v 23). Since we can rely on the constant renewal of God's kindness, there is always hope, and because there is always hope, it is fitting for man to bear his suffering patiently in the knowledge that God sends it for his own ultimate benefit. Having delicately reached this point, Jeremiah now teaches the suffering people the proper way to respond to their suffering. [1] We must always wait for God's salvation (v 26). [2] It is necessary to bear our suffering with patience (v 27). [3] We must "sit alone and keep silent"(v 28) - i.e. enter into deep personal self-reckoning without railing against fate. Here in **Eichah** is one of the foundations of the pathway of **hitbodedut** - secluded meditation and prayer - that Rabbi Nachman of Breslov emphasized more than anything. [4] We must "put our mouths in the dust" (v 29). Dust or earth is **aphar**, the vessel that receives the three higher elements of Fire, Air and Water. **Aphar** is **Malchut**, the acceptance of God's kingship, which we do through prayer. [5] We must "turn the other cheek" to our detractors (v 30), for it is through the silence in which we bear their insults that we attain God's glory (Likutey Moharan I, 6).

Continuing on his delicate path of helping the people to accept and come to terms with their suffering, the Elegist explains beginning in the eleventh triplet (vv 31ff) that God will not reject Israel forever (v 31), and that if He has afflicted them, He will eventually have mercy (v 32), for His chastisements are not sent arbitrarily (v 33ff). Addressing deep questions about the justice of God's providence (which is also the subject of the book of Job) Jeremiah affirms that the Righteous God never twists any man's judgment, and that nothing in the world comes about except through the command of the King (v 37).

"Out of the mouth of the Most High do not the bad things come and the good?" (v 38). The original Hebrew words of this verse are necessarily susceptible to a variety of interpretations that may even appear contradictory to one another. This is because the verse contains the mystery of how good and evil emanate from the One God, who is perfect goodness. Rashi (ad loc.) paraphrases: "If I were to come to say that it was not from His hands that this evil came upon me but that it was a chance occurrence that happened to me, this is not so. For whether bad things or good things occur, 'Who is this that spoke and it came to be if not that HaShem commanded it?' (v 37). 'Why then does a man complain while he yet lives, a man over the punishment of his sins?' (v 39). Each man must complain about his own sins because it is they that bring evil upon him. 'From the mouth of the Supreme it does not go forth' (v 38): Rabbi Yochanan said, From the day that the Holy One blessed be He said, 'See, I have set before you, life and goodness, death and evil' (Deut. 30:15) [i.e. man has been given free will], 'the bad and the good do not go forth from His mouth', but rather, evil comes by itself to those who do bad while goodness comes to those who do good. Therefore, what should a man complain and be upset about if not about his own sins?" (Rashi on v 38).

The moral is clear: "Let us examine and search out our ways and return to HaShem" (v 40). "Let us lift up our **hearts** to our **hands** to God in heaven" (v 41) - It is not enough merely to stretch out our **hands** in prayer: our **hearts** must be in our prayers - we must be sincere and mean what we say, not like those who "immerse in the mikveh while still clutching the defiling unclean creature in their hand", verbally expressing their intention to repent while still holding onto their bad ways (see Ta'anit 16a).

"We have sinned and rebelled, but You have not forgiven us" (v 42). This verse marks a transition from the Elegist's exhortations about prayer and repentance to a further outpouring of the pain, grief and tears caused by Israel's protracted suffering - for he knows that even his wise advice in the previous section (vv 21-41), cannot that quickly assuage the pain and hurt. Yes, we continue to weep - and we will weep "until Hashem will look down and see from heaven" (v 50). Again and again the Elegist delicately steers us back to knowing that we must turn only to God. "I called Your Name, HaShem, from the bottommost pit" (v 55). The following verse, "You have heard my voice; hide not Your ear at my sighing" (v 56) is among the six verses customarily chanted in unison by the congregation immediately prior to the blowing of the Shofar in the synagogue on Rosh HaShanah.

The final section of this elegy (vv 57-66) are a ringing affirmation of faith that God will redeem Israel and wreak His vengeance on their enemies for all their evil.

CHAPTER 4

As discussed in the commentary on **Eichah** Chapter 1, the elegy contained here in Chapter 4 was said by the rabbis of the Talmud to have been composed by Jeremiah on the death of the saintly King Josiah in Megiddo at the hands of Pharaoh Necho (II Chronicles 35:25; Rashi ad loc.).

"How is the gold become dim!" (v 1) - "This lament was said over Josiah, and with it he wove in the other children of Zion" (Rashi on v 1). Rashi here is explaining why it is that if this is an elegy for Josiah, almost all of its contents relate not specifically to the slain king but to the entire people. The elegy is truly about the loss of Josiah, whose importance lay in the fact that he "went in the ways of David his father without turning to the right or the left" (II Chron. 34:2). As such Josiah was the last hope of Judah - had he had time to complete his mission of bringing the people to genuine repentance, he could have saved Jerusalem from destruction, and thus he had the potential to be Mashiach (as he is indeed called here in verse 20). But he was cut down in his very prime and his death sealed the fate of Jerusalem, making the destruction of the Temple and the cruel exile all but inevitable.

Thus, with the death of Josiah twenty-two years prior to the actual destruction, Jeremiah already prophesied the horrors of the coming calamity. "The hallowed stones are poured out at the top of every street" (v 1) - "these are the children, who radiated like precious jewels. And there is also a Midrash telling that Jeremiah gathered every cupful of blood that flowed out of each of Josiah's arrow wounds and buried it in its place, chanting, 'The hallowed stones have been poured out...'" (Rashi on v 1).

The children are cast out like broken shards (v 2). Their starving mothers, who ignore their pleas for food in order to find something to eat themselves, have been reduced to a cruelty that even jackals do not show to their young (v 3, see Rashi). Those brought up in the lap of luxury are thrown out on the streets clutching at the garbage heaps (v 5). Even as Jeremiah depicts the horror, he weaves in his teaching about its cause: "For the sin of the daughter of my people is greater..." (v 6). The fire that was to consume Zion was from God (v 11). The enemy was able to do the unthinkable and enter the gates of Jerusalem "on account of the sins of her prophets, the transgressions of her priests" (vv 12-13).

Verse 15 portrays the terrible victimization of Israel in their places of exile, rejected as an unclean caste by the sanctimonious nations. The face of anger God shows them in their exile is the penalty for their having failed to give the proper respect to their priests and elders in their time of tranquility (v 16, see Rashi).

"As for us, our eyes do yet fail for our vain help: in our watching we have watched for a nation that could not save" (v 17). The kings of Judah who followed Josiah expected that Egypt would intervene to save Israel from the clutches of Babylon, but in vain (see Rashi ad loc.). In our time, it seems that many in Israel somehow expect the country they see as her closest ally to come to her defense, but as the threats around little Israel grow ever more menacing with the apparent complicity of her ally, it seems that any hopes that this ally will ever help may also prove to have been in vain.

After the Elegist's depiction of the horrors of the calamity that was to come as a result of the death of Josiah, we now understand why it was such a disaster that "The breath of our nostrils, HaShem's anointed, has been captured in their pits - he of whom we said, 'Under his shadow we shall live among the nations'" (v 20).

The concluding verses of this elegy promise that God will take vengeance upon the nations that persecuted Israel and destroyed the Temple. Although Jeremiah was living at the time of the destruction of the First Temple by the Babylonians, he already sees prophetically to the eventual destruction of Edom, i.e. Rome, which perpetrated the destruction of the Second Temple.

Targum on verse 21 identifies "the daughter of Edom who dwells in the land of Ootz" with "**Koustantina** (=Constantinople), the city of the wicked Edom that was built in the land of Armenia with a great population from the people of Edom - upon you too is He destined to bring punishment, and the Persians will destroy you." Constantinople was indeed until its demise in the Middle Ages the center of the Latin Empire, which was actually called the Roman Empire. The Talmudic rabbis had a tradition that "Rome is destined to fall by the hand of Persia" (Yoma 10a) and "this will take place just before the coming of Mashiach" (Tosfot on Avodah Zarah 2b). Zion's punishment will then be complete, and they will know no more exile (v 22).

CHAPTER 5

"Remember, HaShem, what has come upon us; look and see our shame" (v 1). The concluding chapter of **Eichah**, unlike all the previous chapters, is not an alphabetical acrostic. It is a prayerful elegy enumerating the painful details of Israel's terrible suffering at the hands of the nations throughout their various exiles.

"Because of this our heart is faint" (v 17). The Hebrew word translated here as "faint" has the connotation of menstrual impurity (cf. Lev. 12:2, 15:33 & 20:18). In the words of the Midrash: "On account of the fact that a menstruating woman has to separate herself from her house for a number of days, the Torah calls her 'faint'. How much more so are we - who have been separated from the House of our life and from our Temple for so many days and so many years - called 'faint', and that is why it says, 'Because of this our heart is faint'" (Eichah Rabbah).

"But You, HaShem, dwell forever. Why do You forget us forever and forsake us for so long? Turn us to You, HaShem, and we will return; renew our days as of old!" (vv 19-21).

With this prayer for God to turn our hearts to Him in repentance the Elegist concludes **Eichah** - **Ayekah**? "Where are you???" - a call to repent. Since verse 22 has a negative tone, it is customary to repeat verse 21 thereafter in order to conclude the reading of **Eichah** on a positive note.

This final chapter of **Eichah** is included in the readings included in **Tikkun Rachel**, which is the first part of **Tikkun Chatzot**, the Midnight Prayer, recited every night by the very devout. **Tikkun Rachel** consisting of laments over the destruction of the Temple is recited only on those weekdays on which Tachanun is recited but not on Sabbaths, festivals and other days with a semi-festive character. However, the second part of **Tikkun Chatzot**, known as **Tikkun Leah**, may be recited every night of the year (see "The Sweetest Hour" by Rabbi Avraham Greenbaum, Breslov Research Institute).

קֹהֶלֶת

ECCLESIASTES

CHAPTER 1

Kohelet is the "pen name" of King Solomon. The name comes from the Hebrew root **kahal**, which means a "gathering" or "assembly". The Hebrew grammatical form of **Kohelet** means "the gatherer", and the name signifies that "he gathered much wisdom" (Rashi on v 1). It also signifies that he assembled the people (cf. Deut. 31:12). In the words of Midrash **Kohelet** Rabbah: "Why was Solomon called **Kohelet**? Because his words were spoken in the assembly of the people, as it is written, 'Then Solomon gathered (yak'hal) the elders of Israel' (I Kings 8:1)". Likewise,the traditional name for Kohelet, **Ecclesiastes**, is from the Greek word **ecclesia**, a regularly convoked assembly, and **Ecclesiastes** is one who takes part in this assembly - i.e. the Preacher.

"The words (**divrei**) of Kohelet..." (v 1) - "Wherever the text says **divrei**, 'the words of', these are words of rebuke" (Rashi ad loc.). Solomon son of David - "a king the son of a king, a tzaddik the son of a tzaddik" (Midrash) - had pursued wisdom all his life. "When God said to Solomon, 'Ask what I should give you' and he asked not for silver and gold but only that 'You should give Your servant an understanding heart', holy spirit immediately rested upon him and he composed the book of Proverbs, Song of Songs and Kohelet" (Midrash Kohelet Rabbah). Solomon wrote Song of Songs in his youth, on the day of the dedication of the Temple; then in his prime he composed Proverbs, the rich fruits of his wisdom. But having reached the very heights, he fell to the lowest depths (as we shall see in the commentary on v 12). Finally, at the end of his life, after having seen everything, he composed Kohelet - his last testament to his people: **rebuke**.

The wisest man that ever lived comes in Kohelet to clarify what is man's destiny and purpose in this world, and what he should do to fulfill it. Everything leads up to the conclusion of the work: "The end of the matter, when all is said and done: Fear God and keep his commandments, for that is the whole duty of man" (Kohelet 12:13). The intent of Kohelet may to some extent be compared with that of the book of Job, which also examines man's existential situation and possible solutions as to how we may come to terms with it. While the approach and structure of the two works are radically different, they both consider the most fundamental questions in life with astonishing boldness and candor.

Perhaps it was this very boldness and candor that almost lost the book of Kohelet its place in the Bible canon ordained by the sages, who argued as to whether it should be included. "The sages sought to hide away Kohelet because his words contradict one another. Then why did they not hide it away? Because it begins with words of Torah and ends with words of Torah." (Talmud Shabbat 30b, where the "contradictions" between Kohelet 7:3 and 2:2 and between 8:15 and 2:2 are reconciled). The dispute over the inclusion of Kohelet in the canon is also discussed in Mishnah Yadayim 3:5, where the Tosephta explains that those opposed to its inclusion maintained that it consisted of Solomon's own wisdom.

The prevailing opinion, however, is that it was composed through holy spirit. For this very reason, we must bear in mind that in our study of the divinely-inspired last testament of the wisest man that ever lived, we can touch little more than the surface of a work that is replete with infinite layers upon layers of P'shat (simple meaning), Remez (allusion), Drush (midrashic interpretation) and Sod (esoteric wisdom). As we learn these holy words, our aim should be to derive personal lessons that we can apply in our own lives as to how to know and fear God and serve Him through practical action: **Asiyah**.

THE PROLOGUE

The opening section of Kohelet (vv 2-11), a complete parshah in itself, is a hauntingly poetic evocation of man's existential situation in this world of endless repeated cycles - the cycles of the generations, the planets, the waters of the rivers and the sea.

"Vanity (1) of vanities (2)...vanity (1) of vanities (2), all is vanity (1)" (verse 1). The Hebrew word traditionally translated as "vanity", **hevel**, means a "vapor", something barely substantial or tangible. Taking into account the singular and plural forms of the word **hevel** in the verse, a total of **seven** "vanities" are enumerated, corresponding to the Seven Days of Creation and the seven "Sefirot of Construction" (Chessed – Gevurah – Tiferet – Netzach – Hod – Yesod – Malchut) "Kohelet cries out and complains that the entire work of the Seven Days of Creation is all vanity of vanities!!!" (Rashi on v 2).

"What profit does a man have in all his labor with which he labors under the sun" (verse 3)? In this verse King Solomon poses man's most fundamental existential question: What is the purpose of all his efforts in this world? The Talmud points out that Solomon is specifically asking about man's efforts "under the sun". "It is from his labor 'under the sun' that he has no profit, but his labor in the realm that existed before the sun he does have profit. And which is that? This is his labor in the Torah!" (Shabbat 30b). In other words, Solomon is asking what people gain when they devote all their endeavors to the transient material world instead of laboring in Torah, which brings an eternal reward.

"...Under the sun" (v 3): "This signifies ever-changing time. For the sun alone gives birth to time, for the day depends on the sun from the time it rises to the time it sets, while night is from the time the sun sets until the time it rises. Likewise sowing and harvesting, cold and heat, summer and winter all depend on the inclination of the sun to the north or south. Even though the moon and stars all have their influence, it cannot be compared to that of the sun" (Ibn Ezra ad loc.) "Therefore, the sun is called the 'king of the skies' (Jeremiah 44:17). Solomon is saying: What is the benefit of all of a person's acquisitions in this world when surely tomorrow he will die taking nothing in his hand?" (Metzudat David on v 3).

"One generation passes away, and another generation comes..." (v 4) - "No matter how much the villain toils to steal and rob, he cannot outlive and enjoy his gains because his generation passes away, and another generation comes and takes everything from the hands of his children, as it says, 'his children will conciliate the poor'" (Job 20:10; Rashi on v 4). "...but the earth endures for ever" (v 4) - "And who are those who endure? The meek and lowly who lower themselves down to the earth, as it says, '...and the meek shall inherit the earth'" (Psalms 37:11; Rashi on v 4).

Verses 5-6 describe the endless daily circuits of the sun in summer and winter, while verse 7 evokes the endless recycling of water from the rivers into the sea and back again to the rivers. "All things are labouring..." (v 8) - "This continues from the question above, 'What profit does a man have...' (v 3): If instead of engaging in Torah one follows idle pursuits, they all involve constant labor and he cannot attain everything. If he goes after sights, his eye will not be satisfied; if he goes after sounds, his ear will not be filled" (Rashi on v 8).

"That which has been is that which shall be, ...and there is nothing new under the sun" (v 9). This refers to the created material world, but not to the realm of the Torah, where our studies can constantly generate new understandings (**chiddushim**; see Rashi on v 9). "He is saying that just as there is nothing new in the created world, so this fundamental fact will never change - that nothing in this world ever yields the gains for which one hopes in one's labor and exertion, just as nothing ever has in the past"

(Metzudat David ad loc.). Even if we imagine we have found something new "under the sun" that might indicate that this fundamental fact of the futility of devotion to material pursuits has changed, this is an illusion, because this seemingly new thing has in fact already been (v 10). It is just that nobody is left from the earlier generations to remember it, just as nobody in generations to come will remember us (v 11).

"I, KOHELET WAS KING OVER ISRAEL IN JERUSALEM" (v 12)

Following the prologue to his book, King Solomon now presents his "credentials" for writing it. "I, Kohelet **was** king..." (v 12). "King over all the world. Then in the end king over Israel. Then in the end king over Jerusalem alone. And finally, over nothing but my walking stick! For it says, 'I **was** king in Jerusalem ' - i.e. but now I am not king" (Rashi ad loc.). "When King Solomon sat on his royal throne his heart swelled because of his wealth and he transgressed God's decree, gathering many horses, chariots and riders, silver and gold, intermarrying with foreign nations. Immediately God's anger was aroused, and He sent Ashmodai king of the demons to drive him from his royal throne. He took the ring from his hand, forcing him to wander around in exile in order to chastise him. He went around all the cities of Israel weeping and crying, 'I am Kohelet, who was called Solomon. Before this I was king over Israel in Jerusalem!!!'" (Targum Yonatan verse 12).

Just as the most successful of worldly kings, Nebuchadnezzar, was driven from his throne and brought down to the level of a wild beast in order to chastise him for his pride (Daniel chapter 4), so King Solomon, the Torah king who literally had everything - wisdom, wealth, women, power, glory, palaces, gardens, attendants, singers - had to be cast down to the very bottom in order to rise to the ultimate wisdom.

"I gave my heart to seek and search out through wisdom..." (v 13). Rashi (ad loc.) explains that Solomon used his Torah wisdom to contemplate and understand the whole futile world of wickedness "under the sun", coming to the conclusion that everything was created by God to test man through being exposed to the need to choose between life and goodness on the one hand and death and evil on the other (cf. Metzudat David ad loc.).

In vv 16ff Solomon explains that even the pursuit of wisdom can be dangerous and break a person's heart - "for with too much wisdom a person depends on his own wisdom and does not avoid what the Torah prohibits, causing God great anger" (Rashi on v 17). Moreover, "a wise person understands the true nature of men's deeds and when he sees that they are not good, he himself becomes angry because these things are contrary to his will, and anger is very damaging. And someone who understands one thing from another increases his pain because he can now understand the consequences of his own faulty behavior and this brings pain to his heart" (Metzudat David on v 18).

CHAPTER 2

"I said in my heart, 'Let me try you (i.e. myself) with mirth...'" (v 1). In the words of Rashi (ad loc.): "Since it is so (i.e. since wisdom is dangerous and painful) let me stop pursuing wisdom and devote myself to **Simchah** (happiness and joy) at all times". Those seeking to fulfill Rabbi Nachman's "great mitzvah to be in Simchah at all times" will surely want to know the lessons Kohelet teaches based on his trying out the path of happiness and joy as an answer to man's existential dilemma.

These lessons are brought out in the Talmudic resolution of one of the apparent "contradictions" in Kohelet. Here he says, "I said of laughter, 'It is mad' and of Simchah, 'What does this accomplish'" (v 2) whereas later on he says, "And I **praised** Simchah." (ch 8 v 15). "'And I praised Simchah.' - This is the Simchah of a mitzvah. '...and of Simchah, What does this accomplish?' - This is Simchah that is not connected with any mitzvah. This comes to teach you that the Shechinah does not rest in a state of sadness or lethargy or through laughter, light headedness, chatter and idle pursuits but through the Simchah of a mitzvah" (Shabbat 30b).

In verse 3 Solomon explains that in pursuit of his goal of understanding if Simchah is the purpose of life, he sought to continue guiding his heart with wisdom while simultaneously indulging in "wine" and laying hold of "folly" (**sichlut**). The latter refers to all the things that people crave for in the material world, such as beautiful buildings, musical instruments, etc. (see Metzudat David ad loc.).

In verses 4-10 Solomon describes his palaces, orchards, gardens, fountains, servants, sheep and cattle, gold, silver and other treasures and delights. "Does the text tell us only about Solomon's wealth? It is surely speaking only about Torah...'I built myself houses' - synagogues and study halls. 'I planted vineyards' - these are the Torah scholars, who sit in rows as in a vineyard. 'I made myself gardens and orchards' - these are the **Mishnayot**. 'I planted in them every kind of fruit tree' - this is the Talmud. 'I made myself fountains of water' - these are the preachers. 'To water the forest with them' - these are the children. 'I acquired male and female servants' - these are the gentiles. 'And also cattle, oxen and sheep' - these are the sacrifices. 'I also gathered silver and gold' - these are words of Torah. 'I acquired men singers and women singers' - these are the Tosephtas. '...and delights' - these are the aggadot (narrative midrash)" (Kohelet Rabbah).

"...and **this** was **my** share from all my labor" (v 10) - "And after my having done all this, I have nothing from all of it except **this**. One of the pair of Talmudic rabbis, Rav and Shmuel, said that **this** refers to his walking stick while the other said it refers to the earthenware pot from which he drank" (Rashi ad loc.; Gittin 68b). In other words, after his downfall, left with nothing but his stick and a primitive mug, Solomon realized that all his endeavors to pursue Simchah "under the sun" were nothing but vanity and striving after wind (v 11).

Having followed one possible answer to the existential dilemma to its ultimate conclusion only to find it a dead end, in verse 12 Solomon turns to clarify how the pathway of wisdom (i.e. Torah wisdom, Rashi on v 12) is superior to madness and folly (i.e. sin and the embrace of the material world). "For what can the man do who comes after the king?" (v 12) - "How can a man despise folly as if he is wiser than the King of the world, seeing that He has already created folly? Even though it is proper to despise folly, nevertheless He has not created it for nothing, for the superiority of wisdom is revealed precisely through the contrast with folly, without which the beauty of wisdom would not be recognized, because a thing can only be known in relation to its opposite, just as the benefit of light is known only through darkness, which is its opposite." (Metzudat David on vv 12-13).

In verses 14ff Solomon explains that wisdom is superior to folly even though the wise man and the fool both die in the end. This existential fact poses a challenging question to the wise man (v 15), but Solomon rejects the possibility that the eternal destiny of the wise man after death could possibly be identical with that of the fool (v 16, see Targum Yonatan, Rashi and Metzudat David ad loc.).

In verses 17ff Solomon explains another vexing issue for the wise man - that after all his efforts "under the sun", when he leaves this world all his achievements are liable to fall into the hands of someone who may not be wise or worthy at all. The issue was greatly sharpened for Solomon himself by the fact that he knew prophetically that in the reign of his son and successor Rehaboam, the kingdom would split, leading to the eventual destruction of Jerusalem and the Holy Temple and the exile of Israel (see Targum Yonatan Kohelet 1:2).

This thought almost brought Solomon to the point of despair (v 20) until he came to a new conclusion: "There is nothing better for a man than that he should eat and drink and that he should make his soul enjoy good in his labor" (v 24). "Rabbi Yonah said: 'Wherever the concept of eating and drinking appears in this Megillah, it is speaking of Torah and good deeds'" (Kohelet Rabbah). In other words, true joy in this world comes through doing one's best to pursue the path of Torah and mitzvot. "...But this also I saw - that this is from the hand of God" (v 24). It is a gift of God to reach this level. If so, we must earnestly ask and beg Him to grant us this precious gift.

CHAPTER 3

The conventional chapter breaks in Kohelet in our printed Bibles whether in Hebrew or translation are mainly for convenience of reference but do not correspond to section-breaks (parshiyot) in the hand-written Hebrew scrolls, where the entire Megillah consists of only three parshahs: (1) The "prologue" – Kohelet ch 1 vv 1-11; (2) The lengthy section from ch 1 v 12 to ch 6 v 12; (3) The lengthy section from 7:1 to the end of the book.

The first verse of our present chapter is thus the direct continuation of the preceding passage, which ended in the last verse of the previous chapter (2:26) with the contrast between the chosen Tzaddikim to whom God grants true wisdom and joy in life as opposed to the sinner who tries to make gains by force, only to end up seeing them pass to the righteous.

The futility of trying to force matters in order to make gains in this world is underlined by Kohelet's exploration - beginning in verse 1 of the present chapter - of how God has already foreordained the entire order of time in creation, so that if a person makes unlawful gains today, he will be brought to justice tomorrow, whereas if he had trustfully waited for the right time, he could have made legitimate gains.

"To everything there is a season, and a time to every purpose under the heaven" (v 1) - "Let not he who gathers vain wealth rejoice, for if it is now in his hand, the time will come when the righteous will inherit it, except that the time has not yet come because everything has a fixed time when it will come about" (Rashi ad loc.).

TWENTY-EIGHT TIMES

Each of the seven verses from v 2 to v 8 contains two pairs of contrasting "times", making a total of twenty-eight different times. All of the various different changing times in the entire creation are subsumed under these twenty-eight paradigmatic "times", which span everything from birth to death (v 2) from total war to complete peace (v 8). God is perfect unity, but His creation is one of multiplicity, all of whose many facets are crafted to bring the whole, stage by stage, to perfect repair. Thus, these twenty-eight times of creation are rooted in the twenty-eight Hebrew letters of the first verse of the Torah (Gen. 1:1), which are the root and power (**Ko-ach**, Kaph 20 & Chet 8 = 28) of all creation.

Many Midrashim explore the different connotations of the various "times" in our text, which relate not only to the life of the individual but to that of entire nations. Rashi's explanations are as follows: "There is a time to give birth..." - after nine months; "...and a time to die" - after the appointed life-span of each generation. "A time to plant..." - a nation and a kingdom; "...and a time to uproot" - the time will come for it to be uprooted. "There is a time to kill..." - a complete nation on their day of retribution; "...and a time to heal" - to heal their destruction. "There is a time to weep..." - on Tisha B'Av; "...and a time to laugh" - in time to come... "A time to lament..." - when mourning the dead; "...and a time to dance" - in honor of brides and grooms. "A time to throw stones..." - these are the youths of Israel, who were cast out at the time of the destruction of the Temple, as it says, "the holy stones have been poured out" (Lam. 4:1); "...and a time to gather in stones" - to gather them in from the exile. "A time to embrace..." - as when God "attaches" Israel to Himself like a belt (Jer. 13:11); "...and a time to refrain from embracing" - as when God "banishes the man=Israel" (Is. 6:12). "A time to seek..." - the outcasts of Israel; "...and a time to lose" - those lost in exile. "A time to keep..." - "HaShem will bless you and keep you" (Num. 6:24); "...and a time to cast out" - "And He cast them out to another land" (Deut. 29:27). "A time to tear apart..." - the kingdom of David; "...and a time to sew" - to join back the Ten Tribes with the House of David. "A time to be silent..." - sometimes a man says nothing and gains a reward, as in the case of Aaron the High Priest (Lev. 10:3); "...and a time to speak" - "Then Moses sang" (Ex. 15:1), "and Deborah sang" (Judges 5:1). "A time to love..." - "And I shall show you love" (Deut. 7:13); "...and a time to hate" - "for there I hated them" (Hosea 9:15).

Having surveyed all these different times, Solomon moves to the inference he wants to make about the futility of trying to make gains by force. "What profit does the worker have from his toil" (v 9). Rashi explains: "What profit does the worker of evil have from all his toil - his time will also come, and everything will be lost!" (Rashi on v 9). "He has made everything beautiful in its time" (v 11) - "Everything that the Holy One blessed be He has created in His world is all beautiful, but only when one uses each thing in its own appointed time, not at any other time" (Metzudat David). Instead of trying to force matters **now**, one should trust that God will send what one needs at the right time!

"...also He has put the world in their hearts without man being able to find out the work that God has made from beginning to end" (v 11). Rashi explains: "Although He has put the wisdom to understand the world in people's hearts, He did not put all of it into the heart of each and every person. Rather, one person has a small portion and someone else another, in order that man should never be able to fathom and understand God's entire work. This way he never knows when his time of judgment will come and how he will stumble. The purpose is that he should set himself to repent and live in a state of anxiety, saying, 'Today or tomorrow I will die'" (Rashi ad loc.). In the light of Rashi's explanation, we see that Kohelet is giving expression to man's basic existential predicament, which derives from his having only partial knowledge and understanding of the world around him and the consequences of his deeds. This indeed is what gives man his freedom, for if he had perfect knowledge of the evil his bad deeds cause to himself, he would never do them.

Thus, Kohelet comes to his conclusion: "I **know** that there is nothing better for them than to rejoice and to do good in his life" (v 12) - "There is nothing better for a person than to rejoice in his share and do good in the eyes of his Creator as long as he is still alive" (Rashi). This is further reinforcement of the point made earlier, "There is nothing better for a man than that he should eat and drink." (Kohelet 2:24) - i.e. eat and drink Torah and good deeds - for these are the ways that God knows will bring him true gain, for God has perfect knowledge of all the different pathways and their consequences to all eternity.

"I **know** that whatever God does, it shall be forever..." (v 14). God has created all of the twenty-eight paradigmatic "times" and their offspring in order to bring the universe to ultimate perfection. If the times change, sometimes very dramatically (as in the case of Noah's flood, see Rashi), the only purpose is to bring men to know that there is a God and to fear Him. There is thus no point in men's trying to force matters in order to make unlawful gains through robbery, exploitation and the like, because it is a fundamental law of creation that "God seeks out the persecuted" (v 15) - "He exacts retribution from the persecutor, so what does the worker of evil gain from all his toil?" (Rashi ad loc.).

"And I have seen yet more under the sun..." (v 16). Kohelet now brings a further observation about this mysterious creation and its many paradoxes: "...in the place of righteousness there is iniquity" (ibid.).

With bold candor, Kohelet confronts the fact that in our world here "under the sun", we witness again and again the most abominable wickedness perpetrated under the guise of Justice and Equity.

"But I **said in my heart**..." (v 17). Kohelet knew that we must not let the outer appearance of this world reduce us to cynicism. He answered his own doubts about the justice of creation with his firm conviction that "...God shall judge the righteous and the wicked" (ibid.). The reason is because "there is a time for every purpose" - as explained at length earlier in the enumeration of the Twenty-Eight Times: God has all the time in the world to do perfect justice "...over all the work there". "Over all the work that a man did, there (i.e. in the judgment after death) they will judge him when the time of retribution comes" (Rashi ad loc.).

This leads Kohelet to give expression to another article of conviction in verse 18 as the verse is explained by Rashi: "Having seen all this, namely that men have adopted the arrogant trait of ruling and lording it over those weaker than themselves, I know that the Holy One blessed be He will make them know that their power is nothing, and so too that of lords and kings, for they are simply like animals and wild beasts - out for themselves".

This brings Kohelet to muse on the mysteries of the body and the soul and the differences between man and the animals. When a man dies, his cadaver may seem to be no different qualitatively from that of an animal - so where is his superiority and success? But "Who knows whether the spirit of the children of men goes upwards and the spirit of the animal goes downwards to the earth?" (v 21). "'Who knows' - i.e. he who knows and understands, knows that man's soul goes above after death to stand trial, while the soul of the animal goes down to the earth and she is not required to give a reckoning and accounting. The moral is that man must not conduct himself like an animal that does not care what she does" (Rashi on vv 20-21).

At last comes the moral of the whole discussion: "So I saw that there is nothing better than that a man should rejoice in his work, for that is his portion." (v 22). Again, this harks back to v 12 in the present chapter and ch 2 v 24: Man should rejoice in the labor of his own hands and eat - Torah and mitzvot - for this is the share given to him by Heaven and in this he should rejoice. What point is there in amassing ill-gotten gains if he will not see what his children will do with them when he dies? (see Rashi on our verse).

CHAPTER 4

"So, I returned and considered all the oppression under the sun..." (v 1). "'I returned, i.e. I changed my mind and went back on what I had thought, that it is good for a man to rejoice, on account of the fact that he is unable to rejoice and be happy. This is because there is robbery in this world, and his property will be taken from him by force, or he will be exploited when some judge or officer takes a bribe or by a thief" (Ibn Ezra ad loc.).

With further daring candor, Kohelet confronts the terrible cruelty of this world, where the oppressed shed tears again and again yet no-one comforts them. It is noteworthy that the phrase "they have no comforter" is repeated twice in the verse in order to give emphasis to their helpless misery.

While Ibn Ezra's above-cited explanation of the verse addresses the material exploitation and oppression of men by men in this world, Rashi illumines the esoteric dimension of the verse in his comment that the tears of the oppressed are those of the wicked in hell, who instead of the Torah embraced this world "under the sun", and who now weep over their souls which are oppressed by the cruel vengeful angels of destruction (see Rashi on v 1). Are we not all robbed in this world by the wicked Evil Inclination, which tempts and tricks us into doing wrong, leaving us bereft of goodness having to face terrible retribution? From the depths of the existential mire in which we find ourselves, is it any wonder that Kohelet goes on to praise those who are already dead (v 2) and to say that it would be better not to be born at all (v 3)?

So, what are we supposed to do in this world? Even people's good deeds are motivated by jealousy of others etc. "Again, I saw all the labor and every skill in work, that it comes from a man's rivalry with his neighbour..." (v 4).

Are we then to fold our arms and do nothing? "The **fool** folds his hands and eats his own flesh." (v 5) - "The fool is the wicked man, who makes no effort to labor honestly and robs to eat" (Rashi). We may not desist from our labors for good in this world, even if we have mixed motives. "Better is a handful with quietness than both hands full of labor and striving after wind" (v 6). "It is better to acquire a modicum of possessions through one's own toil, thereby giving pleasure to his Creator, than to acquire many possessions sinfully, causing vexation and anger before Him" (Rashi ad loc.).

"Then I returned, and I saw a vanity under the sun" (v 7). Having established that we are to toil in the Torah and mitzvot, Kohelet goes a step further in verses 7-12 with his observations about how partnership and teamwork are better than trying to go it alone. A person may have great ambitions, but if he will not join and couple - with a friend, a partner, a wife etc. - selfishly wanting all the gains for himself, this is vanity. God wants us to link up and join together in our work to repair the creation.

Then who will lead us? "Better is a poor and a wise child than an old and foolish king..." (v 13). "The poor, wise child is the good inclination (**Yetzer Tov**). And why is it called a child? Because it does not enter a man until the age of 13. It is wise because it gives the person the intelligence to follow the path of good. The old and foolish king is the evil inclination (**Yetzer Ra**), which rules over all the person's limbs. It is 'old', because from the moment the baby is born it is put in him, as it says, 'Sin crouches at the entrance' (Gen. 4:7). It is 'foolish' because it leads the person astray on the path of evil. It 'does not know to take care anymore' because having become old in his ways, the person does not accept rebuke" (Rashi on v 13).

"And I saw all the living who wander under the sun - they were with the second child who was to rise up in his stead" (v 15). "All the living" are those who are righteous in their deeds. What caused them to be alive under the sun - their going after the second child, which is the good inclination" (Midrash Kohelet Rabbah).

However: "There is no end of all the people who come to acclaim the one who goes before them and also those who come after shall not rejoice in him, for this too is vanity and vexation of the spirit" (v 16). This verse is speaking of the foolish and wicked people who follow the old and foolish king. "There is no end to all the generations that the Evil Inclination has destroyed, and also those who come after will not rejoice if they obey him" (Midrash Kohelet Rabbah).

Kohelet has taught us to follow the poor wise child, the Good Inclination and travel the path of the Torah and the mitzvot. Finally, in verse 17 he teaches that we should be quick and eager to heed the Torah, doing good from the outset, rather than being lax and careless, ending up having to bring the sacrifices of fools - sin and guilt offerings. "Guard your legs when you go to the House of God..." (v 17). Besides the plain meaning of this verse, it is also the foundation for the law that in preparation for prayer we must cleanse ourselves of our bodily wastes, which come from between the legs (Berachot 23a).

May God help us to follow His path and purify ourselves so as to come to His House and serve Him in truth! Amen.

CHAPTER 5

Kohelet cautioned in the last verse of the previous chapter to "Guard your foot when you go to the house of God..." (Koh. 4:17). In verses 1-6 of the present chapter he continues to give advice about the proper way for man to relate to God.

"Do not be rash with your mouth and let not your heart be hasty to utter a word before God..." (v 1). All too often people are quick to protest against what they perceive as the injustice of His dealings with them or with others and to doubt and question His providence, as in the case of those who ask where He was in the Holocaust. Kohelet cautions us to remember that we are puny, transient creatures on earth, while God is in heaven, way above our realm, and we cannot expect to understand His ways. Therefore, we should be sparing in our words, for "silence is a protective fence for wisdom" (Avot 3:17), whereas talking too much is the hallmark of the fool (verse 2).

"When you make a vow to God, do not delay paying it..." (v 3). A vow is a solemn verbal commitment that a person makes, binding himself to perform a certain meritorious act, give to charity, offer a sacrifice etc. In the case of charity, people often make commitments in the heat of the moment - sometimes to impress others, or simply to get the charity-collector off their back - only to go cold afterwards and find every reason to defer and forget their obligation. But Kohelet teaches that it would be better not to make the vow than to make it and fail to pay (v 4).

"Do not let your mouth cause your flesh to sin and do not say before the **Mal'ach**, messenger, that it was an error..." (v 5). Rashi interprets this verse as a continuation of the counsel against taking a vow that one fails to fulfill. This can bring down retribution on a person's "flesh" - his offspring. According to this interpretation, the "messenger" is the charity officer who comes to collect the sum pledged in public. However, the Targum and Midrash give the verse a broader application to sinful speech in general – **Lashon Ra** - which brings the punishment of Gehinnom on the person's very flesh, limbs and body. According to this interpretation, the **Mal'ach** is the cruel accusing angel who grills and punishes the person after death. It will harm the sinner even more if he claims he made his disparaging remarks innocently.

"For this comes about through the multitude of dreams and vanities and many words..." (v 6) - "Dreams, vain prophets and many other things may tell you to separate yourself from God! Don't listen to dreams but just **fear God**" (Rashi). "Even if the master of dreams tells a person that he is to die tomorrow, never despair of the power of prayer" (Berachot 10b).

"If you see the oppression of the poor and the violent perversion of judgment in the state, do not marvel at the matter..." (v 7). Ibn Ezra (ad loc.) explains the connection between this verse and the verses that preceded it: "You may think that He does not keep watch on what you say because you see the violent perversion of justice and nobody comes to save the oppressed. Know that there is a Watcher who sees this corruption". In the words of Metzudat David: "Do not wonder why God shows patience and does not exact retribution. For there is One who is high above all the high ones and rules over them all at every moment, but He waits until the sinners' measure is complete and only then exacts retribution. '...And there are higher ones over them': He has many agents who are high above the men of that state and can rule over them and through them repay them for their deeds" (Metzudat David ad loc.)

"Moreover, land has an advantage (**yitron**) for everyone (**ba-kol**)..." (v 8). According to the simple interpretation of this verse, "after he has finished giving instructions about fear of God, he comes back to teaching about the affairs of this world, discussing what occupation can best enable a person to make a living without sinning" (Ibn Ezra ad loc.). Lovers of the land will rejoice to hear that agriculture is the first choice. According to this interpretation, even a king is beholden to the field, for without it there is nothing to eat (see Targum). However, Rashi and Metzudat David see the verse as the continuation of the previous verse, rendering the Hebrew word **yitron** (translated above as "advantage") has having the connotation of overweening pride (from **yeter**, too much). According to this interpretation, the punishment of those who pervert justice in the state may be sent **ba-kol** - "through everything", i.e. through any of His many agents (as in the case of the Roman emperor Titus, who suffered agony for years as his brain was eaten alive by a mosquito). The "king" who is beholden to the field is the Holy One blessed be He, who toils on behalf of Zion (which has been ploughed as a field) in order to avenge her shame at the hands of those who destroyed her and to pay a reward to those who build her" (see Rashi on v 8).

Similarly, verse 9 - "He who loves money will not be satisfied with money... - is subject to a variety of interpretations on the simple (**p'shat**) and midrashic levels. On the level of **p'shat**, the whole passage in verses 9-16 is a teaching about the folly of people's unquenchable craving to amass wealth, which can cause them the greatest harm, while those who toil honestly, satisfied with their lot, sleep sweetly without anxiety. On the level of Midrash, Rashi explains that "He who loves money" refers to one who loves the mitzvot. Such a person will never be satisfied even after performing many mitzvot as long as they do not include at least one specific and highly conspicuous mitzvah, such as the building of a synagogue or the writing of a beautiful Sefer Torah (Rashi on v 9).

"Sweet is the sleep of the laboring man, whether he eats little or much..." (v 11). Targum's rendering of this verse is: "Sweet is the sleep of a man who labored wholeheartedly for the Master of the World and he has rest in his grave, whether he lived few years or many, because he worked for the Master of the World in this world, and in the World to Come he will inherit the work of his hands and have the wisdom of God's Torah. And when a man who was rich in wisdom and toiled and made efforts in it in this world lies in his grave, his wisdom will dwell upon him and will not leave him alone, just as a wife does not leave her husband alone to sleep."

In verses 12-16 Kohelet preaches against the folly of wanting great wealth, which may be kept by its owner to his hurt. If the person has no true enjoyment from his wealth, his entire life and all his efforts will have been in vain when he goes naked and bereft to his grave.

Verses 17 and 18 return to the same conclusion about the answer to man's existential predicament as Kohelet gave in chapter 2 v 24 and chapter 3 v 12: "What I have seen is that it is good and beautiful to eat and drink and see good in all one's labor in which he toils under the sun..." (v 17) - "To eat and drink, i.e. to toil in the Torah, which is a good teaching, and not to amass great wealth but to rejoice in the portion he has been given, for that is his share" (Rashi ad loc.)

CHAPTER 6

In contrast to the honest laborer who is satisfied with his lot, the man who has wealth, possessions, honor and long life but no enjoyment from them is worse off than a still-born foetus that had no life at all (vv 1-6). Rashi on verse 3 cites King Ahab as an example of the case of one who has no enjoyment since he had many children and great wealth, but he coveted what belonged to others and had no satisfaction from his own wealth, and in the end, he was eaten by the dogs. On the level of Midrash, "Even if a Torah scholar has 'wealth, possessions and honor' - i.e. he knows Bible, Mishnah and

Aggadah, but 'God does not give him the power to eat of it' - i.e. he does not attain to the level of understanding Talmud and therefore is unable to determine the correct legal ruling - then 'a stranger will eat it' - this is the master of Talmud" (Rashi on v 2).

"For all a man's labor is for the sake of his mouth..." (v 7) - "That he should eat in this world and the World to Come" (Rashi).

"For what advantage does the wise man have over the fool or over the poor man who knows how to make his way among the living?" (v 8). Even one who is "rich" in wisdom but has no satisfaction from his "wealth" (as in the case of the scholar who does not know how to give practical rulings) is no better than the fool, or the poor man who is satisfied with his portion and who knows how to reach the life of the World to Come through the simple performance of the mitzvot (see Rashi on v 8).

"Better is the sight of the eyes than the wandering of the soul..." (v 9) - "It would be better if a man would see with his eyes the journey of the soul after death and to which place the soul of the righteous goes and to which place that of the wicked man goes, for if so, he would understand the difference between them, and as a result he would straighten his path" (Metzudat David ad loc.). For even the greatest man cannot escape "the one who is mightier than he" (v 10) - i.e. the angel of death (Rashi).

We therefore need to find out "...what is good for a man in life during the limited number of days of his life of vanity..." (v 12), because life passes like a shadow. "With only this verse I would not know if it is like the shadow cast by a wall or a palm tree, which have some substance. But King David came and specified: "His days are like a **passing** shadow" (Psalms 144:4) - like the shadow of a bird that flies past and its shadow flies off with it" (Kohelet Rabbah).

CHAPTER 7

The letter Tet at the head of the Hebrew word **tov** ("good", "better") with which Chapter 7 begins is traditionally written large (**rabati**) in the parchment scroll, emphasizing how much better is a good name than even the best oil. Above all else is the Name of HaShem, to which the verse alludes on the level of **sod** (esoteric wisdom). In the handwritten Hebrew scrolls this large letter marks the beginning of a new Parshah (section) of the Megillah, which runs continuously without any further breaks until the end of the book.

Compared to the earlier part of the work, this last section often seems to be less of a continuous discourse and more of a succession of proverbs, each of which is a precious jewel joining with those that precede and follow it to make a Torah mosaic providing the deepest insights into the meaning and purpose of life in this world with its many paradoxes and mysteries, in order to clarify how man should best spend his days of vanity here.

The present commentary, which is largely based on Targum and Rashi, seeks to throw light on the **P'shat** (plain meaning) and **Remez** (allusions) contained in these verses while touching only in passing upon some of the many levels of **Drash** (rabbinic interpretation) and **Sod** (esoteric wisdom) they contain.

Verse 1: "A good name is better than precious ointment..." - "Better is the good name that the righteous acquire in this world than the anointing oil that was poured on the heads of kings and priests. And better is the day on which a man is released and lies in his grave with a good name and with merit than the day on which a wicked man is born into the world" (Targum Yonatan).

Verse 2: "It is better to go to the house of mourning..." - "It is better to go to the house of a man who is in mourning in order to comfort him than to go to the house of drinking and lasciviousness, because everyone must eventually go to the house of mourning, because the decree of death applies to everyone, and by going to the house of mourning the righteous man will take to heart the fact of death and let go of any evil in his hands and return to God" (Targum).

Verse 3: "Anger is better than laughter..." - "Better is the anger which the Master of the World displays to the righteous in this world than the smile He shows to the wicked, because the frown on the face of the Shechinah brings dearth and retribution into the world in order to rectify the hearts of the righteous so that they should pray to the Master of the World to have mercy on them" (Targum).

Verse 4: "The heart of the wise is in the house of mourning..." - "The heart of the wise dwells on the destruction of the Holy Temple and is pained over the exile of Israel, whereas the heart of fools is filled with the joy of their house of follies: they eat and drink and indulge themselves, paying no attention to the suffering of their brothers" (Targum).

Verse 5: "It is better to hear the rebuke of the wise..." - "It is better to sit in the study hall and listen to the rebuke of a Torah sage than to go to hear the jingles of fools" (Targum).

Verse 7: "For the oppressor mocks the wise man..." - "For the oppressor mocks at the wise man because he does not go in his way, and with his evil words he can destroy the wisdom in the heart of the sage that was given to him as a gift from heaven" (Targum). "When the fool taunts the sage, he can throw him into confusion and cause him to stumble, as in the case of Datan and Aviram, who taunted Moses (Ex. 5:21) until he spoke against the Holy One (ibid. 6:1) with the result that he did not enter the Promised Land" (see Rashi on our verse).

Verse 8: "Better is the end of a matter..." - "Better is the end of a matter than its beginning. For at the beginning a person does not know what will be at the end, but at the end of something good, a person knows that it is good. And better in God's eyes is the man who is in control of his spirit and subdues his evil inclination than the one who goes in the arrogance of his spirit" (Targum).

Verse 9: "Do not be hasty in your spirit to be angry..." - "If rebuke is sent to you from heaven, do not be quick to let your soul rage and speak rebellious words against heaven. For if you are patient your sins will be forgiven, but if you rebel and rage, know that anger dwells in the lap of fools until it destroys them" (Targum).

Verse 10: "Do not say, 'How was it that the former days were better?'..." - "In your time of trouble do not say that the reason why there used to be good in the world was because the earlier days were better. For the reason is because the deeds of the people of that generation were more beautiful than now and this was why they were sent good. Not with wisdom do you ask about this" (Targum).

Verse 11: "Wisdom is good with an inheritance..." - "Even if someone has a house, wealth and an ancestral inheritance, wisdom is still of benefit, because without it his inheritance will not endure in his hands" (Metzudat David).

Verse 12: "For whoever is in the shade of wisdom is in the shade of wealth..." – "For when a person takes refuge in the shade of wisdom, likewise he can take refuge in the shade of wealth as long as he performs charity with it. But the excellence of knowledge of the wisdom of the Torah is that it brings its owner from the cemetery to the life of the world to come" (Targum).

Verse 13: "Consider the work of God..." - "Consider the work of God and His might. For He has made the blind, the hunchback and the lame prevalent in the world, but who is wise enough to rectify a single one of them except for the Master of the World, who caused them to be flawed?" (Targum).

Verse 14: "On the day of goodness, be good..." - "On the day that God does goodness to you, you too be good and do goodness to the entire world, in order that no evil day should befall you."

"...God has made the one corresponding to the other..." (verse 14). On the level of **sod** (esoteric wisdom) this verse is frequently cited in the literature of Kabbalah and Chassidut as an allusion to God's creation of the **Sitra Achra** ("the Other Side", source of the bad days, bad times) as the counter-image of the Side of Holiness (source of the good days, good times) in order to give man the freedom of choice between good and evil in this world, so as to test him and enable him to earn his reward in the world to come.

Verse 15: "I have seen everything in the days of my vanity: there is a righteous man who perishes in his righteousness..." - "Good and evil are sent into the world through God's decree on account of the destinies with which people are created. For there is a righteous person who perishes in his righteousness in this world while his merit is guarded for him in the world to come, and there is a guilty person who lives a long life despite his sins, but the account of his evil awaits him in the world to come in order to exact retribution from him on the great Day of Judgment" (Targum).

Verse 16: "Do not be over righteous..." - "Do not be over righteous at the time when a sinner is condemned to death in your law court so that you take pity on him so as not to kill him. And do not be excessively wise so that you follow the wisdom of the wicked in your generation: do not learn from their ways, for why should you ruin your ways?" (Targum).

Verse 17: "Do not do much wickedness..." - "Do not go after sinful thoughts in your heart so as to be exceedingly sinful and do not keep your path far from the study house of God's Torah so as to be a fool - for why should you cause death to your soul and cause the years of your life to be cut short so that you die before your time?" (Targum).

Verse 18: "It is good that you should take hold of this but do not withdraw your hand from that..." - "It is good for you to rejoice in the affairs of this world and benefit yourself as traders do, but also do not abandon your share in this book of the Torah."

"...for he that fears God fulfills his duty according to them all" (v 18). This rendering of the closing words of the verse is intended to bring out the halachic prescription which it contains. Many different and often apparently conflicting halachic opinions and approaches are found in the Talmud and among the various Poskim (legal authorities). Where possible, a God-fearing Jew strives to take account of as many of the different opinions as possible in the way he performs the various commandments, and it is this principle that guides the rulings of the Torah Codes (Mishneh Torah, Shulchan Aruch, Mishnah Berurah etc.).

Verse 19: "Wisdom strengthens the wise more than ten rulers who are in the city." "The 'ten rulers' are the ten things that make a person guilty: his two eyes, which show him sinful things, his two ears, which make him listen to idle matters, his two hands, with which he robs and oppresses, his two legs, which transport him to the sin, and his mouth and heart" (Rashi ad loc.). "Wisdom means repentance and good deeds" (Nedarim 32b).

Verse 20: "There is not a just man on earth..." - "...but if a man has sinned, he should make sure he repents before he dies" (Targum).

Verses 21-22: "Another benefit of wisdom is that it will teach you not to pay attention if people speak to you insultingly and disparagingly. Do not listen and pay attention even if it is your servant who insults you and you have it in your power to take vengeance on him. For you know in your heart that you have many times cursed others." (Metzudat David).

Verses 23-24: "All this I tried with wisdom…" - that is the Torah. "…I said, I will be wise, but it was far from me." And what is this that was far? "Far is what was" - i.e. the far off things that took place at the very formation of the creation. This is "...deep, deep - who can find it out?" One is not permitted to speculate about them and ask what is above and what is below, what is inside and what is behind (Rashi).

Verse 25: "I cast about in my mind to know and to search..." - "...To find out the calculation of the reward of the deeds of the righteous and to know the retribution for the sins of the fools and the intelligence and trickery of the government (**Malchut**)" (Targum).

Verse 26: "And I find more bitter than death the woman whose heart is snares and nets and her hands are fetters..." - "This 'woman' refers to heresy" (Rashi). This "woman" is thus none other than the "strange woman" against whom Solomon warns repeatedly in the book of Proverbs (2:16ff, 5:3ff etc.).

Verse 27: "Behold this I have found, **says** Kohelet..." It is noteworthy that in this verse, the Hebrew word for "says", **amrah**, is in the feminine form, which agrees with the grammatical form of **Kohelet**, which is also technically feminine, even though in other appearances of the name Kohelet in the Megillah the accompanying verbs are in the masculine form (1:2; 12:8, 9 and 10). Rashi here renders: "Says the assembly (**kevutzah**, fem.) of wisdom, and says his intelligent soul (**Nefesh**, fem.), which gathers wisdom".

"…counting one thing to another to find the sum" (v 27) - "I drew a line joining one constellation with another to find the sum of the sons of man - what will be at the end" (Targum).

Verse 28: "...One man among a thousand I have found, but a woman among all those I have not found" - "I have not found anyone whole and righteous without flaws from the day the first man was born until the righteous Abraham, who was found faithful and worthy among the thousand kings that gathered to make the Tower of Babel. And I did not find a single worthy woman among all the wives of those kings" (Targum). "It usually happens in this world that a thousand enter into the study of the Bible but out of them only a hundred emerge fit for the Mishnah, and out of those hundred who entered into the Mishnah only ten go forth to the Talmud, and of those ten who enter into the Talmud, only one is fit to give legal rulings - i.e. one in a thousand" (Rashi).

Verse 29: "...God has made man upright, but they sought out many calculations" - "HaShem made the first man worthy and righteous but the serpent and Eve deceived him into eating the fruit of the Tree of Knowledge of Good and Evil and brought down death upon him and all the generations of the earth, and they sought out many calculations in order to bring disaster upon the generations of the earth" (Targum).

CHAPTER 8

Verse 1: "Who is like the wise man and who knows the interpretation of a thing?..." - "Thus, we find that through Daniel's wisdom in the fear of heaven, the secrets of the interpretation of dreams were revealed to him" (Rashi).

In verse 2, Kohelet counsels that the greatest wisdom is to observe the word of God's mouth - the Torah - which Israel are sworn to keep.

Verse 3: "Be not hasty to go out of His presence..." - "In the time of God's anger, do not leave off praying before Him. Beg Him for mercy so that you do not get involved in something evil, for HaShem is the Master of the World: He does everything that He desires" (Targum).

Verse 5: "He who keeps a commandment shall know nothing evil..." - "Whoever fulfills a mitzvah in the proper way will not be the recipient of bad news" (Shabbat 63a).

Verse 6: "For every matter (**chefetz**) has its time and judgment (**mishpat**)..." - "When a person follows his own desire (**chefetz**) and violates the law of Torah, there is a time to exact retribution, and justice and punishment stand ready" (Rashi).

Verses 7-8: Man does not know when the time of retribution will come: no-one warns him, and it is impossible to keep one's soul in one's body because one has no control on the day of death.

Verse 9: "…There is a time when one man rules over another man, to his own hurt." This verse alludes to the mystery of how the **Sitra Achra** (the "other", impure side of creation) may hold the righteous in subjection for a certain period, but the ultimate purpose is to bring about the overthrow of the wicked (as in the case of Amalek, Pharaoh, Nebuchadnezzar and Sennacherib, all of whom held Israel in subjection but were eventually destroyed, see Rashi).

Verse 10: "And in truth I saw how the sinners were buried and they were destroyed from the world and removed from the holy place where the righteous dwell, and they went to be burned in Gehinnom on account of their evil sins of robbery, oppression and theft, and they were forgotten from among the dwellers of the city, and just as they did to others, so they had done to them" (Targum).

Verse 11: It is because God is patient and slow to exact retribution that people imagine they can escape the consequences of doing evil.

Verse 14: "There is a vanity that is decreed on the face of the earth: this is that there are cases of Tzaddikim who suffer evil as if they had acted like sinners, and there are sinners who receive a flow of good as if they had acted like Tzaddikim, and I saw with holy spirit that the evil that befalls the righteous in this world is not because of serious sins but in order for them to pay the penalty for any light sins they may have committed in order for their reward to be complete in the world to come. But the good that comes to the sinners in this world is not because of their merits but in order to pay them the reward for any minor merits they may have so that they may eat their reward in this world in order to destroy their share in the world to come" (Targum).

Verse 15: "And I praised **Simchah**!!!..." The Talmudic reconciliation of the apparent contradiction between our present verse and **Kohelet's** earlier question, "What does **Simchah** accomplish???" has already been discussed in **Know Your Bible** commentary on Kohelet 1:17. Whereas there he was referring to fools' happiness, our present verse speaks about the holy **Simchah** of keeping the Torah.

This verse is seen as the **Binyan Av** (paradigm case) proving that wherever Kohelet speaks about "eating" and "drinking", he is talking about taking joy in the study of Torah, observance of the mitzvot and the performance of good deeds, for this alone is what accompanies man to the grave after all his toil in this world (Kohelet Rabbah).

CHAPTER 9

In the closing verse of the previous chapter Kohelet declared that "a man cannot find out the work that is done under the sun" (Kohelet 8:17) - "The creatures are unable to fathom the ways of the Holy One blessed be He and understand what is the reward for men's actions under the sun, because they see the wicked succeed while the righteous keep sinking lower" (Rashi).

Yet even though His ways may be incomprehensible, in the opening verse of our present chapter Kohelet affirms that "...the righteous and the wise and their deeds are in the hand of God..." That is to say, there is a special divine providence which governs all those who endeavor to go in God's ways. "He helps them and He judges them in order to benefit them in the end" (Rashi). God does not love or hate one person more than any other even when He helps one more than another in his endeavors to serve Him. Rather, "...all is before them" - i.e. everyone has free will. If there is a difference in the degree of divine assistance apparently given to different people, this is in proportion to the goodness of each person's intentions in his efforts to serve Him (Sforno on v 1).

Notwithstanding the special providence that God extends to those who serve Him, we must confront the fact that "...there is one event to the righteous and to the wicked, to the good and pure and to the impure..." (verse 2). This is death, which makes no discrimination whatever between one person and another. How to come to terms with this key factor in our existential predicament in this world is the theme of the passage in verses 2-12.

What can be so confusing to us is precisely the fact that even the best of people apparently come to the same bad end as the worst. Thus the midrashic interpretation of verse 2 cites the parallel fates of the righteous Noah and the wicked Pharaoh Necho, both of whom limped; of the good Moses and the pure Aaron on the one hand and the impure Ten Spies on the other, none of whom were permitted to enter the Promised Land; of King Josiah, who sacrificed to God and King Ahab, who did not sacrifice, both of whom were killed by arrows; and of Tzedekiah, who swore and broke his oath, and Samson, who took oaths very seriously (Judges 15:12), both of whom had their eyes gouged out.

As a result, "...the heart of the sons of man is full of evil..." (verse 3) - "Because they say that there is no retribution against the wicked, but everything is pure chance" (Rashi ad loc.).

But "for him that is joined to all the living there is hope..." (verse 4) - "Whoever attaches himself to all the teachings of the Torah so as to acquire the life of the world to come has hope" (Targum). "For as long as he is alive, even if he has been wicked and attached to other wicked people, he can still repent before his death".

"...For a living dog is better than a dead lion" (verse 4) - "Nevuzaradan (Nebuchadnezzar's captain, who executed the destruction of the Temple) was a wicked servant but he converted before he died and was thus better off than Nebuchadnezzar his master, who was called a lion (Jer. 4:7), and who died in his wickedness and lies in hell while his servant sits in the Garden of Eden" (Rashi). "When King David died, it was Shabbat, and Solomon sent a message to the sages in the study hall asking what to do because his father's body was lying in the sun and the household dogs were hungry. They replied that the maximum that would be permissible would be to cut up carrion meat to throw to the dogs (to divert them from the body), and the only way the corpse (which was **muktzeh**, not to be touched on Shabbat) could be moved would be if this were done indirectly, as by carrying it together with a loaf of bread or a baby. This was a case where a living dog was better off than the dead 'lion' - David" (Shabbat 30b).

Verse 5 teaches the fundamental article of Torah faith that as long as a person is alive in this world of **Asiyah**, action, he can repent, serve God and acquire merits, but after death "they do not have a reward any more" - "There is no possibility for them to fulfill any further commandments in order to receive a reward for their performance" (Metzudat David).

Verse 6: "Also all their love and their hatred and their envy are now long perished...." - "After the death of the wicked, there is no further need for them. Their love, hate and envy are already perished from the world, and they have no good share with the righteous in the world to come, nor do they have any benefit from all that is done in this world beneath the sun" (Targum).

On the other hand, verse 7 addresses those who follow the path of righteousness: "Go, eat your bread in joy...." (v 7) - "You, the tzaddik, whose good deeds God has already accepted and who will merit the World to Come: go eat your bread in joy" (Rashi). "Solomon said with a prophetic spirit from God: The Master of the World is destined to say to all the Tzaddikim - to each and every one by himself - Go and joyously taste the bread that has been prepared for you in return for the good bread that you gave to the poor and needy when they were hungry, and with a good heart drink the wine that has been hidden away for you in the Garden of Eden in return for the wine that you poured out for the poor and needy when they were thirsty" (Targum).

Thus, after death, the destiny of the souls of the righteous is quite different from that of those of the wicked, and it therefore behooves the righteous to do everything in their power to acquire merits as long as they are alive in this world. Therefore - "Let your garments always be white..." (verse 8): "Rabbi Yochanan ben Zakkai said: If the verse is talking literally about white garments and good oils, we see how many white garments and good oils the idolaters have! Rather, the verse is talking only about mitzvot and good deeds. Let your garments always be clean of sins, and never let the oil of mitzvot and good deeds be lacking from upon your head" (Shabbat 153a).

"See life with the wife whom you love all the days of your vanity..." (verse 9). Our sages interpreted this prescription to "see **life**" with your wife as a counsel to pursue a worthy occupation in order to make a livelihood, learning from our verse that just as a father has an obligation to help his son to marry, so he must teach him a trade (Kiddushin 30b). "See and understand that you must learn a craft in order to make a living together with your study of the Torah. And if you do so, your share will be life in this world through the livelihood you gain from your craft, and life in the world to come. For toil in both of them - Torah and making a living - causes sin to be forgotten" (Rashi on verse 9).

"Whatever your hand finds to do, do it with your strength..." (verse 10). In this verse, Kohelet drives home the message that "...there is no action or reckoning...in She'ol where you are going". After death, it is impossible to take any further **action** in order to acquire merits to be added to the **reckoning**. For the only place of action is this world of **Asiyah**. Accordingly, as long as we are alive here, we must apply ourselves with all our strength to the acquisition of merit through mitzvot and good deeds. This is because neither the swift nor the mighty nor the wise nor those of understanding can escape death, which spells the absolute end of the period assigned for action and endeavor (verse 11). Man never knows when his time will come: we are helplessly trapped in this world - like fish in a net or birds in a trap (v 12).

Since the key to our taking advantage of our life in this world to acquire merits lies in **Chochmah**, Kohelet now turns to acclaim the virtues of **Chochmah** in the closing verses of our present chapter (ch 9 vv 13-18) and opening verses of the next (ch 10 vv 1-4). "Having said above that the wise do not necessarily have bread (v 11), he now goes back to praising wisdom, for even though it may not help to bring in bread, one should not reject it because there is a certain wisdom that is of great importance in this world" (Metzudat David). The "wisdom" to which Kohelet refers is not a matter of intellectual brilliance but rather the practical Torah wisdom that enables us to escape the traps of the evil inclination.

"There was a little city and few men within it..." (v 14). The allegory of the "little city" is explained in the Talmud: "The 'little city' is man's body. The 'few men' in it are the limbs of the body. The 'great king' who comes against it is the evil inclination, while the 'poor wise man' found there is the good inclination, which saved the city through wisdom, i.e. repentance and good deeds. But '...nobody remembered that poor man' (v 15), because at the hour when the evil inclination holds sway, nobody remembers the good inclination" (Nedarim 32b). The allegory of the "little city" in this passage harks back to the allegory of the "poor wise boy" who came to rule the country in Kohelet 4:13-15.

"Wisdom is better than instruments of war, but one sinner can destroy much good" (v 18) - "A person should always look at himself as if he is half guilty and half worthy, and therefore if he performs a single mitzvah, happy is he because he swings himself into the scale of merit, but if he carries out one sin, woe is he because he swings himself into the scale of guilt. On account of a single sin that a person commits, he may lose many benefits" (Kiddushin 40b).

CHAPTER 10

The opening verses of chapter 10 continue with the praises of wisdom and the disparagement of folly. The same destructive power of folly that was the subject of the last verse of the previous chapter is the theme of verse 1 of our present chapter. "Dead flies cause the perfumer's oil to give off a foul odor..." (v 1): "For example in wintertime when flies have no strength and are near death, even if a single one falls into perfumer's oil and gets mixed up in the spices, it makes it give off a foul odor causing a scum with little bubbles to rise to the surface. In the same way a little folly can have more weight than wisdom and honor because it can swing everything into the scale of guilt" (Rashi).

Verse 2: "A wise man's hand inclines to his right hand (**Chessed**, expansive kindness, revelation) but a fool's heart is to his left (**Gevurah**, strength, constraint, restriction and concealment)". "The heart of the wise is directed to the acquisition of the Torah, which was given from God's right arm, while the heart of fools is bent on the acquisition of wealth, silver and gold" (Targum).

Verse 3: "Even in the way the fool walks his heart is lacking and he tells everyone he is a fool". "The fool thinks that everyone else is stupid, but he does not realize that he is the one who is stupid while others are wise" (Kohelet Rabbah).

Verse 4: "If the spirit of the ruler rises against you, do not leave your place...." "If the spirit of the evil inclination rules in you and attacks you, do not abandon your good place - the good practices you have been following - for the Torah was created as a healing remedy in the world in order to cause many sins to be forgiven and forgotten by God" (Targum).

In verses 5ff Kohelet continues his moral discourse on the path of life which the righteous should follow with a bold and candid examination of one of the greatest challenges that this world of mysterious paradoxes presents to our faith in God's justice. "There is an evil that I have seen under the sun - it is **like a mistake** that went forth from before the Ruler: folly is set in great dignity while the (spiritually) rich sit in a low place" (vv 5-6). Many sincere people are indeed deeply perplexed by the seeming injustice whereby the most unworthy people enjoy glory and splendor while the truly worthy seem to be despised and rejected. It seems all wrong - like some kind of **error** perpetrated by the Ruler of the world!!! How could this be???

Targum's rendering of verses 6-7 is: "God has given the wicked, insane Edom mighty good fortune and heaven-sent success and his forces are haughty and multitudinous, while the House of Israel are subject to him in exile, and because of their many sins those who were wealthy have become poor and sit in lowliness among the nations. King Solomon said through the spirit of prophecy: I have seen nations that were formerly subject to the House of Israel holding sway and riding horses like governors, while the nation of the House of Israel, their masters, walk like servants on the ground".

While the warning in verse 8 that "he who digs a pit will fall into it..." applies to the machinations of any wicked person, Targum's rendering follows on from his application of the previous verses to Israel: "The Attribute of Judgment spoke up and answered: They themselves brought all this upon themselves, for just as when a man digs a pit at the crossroads he is brought there to fall into it, so the nation that transgressed God's decree and attacked the fence of the world will fall into the hand of a wicked king who will bite them like a serpent" (Targum on v 8).

Verse 10: "If the iron is blunt and one does not whet the edge, then one must put in more strength..." - "When the people of Israel sin and cause the heavens to become hard as iron so that no rain falls, if that generation does not pray before God the whole world is ruined by famine. But when they repent and gather together and overcome their evil inclination, appointing prayer leaders to beg for mercy before God in heaven, they find favor" (Targum).

Verse 11: "If the serpent bites and cannot be charmed, then there is no advantage in the master of the tongue" - "When fiery serpents are let loose to frighten and harm the world, it is because of the sins of Israel in not engaging in words of Torah uttered in a whisper. Likewise, there is no benefit to a person who speaks **Lashon Hara** (evil speech) because he is destined to burn in the fire of hell" (Targum).

Following further disparagement of those who follow the path of folly in verses 12-15, Kohelet continues in verses 16-17 by contrasting the fortune of the land (=Eretz Israel) when under the rule of a king and judges who behave like young lads with its fortune under the rule of those whose might is combined with wisdom and understanding (see Rashi ad loc.). We badly need the latter today.

Verse 18: "By much slothfulness the beams collapse..." - "When a person fails to fix a small crack in the roof of the house the entire structure will collapse" (Rashi). Don't leave little flaws to become bigger.

Verse 19: "For laughter they make bread, and wine will bring joy to the living, and money answers over everything." - "For laughter the righteous make bread to feed the hungry poor, and the wine that they pour for the thirsty will be for them for joy in the world to come, and their redemption money will testify to their merit in the world to come in the eyes of all" (Targum).

Verse 20: "Do not curse the king even in your thought..." - "Do not anger the King of the world" (Rashi). Do not think that your words and thoughts are not heard and registered! "At the hour when a man sleeps, the body tells the lower soul and the lower soul tells the higher soul, and the higher soul tells the angel and the angel tells the cherub and the cherub tells the master of wings - that is the Saraph-

and the Saraph takes the word and tells it before the One Who spoke and brought the world into being" (Kohelet Rabbah).

CHAPTER 11

Our allotted time in this mysterious world of paradox is very short. Kohelet moves towards the conclusion of his work with a few last words of counsel as to what we should do here to make the best of our situation.

"Cast your bread upon the water, for you shall find it after many days" (v 1) - "Practice goodness and kindness even to a person whom your heart tells you that you will never see again, like a person throwing food into the water, for the days are coming when you will receive your reward" (Rashi).

Verse 2: "Give a portion to seven and even to eight...." The simple meaning of the verse is that one should give a share of one's food and drink to seven needy people and even to another eight who come after them, without saying "That's enough" (Rashi). On the level of Midrash, "Rabbi Yehoshua says, 'Give a share to seven' - These are the seven days of Pesach; '...and even to eight' - these are the eight days of Succot, while the word 'even' (**gum**) comes to include Shavuot, Rosh HaShanah and Yom Kippur" (Eiruvin 40b). "Rabbi Eliezer says, 'Seven' refers to the seven days of the week. Give one day, Shabbat, as the share of your Creator! Eight refers to circumcision on the eighth day" (Kohelet Rabbah).

Verse 3: "If the clouds are full of rain, they empty themselves upon the earth..." - "If the clouds are full of water, they don't keep it for themselves but pour it out onto the ground, and then the ground gives rise to vapors so that the clouds become filled up again. Similarly, a person who has wealth should not keep it all for himself but rather, he should share his blessings with others. Then, when his time of need comes, he will receive blessings from others. As long as a tree provides fruit, people come to water it, but if it falls, nobody comes to tend it anymore since it gives no fruit. Similarly, if a person does not give help to others, nobody will help him in his time of need" (Metzudat David).

Verse 4: "One who waits for the wind will not sow, and one who watches the clouds will not reap." Even though the wind may help the sower by spreading the seed, if he waits for the perfect wind to blow he will never sow! Likewise, if we wait for perfect circumstances before carrying out our mitzvot and good deeds, we will never do what we have to do. We must understand that nothing can ever be completely perfect in this world, but we have to carry out our obligations **now**!!! Verse 5 thus goes on to teach us that man can never have full knowledge of all aspects of God's creation, just as he cannot know the nature of an embryo while it is still in the womb. He should therefore perform acts of kindness, marry, have children, study the Torah etc. without worrying if he might go lacking materially as a result, because he cannot know God's decrees as to who will be poor and who will be rich (see Rashi ad loc.).

Verse 6: "In the morning sow your seed and in the evening do not withhold your hand..." - "If you learned Torah in your youth, learn Torah in your old age; if you taught students in your youth, teach students in your old age; if you had a wife and children in your youth, marry a woman with whom to have children in your old age; if you practiced charity in your youth, practice charity in your old age" (Rashi).

Verse 7: "The light is sweet..." - "The light of the Torah is sweet, enlightening darkened eyes so that they see the glory of the face of the Shechinah, which in time to come will illumine the faces of the Tzaddikim, making them as beautiful as the sun" (Targum).

Verse 8: "For if a man lives many years..." - Once again, Kohelet reminds us to rejoice in the share God has given us in this world and use our precious time here to acquire many merits. For the "days of darkness" that come after the death of the wicked are longer than the days of their life in this world, and only merits - Torah and mitzvot - can save us from this darkness (see Rashi ad loc.).

Verse 9: "Rejoice, young man, in your youth..." - "This is like a man who sarcastically tells his servant or his son, 'Go ahead and sin! Sin! For the time will come when you will be punished for all of them!' Likewise, the wise man here says, 'Rejoice, young man, in your youth and go after the ways of your heart...but be assured that the Judge will bring you to judgment for all this'" (Rashi ad loc.).

Verse 10: "And put aside anger from your heart and remove evil from your flesh..." - "Put aside the things that make God angry and remove the evil inclination from your flesh so that you will have a heart of flesh" (Rashi ad loc.).

CHAPTER 12

"And remember your Creator (**Bor'echa**) in the days of your youth..." (verse 1). The letters making up the Hebrew word **Bor'echa**, "your Creator" also spell out the words **be'ercha**, "your well" and **bor'cha**, "your pit". It was on this verse that Akavia ben Mahalalel based his teaching, "Gaze on three things and you will not come to sin. From where did you come? A putrid drop (the 'well' from which you were drawn). Where are you going? To a place of maggots and worms (the grave or 'pit'). And before whom will you have to give an account and a reckoning - your Creator" (Yerushalmi Sota 2:2).

Verse 1 warns about the onset of "...the years of which you will say, I have no pleasure in them;" - i.e. the final years of life - thereby introducing the haunting and evocative passage in verses 2-7, which our sages taught to be an allegory about the pains and troubles of old age and bodily deterioration (Talmud Shabbat 151b). Rashi explains the details of the allegory as follows:

"Before the sun and the light, the moon and the stars are darkened..." - The "sun" is the forehead, which shines and radiates when a person is young, but which brings up wrinkles when he is old and does not shine. The "light" is the nose, which is the glory of the face. The "moon" is the soul, which radiates to a man, but when it is taken from him there is no light in his eyes. The "stars" are the cheeks. "...and the clouds return after the rain;" - a person's light is darkened after his tears of weeping over the many troubles he has endured.

"On the day when the keepers of the house tremble..." - These are the ribs and flanks, which protect the entire hollow of the body, "...and the strong men bow themselves..." - these are the legs, on which the whole body rests, "...and the grinders cease because they are few..." - these are the teeth, most of which fall out in old age, "...and those looking out of the windows are dimmed," - these are the eyes.

"And the doors are shut in the street..." - These are the bowels, "...when the sound of the grinding is low..." - this is the sound of the digestive organs grinding up the food, "...and one starts up at the voice of the bird..." - when a person is old, even the sound of a bird can wake him, "...and all the daughters of music are brought low;" - An aged person has no interest in listening to singers (cf. II Sam. 19:36).

"When they are also afraid of that which is high, and terrors are in the way..." - An old person is afraid to go out into the streets for fear of stumbling on little bumps and clods, "...and the almond tree blossoms..." - this is the thighbone, which protrudes in old age like the blossom of a tree, "...and the grasshopper drags itself along..." - a person feels his buttocks like a heavy weight, "...and the caperberry fails..." - the desire for women departs, "...for the man goes to his eternal home..." - the grave,"...and the mourners go about the streets."

"...Before the silver cord is loosed..." - This is the spinal cord, which is white like silver but which after death shrivels and dries and becomes crooked inside the vertebrae, becoming like a chain, "...or the golden bowl is shattered..." - this is a man's member, which used to gush with water, "...and the pitcher is broken at the fountain..." - this is the stomach, which bursts after death, "...and the wheel is broken at the cistern;" - the eyeball disintegrates in its hollow. "...and the dust returns to the earth as it was, and the spirit returns to God who gave it."

In addition to the above explanation of Kohelet's allegory of old age and decline, Rashi also gives an equally detailed explanation of the same allegory as Solomon's call to Israel to remember their Creator while the Temple still stood, before the onset of the exile, when the light of Torah and the sages would become dimmed as trouble after trouble would strike.

Kohelet now sums up his rebuke and final testimony to Israel in the same words with which he began: "Vanity of vanities. all is vanity" (chapter 12 v 8 harking back to chapter 1 v 2). That which does not endure - this world - is mere vapor and vanity, and therefore we should focus all our efforts on keeping God's Torah in order to attain the enduring life of the World to Come.

If we ask why we should heed Kohelet rather than any other wise preacher, smart thinker or philosopher, he explains: "And more than Kohelet's having been wise, he also taught wisdom to the people and weighed and sought out and set in order many proverbs" (v 9). In the words of Rashi: "Kohelet was even wiser than might appear from what is written in this book. He made 'handles' for the Torah, which was like a box without any handles to hold onto it. Thus, he instituted the laws of **Eruvs** as a fence around the keeping of Shabbat, and washing of the hands as a fence to purity, and he prohibited 'secondary' incest relationships as a fence against incest."

"Kohelet sought to find out acceptable words..." (v 10). Metzudat David (ad loc.) explains: "Everything he wanted to know he sought to discover, and he exerted himself to find out the truth." The Talmud comments on this verse: "Kohelet sought to be like Moses, but a heavenly voice came forth and told him: 'and words of truth written in proper form' - 'And no other prophet arose in Israel like Moses'" (Deut. 34:10; Rosh Hashanah 21b).

"The words of the wise are like goads..." (v 11) - "Just like the goad directs the plow-ox in its furrow, so the words of the wise direct a man in the pathways of life" (Rashi ad loc.).

There is no end to the books of wisdom that could be written. We should not say that if we cannot complete studying them all, it is not even worth starting. For the moral - the "bottom line" - can be stated very simply: "The end of the matter, when all is said and done: Fear God and keep his commandments! For that is the whole duty of man!" Amen.

אסתר

ESTHER

CHAPTER 1

In the public reading of the Torah in the synagogue, only one person at a time may read aloud to the congregation, because hearing more than one voice would be distracting to the listeners. However, so beloved is the story of the Purim miracle told in Megillat Esther that the halachah permits two or even ten people to read aloud at the same time. The reason given for this is precisely because the Megillah is so beloved (Megillah 21b; Shulchan Aruch Orach Chayim 690:2): it is intrinsically captivating.

Although the book of Esther is not strictly speaking considered a prophetic work, the sages were agreed that it was written by Esther and Mordechai through Ru'ach HaKodesh, "holy spirit", and the text of this deeply veiled allegory is laden with layer upon layer of meaning and allusions.

"Where in the Torah do we find an allusion to Esther? In the verse, 'And I shall surely hide (**asteer**) My face on that day.'" (Chulin 139b). The "face" of God is His revealed presence. Esther alludes to the concealment of His presence in exile as a result of Israel's sins. Yet the story of Esther proves that even when His presence is concealed, God is in complete control of everything. The revelation of God's power through the miracle of Purim came about in the merit of the Tzaddik Mordechai. "And where in the Torah do we find an allusion to Mordechai? In the pure myrrh of the holy anointing oil made by Moses, which in Hebrew is **Mar D'ror** (lit. "master of freedom") and in the Aramaic Targum is **Meira Dechya**=MoRDeCHaY" (Chulin ibid.)

With the killing of Nebuchadnezzar's son (or grandson) Belshazzar and the fall of Babylon to Darius the Mede and his son-in-law Cyrus king of Persia, the focus of power shifted to their twin empires of Medea and Persia, centered in the western regions of present-day Iran. With the collapse of Babylon and the consolidation of the Persian Empire many of the exiles from Judea, including Mordechai and his orphaned protégé Esther, moved to Shushan (Susa or Seleukia, about 150 miles east of the R. Tigris in Khuzestan province of Iran). According to the dating system of Midrash Seder Olam, the fall of Babylon took place in the year 3389 (=371 B.C.E.) exactly 70 years after Nebuchadnezzar rose to power. Even the greatest Tzaddikim were confused as to why the Temple was not then rebuilt since Jeremiah had apparently prophesied that God would punish Babylon and restore the people to Jerusalem after seventy years (Jeremiah 29:10; cf. Daniel 9:2 and commentators there). They did not realize that the Temple itself could not be rebuilt until seventy years after its destruction, which had taken place eighteen years after Nebuchadnezzar rose to power. The redemption prophesied by Jeremiah was the first wave of returning exiles under Zerubavel, which took place in the first year of the reign of Cyrus and with his encouragement (Ezra 1:1). But Cyrus reigned no more than two years, and when Ahashverosh (Ahasuerus) ascended the throne of Persia (in 3392=368 B.C.E.), royal support for the rebuilding of Jerusalem ceased as a result of letters of denunciation sent to the new king by the returning Jews' adversaries, who according to rabbinic tradition were the sons of Haman (Ezra 4:6). Ahashverosh's feast, at which he brought out the vessels captured by the Babylonians from the Temple in Jerusalem (Esther 1:7), was intended to celebrate the uneventful passing of the prophesied date of the restoration, which the gentiles took as a sign that it would never take place.

The thwarting of the rebuilding of Jerusalem and the Temple undoubtedly generated the darkest despair among the exiles in Shushan, many of whom reacted by allowing themselves to fall into laxity in their Torah observance, as exemplified by their participation in Ahashverosh's feast (Esther 1:5, see Targum there). The deepening Jewish assimilation was itself the fulfillment of God's warning in the Torah that "I shall surely hide My face on that day". But despite the fact that his Jewish brothers were running to join the gentiles in their celebrations in Shushan, Mordechai refused to participate in the consumption of **treif** (unkosher food), just as his saintly counterpart Daniel had refused in Babylon (Targum on Esther 1:5; Daniel 1:8). Purity of the food we ingest is the foundation of purity of mind and soul.

Through Mordechai's outstanding sanctity and that of Esther, they were worthy of one of the greatest miracles of all time: everything was completely turned around (**ve-nahaphoch hoo**, Esther 9:1), with the result that "the Jews fulfilled and took upon themselves (**keeyemoo ve-kibloo**) and their seed." (Esther 9:27). The sages taught that the phrase **keeyemoo ve-kiblooo** implies that the Jews **fulfilled** (**keeyemoo**) in the days of Ahashverosh what they had already **received** (**kibloo**), i.e. the Torah which they received at Sinai. Out of despair and assimilation came a national return to the ancestral Torah, and the Second Temple was built shortly afterwards. The Purim miracle took place in the thirteenth year of the reign of Ahashverosh in 3405 (=355 B.C.E.) while the Second Temple was built in 3408 (352 B.C.E.).

Yet this great salvation was only revealed at the very climax of the story of Purim, which began with the most terrible darkness in which Mordechai and Esther had only their perfect faith in God to sustain them. In the book of Esther more than anywhere else in the Bible, the hand of God is concealed to the point that the very Name of God does not even appear explicitly anywhere in the Megillah. It appears only in ways that are not discernible to the casual reader: for example, the initial or concluding Hebrew letters of certain phrases spell out various names of God. At least forty such cases are listed in the Kabbalistic Kavanot. (One of the most obvious examples is Esther 5:4, **Yavo HaMelech VeHaman Hayom**). Although the Megillah appears to be talking about King Ahashverosh, the text frequently refers simply to **HaMelech** (the King). The sages teach that this term simultaneously refers to the temporal Ahashverosh while also alluding to the King of kings (Midrash Esther Rabbah). The story of Purim apparently unfolds like a completely natural series of events, but as it develops, it becomes visible that each event was flawlessly planned and designed by the Ruler of all the world to teach a great lesson in how His providence governs every single detail of creation. How often the most enormous consequences flow from a single slight gesture or movement that nobody could have imagined would bring so much in its train.

The essence of the story of Purim is nothing less than God's war against evil from generation to generation "for HaShem will have war with Amalek from generation to generation" (Exodus 17:16). Amalek is the embodiment of the evil of the primordial serpent, glorying in cruelty, bloodshed and murder of men, women and children accompanied by the amassing of God-denying power and wealth. The extirpation of Amalek, who had perpetrated a barbaric attack on the newly freed people of Israel immediately after their exodus from Egypt, was the second of three commandments they were instructed to fulfill after their entry into the Land of Israel. The first was to appoint a king. He was to lead the people in fulfilling the second of these commandments by making war against Amalek. This was the necessary preparation for the fulfillment of the third, the building of the Temple in Jerusalem (Rambam, Laws of Kings 1:1).

The first king of Israel, the Benjaminite King Saul, was intended to fulfill the second commandment by wiping out all the Amalekites. However, Saul failed because he allowed the people to leave the Amalekite king Agag alive, and the latter succeeded in fathering a child even after his capture, before being hacked to death by the prophet Samuel (I Samuel ch 15). Because of Saul's failure, Samuel told him: "God has torn the kingship over Israel from you today and He has given it to your companion who is better than you" (I Samuel 15:28). This was David, from the tribe of Judah.

It was Mordechai and Esther who brought about the **tikkun** ("repair") of the terrible flaw left by King Saul in the form of Agag's descendant, Haman, who tried to destroy the entire Jewish people. Just like Saul, Mordechai was from the tribe of Benjamin (Esther 2:5), and moreover, he was the descendant of Shimi, who had come out to deliver the worst curses against King David when the latter fled from Jerusalem to escape Absalom (II Samuel 16:5-10). When David returned to Jerusalem after the thwarting of Absalom's rebellion, he spared Shimi, who was able to bear a son before eventually being killed by King Solomon (II Kings 2:8 & 40ff). Not only did Mordechai and Esther rectify Saul's flaw through the downfall of the Amalekite Haman. They also rectified the breach between the tribes of Benjamin and Judah, because Mordechai the Benjaminite is specifically called **Mordechai Ha-Yehudi** (Esther 2:5) - the Judean. To repair the **Malchut**, "kingship" having been taken from King Saul and given "to your companion who is better than you", the royal title of Queen was taken from Vashti and "the king will give her **Malchut** to her companion that is better than she" (Esther 1:19). Thus, it was that Saul's descendant, the royal Esther, became queen.

The **tikkun**, "repair", accomplished by Mordechai and Esther is expressed in the language of Kabbalah by Rabbi Moshe Chayim Luzzatto (RaMChaL) in his Kavanot (1st edition p. 138, Secret of Purim and Reading the Megillah):--

In the days of the exile in Babylon the Shechinah was turned away "back to back". It was necessary to build her in order for her to return "face to face". This is accomplished through Abba and Imma, which enter into her and build her. Now Yesod of Abba is long and goes out from Yesod of Imma, and it enters into Yesod of Zeir Anpin as well, unlike Yesod of Imma, which ends at the chest. Even in Nukva (=Shechinah) Yesod of Abba also reaches her Yesod, and indeed her Yesod is short so that the part of Yesod of Abba that is clothed therein protrudes even more. It was from this aspect that the soul of Mordechai the Tzaddik was drawn. This took place immediately before the redemption. The wicked Haman wanted to thwart the building of this Nukva and to thwart Mordechai. Mordechai received an illumination from the above-mentioned aspect, which is his root, which had already been in existence for a very long time, and Haman, who was jealous of him, wanted to thwart him and thwart the whole repair. But the Holy One blessed be He performed a miracle and the **Mochin** ("brain power") began to return to Zeir Anpin. This is the secret of "the sleep of the king fled" (Esther 6:1). This did not negate Mordechai, because the illumination which he had attained remained in all its strength, while Haman became weak and fell before him so that he was unable to harm the Jews, because the King of the Universe was already aroused. Mordechai's illumination strengthened him and enabled him to accomplish the great feat of saving Israel. Esther is the Malchut, which was for Mordechai a "daughter" (**bat**) and a "house" (=wife, **bayit**) through the mystery of the repair of the Nukva. (Ramchal, Kavanot).

Lovers of Rabbi Nachman will be delighted to know that **Esther** has the numerical value of 661 =**Tikkun HaKlali**, the Complete Remedy!!!

Chapter 1 Verse 1: "And it was (**Vayehi**) in the days of Ahashverosh…" - "We have a tradition handed down from the Men of the Great Assembly that wherever the text says, 'and it was (**Vayehi**) in the days of…' it means they were days of suffering, **Vay!!!**" (Megillah 10b).

Vv 1-8 illustrate the wealth, grandeur and magnificence of Ahashverosh's world center, capital of an enormous empire of hugely diverse nations, languages and cultures.

V 9: Queen Vashti was the daughter of Belshazzar and because of her own lineage from Nebuchadnezzar was somewhat contemptuous of Ahashverosh, whom she saw as a self-made upstart (cf. Megillah 11a, "he made himself ruler"). Our sages taught that through the hidden hand of God, Vashti was smitten with leprosy on the day Ahashverosh called her to appear naked except for her crown at his banquet, and she did not wish to go out of shame. She was afflicted by leprosy as punishment for having forced Jewish girls to work for her naked even on Shabbat.

V 16: "And Memuchan answered..." Having been mentioned last among Ahashverosh's advisors (v 14), why did he jump in first to tell the king to have Vashti killed? Our sages teach that this **Memuchan** was none other than Haman (Targum ibid. etc.), who was **muchan**, prepared by God for the purpose of bringing about punishment. What motive had Haman for wanting to kill Vashti? It is said that he knew from astrology that he would die at the hand of Ahashverosh's wife, and he mistakenly thought that this prediction referred to Vashti when in fact it referred to Esther. By killing Vashti Haman wanted to get Ahashverosh to marry his own daughter so that he himself could then become king.

CHAPTER 2

Verse 5: "There was a Yehudi man (**ish**)…" - "this teaches that Mordechai in his generation was the equivalent of Moses in his generation, as it is written, "And the man (**ish**) Moses was very humble" (Numbers 12:3; Midrash Esther Rabbah).

Mordechai's proactive genius was displayed in his allowing Esther to be taken to Ahashverosh when he could have hidden her away from the king's talent scouts. Mordechai had perfect faith that if God sent such an opportunity to win the jackpot and propel his adoptive exile daughter directly onto the throne of the world empire of the time, there must be some great purpose in it.

Verse 15: "…And Esther found favor (**chein**) in the eyes of all who saw her." The attribute of **chein**, charismatic charm and favor, is precisely the attribute of **Malchut**. "In the eyes of all who saw her" = "this teaches that each and every person imagined she was from his people" (Megillah 13b). "In the eyes of all who saw her" - "in the eyes of the supernal beings and in the eyes of the beings of the lower world" (ibid.).

Verses 21-3: The apparently quite irrelevant conspiracy of Bigtan and Teresh, which was thwarted by Mordechai, archived in the king's book of chronicles and promptly forgotten by everyone, eventually turns out to have been the event that brings about the denouement of the whole story, because Ahashverosh wanted to belatedly reward Mordechai just when Haman was on his way in trying to get him hanged (Esther 6:1-10). "God prepared the remedy for Israel's trouble even before He brought the trouble upon them" (Rashi on Esther 3:1).

CHAPTER 3

V 1: "After these things Ahashverosh promoted Haman..." Ahashverosh's feast had taken place in the third year of his fourteen-year reign (Esther 1:3), while Esther became queen four years later, in the seventh year of his reign (Esther 2:16). It was not until five years after that, in the twelfth year of Ahashverosh's reign, that Haman laid his plot to exterminate the Jews (Esther 3:7). During all these years Haman kept himself busy. Targum Yonatan (on Esther 3:1) states that he traveled in person from Shushan to Jerusalem to prevent the building of the Temple [not unlike the foreign "activists" until today who travel to Israel to monitor and thwart every move Jews make to assert their sovereignty in their land]. Targum continues: "The attribute of Justice rose before the Master of the World to accuse Haman. but the Master of the World answered, 'So far, he is not well known in the world, leave Me until he becomes great and known to all the nations and then I will exact punishment from him for all the persecution perpetrated by him and his fathers against the House of Israel.'" God allows the wicked to rise to the very peak of their power and fame before casting them down, and His glory is thereby enhanced.

Vv 2-4: "And all the king's servants bowed..." Haman hung an idolatrous figurine on his coat so that all who bowed to him to show their respect were also bowing to the idol (Targum Yonatan etc.). [Such personality cults should not surprise us since in our day entertainment and other celebrities are explicitly referred to as idols.] Targum states that Mordechai would not bow to Haman for two reasons.(1) Mordechai would never bow to an idol since this contravenes the Second Commandment.

(2) In any case Haman was Mordechai's slave ever since one time when Haman had nothing to eat and sold himself to Mordechai for bread - this Midrash echoes the fact that Esau had sold the birthright to Jacob for food and was thus subject to him (cf. Genesis 27:37; cf. also Rabbi Nachman's story of "The Exchanged Children", a major theme of which is the mystery of Jacob and Esau).

Vv 5-6: The thought of taking personal vengeance on Mordechai was not to appease Haman for the affront to his self-importance. Only the destruction of Mordechai's entire people could assuage his wrath because the existence of even a single remaining adherent to the Sinaitic Covenant would always be a slap in the face to Haman's worldview.

V 7: Like many prominent world leaders through history up until the present day, Haman used astrology and occult arts to accomplish his goals. The Second Targum on Esther, which is far more elaborate than Targum Yonatan, bringing a rich array of supplementary Midrashic lore, tells how Haman rejected month after month as being unsuitable for scheduling his planned extermination of the Jews because each month had some Jewish festival in whose merit they would be protected. The reason why Haman chose the twelfth month - Adar - was because it was on the 7th of Adar that Moses had left the world, and the loss of their leader left Israel completely vulnerable.

V 8: Haman's artful speech to Ahashverosh is one of the outstanding all-time masterpieces of anti-Semitic insinuation and slander.

Vv 9-11: Haman offered to pay ten thousand talents of his own silver to Ahashverosh in order to "buy" the Jews from him so that he could then do to them as he pleased. (The reason for the sum of 10,000 talents of silver that Haman offered was that this was equivalent to paying one zuz for each of the 600,000 Israelites who went out of Egypt.) Yet we see from verse 11 that Ahashverosh did not even take the money, telling Haman he could keep it as a gift: "The money is given to you and the people to do with them as is good in your eyes". This shows that Ahashverosh was quite as happy as Haman at the thought of getting rid of the Jews, who were an affront to his own world-view as well. Rather than taking anything from Haman, Ahashverosh **gave him** his own ring: i.e. he gave Haman authority to do whatever he wanted. "Rabbi Abba bar Kahana said: "The removal of Ahashverosh's ring accomplished more than forty-eight prophets and seven prophetesses who prophesied to Israel. None of them succeeded in persuading Israel to repent, but the removal of the ring [and the dire threat of extermination to which this led] caused them to repent!" (Megillah 14a).

Vv 12-15: Haman now set in motion the enormous governmental apparatus across the entire vast, sprawling Persian empire in order to execute his dastardly Jihadist plot of staging a global one-day massacre of all the Jewish men, women and children everywhere and anywhere on the 13th of Adar.

V 16: "...and the city of Shushan was in consternation" - because the exultation of all the Jews' enemies was mixed with the sound of Jewish wailing (Targum Yonatan).

CHAPTER 4

Verses 1-3: "And Mordechai knew..." - "The master of the dream told him that the Heavenly Court had agreed to the decree because they had bowed to the idol in the time of Nebuchadnezzar (Daniel ch 3) and enjoyed themselves at Ahashverosh's banquet" (Rashi). Mordechai now showed his mettle as Tzaddik of the Generation, single-handedly going out to arouse the people and induce them to repent. With the dire decree staring them in the face, the people finally began to do so.

Vv 5ff: "Then Esther called for Chatach..." According to rabbinic tradition, the go-between who went back and forth from Esther to Mordechai was none other than Daniel, who had been the leading advisor of Nebuchadnezzar, Belshazzar and Darius the Mede. He was called **Chatach** because "all the matters of the kingdom were determined (mith**chat'ch**im) in accordance with the words of his mouth" (Targum Yonatan). Our text tells us that Chatach went from Esther to Mordechai and back again. However, while in verses 10-12 we see that Esther gave Chatach instructions for a second mission to Mordechai, Chatach's name is not mentioned again thereafter, while in verse 12 it is written that "...**they** told Mordechai the words of Esther". Targum Yonatan on verse 12 tells that Haman (who was obviously a control-freak) saw that Chatach-Daniel kept on coming and going to Esther and promptly killed him. Indeed, a tomb said to be that of Daniel exists in Shushan. Targum on v 12 tells us who **they** were.

V 11: "All the king's servants and the people of the king's provinces know that every man and woman who comes to the inner courtyard of the king without being called is to be put to death." Targum states that Esther told Mordechai that Haman had instituted that nobody could go into the king without his permission, which again testifies to his having been a paranoid control-freak.

V 12: "And they told Mordechai the words of Esther." Since Chatach-Daniel had been killed, it was the angels Michael and Gabriel who now relayed Esther's message to Mordechai, who sent them back to her with his reply (Targum Yonatan).

Vv 13-14: Mordechai's reply to Esther shows his complete faith that even if she did not go to the king to try to intercede for the Jews, relief and deliverance would definitely come to them from elsewhere: no one individual is indispensable because God has many messengers!

V 15-16: Esther stood to lose everything if her mission was unsuccessful. The rabbis taught that Mordechai had taken Esther as his wife (darshening the word **bat**, "daughter", in Esther 2:7 as **bayit**, "house"=wife). Having originally been taken to Ahashverosh **b'o-ness**, "under duress", she was still halachically permitted to go back to her husband Mordechai since only a priest is forbidden to take back his wife if she is raped, but not an Israelite. However, the moment Esther went into Ahashverosh **of her own free will**, her adultery was intentional, and she would subsequently be forbidden to Mordechai in any event -- even if failed in her mission. Despite the fact that the erratic and unpredictable Ahashverosh was quite likely to kill Esther for coming to him of her own volition (just as he had killed Vashti for showing that she had a mind of her own), Esther was willing to sacrifice her entire life and future in order to save her people. "Go gather together all the Jews who are present in Shushan and fast for me." Esther knew that her only chance of success was if all the Jews repented.

V 17: "So Mordechai went his way (**va-ya-avor**)." The root of **va-ya-avor** is **avar**, which has the connotation of transgression. The rabbis stated that Mordechai "transgressed" because he agreed to the public fast despite the fact that it took place during the festival of Pesach when fasting is normally forbidden (Rashi on Esther 4:17).

It must be understood that while the events described in Esther 1:1-3:6 were spread out over **nine years**, the events described from 3:7 until 8:2 were concentrated in the space of **five days**. Haman cast lots at the beginning of the month of Nissan, and the decree became public knowledge on the 13th of Nissan (Esther 3:12). Mordechai went into action immediately, and his exchanges with Esther took place on the very same day. The three-day fast called by Mordechai started on the 14th of Nissan and continued on the 15th and 16th (both of which were Yom Tov in Shushan since it was in the Diaspora). It was on the 16th of Nissan - the third day of the fast -- that Esther invited Ahashverosh and Haman to the first banquet (Esther 5:4) and it was held on the same day. Ahashverosh's sleep was disturbed that night (eve of the 17th of Nissan, Esther 6:1) and the second banquet, Haman's downfall and hanging took place the next morning - the third day of Pesach. Despite the fact that we today celebrate Purim in Adar, which is when the decree of extermination was intended to be fulfilled, the actual miracle took place during Pesach, the festival of redemption.

Verses 21-3: The apparently quite irrelevant conspiracy of Bigtan and Teresh, which was thwarted by Mordechai, arrived in the king's chronicles and promptly forgotten by everyone, eventually turns out to have been the event that brings about the denouement of the whole story, because Ahashverosh wanted to belatedly reward Mordechai just when Haman was on his way in trying to get him hanged (Esther 6:1-10). "God prepared the remedy for Israel's trouble even before He brought the trouble on them" (Rashi on Esther 3:1).

CHAPTER 5

V 1: "And it was on the **third** day..." - "Israel are not left in trouble for more than three days. Joseph put his brothers 'into custody for **three** days' (Genesis 42:17); Jonah was in the belly of the fish '**three** days and three nights' (Jonah 2:1); and in time to come, 'on the **third day** He will raise us up and we shall live in His presence' (Hosea 6:2)" (Midrash Esther Rabbah).

"...and Esther clothed herself in royalty" - "The verse should have said 'she clothed herself in garments of royalty'. Rabbi Chaninah said, 'She clothed herself in holy spirit, as it says, "and the spirit **clothed** Amassay" (1 Chronicles 12:19). From here we learn that Esther was a prophetess'" (Talmud, Megillah 14b).

"...and she stood in the inner court of the king's house over against the king's house." In accordance with the principle that when the word **melech** appears in the Megillah without further qualification it alludes to God, this verse is interpreted to mean that Esther prayed before the Heavenly Temple, which is aligned directly with the earthly Temple in Jerusalem (cf. Targum Yonatan).

V 2: "And it was when the king saw Esther the queen standing in the courtyard." - "When she reached the chamber of the idols, the Divine Presence left her. At that moment, she said, 'My God, my God, why have You abandoned me?' (Psalm 22:2). Immediately, the king saw her and she found favor in his eyes" (Megillah 15b). It is customary to recite Psalm 22 on Purim at the end of the morning prayers. The "deer of the morning" alludes to the Shechinah.

V 3: "Then the king said to her, 'What is your wish. it shall be given to you even up to half the kingdom.'" The simple meaning is that Ahashverosh said that even if she asked for half the kingdom he would give it to her, but Targum Yonatan renders: "Even if you ask for half my kingdom I will give it to you but not if you ask to build the Temple which stands on the boundary of half my kingdom: that I will not give you, because I have made an oath to Geshem the Arab and Sanvalat the Horonite and Toviah the Ammonite slave (see Nehemiah 2:19) not to permit it to be built, because I am afraid of the Jews in case they will rebel against me, so I cannot grant this request but I will grant you anything else you ask."

Vv 4-9: What was in Esther's mind when she did not give the king an answer at the feast that same day but instead pushed him off to the next day? Some explain that despite the three-day fast of the Jews, Esther as yet still saw no sign of redemption. It was only the next day, after Haman had already begun to fall when he had to dress Mordechai in finery, that Esther knew that God was smiling and that she could ask Ahashverosh for what she really needed with impunity.

V 9: "Then Haman went out that day joyful and with a glad heart." Pride comes before a fall!

"But when Haman saw Mordechai in the king's gate and that he did not stand or stir for him." Not only would Mordechai not bow to the idolatrous figurine that Haman wore. When Haman passed by, Mordechai - who was sitting in his Sanhedrin, "the King's gate" (Deut. 16:18) - merely stretched out his right leg and showed Haman the deed of purchase attesting to how he had once purchased him as his slave in exchange for bread (Targum Yonatan). This appears to allude to how Jacob holds Esau by the heel (Gen. 25:26).

V 10: Targum Yonatan includes the interesting information that Haman's wife Zeresh was the daughter of Tatnai, governor of the Persian imperial provinces "over the river", i.e. west of the Euphrates, including the Land of Israel. We have encountered Tatnai in Ezra 5:3ff as a key figure in the diplomatic efforts made by the adversaries of the Jewish returnees from Babylon to Jerusalem to impede the building of the Second Temple. It would make sense that as an Edomite-Amalekite, Haman's origins lay in the desert regions south and east of the Dead Sea, which were part of the provinces "over the river" under the governorship of his father-in-law Tatnai.

V 14: In elaborating the counsel of Haman received from his wife and friends, Targum Yonatan explains that they detailed various failed plots to kill Tzaddikim: "If he is one of the Tzaddikim, then if we kill him by the sword, the sword will turn around and strike us. If we stone him, David already stoned Goliath. If we roast him in a copper pot, King Menasheh already escaped from such a pot (II Chronicles 33:11ff). If we throw him into the sea, the Israelites already split the sea and passed through on dry land. If we throw him into a fiery furnace, Chananiyah, Misha'el and Azariah already escaped from such a furnace. If we throw him into the lion's den, the lions left Daniel unharmed. If we throw him alive to the dogs, the mouths of the dogs were closed when Israel left Egypt. If we exile him to the wilderness, they were already fruitful and multiplied in the wilderness. If we throw him into prison, Joseph came out of prison to rule. If we stick a knife in his neck, the knife could not harm Isaac's neck. If we gouge out his eyes he will kill us like Samson killed the Philistines. We don't know what to do. The only solution is to set up a great **tree** (etz) for gallows at the gate of his house so that all the Jews and all his friends will see." (Targum Yonatan on v 14).

"Where in the Torah is there an allusion to Haman? In God's words to Adam after his sin: 'Is it that you have eaten from the tree that I commanded you not to eat from it?' (Genesis 3:11; Talmud Chulin 139b). The Hebrew for "is it that... from" is **ha-min** (grammatically the **ha** is interrogative, while **min** means "from"). Since Hebrew is written without vowels, these letters could equally well be read as **ha-man**. Haman was the embodiment of the serpent that caused man to eat from the tree of knowledge of good and evil. Haman's **tree** was **fifty** cubits high, corresponding to the fifty gates of the unholy Binah ("Understanding") whose power he wanted to use to destroy Mordechai, the Tzaddik of the Generation, who was teaching his people to reach God through the Fiftieth Gate - prayer. Thus, the Midrash tells that when Haman passed Mordechai as he sat teaching his students, he asked him what he was teaching. Mordechai told him he was explaining the laws of the Omer offering, which would have been offered on the second day of the festival of Pesach had the Temple been standing. The Omer offering begins the 50-day count to the festival of Shavuot celebrating the Giving of the Torah, corresponding to the 50th Gate.

CHAPTER 6

V 1: "On that night the sleep of the king was disturbed." It is customary for the **Ba'al Korei** reading the Megillah in the synagogue to raise his voice while saying these words, because the king's disturbed sleep was the root of the miracle (Shuchan Aruch, Orach Chaim 690:15, Mishnah Berurah #52).

"Why was his sleep disturbed? He was trying to understand why Esther had also invited Haman to the feast, and he began wondering if they might not be plotting to kill him. He thought to himself: 'Is there nobody who loves me enough to warn me? Could it be that someone did me some favor and I never paid him back, and as a result people are holding back from revealing information to me?' He immediately gave instructions to bring the book of records!" (Talmud, Megillah 15a).

V 2: "And it was found written." If something written in the world below for the merit of the Jews was not erased, how much more can that which is written above [God's promises in the Torah] never be erased" (Megillah 16a).

V 6: "And Haman came, and the king said to him, 'What shall be done to the man whom the king delights to honor?' " If Ahashverosh had asked Haman directly what should be done to his arch-enemy Mordechai, he would surely have given a very negative reply. Ahashverosh thus phrased the question in such a way that Haman would not know whom he intended to honor - and of course the pompous Haman immediately assumed it was himself and answered in the grandest terms. A somewhat parallel method of ascertaining indirectly what a person really thinks was used by the prophet Nathan when he went to David to reprove him for having taken Batsheva (II Samuel 12:1ff).

"And Haman said in his heart, 'To whom would the king delight to give honor more than to myself?' " - "The wicked are in the power of their own heart, and thus, 'and Esau said **in his heart**' (Gen. 27:41), 'and the wicked says **in his heart**' (Psalms 14:1), 'and Jeraboam said **in his heart**' (I Kings 12:26). But in the case of the Tzaddikim, their hearts are under their control, and thus 'Hannah spoke **to her heart**' (I Sam. 1:13), 'and Daniel put it **upon his heart**' (Daniel 1:8) 'and David spoke **to his heart**' (I Sam. 27:1), and in this they are like their Creator, of Whom it is written, 'And HaShem said **to his heart**' (Gen. 8:21; Midrash Esther Rabbah).

V 12: "But Haman was pushed back to his house **mourning** and **with his head covered**" - "Haman was going on his way through the streets leading Mordechai when they passed through the road where Haman's house was situated. Haman's daughter, who was standing on the roof, saw them and assumed that the person riding the horse was her father and the person walking in front of him was Mordechai. She took the toilet pan and threw it at the one walking in front, but when she looked and saw that it was her father she fell from the roof to the ground and was killed. This is why Haman was **mourning**, over his daughter, **with his head covered** - because of what had happened (Megillah 16a).

CHAPTER 7

Seeing Esther invite Haman to her feast with the king had brought the Jews of Shushan to the highest peak of Teshuvah. Previously they believed that in the Jewish queen they had a strong ally in the royal household who might yet save them by asking the king to kill Haman, but here she was inviting their worst enemy to her feast! "At that moment, the entire house of Jacob poured out their hearts and trusted only in their Father in Heaven" (Targum Yonatan on Esther 5:14).

Vv 1-2: "So the king and Haman came to drink with Queen Esther. And the king said again to Esther on the second day at the feast of wine, 'What is your petition… even to half the kingdom?'" Targum Yonatan explains here as on Esther 5:6 that when Ahashverosh offered Esther up to half the kingdom, he was explicitly refusing to allow the rebuilding of the Temple, except that in his explanation of the present verse, Yonatan adds that the king said to Esther, "Wait until your son Darius will grow up and inherit the kingdom and that too will be done".

Vv 3-4: The directness, simplicity and heart-rending pathos of Esther's plea to the king to save herself and her people from destruction makes this a model that all of us can follow in our prayers to God to redeem Israel.

"…for the oppressor is not concerned about the damage to the king" – "Esther was saying to Ahashverosh, 'This oppressor [Haman] does not care about any loss to the king! He was jealous of Vashti and killed her, and now he has become jealous of me and wants to kill me!' " (Megillah 16a).

By openly identifying with the Jews, Esther finally revealed her origins and people to Ahashverosh for the first time since Mordechai had instructed her not to do so (see Esther 2:20).

V 5: "And the king Ahashverosh said, and he said to Esther the queen." In this verse the word **va'yomer**, "he said" is repeated twice. While the second **va'yomer** is directed to Esther, the first **va'yomer** is not directed to anyone and is apparently redundant. Thus Rashi (ad loc.) states: "In every place where a verse reads **va'yomer…va'yomer** twice, this is can only be explained through Midrash. The Midrashic teaching that comes out from this verse is that previously Ahashverosh had spoken to her through an intermediary, but now that he knew that she was from a family of kings [Saul] he spoke to her himself directly (see Megillah 16a).

Vv 6-8: With Haman now falling faster and faster, his every move just made things worse. He tried to appeal to Esther, but when the king saw him falling over Esther's couch he was all the more convinced that Haman was up to no good.

V 9: "And Charvonah, one of the chamberlains, said before the king, 'Also see the gallows fifty cubits high that Haman made for Mordechai who spoke good for the king.'" Charvonah's timely intervention settled Haman's fate. Some rabbis said that it was Elijah the prophet who appeared to the king in the guise of one of his chamberlains (see Ibn Ezra on this verse). However, the opinion of Rabbi Elazar in the Talmud is that Charvonah had in fact been in on Haman's conspiracy to have Mordechai hanged but that when he saw that Haman was obviously going down fast he quickly abandoned the sinking ship and changed his colors (Megillah 16a; cf. Targum Sheini on Esther 7:9).

V 10: "And they hanged Haman on the gallows that he prepared for Mordechai." - "He hewed out a pit and dug it out, and he fell into the ditch which he made" (Psalms 7:16). Similarly, Jethro saw the hand of God's justice in the way that the Egyptians were drowned in the waters of the Red Sea after having plotted to drown the Hebrew babies in the waters of the river (Exodus 18:11, see Rashi ad loc.)

CHAPTER 8

Verses 3-6: "And Esther spoke once more before the king." The death of Haman had removed the Jews' worst persecutor but it did not undo the fact that a few days earlier messengers had been dispatched at top speed to all the provinces of the empire telling all the gentiles to mobilize for the 13th of Adar to exterminate, kill and destroy all the Jews, young and old (Esther 3:12-15). This was why Esther now asked Ahashverosh to revoke the letters Haman had sent out in the name of the king.

Vv 7-8: Ahashverosh replied that this was impossible, because "writing that is already written in the king's name and sealed with the king's ring cannot be revoked". This was in accordance with a law in the empire of the Medes and Persians that once promulgated, no governmental decree could ever be changed, as we find in Daniel 6:16, where even Darius king of Medea was unable to intervene to save his favorite Daniel from the decree made by his ministers to kill anyone found worshipping any other god besides the king. Our present text also alludes to the impossibility of changing even a single word or letter of the Torah.

Nevertheless, Ahashverosh now gave Mordechai and Esther permission to promulgate a new decree in the name of the king that would not revoke the previous decree but would allow the Jews to stand up against their enemies on D-Day, the 13th of Adar, and do to them exactly what they sought to do to the Jews.

V 10: "…and he sent letters in the hand of couriers on horseback riding on the swift horses used in the royal service bred from the stud mares." The phrase "used in the royal service bred from the stud mares" is a translator's device to find an intelligible rendering for the Hebrew/Persian words **ha-achashtranim b'ney haramachim**, whose exact meaning is not known. Targum renders **ha-achashtranim** as **artoulyoney**, which has the connotation of "naked" and apparently refers to the riders, who were stripped to the minimum gear necessary in order to be able to travel at top speed. Targum explains that the runners had their spleens removed and that the soles of their feet were arched so that only their toes touched the ground. Using couriers of this kind was the only way to communicate at high speed across a vast empire in the days before phones, faxes, the Internet and satellite technology.

V 11: The king permitted the Jews not only to defend themselves and kill and destroy their enemies [which the United Nations and Israel's "allies" still do not allow until today] but also authorized them "…to plunder their goods". The last provision was exactly parallel to the provision made in Haman's letters that the enemies were to plunder the Jews (Esther 3:13). However, when it came to it, the Jews did **not** plunder their enemies (Esther 9:10), thereby showing everyone that they did not do what they did for monetary gain (Rashi on Esther 8:11).

Vv 15-16 are two of the four "Verses of Redemption" (together with Esther 2:5 and 10:3) that are read out aloud, each in its proper place, by all the congregation during the public reading of the Megillah prior to their being read out of the scroll by the **Ba'al Korei** ("reader"; Shulchan Aruch, Orach Chaim 690:17).

"The Jews had light and gladness and joy and honor." - "Light" is Torah; "Gladness" is **YomTov**, festive celebration; "Joy" refers to circumcision, while "honor" refers to Tefilin (Megillah 16b).

V 17: "And many of the people of the land became Jews." Seeing the hand of God in the miracle performed for the Jews convinced them to become converts.

CHAPTER 9

Verse 1: "…and it was turned to the contrary." Through the grace of Heaven and in the merit of the patriarchs (Targum), in the Purim miracle, everything was turned around diametrically opposite to the way it all seemed at first. For this reason, the celebration of Purim every year on the anniversary of the miracle is also characterized by turning everything around, such as by wearing disguises, joking and upsetting many of the social conventions that govern normal everyday life (as long as this does not turn nasty in any way).

Vv 2: On the very day that had been designated by Haman's lot for the destruction of the Jews and what he hoped would be the death of their faith, they suddenly staged a one-day national Intifada against their enemies throughout the Persian empire, with complete success. Not only was this Jewish Intifada accomplished without the international chorus of condemnations, UN resolutions, sanctions etc. etc.

that follow any genuine act of Jewish self-defense today; it was actually carried out with the full support of the Persian imperial governmental apparatus.

V 4: "For Mordechai was great in the king's house." This depiction of Mordechai's greatness is reminiscent of the description of Moses' greatness in Egypt, "for the man Moses was very great in the land of Egypt in the eyes of Pharaoh's servants and in the eyes of the people" (Exodus 11:3).

Vv 5-18: Following the general account of the Purim miracle in the previous verses, the text now details (1) how the Jews rose up and killed their enemies throughout the Persian empire on the 13th of Adar and rested and celebrated on the 14th; (2) what they did in Shushan the capital, where they needed a second day to complete the work and only rested on the 15th of Adar. This narrative completes the story of the Purim miracle and also explains the reason why Purim is celebrated throughout the world on the 14th of Adar except in Shushan and certain other ancient walled cities, where it is celebrated on the 15th, as we read below in vv 19ff.

V 6: "And in Shushan the capital the Jews slew and destroyed five hundred men." Targum adds that these were all high-ranking members of the house of Amalek.

Vv 7-9: In the handwritten parchment scroll of Megillat Esther it is obligatory to write the Hebrew word **ish** at the end of verse 6 and the names of the ten sons of Haman who were killed one under the other, each at the beginning of a new line, while the ten occurrences of **ve-et** are written one under the other at the end of each line. Each name is thus separated by a wide space from the **ve-et** that follows it at the end of the line. This way of writing the names is identical with the way the names of the 31 defeated kings of Canaan are written in the parchment scroll in Joshua 12:9-24. Separating the words with wide spaces is also how **Shirah**, "song", is written, as in the case of Israel's song after crossing the Red Sea (Exodus ch 15) and the Song of Deborah (Judges ch 5). However, in **Shirah**, the first, third and fifth lines etc. are written with one word at the beginning, middle and end of each line, while the second, fourth and sixth lines etc. have only two words each of which is positioned where the spaces between the words appear in the lines above and below them. This arrangement of the text of **Shirah** has the appearance of a solid brick wall. However, in the case of the names of the kings of Canaan and the sons of Haman, nothing is written in the middle of each line. This signifies that there is nothing to support the entire structure from collapsing, and that once it has collapsed it can never stand up again (Megillah 16b).

Vv 11-15: King Ahashverosh appears to have been anxious to monitor what was going on in his kingdom, but through the hand of Heaven he did not try to interfere, and when Esther explained that in Shushan more time was needed to complete the work, he gave the green light to go ahead. In verses 6ff the text only said that the sons of Haman were killed. Now in verse 13, Esther requested that their corpses should be strung up on the tree-gallows Haman had made. This was doubtless in order to strike fear into the hearts of the Jews' enemies. Targum Sheini on Esther 9:23 explains what made Esther violate the Torah prohibition against leaving the corpse of an executed criminal hanging from the tree for more than a few moments before nightfall (Deut. 21:23). "Esther answered and said to them, Because King Saul killed the Gibeonite converts, his sons were hanged for six months (II Samuel 21:8ff). If this was done because their father killed Gibeonite converts, how much more should Haman and his sons, who wanted to destroy the entire House of Israel, be left hanging for ever."

Targum Yonatan and Targum Sheini on verse 15, both give detailed though slightly different mathematical explanations of exactly how Haman and his ten sons were hung on the fifty-cubit tree, one underneath the other, with equal spaces between them. Haman (disunity, separation) had wanted to extirpate Mordechai to the point that he and his people and everything they represented would be completely forgotten. On the other hand, Mordechai and Esther specifically wanted to have Haman and his sons "hung from the tree" - the tree of the Torah - to show that even evil has a place in the creation of the One God, and that the ultimate destiny of evil is to hang there, dead and completely defeated, to show that God rules over all.

Verse 19ff. Having completed the story of the Purim miracle, the Megillah now explains how Mordechai and Esther instituted the celebration of the festival of Purim the following year and every year forever afterwards in order to remember the miracle and give thanks and praise to God for it. The Torah forbids adding to the 613 commandments given in the Five Books of Moses, but the miracle of Purim was outstanding because without it, there would have been no Jews left in the world to keep the Torah. For this reason, the sages of the generation agreed with Mordechai and Esther in establishing the celebration of Purim not as a new commandment **Mi-D'Oraita** but as an institution **Mi-Divrey Sofrim**. Their initiative in writing and disseminating the Megillah as part of the **Ketuvim**, "holy writings" in order to explain the reasons for their institution has its foundation in God's words to Moses after the battle against Amalek: "Write this for a memorial in a book" (Exodus 17:14). The annual Purim exercise in heightening our consciousness of God's eternal war against Amalek is also an aspect of the Torah commandment, "Remember what Amalek did to you." (Deuteronomy 25:17ff).

V 20: "And Mordechai wrote these things." - "This refers to this very Megillah just as we have it" (Rashi). After the Purim miracle, the first step in the institution of the festival was its celebration for the first time one year after the actual miracle.

V 22 refers to the three main Mitzvot of Purim besides the reading of the Megillah:(1) feasting; (2) sending of two portions of ready-to-eat food to at least one friend and if possible to many more; (3) giving gifts of charity to at least two poor people and preferably to many more.

V 25 on the simple level refers to Ahashverosh's having given permission in writing (**im ha-sepher**) to the Jews to rise up against their enemies to thwart the earlier decree to exterminate them. The phrase **im ha-sepher**, "with the book", is also taken by Targum Sheini as an allusion to the Torah commandment to "blot out the memory of Amalek from under the heavens" (Deut. 25:19).

V 26: The festival is called **Purim** because everything started with Haman's casting of the lot - **pur** (Esther 3:7). He himself thereby predestined the day of his own destruction. We also see from this verse that Megillat Esther is called an **igeret** ("letter"), from the root **agar**, to "gather" (cf. Proverbs 6:8), since it gathers and puts together all the events that make up the story (Ibn Ezra). However, in Esther 9:32 the Megillah is called **sepher**, a "book" or "scroll" from the root **saper**, to recount or relate. The word Megillah is from the root **galah**, "reveal". As discussed in the commentary on Esther chs 1-2, the light that was revealed through the miracle of Purim derives from the Kabbalistic Partzuf of **Abba**, and in this aspect the Megillah is called **sepher**. However, this light had to spread and be revealed in all the worlds, and in this aspect the Megillah is called **igeret**, which could loosely be translated as a "broadsheet". For this reason, it is customary for the reader in the Synagogue to unroll and spread out the entire Megillah before reading it (somewhat as one spreads a newspaper over a table), alluding to the spread of the light of **Abba** in all the worlds.

V 27: The acceptance by all the Jews of the injunction to celebrate Purim every year for ever was a **Kabbalah**, an "undertaking" which under the laws of Nedarim ("vows") applied not only to themselves but also to all their offspring to all the generations. The celebration of Purim is thus binding on every Jew until today.

V 28: "…and these days should be remembered and observed." We **remember** them through the reading of the Megillah on Purim night and morning, and we **observe** them through the giving of charity to the poor, sending portions of foods to our friends, and feasting. The Hebrew phrase **nizkarim ve-na'asim** also alludes to the fact that every year during this season the same light that shone in the time of Mordechai and Esther shines all over again and the same events are repeated cyclically though often in a new guise. "…and these days of Purim shall not pass from among the Jews and their memory shall not cease from their seed". This teaches that Megillat Esther will never become defunct - not even in the end of days. Rabbi Nachman taught that originally all beginnings were traced to the Exodus from Egypt, but he hinted that now all beginnings come from the Purim miracle (Likutey Moharan II:74). As we today watch the rising power of Persia-Iran and her leader's publicly stated desire to destroy Israel, we should ponder the miracles that God performed for our ancestors in that very country of Persia and trust that if we repent with the same fervor as our ancestors then, God will surely save us from all our enemies and everything will be turned to the contrary!!!

Vv 29ff: After the celebration of the first Purim one year after the actual miracle, Esther and Mordechai established Purim as an annual festival forever after. This is why they wrote "this **second** letter of Purim".

V 30: "…words of peace and truth". Mordechai taught a lesson in effective outreach: start with **peace** and lead into **truth**.

V 31: "…as they had decreed for themselves and for their seed with regard to the fastings and the order of lamentation". Ibn Ezra points out that after the destruction of the First Temple the Jews took upon themselves the four-annual public fast days mourning the breach of the Jerusalem walls and the burning of the Sanctuary (the 17th of Tammuz, 9th of Av, 3rd of Tishri and 10th of Tevet, cf. Zechariah 8:19). Having taken upon themselves fasts of mourning, they now took upon themselves to celebrate the great miracle of Purim with eating and drinking.

CHAPTER 10

The Megillah started with Ahashverosh, and he is mentioned here at the end in the unpopular role of imposing taxes on his entire empire. However, Targum Sheini indicates that in recognition of the great miracle performed for them, the Jews were relieved of having to pay these taxes. However, the leading personality at the end of the Megillah is not Ahashverosh but rather the real hero of the whole story, Mordechai HaYehudi. He was beloved by "most" of his brothers but not all, because, as Ibn Ezra points out (on Esther 10:3), it is impossible for someone to please everyone owing to the natural jealousy that exists even between brothers. Notwithstanding this jealousy, Mordechai was always "seeking the good of his people and speaking peace to all his seed", and thus the Megillah ends with what we all await daily: **Shalom**.

דניאל

DANIEL

CHAPTER 1

There could be few better introductions to the book of Daniel than the opening words of R. Avraham Ibn Ezra's commentary thereon: "This is the book of the man greatly beloved, in which the most glorious of things are spoken, with prophecies some of which have already come about and others that are still destined to come about. Each thing is expressed with brevity in mysteries and riddles, while its secrets reside with the angels above - secrets that stand upon all the foundational elements - and its commentators have not succeeded in penetrating its secret. Each one explains as far as his hand reaches, but the feet of all of them are unsteady when it comes to the time of the destined end."

The rabbis said: "If all the wise men of the nations of the world were on one side of the scale and Daniel on the other, he would outweigh them all" (Yoma 77a). Daniel himself was considered not a **prophet** (**Navee**) but a wise and saintly **sage** (**Chacham**), yet he saw what even the prophets did not see" (Sanhedrin 93b; see Daniel 10:7).

From the point of view of historical narrative, the book of Daniel takes up the story of the exile of Judah in Babylon from the time of the first phase of the exile, which took place under King Yeho-yakim, as told in II Kings ch 24. This was eighteen years before the destruction of the Temple and, together with the exile of Yeho-yakim's son Yeho-yachin a year later, brought to Babylon the very flower of the Judean population, including all those righteous Judeans who heeded the message of the prophets of the time and accepted the decree of exile with resignation instead of trying to fight it.

Nebuchadnezzar was a ruthless but highly complex and very deep world ruler who was determined to use the minds and intellects of the very cream of the captive Judeans to serve his needs in governing and expanding his empire. "Because you did not serve HaShem your God. you shall serve your enemies" (Deut. 28:47). "If you had been worthy, you would have been called My servants, but now that you have not been worthy, you are servants of Nebuchadnezzar and his companions" (Yalkut Shimoni).

Nebuchadnezzar ordered his chief minister to choose an elite of good-looking, super-intelligent and wise Judean children who would be well fed and specially educated for service in his court. One of the requirements was that "they must have the ability to stand in the palace of the king" (v 4). The Talmud picturesquely explains this to mean that they would have to be able to control themselves so as not to laugh, chat or fall asleep during lengthy court sessions as well as holding themselves in if they felt the need to relieve themselves (Rashi ad loc., Sanhedrin 93b).

Daniel was determined not to defile and sully himself with the royal food that was provided for these privileged Judean captive children, exemplifying the very first rule of Jewish spiritual survival in exile: **meticulous observance of the laws of Kashrut** (spiritual purity of food). Daniel and his companions understood that the food we ingest nourishes not only our physical bodies but fuels and influences our very minds and souls. They knew that ingesting the royal food, whose ingredients and methods of preparation went contrary to Torah law, would corrupt their subtlest spiritual sensitivities and indeed their entire outlook on everything, destroying their Jewish purity. With a courage, comparable to that of Joseph in his years of captivity in Egypt, they secured the agreement of the king's catering officer to test them out on a diet of vegetables and water for ten days in what must have been one of the first macrobiotic experiments in history. They had astounding success, proving healthier than all the other children who did eat the king's food.

When Daniel and his companions were finally taken before Nebuchadnezzar, they brought about a great sanctification of the Name of God even in exile, showing that it was precisely the Torah-observant Jewish captives who outweighed all the sages, wizards and diviners of the Babylonian empire.

The closing verse of our present chapter (v 21) which tells us that Daniel remained in a position of influence until "the first year of King Koresh (=Cyrus)", is open to a variety of interpretations (see Rashi ad loc.) Some rabbis held that Daniel retained his influence only until the reign of Koresh I, who ruled before Ahashverosh, while others held that he remained until the reign of Koresh II (=Darius II) who ruled after Ahashverosh (Megillah 15a). The chronology of the empires that succeeded that of Babylon will be discussed in later commentaries.

CHAPTER 2

Although the dream of Nebuchadnezzar is dated in our text as having taken place in "the second year of the reign (**Malchut**, kingship) of Nebuchadnezzar." (v 1), Rashi (ad loc.) points out that this cannot be taken literally since Daniel was not yet in Bablyon. What the text means is that this was in the second year after the destruction of the Temple, for then Nebuchadnezzar attained the height of temporal, unholy **Malchut** when he displayed his brazen arrogance in entering into the Sanctuary of the King of the Universe.

After his dream, "his spirit was troubled", **vatit-pa'em rucho**. Nebuchadnezzar's dream is compared to Pharaoh's dream of the seven cows and seven ears of corn, except that in Pharaoh's case, it says **vati-pa'em rucho** (Gen. 41:8), whereas in the case of Nebuchadnezzar the grammatical form of the Hebrew verb is the "doubled" **hitpa'el - vatit-pa'em rucho** implying double trouble, because on waking up, Pharaoh forgot the interpretation but did remember the dream, whereas Nebuchadnezzar forgot both the interpretation **and the dream itself**.

Metzudat David on verse 2 explains that the **Chartoomim** that Nebuchadnezzar summoned to tell him what he had dreamed and what it meant were experts in natural sciences and psychological explanations of dreams while the **Asaphim** were medical doctors who understood how bodily changes are reflected in the pulse, urine etc. The **Mechashphim** were astrologers who used the positions of planets etc. in interpreting various phenomena including dreams, while the **Kasdim** were experts in the constellations and could understand a person's destiny by knowing the hour at which he was born. Rashi (on Daniel 1:20) says the **Chartoomim** used to use human bones for divination.

In response to Nebuchadnezzar's outlandish demand to be told the very dream that he himself had forgotten, the **Kasdim**, who had the reputation for being the most deeply immersed in the occult arts as well as the cruellest, switched into speaking Aramaic - the lingua franca of Mesopotamia and Syria - so that everyone present should be able to understand and see how ridiculous the king's demand was in order to shame him into backtracking. Much of the rest of the book of Daniel is written in the same courtly Aramaic, with its very stately cadences and a style somewhat more ornate than the classic chiseled simplicity of biblical Hebrew.

The **Kasdim** explained to the king that he was asking for something far too weighty "and there is no one else (**aharan**) who can tell the king except the gods, whose dwelling is not with flesh" (v 11). The Midrash states that (by reading the letter **Chet** of **acharan** as a **Heh**) the **Kasdim** were saying that "there is no **Aharon**" - i.e. the only person who could have told the king his dream would have been **Aharon** the High Priest - i.e. the High Priest of the destroyed Temple in Jerusalem, who could have consulted the **Urim ve-Turim**. Nebuchadnezzar was enraged because those same **Kasdim** had advised him to destroy the Temple, and this is why he now ordered them all to be killed (Rashi on v 11).

The decree extended to all the wise men in Babylon, including Daniel and his companions Chananiyah, Misha'el and Azariah, but through the power of their sanctity and prayer and Daniel's exalted holiness, God revealed the secret of the dream to him. Like Joseph when he explained to Pharaoh the meaning of his dream, Daniel emphasized to Nebuchadnezzar that God alone had the power to reveal the dream and its meaning to him - as if Daniel himself were a mere channel (v 27): Daniel's whole purpose was to **sanctify the name of God**.

With the collapse of the Davidic kingdom of holiness as a temporal world power, the **Malchut** had fallen to the **Kelipot** ("husks"), of which - after Pharaoh king of Egypt - Nebuchadnezzar was the golden **head**. Thus, in the second year after the destruction of the Holy Temple in Jerusalem, Nebuchadnezzar in his dream envisaged **himself** and all that would come after him until the end of time as the unholy **Malchut** worked its way through to the end of its internal logic, leading eventually to its own destruction by the **Malchut** of **Mashiach** (the stone that smashes the statue).

We are blessed to have very great rabbinic commentators on the book of Daniel. Besides Rashi and Metzudat David, the standard classical commentators, we also have the outstanding commentary of **Rabbeinu Saadia Gaon** (892-942, Egypt and Israel) and that of R. Avraham **Ibn Ezra**, both of which provide crucial insights into the meaning of the imagery in Daniel's visions.

All the commentators are agreed that the golden head of the statue is Nebuchadnezzar while the silver chest and arms are the empires of Medea and Persia that followed (as we will read later on in Daniel, Ezra and Nehemiah and also in Esther). All are agreed that the bronze belly and thighs allude to the Greek empire that started with the conquests of Alexander of Macedon. R. Saadia Gaon states that some commentators identified the iron legs exclusively with Aram (=Edom, Rome), but he takes issue with this as it leaves no room for the empire of Ishmael. He himself endorses the view that the fourth kingdom is divided between Aram (iron) and Ishmael (clay). As to their being "iron mixed with miry clay, they shall mingle themselves with the seed of men": this signifies that Jewish seed will be mixed in with these peoples as will the seed of many other peoples living with them - except that they will not be truly attached to one another just as iron and clay don't hold together.

[We can see aspects of this end-of-time prediction in today's kind-of alliance between Britain-U.S.A. and Saudi Arabia etc. The degree of intermingling of Jewish seed in many nations can be gauged from today's rates of intermarriage and assimilation.]

All the commentators are agreed that the stone that smashes the statue (v 34-5) - which Daniel explains as the **Malchut** that will never ever be destroyed - is the **Malchut** of Melech HaMashiach that we are awaiting soon in our times.

On hearing Daniel tell him his dream and its meaning, both of which Nebuchadnezzar knew but had forgotten, the king fell down to worship him like a god - but Daniel refused to be treated as a god and did not accept the king's gifts, because Daniel knew that God exacts retribution not only from idol worshippers but also from the gods they worship (Bereishit Rabbah 96).

CHAPTER 3

Having heard Daniel's interpretation of his dream - that the empires of the nations would be destroyed while the kingdom of Israel would endure - Nebuchadnezzar was determined to make Israel stumble and find a way to destroy them, and this was why he immediately built his golden idol (R. Saadia Gaon). ARI explains that the idol was **sixty cubits high** corresponding to the six main Sefirot of Chessed – Gevurah – Tiferet – Netzach – Hod – Yesod, each of which is composed of all ten Sefirot

(6 x 10 = 60). Nebuchadnezzar sought to turn the Kindness of Zeir Anpin into severe Judgment (Sefer HaLikutim, Daniel).

It is said that he chose to erect his idol in the Valley of Doura (v 1) because this was where Adam's buttocks were formed. R. Saadia Gaon states that the Valley was full of the bones of Israelite exiles from the tribe of Ephraim who had been slain by the **Kasdim**, and the king wanted to frighten all his subjects into submission. In revenge for Nebuchadnezzar's brazen arrogance, God commanded Ezekiel to bring the dry bones back to life in this same Valley of Doura (Sanhedrin 92b).

It seems as if Nebuchadnezzar wanted to establish a new world religion, which would explain why he brought together such a huge array of officials and representatives of so many different lands (v 2). For the jubilant inauguration of his idol he assembled an enormous symphony orchestra: the list of the many different kinds of instruments includes many that had formerly been played in the Temple in Jerusalem.

The Chaldean slanderers who denounced Daniel's three companions, Chananiyah (Shadrakh), Misha'el (Meishakh) and Azariah (Abed-nego), to Nebuchadnezzar were jealous of the fact that at Daniel's request they had been appointed to supervise all the royal ministers (Daniel 2:49).

When Nebuchadnezzar threatened the three with burning in his furnace and arrogantly asked them, "Which god will save you from my hands?" (v 15), they replied without hesitation that the God they served had the power to save them, and that even if He did not - for they did not rely on their own merits or on miracles - they would still not worship Nebuchadnezzar's idol. In other words, they were ready to sacrifice themselves even without being saved.

In the words of the Midrash, the three companions told Nebuchadnezzar: "When it comes to all the various taxes you impose on us you are king, but if you are telling us to worship idols, you and a dog are just the same and you are no king" (Yalkut Shimoni). It was this that enraged the king (v 19) causing him to have the furnace stoked sevenfold. The fourth figure that Nebuchadnezzar saw walking unscathed through the fire was the angel Gabriel, "who was following after the three companions like a student after his teacher, to teach you that the Tzaddikim are greater than the ministering angels! When Nebuchadnezzar saw the angel Gabriel, he immediately recognized him and all his limbs quaked and trembled. He said, 'This is the angel I saw in Sennacherib's war, and he appeared like a river of fire that burned up his entire camp'" (Yalkut Shimoni).

Nebuchadnezzar's recognition of the saving power of HaShem was a great **sanctification of His Name** during the very exile of Israel - and as we see from vv 31ff, Nebuchadnezzar wrote a letter to all the peoples of his empire praising the supreme God. A number of the beautiful Aramaic phrases from this letter are woven into the Shabbat table song **Kah Ribbon** found in most Siddurs and collections of Shabbat Zemirot.

CHAPTER 4

In order to interpret yet another of his mysterious and terrifying dreams, Nebuchadnezzar felt obliged to turn again to Daniel, "...because I know that the spirit of the Holy God is with you and no secret is withheld from you" (v 6).

The essential moral of the dream is that man's pride - a trait associated with human **Malchut**, kingship, government, power - is an affront to God, Who brings down and humbles the mighty in order to teach them that everything they have is only His gift.

Nebuchadnezzar had ascended to the greatest heights as a conqueror and ruler of a world empire. He had built up Babylon as an enormous metropolis whose magnificent buildings were the very wonder of the world. But he said in his heart, "My power and the strength of my hand has made for me all this might" (Deut. 8:17). He had to learn the same lesson that we all have to learn: that no matter what we may have achieved, whether materially or spiritually, there is no place for vanity and arrogance because everything we have has been given to us by God not because of our own intrinsic worth or merit but only through His kindness and compassion.

The great tree in Nebuchadnezzar's dream with its beautiful branches and abundant fruit providing food for all, shade for all the animals and branches for all the birds, was none other than the king himself, who is the **Parnass** - provider of livelihood and sustenance for all. Thus, **Malchut** is called the **Parnass**, source of **parnassah**.

It was Rabbi Nachman of Breslov who revealed that the angel that came to cut down Nebuchadnezzar's mighty **Malchut** and teach him the lesson of his life was a manifestation of the soul and spirit of **Rashbi** - Rabbi Shimon Bar Yochai, author of the outstanding kabbalistic treasure, the holy Zohar. In verse 10, "a watcher and a holy one came down from heaven", the initial letters of the Hebrew words, **E-er V-kadeesh M-in SH-emaya Na-heet**, are an anagram of the name Shim'on (Preface to Likutey Moharan Part I).

To teach Nebuchadnezzar his lesson and humble his arrogant heart, he was to be literally cast down from his kingship and transformed into a beast living wild with the animals eating grass and moistened with dew. Stripped of his human intellect and sensibilities, he would have the heart of a beast for seven years.

The decree against Nebuchadnezzar is reminiscent of the similar decree against his counterpart on the side of holiness, King Solomon, who was tricked by Ashmodai ("Asmodeus") king of the demons into giving him his protective ring, after which the demon king banished Solomon from his kingdom forcing him to wander for years until he was restored (Targum and Rashi on Ecclesiastes 1:12; Sanhedrin 20b).

King Solomon recorded the moral of what he learned about the world during his period of humiliating banishment in the last work of his life, Ecclesiastes. Daniel spelled out the essential lesson that Nebuchadnezzar was to learn from his banishment here in our chapter, v 22: "You will be driven from men and your dwelling will be with the beasts of the field... until you know that the Supreme God rules over the kingdom of men and that He gives it to whoever He pleases".

Ordinary citizens like ourselves should also learn from this that it is God who has appointed all of the world leaders of today, and He alone decides whom to raise up and whom to bring down. Instead of complaining about our "leaders" we should ask what we can do to improve things in the realm where we have influence: the spiritual realm.

Each one should also take to heart the existential message of this chapter to all men - for there comes a time when each one of us must meet our end, and the body goes back to the earth from which it came, and the soul returns to her Maker.

Having interpreted Nebuchadnezzar's dream, Daniel advised him to redeem his sins with charity. The rabbis taught that Daniel was punished for advising the wicked Nebuchadnezzar how to save himself, because "Charity elevates a People (=Israel), but the kindness of the nations is a sin" (Proverbs 14:34). "All the kindness that the idolatrous nations perform is accounted to them as a sin because they do it only in order for their power to endure" (Bava Batra 10b). Some say Daniel's penalty was to be thrown into the lions' den, while others say that Daniel is identical with Chatach (Esther 4:5-6 & 9) who was killed by Haman (Bava Batra 4a).

For a whole year Nebuchadnezzar gave charity to support the exiles from Judea, who had been reduced to begging (Rashi on v 24) but one time he heard the noise of the crowds of poor people he had agreed to support, and he regretted not having used the money to embellish Babylon even more grandiosely. He decided to stop giving charity (Rashi on v 25), and: "At the end of twelve months he was walking in the palace... and said, ''Is this not great Babylon that I have built up by the might of my power.'" (vv 26- 27). No sooner had the words left his mouth than the decree as foretold in his dream was fulfilled exactly as Daniel had interpreted it, and Nebuchadnezzar was banished from his kingdom until he learned the truth.

CHAPTER 5

According to the dating system of Midrash Seder Olam, Nebuchadnezzar had come to power in Babylon in 3319 (441 B.C.E.) and ruled for 45 years until his death in 3364 (396 B.C.E.). He was succeeded by his son Eveel Merodakh, who ruled for 23 years, after which Belshazzar, Nebuchad-nezzar's second son (Rashi on v 1), ruled for two years until 3389 (371 B.C.E.) It was in that year that Darius king of Medea fought against Belshazzar, killed him and captured Babylon, as recorded in the closing verse of our present chapter (v 30). Thus, Babylon ruled for a total of 70 years.

Rashi (on verse 1) says, "We find in Josephus that Belshazzar fought against Darius the Mede and Cyrus (Darius' son-in-law) by day and conquered them in battle, and in the evening he made his great feast, and it was during the meal that his enemies returned and fought against the city and conquered it."

Nebuchadnezzar may have learned God's lesson, but he failed to teach it to his son Belshazzar, who at the height of his drunken jubilation over his imagined victory ordered the gold and silver vessels that Nebuchadnezzar had looted from the Holy Temple in Jerusalem to be brought out for use in his idolat-rous feast.

THE ORIGINAL WRITING ON THE WALL

The mysterious message of doom that appeared on the walls of Belshazzar's palace at the height of the banquet was inscribed by the fingers of a frightening human-looking hologram of a hand. The Talmud (Sanhedrin 21b-22a) brings a variety of opinions about why neither the king nor any of the Chaldean sages, wizards, astrologers, necromancers or other diviners could decipher the writing. One is that the script in which the Torah scroll was written changed in the days of Ezra (which were now beginning with the demise of Babylon) and no-one knew the new script. Other opinions hold that in any case the message was written in the **Atbash** cipher (where Aleph is replaced with Tav, Beit with Shin, etc.).

It would appear that since the death of Nebuchadnezzar, Daniel had been relegated to a position of lesser influence, but now while everybody panicked, the Queen (Mother?) suddenly remembered the divinely-gifted grace-crowned Daniel, who was summoned to foretell the imminent first stage in the collapse of Nebuchadnezzar's dream-image of gold, silver, copper, iron and clay as he had originally interpreted it (Chapter 2) - the fall of the golden head, Babylon.

Daniel rejected the gifts of purple robes, gold chains and rule over one third of the empire that Belshazzar offered him in return for deciphering the message. Daniel did everything not for gain but only **Li-Shmah,** in order to sanctify the Name of God. Despite the fact that in speaking to Belshazzar he knew he was addressing another world autocrat no less arrogant and ruthless than his father, Daniel did not shrink from delivering his message of reproof and doom. After reminding Belshazzar of the forgotten lesson learned by Nebuchadnezzar, he says, "You his son Belshazzar... have not humbled your heart..." (v 22). "You took the Temple vessels and used them to praise gods of silver and gold, copper, iron, wood and stone that do not see or hear or know anything, but you gave no honor to God, in Whose hands are your soul and all your ways" (v 23).

Each generation has to learn the same lesson again. The days of Babylonian supremacy had been numbered and were now complete. Belshazzar had been weighed in the scales and found wanting, and the Babylonian empire therefore broke in pieces as the ascendant star of Medea rose over the world.

CHAPTER 6

Darius the Mede conquered Babylon in 3389 (371 B.C.E.) and thus the center of power moved northeast across from Babylon to the Medean capital of Ahmata (present-day Hamadan in western Iran approximately midway between the Caspian Sea and the Persian Gulf). Darius ruled for only one year before he was killed, after which the center of power moved again, this time to neighboring Persia, with its capital in Persopolis (near present-day Shiraz in south west Iran).

Our text (v 1) notes that Darius was sixty-two when he took power, from which we may learn that he was born in the same year that Nebuchadnezzar took King Yeho-yachin of Judah into exile in Babylon: thus, at the very moment that Nebuchadnezzar was building his empire, God had already prepared its nemesis! (Rashi ad loc.)

Darius was another world emperor, although apparently somewhat mellower than the cruel, ruthless tyrants who preceded him. Our present chapter gives us something of a feel for the extensive governmental apparatus of satraps and presidents that was necessary to rule over this patchwork empire consisting of peoples of so many different cultures and languages.

Daniel, who had foretold the downfall of Belshazzar's Babylon at the hands of Darius and who immediately became the latter's favorite advisor, was appointed to supervise the entire apparatus, being placed above all the satraps and their presidents - which caused intense jealousy on their part. It is a sign of the balance of power that prevailed in Darius' regime that the satraps and presidents were not only capable of getting their own legislation passed (vv 8-10) but could even force the king to keep to their laws against his will (v 16).

Having failed to find anything incriminating in Daniel's personal conduct, these prototypical anti-Semites decided to catch him out on religious grounds by instituting a new personality-cult religion based on emperor worship that predated Roman emperor worship and Christianity by about four hundred years. The satraps and presidents of Medea legislated a new political correctness that forbade anybody to pray to any other god except the emperor.

Quite unfazed, Daniel continued the life of prayer that he had always followed both in his childhood in Jerusalem and ever since he went into exile. Three times a day he would face in the direction of the place of the Temple in Jerusalem, kneeling down to bless, pray and give thanks to God through open windows (v 11). This text is one of the main biblical sources of the laws of prayer (Berachot 31a) including the law that a synagogue should have windows (preferably twelve).

After Daniel was caught praying to the true God and thereby contravening the new law of Persia and Medea that gave the emperor a monopoly on receiving worship, even King Darius was unable to rescue his wise and beloved favorite from being thrown into the lions' den. Beside himself with worry, Darius could not bring himself to eat or sleep and rose with the first light of morning full of foreboding - only to find that Daniel was alive and well, sitting among the peaceful, entranced lions, whose mouths had been closed by God's angel (v 23).

This miracle was another tremendous **sanctification of God's Name** that lives on in a story that has been told and retold from generation to generation. The righteous were redeemed while the wicked slanderers who tried to denounce Daniel got their just deserts and suffered the very penalty they tried to inflict on him, being torn to pieces by the lions.

It is a sign of the enlightened atmosphere that prevailed thereafter under Darius (as under Cyrus of Persia, who followed him) that Darius wrote to all the provinces of his empire telling everyone to revere the God of Daniel, Who "delivers and rescues and works signs and wonders in heaven and on earth..." (v 28).

CHAPTER 7

"There is no before and after in the Torah". The dreams of Daniel recounted in the present chapter are dated to "the first year of Belshazzar king of Babylon" (v 1) which was prior to his overthrow by Darius the Mede who was the central character in the previous chapter.

Daniel is not considered as one of the prophets, yet his dreams and visions reach to the most sublime heights of the universe. The present vision beginning with the four winds churning up the great sea (=Binah, the Sea of Wisdom comprising the 50 - YaM - Gates of Understanding) encompasses the entire sweep of world history from the ascendancy of Babylon until the end of time and the rule of Melech Ha-Mashiach.

A single stone lion is all that remains today in the ruins of ancient Babylon in Iraq to testify to the lost glory of that fallen empire. Many similar carved images of all kinds of fearsome beasts must have adorned the Babylonian capital in its heyday, and these would have helped make the imagery in Daniel's account of his dream of monsters even more real and graphic in the minds of those who heard them in his time and afterwards.

Rashi on verse 4 brings proof texts from Jeremiah 4:7 and 48:40 associating the first monster - the lion with eagle's wings - with the empire of Babylon itself, which in the time of Belshazzar was just about to have its wings clipped and get cut down to size.

The second monster, in the form of a bear, is associated with Persia - then in the ascendant - since "the Persians eat and drink like a bear and are wrapped in a thick coat of flesh like a bear" (Rashi on v 5). The three ribs in its mouth correspond to the three kings of Persia, Cyrus, Ahashverosh and Darius the Persian (Rashi).

The leopard (v 6) is associated with Greece, and its four wings correspond to the four kingdoms into which the Greek empire split after the death of Alexander of Macedon. The Greeks were compared to a leopard because they imposed a succession of evil decrees against the Jews that were like a leopard's spots, each one strange and different from the others (Rashi).

Daniel's vision of the fourth monster came in a separate dream on its own (v 7) because it was more powerful than the three that preceded it (Rashi ad loc.). Rashi and R. Saadia Gaon agree that the fourth monster alludes to Aram (=Edom, Rome) and that its ten horns correspond to the ten emperors up until Vespasian, in whose time the Second Temple was destroyed. Where these two commentators differ is on the identification of the little horn that came up among the others, which had "eyes like the eyes of a man and a mouth speaking great things" (v 8). Rashi identifies this with the ranting Titus, who entered the Temple Sanctuary in Jerusalem with a harlot before desecrating and destroying it. Rashi does not mention the empire of Ishmael (which is less than surprising when we consider that he was living in eleventh century France-Germany in what was part of the well-entrenched " Holy Roman Empire "). On the other hand, R. Saadia Gaon - who lived a century earlier in Egypt and Israel and could witness the rise of Islam from close at hand - identifies the eleventh horn with Ishmael. In R. Saadia's commentary on Nebuchadnezzar's dream of the statue of gold, silver, bronze, iron and clay (Daniel 2:40ff), he discusses in detail the complex interrelationship between Aram and Ishmael and their respective spheres of influence (see also Ibn Ezra on Daniel 2:39). Rambam (Letters) identifies the "mouth speaking great things" with the founder of Islam.

"As I looked, thrones were placed and the Ancient of Days sat..." (v 9). The depiction of the heavenly court sitting in judgment over the world is the source of many kabbalistic teachings about God's providence, including the name given in the Zohar to the divine **Partzuf** ("persona") of Arich Anpin, **Atik Yamin** ("the Ancient of Days"). His "garb like white snow" and "the hair of His head like clean wool" (ibid.) allude to the attributes of loving kindness and compassion that characterize the Partzuf of Arich Anpin.

One by one the successive monsters were cast aside, until the fourth was destroyed and burned up by fire. Their lives were prolonged only "for a season and a time" (v 12) until "one like a son of man came with the clouds of heaven and came to the Ancient of Days." (v13). All the commentators agree that the "son of man" is Mashiach (note that he is **not** called the "son of God"), who will receive "dominion and glory and a kingdom, that all the peoples, nations and tongues should serve him - an everlasting dominion that shall not pass away, and a kingdom that shall not be destroyed" (v 14).

"I came to one of them that stood by" (v 16): it was to an "angel" (=intelligent celestial being) that Daniel turned for an explanation of the vision. The angel told Daniel that in the end the kingdom will be inherited by **Kadishey Elyon**, the "holy ones of the Most High..."(v 18) - these are the restored, rectified saints of Israel.

As to when this will happen, our text is of course famously cryptic. Speaking to Daniel 2,300 years ago, the angel revealed that the eleventh horn would inflict many painful decrees and chastisements upon Israel "for a season and seasons and half a season" (v 25). Anyone who wants to speculate on how long this may be is welcome to do so, but those who believe with simple faith will take on trust the words of R. Saadia Gaon (ad loc.): "All the sages and commentators, including those with genuine Torah knowledge, have found no way to unlock and understand this calculation, and no one knows the secret except God, as it is written, 'For the day of vengeance is in my heart' (Isaiah 63:4). If the heart has not revealed it to the mouth, how would the mouth reveal it to a mere angel? We simply have to wait and hope until He will have mercy on his people and His city. Amen."

CHAPTER 8

The text now reverts from Aramaic to Hebrew for the remainder of the book of Daniel. Chapters 2-7, which were in Aramaic, the lingua franca of the Babylonian and Persian Empires, speak of Daniel's interactions with their rulers and the profound universal lessons they had to learn about how God deals with man "measure for measure". In the coming chapters the lessons are directed more specifically to Israel yearning for the rebuilding of Jerusalem, and they contain a deep **Pnimiut** (interiority) that Hebrew is uniquely fit to express.

DANIEL

Daniel records the graphic external images of his visions, and then tells how angels come to him to interpret and explain them, thereby bringing him to the level of **Binah**. We in turn must rely on R. Saadia Gaon, Rashi and the other great commentators who have come down to us to explain Daniel's visions.

The vision in our present chapter is dated to the third year of Belshazzar, the last king of Babylon. His empire was on the verge of collapse, and we find Daniel in Shushan, which is located in what is now western Iran between Hamadan and Shiraz: it had been the capital of Eilam and now became the main center of the Persian empire.

This vision is the second in a series (v 1) the first of which was in the previous chapter (7). The imagery of these visions is in each case different, but the **nimshal** - the object of the comparison - is the ultimate one: the great sweep of history until the "end of days".

In his vision, Daniel saw himself standing by **Ooval Ooloi**, which some render as the River **Ooloi**, although R. Saadia says there is no river in Shushan and that this was the mighty gate of the city. **Ooloi** would then be related to the word **Eil**, "mighty one" - and this in turn is related to the word **Ayil**, a "ram", one of the creatures Daniel saw, representing the rising star of Persia.

The classical commentators agree that the larger and smaller horns of the ram (v 3) allude respectively to Persia, the greater power, and Medea, the lesser power. Thus, under Queen Esther's Ahashverosh, Persia extended "from India to Africa", while Darius the Mede ruled for only one year before giving over the kingship to his son-in-law, Cyrus of Persia (father of Esther's Ahashverosh).

The goat alludes to Greece. The horn signifies Alexander of Macedon, who defeated Darius of Persia, who was Esther's son. Yet Alexander died at the very height of his power, and his kingdom split into four (v 8).

"And out of one of them came a little horn that became exceedingly great" (v 9). Rashi interprets this horn as alluding to Titus, and he takes the phrase in verse 10 - "And it grew great, even to the host of heaven..." - to refer to his destruction of the Second Temple. On the other hand, R. Saadia Gaon sees this horn as an allusion to the empire of Ishmael (Islam) which took the land of beauty (v 9, =Israel) from the Romans.

"And for an appointed time, it was flagrantly set against the daily sacrifice, and it cast down the truth to the ground..." (v 12). Rashi (ad loc.) says this means that idolatry would be established in Jerusalem instead of the daily Temple offerings.

It is when the focus of the vision moves to Jerusalem, the heart of the world (**Binah**), that Daniel hears a celestial conversation between the angels asking "How long shall be the vision... to give both the sanctuary and the host to be trodden under foot" (v 13). As to the calculation of how long this will be as given in verse 14, Rashi (ad loc.) comments: "The seer was commanded to close up and seal the matter, and even to him it was revealed in a language that is closed up and sealed, and we shall wait in hope for the fulfillment of the promise of our King, even if one 'end' after another passes by."

The angel Gabriel is sent to explain the vision to Daniel - yet the explanation itself is so beyond him that he falls into a slumber until the angel touches him and brings him to his feet (v 18). Gabriel teaches "what will be in the latter end of the indignation, for it is at the end of a long time" (v 19). Rashi explains the "king of fierce countenance" mentioned in v 23 as referring to Titus, who destroyed the Second Temple, but R. Saadia Gaon explains this as a reference to the kingship of Ishmael.(R. Saadia also gives an alternative explanation relating the entire vision primarily to the struggle between Persia and Greece.)

We should remember that at the time of Daniel's vision the destruction of the Second Temple was over 450 years in the future and it was no mean feat to foretell how it would come about. At the same time, the vision is multi-layered, and just as history goes around in cycles, so the imagery can allude to multiple levels all at once.

CHAPTER 9

Very soon after his vision in the previous chapter, Daniel "pondered in the books the number of the years..." (v 2). This was in the first (and only) year of the reign of Darius son of Ahashverosh the Mede. (This was **not** the Ahashverosh of Megillat Esther). Little more than a year after conquering Babylon, Darius the Mede gave over the kingship to his son-in-law Cyrus of Persia, who was the father of Esther's Ahashverosh.

Daniel had watched the fall of Babylon knowing that it had been prophesied by Jeremiah (29:10), who had foretold that at the completion of seventy years of Babylonian power, God would redeem Israel. At first Daniel thought that the building of the (second) Temple and complete redemption would come about seventy years from the time that Babylon had first subjected Israel to her dominion, which was when Nebuchadnezzar conquered King Yehoyakim eighteen years prior to destruction of the First Temple. It was only from the words of the angel at the end of this chapter that Daniel understood that the new Temple would not be built until seventy years after the actual destruction of the First Temple by the Babylonians in the reign of King Tzidkiyahu.

Daniel's response to the seemingly interminable exile was to **pray**. The Tzaddik repents for all Israel, and in his most eloquent prayer for redemption Daniel speaks in the first-person plural, putting fitting words of repentance and supplication into the mouths of all of us. Many phrases and indeed entire passages (vv 15-20) are incorporated into the **Tachanun** supplication as recited on Mondays and Thursdays as well as into many other penitential **Selichot**.

Daniel begins his prayer with the confession of sin (vv 5ff) expressing our deep shame and contrition over the misdemeanors that have led to our national exile. The prayer is designed to guide us to internalize the bitter lesson and moral of the destruction of the Temple and the exile, which came about exactly as the Torah had warned (v 13).

Daniel appeals to God's compassion, arousing the memory of the redemption from Egypt (v 15) as he begs God to turn His anger from Jerusalem.

With hindsight we know that the Second Temple was built in due course, but Daniel was praying eighteen years beforehand at a time when the satraps and governors of Babylon and Persia were no doubt gloating over the exile of the troublesome Jews and drumming in the message that they would never be restored.

Through Daniel's profound faith and earnest prayer, he was "greatly beloved" (v 23) in God's eyes, and was worthy of ascending to the level of **Binah** (v 22), for the angel Gabriel came swooping down from the heavens to further elucidate the meaning of the visions in the previous chapters and enlighten him as to when the Temple would be rebuilt. Rashi (vv 25ff) explains that the cryptic message of the angel alludes to the building of the Second Temple and its subsequent destruction by Titus, and how in the end he will be accursed and lost when the power of his empire is swept away by Mashiach in the war of

Gog and Magog. Although the place of the Temple is presently occupied by non-Jews, this will endure only until the decreed day with the coming of Mashiach.

CHAPTER 10

The vision in our present chapter is dated to the third year of Koresh (Cyrus) king of Persia (v 1). Cyrus was given the kingship by his father-in-law Darius the Mede in the year 3390 (370 B.C.E.) and ruled for only three years. Initially he permitted the rebuilding of the Temple in Jerusalem, but soon afterwards the work was suspended owing to the denunciations against the Jews by their enemies, as we will read in detail in the book of Ezra, which we shall God willing be studying after Daniel.

Rashi (on verse 2) explains that Daniel's period of mourning and abstention lasted for **three sabbatical cycles**, i.e. 21 years, from the time Darius the Mede conquered Babylon (which was when Daniel tried to calculate when the restoration would take place, see ch 9 v 2) until the second year of the reign of Darius the Persian, the son of Esther, under whom the Second Temple was completed.

To abstain from fine bread, meat, wine and anointment for all this time in mourning over the desolation of Jerusalem was an extraordinary feat, and in the merit of his undertaking to do so Daniel was granted the extraordinary vision of the end of time in this and the ensuing chapters. Just as his vision in ch 8 v 2 was by the River **Ooloi**, so the present vision was at the River Tigris, and similarly Ezekiel's vision of the Chariot was at the River Kvar - these are spiritual rivers flowing with the light of divine revelation.

Daniel now saw "the man dressed in linen", whom he describes in truly spectacular terms (vv 5-6). Only Daniel saw this apparition, but "the men who were with me did not see the vision, but great trembling fell upon them" (v 7). According to our sages, Daniel's companions were the prophets Haggai, Zechariah and Malachi (Megillah 3a; Rashi on v 7). Prophets had their own methods of rising to the level where they were worthy to have the voice of God speak through them (see Rabbi Aryeh Kaplan, "Meditation & the Bible"), but even these prophets were unable to see what Daniel, the righteous sage, now saw.

Ibn Ezra on v 5 points out that Daniel's ability to stand in the face of the revelation of an angel exceeded that of Gideon and Samson's parents, Manoah and his wife (Judges 6:22-3 and 13:22). This indicates that **Yeridat HaDorot** (the spiritual decline that occurs from generation to generation) is not necessarily irreversible by Tzaddikim on the highest of levels. Similarly, in recent generations Rabbi Nachman mentioned his having received visits from the guardian angels of nations like Greece (= Russia?) and France (see Tzaddik – Chayey Moharan -- #489).

The "man dressed in linen" whom Daniel saw had also been seen by the prophet Ezekiel prior to the destruction of the First Temple (Ezekiel 9:2; 10:11). The sages identified him with the angel Gabriel (see Yoma 77a) as does Rashi (on ch 11 v 1). Eichah Rabbati states that the "man dressed in linen" serves three functions: (1) Executioner of **Harugey Malchut**, those to be killed on the decree of the King; (2) High Priest - for he wears linen, like the High Priest on Yom Kippur; (3) Heavenly scribe.

As the "man dressed in linen" tells Daniel (v 12), it was in the merit of his having undertaken to fast on behalf of Israel and Jerusalem that his prayers were heard and Gabriel was turned into the defender of Israel.

The "man dressed in linen" opens a chink in the heavy veil that covers over the proceedings before the Heavenly Court, where the guardian angels of the various nations advance their pleas and counter-pleas. The "man dressed in linen" tells Daniel that "the guardian angel of Persia has been standing against me for 21 days [of heavenly time]" (v 13). Rashi explains (ad loc.): "He has been fighting with me in heaven asking for an extension for the empire of Persia in order to keep Israel subject". The "man dressed in linen" has been resisting this, and has now come to enable Daniel to understand what will happen to his people "in the end of days" (v 14). This vision of the future, which begins in the next chapter, covers the entire period of the Second Temple including its destruction and thereafter up until the final redemption.

CHAPTER 11

"As for me, in the first year of Darius the Mede, I stood up to confirm and strengthen **him**" (v 1). It is the "man dressed in linen", the angel Gabriel, who is speaking in this entire chapter, and as explained by Rashi (ad loc.) he stood up to strengthen the angel Michael - Israel's guardian angel - against the pleas by the guardian angel of Persia before the Heavenly Court to intensify Israel's burden of exile.

"And now I will tell you the truth" (v 2): this is the beginning of a very long, involved and detailed prophecy which according to Ibn Ezra (on v 3) covers the entire history of the world from the time of Daniel until the destruction of the Second Temple (vv 5-31) and from then on until the final redemption (vv 32-40).

Verse 2 speaks about the empire of Persia. The "fourth king" mentioned here is Darius the Persian, son of Ahashverosh and Esther, who mobilized his entire empire to fight against Greece and was defeated.

Verse 3 refers to Alexander of Macedon, and verse 4 speaks of how his empire split into four kingdoms.

From that time on the two dominant players on the world scene were the kings of the south and the north. Metzudat David on v 5 identifies the king of the south with Egypt and the king of the north with Greece/Rome. Students of world history may see certain parallels between the back-and-forth conflicts between these two as foretold in this chapter and world conflicts in more recent times. In some respects, the wars between the colonialist empires and their subject nations (the "Third World") and between the West vs. Islam are conflicts between the kings of the north and the south!

Caught somewhere in the middle of the conflicts described in this chapter are Israel, who by the time of the Second Temple period were split into the righteous faithful and the wicked sinners. Rashi and R. Saadia Gaon both interpret v 14 as a reference to the way the "renegades of your people" - the sinners - repeatedly conspired and intrigued with Rome and Egypt, trying to play off the one against the other. The phrase **Bney Poritzey Amecha** ("renegades of your people") is often cited as an allusion to **That Man** (Yemach SHemo OOzichro).

Verse 20 is explained by Rashi as an allusion to the Hasmoneans (the heroes of Chanukah), who overthrew the Greek oppressors. Thereafter, however, the Hasmonean king Hyrkanus conspired with Rome to overthrow his brother Aristobulus, which led to the downfall of the Hasmonean dynasty and ever-increasing intervention by Rome until eventually they became the occupying power and destroyed the Temple. Rome is specifically alluded to in v 21 (see Rashi and Metzudat David).

Verse 31 alludes to the destruction of the Second Temple. Verse 32 speaks of the collaboration between the Jewish renegades and the Romans while the righteous Jews continued in the path of the Torah. Despite the efforts of the latter to teach the people God's ways, verse 33 speaks about their terrible suffering in the tribulations of the long exile after the destruction of the Temple.

Verses 36ff allude to the spectacular successes of Rome and the kings who inherited her mantle, whose policy was to show outward respect to the religious traditions of the people they governed in order to keep control of them (see Rashi on v 39).

The closing verses of the chapter allude to the bitter wars prior to the final redemption of Israel, may it come speedily in our times!

CHAPTER 12

Our present chapter, which concludes the book of Daniel, completes the prophecy that he received from "the man dressed in linen" about the future history of the world until the end of days. This prophecy was granted to Daniel in the merit of his mourning and self-affliction over the desolation of Jerusalem. The prophecy began in the previous chapter with the foretelling of the tangled history of the period of the Second Temple up until its destruction (Daniel 11:2-31), after which it continues with its highly allusive foretelling of the end of days (Daniel 11:32-45; 12:1-13).

"And at that time Michael shall stand" (v 1). Rashi (ad loc.) says that Israel's guardian angel will "stand" in the sense of being stopped in his tracks and silent like one struck dumb when he will see how the Holy One blessed be He will ponder how He can destroy the great armies of Gog and Magog for the sake of small Israel. It will be "a time of trouble such as there never was." (v 1). The rabbis said there will be trouble for the Torah scholars because of their enemies and accusers, and trouble for the whole people because of decree after decree and waves of robbers one after the other (Ketubot 112b).

The good news is that "your people shall be delivered" (v 1) - "the kingdom of Gog will be destroyed, and Israel shall be saved" (Rashi ibid.). [Instead of worrying whether present-day Persia will harm Israel, we should repent with all our hearts and trust in God.]

"And many of those who sleep in the dust of the earth shall awake..." (v 2). This refers to the resurrection of the dead (Rashi ad loc.) - as well, of course, to the tremendous spiritual awakening and the widespread return to the Torah that we witness in our time among Israelite souls that in some cases have been buried in exile and cultural alienation for centuries. This itself is the revival of the dead!

"And those who are wise shall shine like the brightness (**zohar**) of the firmament..." (v 3). This verse is darshened at length in the Zohar, which takes its name from here. The rabbis of the Talmud state that the category of "the wise" includes every **Dayan** ("judge") who judges truthfully as well as those who go around collecting charity, while "they who turn many to righteousness" are those who teach Torah to little children (Bava Batra 8b).

Just like the angels whom Daniel heard asking the "man dressed in linen" - "How long shall it be to the wondrous end?" (v 6) - we too are more than curious to know the answer. The "man dressed in linen" replied most cryptically, "It shall be for a time, times and a half" (v 7). Daniel himself did not understand this answer (v 8), so we should not be surprised that we cannot either. As Rashi says on verse 10, "Many shall purify themselves and make themselves white" - many will try to give a clear explanation of these calculations; "and they will be tried" - it will be a trial to many to understand them; "and the wicked shall do wickedly" - the wicked will miscalculate, and having stumbled they will say there will be no further redemption, "and they will not understand". However, "the wise shall understand" - at the time when the end arrives. (Rashi on v 10). For "in the end they will be granted the wisdom to understand the allusions" (Metzudat David on v 9).

In the words of R. Saadia Gaon (on v 7): "When the generations have descended very low, then all these troubles will come to an end, but we do not know until when they will go on since the angel himself told Daniel that the matters are sealed and closed up, and we certainly do not have the power to understand the secret of these calculations of days and years."

"Happy is the man who waits..." (v 12).

עזרא-נחמיה

EZRA-NEHEMIAH

CHAPTER 1

"And Moses ascended to God..." (Exodus 19:3). "This Ezra ascended from Babylon..." (Ezra 7:6). Citing these two verses and the word they have in common, "ascended", the rabbis compared the stature of Ezra to that of Moses, saying that Ezra too was fit to be the one through whom the Torah was given to Israel (Sanhedrin 21b).

The achievements of Ezra will be discussed later on. His book is a direct continuation of the book of Daniel - the opening verse of Ezra begins with a **Vav**, "**And** in the first year of Cyrus..." (v 1), connecting the narrative in Ezra with what went before in Daniel (Rashi on Ezra 1:1). The book of Ezra tells the story of the return of the exiles from Babylon to Judea and other parts of the Land of Israel and how the Second Temple was built. This book is therefore a most important paradigm for our time, since our task too is to return out of exile and to restore and rebuild our heritage and our Temple. The greatness of the achievement of Ezra and his generation is enhanced by the fact that so far, they had experienced only destruction but as yet no redemption. Even so, they defied all of the many accusers who sought to thwart and discourage them, and with great courage they went up to their land. For us their achievement should serve as a precedent that can guide us in the restoration that we must accomplish.

The return from the exile in Babylon took place **in stages**, the **first** of which is recorded in our present chapter and those that follow it. Although this book was written by Ezra and is called by his name, Ezra himself does not enter the narrative until Chapter 7, which describes the **second** stage of the return.

We have already seen how with the fall of Babylon to Darius the Mede, Daniel "contemplated in books." in order to calculate the number of years that had passed since God's word to Jeremiah "to accomplish seventy years in the desolations of Jerusalem" (Daniel 9:2). As discussed in our commentary there, Darius' capture of Babylon took place exactly seventy years after Nebuchadnezzar had taken Yeho-yakim king of Judah into exile - that was eighteen years before the destruction of the First Temple in the reign of King Tzidkiyahu.

The narrative in the book of Ezra begins "in the first year of Cyrus king of Persia" (v 1), whose reign began within a year of Darius the Mede's conquest of Babylon. With the fall of the Babylonian empire after seventy years, the **first wave** of returnees now went back to Judea and they started laying the foundations of the Second Temple, but - as we will read in the ensuing chapters - their enemies denounced them to Cyrus and he ordered the work to be suspended. There were no further building activities during the whole of the remainder of the reign of Cyrus and throughout that of Ahashverosh, and the building of the Temple was resumed only in the reign of his son, Darius ("the Persian") son of Queen Esther. Thus, from the time of the Aliyah of the first wave of returnees under Cyrus as recounted in our present chapter, it took another **eighteen years** until the Temple was finally rebuilt, exactly seventy years after the destruction of the First Temple.

The leadership of the first wave of returnees will be discussed in the next chapter (Ezra 2). Ezra himself did not go up to Jerusalem with the first wave of returnees because the teacher from whom he received the Torah tradition - Baruch ben Neriyah, who had received it from the prophet Jeremiah - was still alive in Babylon, and Ezra wanted to receive everything possible from his teacher. It was only after seven years, with the death of Baruch, that Ezra went up to Jerusalem with the **second wave** of returnees.

After all the years of exile under the weighty yoke of Babylon, its fall at the hands of Darius the Mede and the subsequent ascent of Cyrus to the throne of Persia were a great relief. "'So,' says Cyrus king of Persia, 'all the kingdoms of the Earth have HaShem the God of Heaven given to me, and He has commanded me to build Him a House in Jerusalem that is in Judah'" (v 2).

God's "command" to Cyrus is contained in the prophecy of Isaiah, who had lived generations earlier yet foretold that Cyrus would restore Israel to their land and have the Temple rebuilt (Isaiah 44:28; see 45:1).

The campaign of Aliyah from Babylon and the other cities of exile to the Land of Israel is somewhat reminiscent of the magnificent enterprise of Aliyah of Jews to Israel over the past centuries rising exponentially since 1948. Like the Aliyah sanctioned by Cyrus, the modern Aliyah has also been supported by many contributions from those who for one reason or another have had to remain in the Diaspora, who have formed local support groups to sustain those going up to the land (see our chapter vv 4; 6).

Cyrus' release of the Temple vessels looted by the Babylonians held forth the promise that redemption was near at hand. They were entrusted to "**Shashbatzar** the prince over Judah", v 8; the rabbis identified him with Daniel, who stood firm six (**shesh**) times when he was in trouble (**ba-tzar**; see Rashi ad loc.).

The thrill and excitement of the return of the exiles from Babylon is captured in the Song of Ascents (**Shir Ha-Ma'alot**) that is traditionally recited on Shabbat and other festive occasions immediately prior to **Birkhat Ha-Mazon**, Grace after eating bread. "When HaShem restored the captivity of Zion, we were like dreamers. Then was our mouth filled with laughter and our tongue with song. He who goes weeping in his way, bearing a bag of seed, shall come back with joy, carrying his sheaves" (Psalms 126:2 & 6).

CHAPTER 2

"And these are the children of the province who went up out of the captivity..." (v 1). Rashi paraphrases, "These are the children of Israel that were from the province of Israel [which was then a province of the Persian Empire] who went up now from the captivity in exile to Jerusalem."

Verse 2 provides us with the names of the leadership of this first wave of Aliyah from Babylon, including some familiar names like Mordechai and Nehemiah. (This Aliyah took place **before** the Purim story, as will be discussed in a future commentary: it would appear that Mordechai must have gone back to Shushan at some point after his Aliyah.)

ZERUBAVEL

The first name in the list of leaders is Zerubavel ben She'alti-el, who in Haggai 1:1 is called "governor" (**Pachat**) of Judea. Zerubavel was heir to the kingship of David, which had very nearly been wiped out completely. Two out of the last three kings of Judah had left no heirs: these were Yeho-yakim, whom Nebuchadnezzar exiled and tortured to death, and Tzidkiyahu, all of whose sons were slaughtered in front of his eyes. The last surviving member of the Davidic dynasty, Yeho-yakim's son, King Yechoniah (Yeho-yachin), whom Nebuchadnezzar had taken into exile in Babylon prior to the destruction of the Temple, also had no heir and was unlikely to have one since he was cruelly imprisoned in Nebuchadnezzar's jail in solitary confinement in a deep narrow pit.

The Midrash tells that the exiled Sanhedrin in Babylon realized the peril hanging over the House of David and turned to the Queen's old nanny asking her to try to influence the Queen to influence Nebuchadnezzar to let Yechoniah be with his wife. Eventually he agreed that she could be lowered down by rope into Yechoniah's prison pit cell, where there was barely room to stand let alone to lie down. In any case, after having been lowered down for this chance-in-a lifetime, Yechoniah's wife suddenly discovered that she had a flow of blood, which meant that relations were forbidden. Yechoniah used to ignore the laws of **Niddah** and **Zivah** when free in Jerusalem prior to his captivity, but, chastened by his sufferings in exile, he had repented and heroically refused to have relations. His wife was hauled up again and mercifully was allowed to purify herself from her flow, after which she was once again lowered down. And through their coming together standing in this cramped dark pit, the House of David was saved from extinction (Vayikra Rabba 19:6). The child born of that union was She'alti-el, father of Zerubavel.

The heirs to the Davidic throne were no longer called kings: in future, the Davidic leadership was primarily spiritual. The mantle of leadership eventually came down to Hillel, whose school became the accepted legal authority by all Jews, and a few generations afterwards it passed down to Rabbi Yehudah, known as **Ha-Nasi**, "The Prince", author of the Mishnah, which is the very foundation of the Oral Torah.

YESHUA THE HIGH PRIEST

In Haggai 1 Yeshua ben Yotzadok is called Ye**ho**shua ben Ye**ho**tzadok. His name (like the name Zerubavel) is familiar to those who read the Haftarot because it appears in the prophecy of Zechariah (2:14-3:7) which is read in the synagogue as Haftarah **twice** every year: on Shabbat Chanukah and also on Shabbat Parshat Beha'alot'cha (third parshah in Numbers, read shortly after the festival of Shavuot.)

Yehoshua was the High Priest and son of a High Priest, but some sources suggest that he might not have served as High Priest had not Ezra - who was greater in Torah and more saintly - remained initially in Babylon (Shir HaShirim Rabbah 5:5). According to Rambam, Ezra did eventually serve as High Priest. In Ezra 10:18 we find that Yehoshua's sons had intermarried, which was a stain on the family. This may be why in these texts his name and the name of his father (Ezra 3:8) are spelled without the letter **Heh**. In its form of Yeshu'a it was a not uncommon name and, despite its having apparently been given to the founder of Christianity, there is no suggestion whatever in our biblical texts that it has any kind of specifically messianic connotation.

THE RETURNEES

Rashi on verse 3 states that in some cases in this chapter the text mentions the fathers or family of the people named, in other cases the Judean towns from which they had originated and to which they now returned (v 70). Even in exile they evidently cherished their attachment to their old homes and never lost hope of returning: Diaspora Jews should take note!!!

Those who returned were not only from the tribes of Judah and Benjamin although the latter were in the majority. The total number of those who returned in this first wave of Aliyah is given in v 64 as 42,360, but the total of all the population figures given in the earlier part of the chapter - which are for members of Judah and Benjamin - is only 30,000. Seder Olam states that the remainder were from other tribes who joined this Aliyah (Rashi on v 64). Although the returning population was initially mainly concentrated in the tribal territories of Judah and Benjamin, we know from many references in the Mishnah as well as from archeological relics that during the four centuries-long period of the

Second Temple the **Yishuv** ("settlement") extended over most areas of Eretz Israel except for certain coastal areas and a strip around Shomron which was inhabited by the **Kootim** whom Sennacherib had settled in place of the Ten Tribes.

YICHUS - "LINEAGE"

We will see in the later portions of the book of Ezra that ethnic self-purification was a very important preoccupation for the leaders of the return, because even before the exile there had been a certain incidence of intermarriage between Israelites and the surrounding Canaanites, Ammonites and Moabites etc. and intermarriage increased when they went to Babylon. One of Ezra's major concerns was to clarify the personal status of the various different categories that made up the Jewish communities in Babylon that were now sending **Olim** to Israel. The fourth chapter of the Talmudic tractate **Kiddushin** begins by stating that Ten **Yichusim** ('categories of pedigree') went up from Babylon: Cohen-Priests, Levites, Israelites, Hallalim (disenfranchised priests), converts, freed slaves, Mamzerim ("bastards"), Netinim (Gibeonites), Shesuki (child of unknown fatherhood) and Asufi (child of indeterminate parentage; Kiddushin 96a). The Talmud explains that Ezra realized that with the return of the people together with the Sanhedrin to Israel, Babylon would be left without a strong rabbinic leadership. He therefore endeavored to empty Babylon of all those whose personal status was questionable so that the purity of the Babylonian community could be maintained, sending them to Israel where the rabbis of the Sanhedrin would be able to adjudicate over their status.

Thus, the list of **Olim** given in our present chapter specifies that some were Gibeonites (vv 43ff) or from among the (non-Israelite) servants of Solomon (vv 55f), while some were unable to tell their parentage or family (v 59). The status of certain priests was indeterminate and would not be able to be clarified "until a priest will stand with the **Urim ve-Turim**" (v 63), i.e. through the holy spirit that will return with the coming of Mashiach.

All these **Olim** did not travel to Israel by plane to Ben Gurion airport, and since the numbers of animals listed (v 66) are considerably smaller than those of the humans, we must infer that the great majority of the latter made the journey on foot. And what a journey it was!!! Traveling with them were **two hundred musicians** (v 65): "Because they were going up joyously from Babylon to Eretz Israel, they **needed** singers to help them turn their journey into an enjoyable walk through abundant **simchah**." (Rashi ad loc.)

CHAPTER 3

From the closing verses of the previous chapter (Ezra 2:68-70) we see that the primary goal of these **Olim** was to return to the House of God in Jerusalem and rebuild it. The present chapter traces the initial steps in the rebuilding of the Temple taken by this **first wave** of returnees.

The journey of the **Olim** across land from Babylon to Israel and their settlement in their old towns and villages in Judea must have taken much of the summer. "And when the seventh month arrived... the people gathered themselves together as one man to Jerusalem" (v 1). The first day of the seventh month (=Tishri) was Rosh HaShanah. Likewise, we will see in Nehemiah ch 8 that Rosh HaShanah was a highly propitious day in the calendar.

"And they set the altar on its bases; for fear was upon them because of the peoples of the lands." (v 3). The "peoples of the lands" were the jealous **Kootim** ("Samaritans") and other inhabitants of the surrounding areas of what was a province of the Persian Empire. As we shall see in the ensuing chapters, these assorted peoples were keeping their eyes skinned on the returning Jews waiting to pounce at any sign of rebellious activity in order to denounce them to the king. [Similarly, today "Peace Now" and hosts of other official and unofficial monitors from all over the world keep their eyes constantly skinned on the Jewish settlers in Judea and Samaria, ready to denounce them the moment they do anything that might suggest they are free people living in their own land.] Rashi on v 3 explains that the reason why Yeshu'a the High Priest and Zerubavel built and offered on the Altar was in order to make a public demonstration that they had authorization from the king of Persia in the hope of forestalling any efforts to denounce them. In the event, they did not succeed, because the accusers were soon writing letters to the Persian king anyway, as we will see in the ensuing chapters. Nevertheless, all of the daily and seasonal public sacrifices as well as private dedications were now reinstituted (v 5).

Seven months later the building work commenced, accompanied by the singing of the Levites (v 9) - what a spectacle that must have been - and the foundations of the new Temple were laid (v 10).

Despite the jubilation of the younger generation over the rebuilding of the Temple, those present who were old enough to remember the Temple of Solomon, which had been destroyed 53 years earlier, cried and sobbed so loudly that they almost drowned out the joyous singing, for this was joy mingled with the sorrow of chastened hearts.

CHAPTER 4

"And the adversaries of Judah and Benjamin heard that the children of the exiles were building the Temple" (v 1). These "adversaries" were the **Kootim** ("Samaritans") and other peoples that Sennacherib had settled in Shomron and the other cities of Israel in place of the Ten Tribes (II Kings 17:24). Their sensors were telling them that a rebuilt Jerusalem would be a serious threat to their comfort as it could herald an Israelite national revival that would bring back the Ten Tribes, who were all too likely to drive them out of the rich and pleasant land in which they had been squatting since the time of Sennacherib. [The present-day "Palestinian" Arab perception of any possibility of a Jewish revival in Israel is based on similar considerations.]

The response of the adversaries to the efforts to rebuild the Temple is an example of the way the **Sitra Achra** (the unholy side) is aroused as soon as there is an arousal on the side of the holy (Likutey Moharan I, 22:7). God sends obstacles in the way of those seeking to accomplish a holy goal in order to increase their yearning and longing to the point where they are able to do so. The time had not yet come for the building of the Second Temple, for it had already been prophesied that it would only be built seventy years after the destruction of the First Temple. Zerubavel and Yeshu'a were obliged to **try** to accomplish the holy task, but as yet they could not succeed.

The first ploy of the adversaries was to propose that they should join with the Jews in building the Temple - in order to be able to stall and sabotage the venture from within. The reply of Zerubavel and the other leaders that "You have nothing to do with us in building a House to our God" (v 3) is one of the main sources for the law forbidding receiving dedications and donations from non-Israelites for incorporation in the actual fabric of the Temple building (Rambam, Hilchot Shekalim 4:8; Erchin 1:11; Matanot Aniyim 8:8).

After this rebuff, the adversaries turned to psychological warfare (v 4) in an attempt to discourage and demoralize the Jews. In addition, they hired lobbyists in the Persian court in order to bring diplomatic pressure to bear on the king to undermine the project. We learn from verses 5-6 that this campaign was sustained for a period of more than sixteen years until the second year of the reign of Darius, king of Persia.

Cyrus I of Persia, in whose reign this campaign started, is identical with Artahshasta in v 7: this was the generic name of the Persian kings just as Pharoah was the generic name of the kings of Egypt. Cyrus reigned only two years (3390-2=370-368 B.C.E.) and was succeeded by Ahashverosh of Megillat Esther fame. The unnamed individuals who "wrote to him an accusation (**sitnah** from the root satan) against the inhabitants of Judah and Jerusalem" (v 6) are identified by Midrash Seder Olam as being none other than the sons of Haman that were eventually hanged. Aside from this reference, the Book of Ezra passes over the events in the reign of Ahashverosh, including Haman's plot against the Jews as foiled by Mordechai and Esther, in complete silence.

Having typified this sixteen-year campaign in general terms in vv 5-6, the text in verse 7 goes back to the very beginning of the period - for as mentioned earlier, Artahshasta is identical with Cyrus, who reigned for only two years before Ahashverosh came to the throne. One of the great paradoxes of Cyrus is that after having grandiloquently sanctioned the building of the Temple (Ezra 1:1ff), he then made a complete about-turn as a result of the diplomatic machinations of the adversaries.

From verse 7 onwards the text shifts into Aramaic, the lingua franca of the Persian empire, as it begins to report the correspondence passing to and fro between the adversaries of the Jews in the province of **Avar Nahara** ("West of the River Euphrates") and the imperial court. The text continues in Aramaic until Ezra 6:19.

The letter from the adversaries to Cyrus is recorded in our present chapter vv 7-16. Having established their credentials as representatives of the peoples moved into Shomron and other locations west of the Euphrates by Assnapar (=Sennacherib, vv 9-10, Rashi ad loc.), they immediately warn the king of serious trouble if the "rebellious, bad city" of Jerusalem (v 12) is ever rebuilt. [Their insinuations bear comparison with the best of latter-day anti-Jewish and anti-Israel incitement.] They warn him that any rebellion by the Jews will hit him hard **in the pocket** as they will cease paying the various poll-taxes and other kinds of tribute into the Persian treasury (v 13). They advise him to check out the imperial records to see if permission was ever granted to the Jews to rebuild their Temple. The bottom line of their message to the Persian emperor was that if the city of Jerusalem were to be rebuilt and fortified, "you won't have any portion west of the Euphrates" (v 16). If anything was calculated to make the king of a new world empire jump it was this reminder of the likely effects of any re-arousal of Jewish imperial expansionism.

In his reply to the adversaries' letter (vv 17-22), which expresses an historical awareness of the great power of Israel under its mighty kings of the past (v 20), Cyrus reversed his earlier endorsement of the project of building God's House in Jerusalem (Ezra 1:1ff). [Similarly, not long after their "Balfour Declaration" of 1917, the British government hastily backtracked from giving genuine support to the building of a Jewish homeland in Palestine, since which time Israel has suffered repeated back-stabbings from this and other professed allies.] Cyrus gave the adversaries carte blanche to interrupt the building of the Temple, which they rushed to do with all haste (v 23), and the work was stopped until the second year of the reign of Darius, king of Persia (v 24). (According to the opinion that Darius was the son of Queen Esther, he would have been no more than about six years old when he came to the throne as Esther became queen in the seventh year of the reign of Ahashverosh, who reigned thereafter for only seven more years until he was killed by one of his servants in 3406=354 B.C.E.)

CHAPTER 5

Our text now fast-forwards from the reign of Cyrus, ignoring that of Ahashverosh and jumping directly to the second year of the reign of Darius, when the building of the Temple was resumed. The prophecies of Haggai and Zechariah mentioned in verse 1 of the present chapter are found respectively in Haggai 1:1ff and Zechariah 1:1ff, both of which are date-stamped to the second year of Darius.

The prophets knew through holy spirit that with the death of Ahashverosh and the ascent of Darius to the throne of Persia, the times had changed and now the moment had come to actually build and complete the Temple, work on which started in earnest.

This holy arousal naturally elicited a counter-arousal on the part of the unholy forces and a new set of adversaries headed by Tatnai, the governor of the Persian provinces west of the Euphrates (v 3), now tried to interfere with the building project. After receiving no comfort from the Jews, they wrote to Darius drawing his attention to the unnatural speed with which the Temple was being built in Jerusalem and the unnatural success of the project (v 8).

It is perhaps a sign of the changed times after the death of Ahashverosh and the ascent of Darius to the throne that the tone of their letter is more subdued than that of the adversaries as recorded in ch 4. Now they only enquired of the new king whether it was correct that the building work proceeding apace in Jerusalem had received the sanction of King Cyrus, and as we shall see in the next chapter, Darius reply was in the affirmative.

CHAPTER 6

A MIRACULOUS FIND

The emperors of Assyria, Babylon and Persia were autocrats who were literally worshipped as gods (Daniel 6:8). The legitimacy of the new Persian king Darius depended on that of his grandfather Cyrus, founder of the empire, and this was why the discovery of a scroll recording an imperial decree from the time of Cyrus was of great significance sixteen years later in the time of Darius, demonstrating to the Jews and gentiles alike that there was a solid imperial precedent for Persia - which had swept away the Babylonian empire - to back the rebuilding of the Temple in Jerusalem.

Several millennia prior to the advent of electronic information storage, the rulers of Egypt, Assyria, Babylon and Persia etc. kept extensive archives of scrolls recording all kinds of governmental decisions and transactions. Some say that **Ahmeta** where Cyrus' decree about the Temple was discovered was the name of the Medean capital (=present-day Hamadan in W. Iran), while others say that it refers to the protective pottery flask or leather pouch in which the document was stored (Rashi, Metzudat David).

The scroll (vv 3-5) gave full confirmation of everything that the priests and leaders of Judea had been saying to their adversaries: they had indeed received royal endorsement from no less than the emperor Cyrus for the building of a splendid Temple in Jerusalem adorned with marble and wood and for the return of the Temple vessels.

In a very pointed snub to the adversaries, Darius instructed them to keep well away and stop interfering with the building project (vv 4-7). More than that, they were to ensure that the returnees had everything they needed for all the Temple sacrifices, including oxen, rams, lambs, goats and salt as well as wheat, oil and wine for use in the libations (v 9).

Darius wanted the returnees not only to offer the Temple sacrifices but also to "pray for the life of the king and his sons" (v 10). The rabbis commented that Darius' charity was not complete as it was motivated by self-interest (Bava Batra 10a). The danger to his life must have seemed very real: his father Ahashverosh had been murdered only two years earlier (just two years after the Purim miracle, which took place in the twelfth year of Ahashverosh's fourteen-year reign). Given that Ahashverosh had initially given his full support to Haman's plot to exterminate all the Jews, his violent death so soon after Haman's downfall must have seemed like a warning from Heaven about the likely fate of those who make trouble for the Jews, giving Darius a strong motive to support the rebuilding of the Temple. We can only speculate what if any influence Queen Esther had over Darius, who was her son.

The adversaries had been diplomatically routed, the prophets were prophesying that the time was ripe to build the Temple, and imperial patronage for the rebuilding had been publicly reaffirmed. Thus, the project now went ahead at full speed. Work on the new Temple commenced in the second year of Darius' reign and continued for four years until its completion in Darius' sixth year. The inauguration of the Second Temple (v 16), seventy-four years after the destruction of the First Temple, is somewhat comparable to the giving of the second Tablets of Stone after the shattering of the first. It is noteworthy that the returnees did not see themselves as Judeans but as representatives of all of the Twelve Tribes of Israel (v 17).

"And the children of the exile celebrated the Pesach..." (v 19). After several chapters in Aramaic tracing the diplomatic process between the imperial court and the governor of the provinces west of the Euphrates and his clique, our text here reverts to Hebrew since the Pesach celebration was a purely internal Israelite affair.

"And the Children of Israel who had returned from the exile ate, as did all who were separated from the impurity of the nations of the earth to join them to search out HaShem the God of Israel" (v 21). Rashi explains that those who had "separated from the impurity of the nations" were **Gerim**, "proselytes" who had converted in Babylon and elsewhere (see Kiddushin 70a; cf. Esther 8:17), for the main purpose of the Israelite descent into exile is to gather in the sparks of holiness that are scattered among the nations and bring them up to the Holy Land.

Verse 22 states that God had made Israel rejoice, "....and He turned the heart of the king of **Ashur** in their favor to strengthen their hands...". This refers to Darius of Persia, whose empire extended over the territories once ruled by Assyria (Metzudat David).

CHAPTER 7

"Now after these things in the reign of **Artahshasta** king of Persia..." (v 1). This is none other than Darius, for as previously mentioned, Artahshasta was the generic name of all the Persian kings just as Pharaoh was the generic name of the kings of Egypt. Since the events in the present chapter took place in the seventh year of Darius' reign, it could be that after the consolidation of his kingship following the assassination of his father Ahashverosh he now preferred to use the hereditary title of the Persian kings.

ENTER EZRA

The seventeen-generation genealogy of Ezra given in our text (which skips over some of the generations mentioned in the parallel genealogy in I Chronicles 5:30ff, Metzudat David on v 1) traces his lineage to Aaron the High Priest through the line of Pinchas son of Elazar.

According to some opinions, Ezra is identical with the prophet Malachi (Megillah 15a; Targum on Malachi 1:1). He is known as **Ha-Sopher**, "the scribe", because he was the towering Torah authority of his time and his influence is felt until today. Since the written scroll of the Torah is the very foundation of all of Judaism, those who were able to write the sacred scroll in accordance with all its conventions and secrets were the most honored of sages. The Hebrew word **sopher** also means to count and tell. The repetition of the word **Sopher** in verse 11 is darshened in Shekalim 13b to indicate that just as Ezra was the scribe, counter and enumerator of the Written Torah, so he was the teller and enumerator of the Oral Torah. Indeed, the enactments of the outstanding rabbis - some of the most important of which were instituted by Ezra - are known as **Divrey Sophrim**, "the words of the scribes".

Verses 7-10 recount the four-month cross-country journey of Ezra and those who joined him in the **second wave** of returnees from Babylon to Jerusalem in the seventh year of the reign of Darius. Ezra came bearing certified documentation from the Persian king (with whose court Ezra obviously had the best of contacts) affirming that: All Israel were free to go up to Jerusalem (v 13); they were to be provided with **money** - silver and gold - to finance the Temple project (v 15); financing for the Temple sacrifices, vessels and all other needs was to be provided through a grant from the royal treasury (v 20); and the Cohen-priests, Levites, the Temple **singers** and gate-keepers and the Gibeonite hewers of stone and wood were to be exempt from imperial taxes (v 24). From this last enactment, the Talmud learns that Torah scholars should be exempt from taxation (Nedarim 62b).

BARUCH HASHEM

Building the Temple in Jerusalem under the patronage of the Persian king was not the same as building it as a free nation in the time of Solomon without being subject to any foreign power. Nevertheless, after seventy years in ruins, the rise of the new Temple was a miracle that was all the greater when seen against the backdrop of the terrible exiles and persecutions that had taken place under Sennacherib king of Assyria and Nebuchadnezzar king of Babylon. This is why Ezra blessed God "…who has put such a thing as this in the king's heart... and has given me grace before the king and his counselors and before all the king's mighty princes..." (vv 27-8).

CHAPTER 8

"Now these are the heads of their fathers' houses and this is the genealogy of those who went up with me from Babylon" (v 1).

When Israel had come up out of Egypt, "and also a mixed multitude went up with them" (Exodus 12:38). The admixture of non-Israelite stock had again and again brought disaster upon the nation. In order to avoid further disasters, Ezra made sure that only those who could establish their Israelite status and lineage would go up with him from Babylon. It is said that one of his main activities there in the years in which he stayed behind before going up to Jerusalem to join the returnees who went in the first wave was to investigate and clarify the status and lineage of all those who were still in exile.

Ezra's journey from Babylon and his arrival in Jerusalem were briefly described in the previous chapter (Ezra 7:7-9). In the present chapter, the text takes us back to the beginning of this journey just before Ezra set off (vv 15ff). The first step was to assemble all the new Olim who would be traveling together across the dangerous territory between Babylon and Israel. They came together at the River Ahavah (which in this case cannot be interpreted as having the connotation of "love" as **Ahavah** here is spelled with a **Vav** and not a **Beit**).

"And we encamped there for three days" (v 15). An interesting law that the Talmud derives from this verse is that someone returning from a journey is exempt from the obligation of prayer for three days (Eiruvin 65a). In the days before jets and super-smooth cars, coaches and the like, travel could be extremely exhausting and debilitating, particularly for these Olim who had just come from the Babylonian villages of their exile together with their wives, children, livestock and possessions. As a general rule, in order to bring ourselves into the right frame of mind for prayer, it is necessary to "camp", unwind and meditate for a while before we open our mouths!

"And I inspected the people and the priests, but I found none of the sons of Levi" (v 15). Rashi on Kiddushin 69a, where this verse is darshened, brings down the tradition that Ezra searched for Levites who would be fit to serve in the Temple but could find only Levites who had bitten off their thumbs with their teeth in the time of Nebuchadnezzar so that when he demanded that they sing him the Temple music, they could honestly reply, "'How can we sing the song of God in a foreign land?' (Psalms 137:4) - we are unable to play our harps". Thus, Ezra found no Levites fit for service - because those who were fit were sitting peacefully and comfortably in Babylon while the **Olim** who went up to Jerusalem were impoverished and burdened with the rebuilding work and in fear of all those around them".

Rashi's evocation of the sharp contrast between the peace and comfort of the exiles in Babylon as opposed to the trials of the **Olim** in Jerusalem could apply equally well today, when the material lives of many Jews in the lusher areas of the present-day Diaspora are often very much more cushioned than those of many Israelis.

A halachic consequence of the absence of fit Levites from Ezra's **Aliyah** was that he penalized the Levites for their failure to return to Israel by awarding the 10% **Ma'aser** tithe on produce that farmers were supposed to give them (Numbers 18:24) to the Cohanim (priests) instead (Yevamot 86b; Rambam Hilchot Ma'aser 1:4).

The Talmud states that it would have been fit for the Israelites to return to their Land in the days of Ezra to the accompaniment of miracles and with the same "high hand" with which they entered under Joshua, except that sin had its effects and they now needed permission from Cyrus and Darius to do so (Berachot 4a). The route from Babylon to Israel passed through lands whose inhabitants had shown extreme cruelty to the Israelites when they went into exile in the days of Sennacherib and Nebuchadnezzar. Moreover, as we have seen from the previous chapters, the territories west of the Euphrates harbored all kinds of adversaries who were very anxious to thwart the returnees. Thus, Ezra's large, straggling cross-country caravan of men, women and children and livestock had the potential for being exposed to great danger. Yet Ezra confesses that he had been "ashamed to ask the king for a band of soldiers and horsemen to help us against the enemy on the road, because we had spoken to the king saying, 'The hand of our God is upon all those who seek Him for good, but His power and His wrath are against all those who forsake Him '" (v 22).

The same positive "spin" that Ezra had used in order to persuade the Persian ruler that God was with the Israelites actually put him in a corner, making it impossible for him to now ask for military protection. An armed escort would have been very reassuring, but the Israelites were forced to put their trust in God alone, and Ezra called for fasting and repentance before they set off (vv 21 & 23). Ezra entrusted the treasures sent by the Persian king and the Israelites who remained in Babylon into the hands of leading priests to carry during the journey (vv 24-29).

"And I said to them, 'You are holy to HaShem; the vessels are holy also'" (v 28). From the comparison in this verse between the holiness of the priests and that of the Temple vessels, which are not allowed to be used for personal benefit, the rabbis learned out that it is forbidden to "use" a Cohen-priest as a waiter or attendant or to perform mundane tasks for one's own benefit (Yerushalmi Nedarim).

Verse 35 tells us that among the offerings offered by the returnees after their arrival in Jerusalem were "twelve he-goats for a sin offering (**Chatat**)" but goes on to say that "all this was a burnt (**Olah**) offering". Since the meat of sin offerings is normally consumed by the priests, why are these sin offerings specifically described as an **Olah**, all of which is consumed on the Altar? The Talmud explains that the twelve goat sin offerings were brought on behalf of the Twelve Tribes in order to expiate the sin of idolatry in the days of King Tzidkiyahu - and the meat of the goat sin-offering for idolatry is **not** eaten by the priests but burned outside the camp (Temurah 15b; see Numbers 15:24 and Rambam Hilchot Shegagah 12:1). In offering sacrifices for all the Twelve Tribes, we see once again how Ezra and the returnees saw themselves as representatives of the entire people of Israel.

CHAPTER 9

The return to Jerusalem and the reinstitution of the Temple rites encouraged a great wave of repentance among the people. The leaders immediately approached Ezra and confessed that the entire nation - Israelites, priests and Levites - had been guilty in Babylon of the same sin of intermarriage that their fathers had committed before the exile with the Canaanite nations and the surrounding Ammonites, Moabites and Egyptians (vv 1-2). Moreover, they admitted that "the hand of the princes and rulers has been chief in this crime" (v 2) [just as it was in the great wave of Jewish assimilation in the last few centuries, which was led by the Rothschilds and similar leading families].

Ezra was surely not unaware of this national flaw, which undermines the very foundations of the people, but the mere mention of it was sufficient to drive him to tear his garments and pull out the hairs of his head and beard in anguish (v 3).

"And at the time of the afternoon sacrifice [shortly after midday] I arose from my fasting" (v 5). From here the Talmud (Megillah 30b) learns that the proper procedure on a public fast day is for the leaders to spend the entire morning investigating the affairs of the community. [A lot could be accomplished if rabbis and community leaders would actually practice this today.]

Ezra's prayer (vv 6ff) puts words of confession, contrition and repentance into the mouths of all Israel. He admits that "we are slaves" (v 9). [In Ezra's day, it was to the Persians, while today it seems to be to the Americans, who appear to dictate most if not all of what Israel does.] "But He gave us grace in the eyes of the king of Persia" (ibid.) This is interpreted by the Talmud as a reference to the overthrow of Haman in the days of Ahashverosh (Megillah 10b).

At the very outset of the new settlement, Ezra delivered a forthright lesson on the Torah condition for successful Israelite possession of the Holy Land: complete separation from the impurity of the idolatrous nations, which means **no intermarriage** (vv 11-14).

In our times, there is hardly a family in all Israel that has been unaffected by the enormous wave of intermarriage in recent centuries, and in many cases the bold steps taken by the returnees in the time of Ezra to cleanse the nation as described in the coming chapter are in practical terms all but impossible in most families. What we can do is to try to do everything possible to cleanse our minds of any foreign ideologies that have knowingly or unknowingly allowed to intermarry into the native Torah way of thinking that is our national heritage.

CHAPTER 10

"Judah has dealt treacherously and a disgusting thing has been done in Israel and in Jerusalem; for Judah has profaned the holiness of HaShem that He loved, and has married the daughter of a strange god" (Malachi 2:11). In the Talmud, Rav Nachman brings this verse as support for the statement by R. Yehoshua ben Korchah that Malachi is identical with Ezra, one of whose greatest achievements was to eliminate the blight of intermarriage that cut at the very foundations of the people.

It was the sight of this saintly priest and prophet in the newly built Temple, praying, weeping and confessing in the name of the entire nation, that brought all the assembled people to a great swell of Teshuvah, with all the men, women and children weeping (v 1).

"And **Shechaniyah** the son of **Yechiel** from the children of **Eilam** answered and said to Ezra, 'We have trespassed against our God and have taken alien women...'" (v 2). It is interesting that in verse 26, where **Yechiel** is listed among the children of Eilam who had taken foreign wives, his son Shechaniyah is **not** mentioned as one of those who had done so. Yet Shechaniyah still stepped forward to "confess". Why?

The Talmud explains by telling how one time while R Judah the Prince was teaching his disciples, he smelled a strong smell of garlic. He told whoever had eaten garlic to leave. His best student, R. Chiya, immediately got up and left, and then everyone else also got up and left. The following morning R. Judah's son Shimon found R. Chiya and asked how he could dare offend his father - until R. Chiya confessed that he had not eaten garlic at all. From whom did R. Chiya learn this way of saving others from embarrassment? From R. Meir. For once a woman came into the Beit Midrash and said, "One of you made me his wife by sleeping with me." On hearing this R. Meir immediately got up and wrote her a Get ("bill of divorce") and on seeing this, all the other students also wrote her a Get. And who did R. Meir learn it from? From Shmuel HaKatan. And Shmuel HaKatan learned it from Shechaniyah the son of Yechiel (Sanhedrin 11a).

Getting up first in front of everyone to confess to having intermarried was a courageous act on the part of Shechaniyah that was intended to make it easier for all those who really were guilty to confess and begin to repair the damage. Shechaniyah asked Ezra to set the process in motion, and the latter - continuing his fasting and repentance - gave orders for all the returnees to assemble in Jerusalem, warning that anyone who failed to do so would be penalized by having all his property declared ownerless (v 8). This verse is the foundation for the law that a Beit Din (a rabbinic court) is entitled to use the sanction of declaring the property of recalcitrant individuals **hefker**, ownerless and free for anyone to take (Shekalim 3b).

This great national assembly was held on the 20th of the month of Kislev (v 9) - which is in December at the height of Israel's rainy season, usually one of the coldest, windiest times in Jerusalem. We can imagine what a chilly, sorrowful occasion it was as the bedraggled crowd confronted the enormity of what they had allowed to happen during their exile. Everyone was willing to do what was necessary to purify the nation, but it was simply too cold to stand outside in the rain now and complete the very delicate and time-consuming work needed to rectify the flaw.

Ezra laid down a timetable for the returnees from the various different cities of the exile to appear together with their elders and judges in order to check into what had happened in each family and separate Israelites from their foreign wives and children. We need only try to imagine what it would take today to separate home-born Jews who have intermarried from their non-Jewish spouses and children in order to get a glimmer of understanding of the enormous, heart-rending enterprise Ezra carried out in his time with priests, Levites and Israelites alike.

NEHEMIAH
CHAPTER 1

The book of Nehemiah is a direct continuation of the book of Ezra. In Ezra 2:2 Nehemiah was numbered among the leaders of the **first wave** of returnees who had gone up out of exile to Jerusalem together with Zerubavel and Yehoshua the High Priest while Ezra remained in Babylon. In Ezra 2:63 Nehemiah was mentioned under his name **Hatirshata** (see Nehemiah 10:2) as having forbidden those priests who were unable to bring written proof of their priestly lineage from eating sacrificial meat.

Nehemiah evidently returned to exile at some point thereafter to join and presumably lead the sizeable communities that remained in Babylon, Persia and other centers. We have evidence in our text of a certain two-way traffic between Israel and the Diaspora of those days, though it was probably less intense than the two-way jet air traffic that exists today between Tel Aviv, Paris, London, New York, Los Angeles and other Jewish centers worldwide. As we shall presently see, Nehemiah rose to a top position in the Persian royal court - in the same tradition of outstanding Tzaddikim like Daniel and Ezra who also had the ear of the emperor kings of their times.

The first wave of returnees had come up to Jerusalem in the first year of the reign of Cyrus of Persia in 3390 (370 B.C.E.). They had laid the foundations of the Temple Altar, but owing to the opposition of the adversaries it was not until eighteen years later that they were able to build the Temple in the year 3408 (352 B.C.E.). Ezra came up from Babylon to Jerusalem seven years later in 3415 (345 B.C.E.), and it was then that he began his work of separating the people from their foreign wives as told in the closing chapters of the book of Ezra.

The book of Nehemiah opens "in the twentieth year" (Nehemiah 1:1) but does not specify in the twentieth year of what! The rabbis learned from **Gezeirah Shavah** with the identical phrase in Nehemiah 2:1 that this was in the twentieth year of **Artahshasta** = Darius king of Persia (Rosh Hashanah 3a, see Rashi on Nehemiah 1:1). This was in the year 3426 (334 B.C.E.) - i.e. **eleven years** after Ezra's Aliyah to Jerusalem.

In other words, with the opening of the book of Nehemiah we have once again fast-forwarded, this time to eleven years after the events described at the end of the book of Ezra, passing over in silence the details of all that happened in the intervening years.

We are not told until the closing words of our present chapter (Nehemiah 1:11) exactly who Nehemiah is. It turns out that he is no less than the personal wine-butler of Darius king of Persia - a prestigious position of influence if ever there was one, since you get the king at his most mellow moments. Of course, a king's butler has to taste the wine every time before he serves it to prove that it has not been poisoned, and since the Persian king's wine was **Yayin Nesech** (idolatrous wine), the rabbis of the time gave a special license to Nehemiah to drink it even though **Yayin Nesech** is normally strictly forbidden for Jewish consumption. This is the reason why Nehemiah was given the name **Hatirshasta**: **hatir** means "permitted", **shata** means "he drank" (see Rashi on Ezra 2:63, Yerushalmi Kiddushin 41b).

It was precisely because Nehemiah was not only a great, open-hearted Tzaddik but also one who had the ear of the king of Persia, head of the great superpower of the day, that it was so fortuitous that Chanani and his companions, visiting the Galut from Jerusalem, came to him and told him the latest news about his brothers in Jerusalem (Nehemiah v 2).

The great jubilation at the time of the Aliyah of Ezra eleven years earlier carrying a letter of authorization from that same king Darius had given way to a cry of pain from the harassed residents of Judah. The walls of Jerusalem were broken down and marauding adversaries were engaged in an intense intifada, burning down the houses without regard for the authority of the king of Persia, who was many, many hundreds of miles away and who in any case had little interest in backing up his letter of authorization by engaging his armies to deal with a local squabble in one of his many provinces.

The news of the plight of the returnees threw Nehemiah into mourning, weeping and fasting, and he offered the eloquent prayer recorded in our chapter, phrases from which are included in some of the prayers and supplications in our Siddur (prayer book) and Selichot (penitential prayers). Nehemiah delicately alludes to God's promise that if the exiles of Israel would repent, He would gather them in to His chosen place (v 9) - as if to say, now that they have returned, please **protect them**!!! Nehemiah continued - since he had some **protekzia** with the king of Persia - asking for God to grant him favor with the king - showing that it is permissible for us to pray for success in our dealings with other people.

In the ensuing chapters, we will see how Nehemiah asked the king of Persia for a temporary leave of absence (which lasted twelve years) in order to go to Jerusalem, where he not only built the city walls to protect the population physically, but also built the spiritual walls of the nation by campaigning against the cruelty of creditors to defaulting debtors and against the desecration of the holy Shabbat.

CHAPTER 2

A unique feature of the book of Nehemiah is that unlike almost all the other narrative portions of the Bible, here the hero of the story writes about his own exploits in the first person singular. Throughout the Torah, Moses, who wrote at God's dictation, described his own deeds as if writing about someone else in the third person [except in certain of his discourses in Deuteronomy]. Samuel did the same when he wrote the book called by his name. While the prophets frequently describe their own spiritual experiences in the first person, Nehemiah alone gives a long, detailed first-person account of his own endeavors in the world of practical action.

In this book, we thus have an intimate picture of how a Tzaddik and a man of **action** and **accomplishment** turned to prayer, faith and trust in God at every step in his activities. Writing about oneself carries some risks: thus, Nehemiah's repeated prayer to God to remember him for good in the merit of his various exploits (Nehemiah 5:19, 13:14 etc.) did not escape the censure of some of the rabbis, who said that as a result his book, although called by his name, was merely appended to the Book of Ezra instead of standing as a complete work in its own right (Sanhedrin 93b).

The conversation between **Artahshasta** (= Darius) king of Persia and his wine butler Nehemiah took place a few months after the latter had received a report of the great plight of the residents of Jerusalem as described in Chapter 1. As Nehemiah was serving the king wine, the latter observed a serious change for the worse in his butler's facial expression. In a verse cited as illumining the effect of the emotions upon the physical body (Likutey Moharan I, 60:6), the king declared that the bad look on Nehemiah's face proved that he harbored bad thoughts in his heart (v 2). The king feared that his butler was trying to get him to drink poisoned wine (Rashi ad loc.).

After Nehemiah had explained that the cause of his anguish was the plight of Jerusalem, when the king asked him what he wanted, Nehemiah first prayed to God in Heaven (v 4, cf. Nehemiah 1:11). He then asked leave of absence from the royal court in order to travel to Jerusalem to take matters into his own hands and rebuild the city. He requested a written guarantee of safe passage through the dangerous western imperial provinces through which he had to pass on his way to Judea as well as for access to the royal forests there for timber for his building project.

"And when Sanbalat the Horonite and Toviah the Ammonite slave heard, it displeased them greatly that there was come a man to seek the welfare of the children of Israel" (v 10). In the eleven years since Ezra's danger-ridden Aliyah to Jerusalem, a new set of adversaries had grown up, for "in each and every generation they have stood up against us to destroy us" (Pesach Haggadah). Sanvalat would appear to have been one of the leaders of the Samaritans (cf. Nehemiah 3:34) while the Ammonites had always been implacable enemies of Israel.

DEMOLITION FOR THE PURPOSE OF BUILDING

Only three days after his arrival in Jerusalem, Nehemiah jumped into action. "And I arose in the night… and I told no one what my God had put in my heart to do in Jerusalem..." (v 12). Ibn Ezra followed by modern Bible translators interpret the verb **soveir** in vv 13 and 15 as meaning that Nehemiah merely **inspected** the city walls, but Rashi (on v 12) and Metzudat David (on v 13) interpret it has having the sense of **shoveir**, "**I broke** the walls", explaining that Nehemiah's intention was to make the breaches in the walls even bigger and more extensive than they already were in order to shock the inhabitants of Jerusalem when they would wake up the following morning so as to spur them into agreeing to join Nehemiah in the urgent rebuilding of the city walls.

Living in the vast urban agglomerations in which over half the world's population resides today, it is harder to appreciate the reason why all ancient cities that were worthy of the name were almost invariably walled for defensive purposes. Indeed, in the times of Sennacherib and Nebuchadnezzar the fortified walls of Jerusalem enabled its inhabitants to survive years of sieges before the city finally succumbed. With the destruction of Jerusalem, the massive wooden gates of the various entrances to the city had been burned, and the charred stones of the walls were weak and crumbling. The ruined walls symbolized the weakness of the Jews and their subject status. The returnees from Babylon who lived in the unfortified city were exposed to constant marauding incursions from their adversaries, and were evidently too weak, demoralized and preoccupied with their day-to-day activities to be able to take decisive action to defend themselves.

By further breaking down the remains of the old walls, Nehemiah did indeed succeed in arousing the inhabitants of Jerusalem to take urgent action to rebuild them (v 17), much to the anger of their adversaries, who immediately accused them of treason against the Persian king. Nehemiah's response was to strengthen himself in his faith in God. His statement to the adversaries that "you have no portion or charity or memorial in Jerusalem (v 20) is one of the main proof texts for the law that no contributions to the walls and towers of Jerusalem are accepted from non-Israelites (Shekalim 4b).

The walls of Jerusalem are also of great halachic significance, as they define the boundaries of the city for the purpose of eating **Kadoshim Kalim** ("light holy offerings" that could be consumed outside the Temple but only within the city walls), **Ma'aser Sheini** (the "second tithe" eaten by its owners in Jerusalem, usually during their visits for the pilgrim festivals) and **Bikurim** ("first fruits", eaten by the priests) etc.

CHAPTER 3

Despite the opposition of their adversaries, Nehemiah and the people of Jerusalem succeeded in building up the walls of the city.

The present chapter is of very great interest in providing us with a detailed topography of the walls of Jerusalem at the start of the Second Temple period including references to gates, springs, pools and strategic strongholds many of which are known until today. While the city was expanded later on in this period, many of the locations mentioned must have been familiar to the Tanna'im and other Tzaddikim of the late Second Temple period about whom we read constantly in the Mishnah and Talmud, such as Hillel and Shamai, Rabban Yochanan ben Zakkai, Rabbi Eliezer, Rabbi Yehoshua and Rabbi Akiva etc.

Part of the beauty of the project of rebuilding the fortifications of Jerusalem about which we read in the present chapter was that it was not an impersonal, monolithic government enterprise using imported foreign laborers having no connection with the city. It was a cooperative venture carried out with their bare hands by the very citizens themselves. Virtually every family took responsibility for a designated section of the city walls and gates. Almost everyone took part - Cohanim, Levites, Israelites and Gibeonites - with very few exceptions (v 5).

The gates of Jerusalem as recorded in this chapter have very evocative names, such as the Gate of the Flocks (v 1) - many animals were brought up to the Temple - the Gate of the Fish (v 2, for Shabbat?!?) - the "Old Gate" (v 6), the Dung Gate (v 14) - known until today as the gate near the Western Wall - the Gate of the Spring (v 15), the Water Gate (v 26), the Gate of the Horses (v 18) which dated from the period of the Kings (II Kings 11:16), the Eastern Gate (v 29) and the Gate of the Guard (v 31).

The adversaries responded to this building project with scorn, derision and vilification of the "wretched Jews" (v 34) echoes of which can be heard until today in the Arab response to the rebuilding of modern Israel. Swollen with arrogance, Sanvalat asked rhetorically, "Will they [the nations] allow them? Will they [the Jews] sacrifice? Will they complete the work in one day? Will they revive the stones out of the heaps of dust seeing as they are burned?" (v 34). Toviah the Ammonite slave further refined the mockery, saying that even a fox would be able to break through their stone wall (v 35).

Nehemiah showed the right way for a Jew to respond to such anti-Semitic abuse, refusing to engage the adversaries but rather turning to God and asking Him to hear their insolence and bring it down on their own heads. Nehemiah and the inhabitants of Jerusalem meanwhile pressed on unperturbed with the work of rebuilding.

CHAPTER 4

Our chapter relates the thickening trouble that now struck the builders of Jerusalem from their adversaries. The opening verse gives us an indication of who these adversaries were. As mentioned in the commentary on Nehemiah ch 2, Sanvalat appears to have been one of the leaders of the inhabitants of Shomron (see Nehemiah 3:34). Toviah was apparently a renegade Israelite who was intermarried with some of the leading Judeans, with whom he had excellent connections (see Nehemiah 6:18). The **Arevim** are likely to have been Ishmaelite tribes who had spread into Eretz Israel from east of the River Jordan, where the Ammonites were also based. The **Ashdodim** were Philistines living in the Mediterranean coastal areas of Israel. All of these elements now gathered together to make war on the Judeans who by rebuilding Jerusalem were threatening the comfortable status quo the adversaries had been enjoying since the exile of the Ten Tribes under Sennacherib and of Judah and Benjamin under Nebuchadnezzar.

Nehemiah's building of the walls of Jerusalem "under fire" or, at the very least, under the constant threat of attack from enemies all around has its parallel in the building of the modern Jewish Yishuv in Eretz Israel, which since its inception has been attended by unremitting belligerence and aggression from Arab and other enemies on every border of the tiny country. The greater the influx of Jews into Israel and the greater their success in building up the country, the greater their enemies' hostility has become, making a mockery of every peace plan that has been devised to try to diffuse it.

The previous chapter gave a general account of the rebuilding of the walls and various gates of Jerusalem. This enterprise, which was executed through each of the different families in the city building their own section of the wall, could not be accomplished in one day. It was a protracted project that left the Jews highly vulnerable to attack in what turned into an enervating war of attrition to the point that "Judah said, the strength of the bearers of the burdens is failing..." (v 4). The repeated helpless sighs heaved daily by the pressured citizens of contemporary Israel echo the same feeling.

The adversaries' plan was to infiltrate Judea in order to spring a surprise attack (v 5). [This is reminiscent of the original Oslo strategy of the "Palestinians" to infiltrate Israel in order to strike with the sudden terror attacks that has become the hallmark of the last decades. This is one of the reasons why the Palestinians have always advocated "open borders" into Israel (but not the other way round), opposing the Israeli separation fence that is a de facto admission of the complete failure of the "peace process".]

In verse 6 we find that Nehemiah receives a warning of the hostile intentions of the adversaries from "the Jews dwelling with them". This is evidence that the returnees were not only concentrated in and around Jerusalem and Judea but were spreading considerably further afield. Indeed, by the time of the later Second Temple period, the Yishuv extended over most of the areas occupied by the earlier kingdoms of Judah and Israel, including the whole Galilee, Mount Ephraim, the Negev and east of the Jordan. The main exceptions were certain coastal areas and the strip of land around Shomron, which was occupied by the **Kootim** ("Samaritans").

The belligerence of modern Israel's enemies has forced her to become a militarized nation in which most members of the workforce, having already performed compulsory full-time army service for a number of years, they have to serve every year in **Milu'im**, "reserve duty", sometimes for periods of up to several months. Somewhat similarly, Nehemiah was forced to build the walls of Jerusalem with a civilian workforce half of whom worked on the building while the other half had to carry out guard duty in order to defend them (v 10). Even those who were engaged in the actual labor had to do so while heavily armed. They were forced to do their work with one hand while holding a sword in the other! Nehemiah himself had to keep a shofar-blower at his side in case there was a need to summon everybody to one place to stave off a sudden attack (vv 11-12).

"So we labored in the work, and half of them held the spears from the time of the breaking dawn until the stars appeared. Likewise, at the same time I said to the people, 'Let everyone lodge with his attendant within Jerusalem so that in the night they may be a guard to us and labor in the day'" (vv 15-16). These verses are likely to be familiar to anyone who has studied the Talmud where it begins in Tractate Berachot, because these are the very first verses quoted by the ShaS from the NaKh (though not from the Five Books of Moses, from which three verses are quoted earlier on the page). These verses from Nehemiah are introduced as proof texts in a discussion about the time when the obligation to recite the evening **Shema** begins - when the stars first appear (Berachot 2b).

Despite the fact that the Jewish laborers were engaged in physically demanding and doubtless very sweaty work during the Israeli summer, they were so busy working and trying to defend themselves that they did not even have time to strip off their clothes and wash!!! (v 17).

CHAPTER 5

Nehemiah did not only have to deal with threats from Israel's external enemies. He was also faced with internal social friction and resentment caused by the great disparity between the "upper crust" of the returnees, who were or had become very wealthy, and the less successful ones, who were not. The latter were small farmers who were trying to scrape a living out of ancestral allotments that had been neglected for over seventy years. Not only did they have to produce sufficient to be able to subsist and cover their basic needs; they also had to pay heavy tributes to the Persian king.

The opening of the present chapter paints a sorry picture of how the poor had fallen into debt and were reduced to selling not only their fields and vineyards but even their very sons and daughters as slaves to the rich just in order to survive (vv 1-5).

The descent of the weaker classes into chronic debt is another feature of the time of Nehemiah that also characterizes modern Israel, where the huge gap between the rich and the poor continues to widen despite major economic growth. The country's enormous security budget sucks money out of the economy, necessitating heavy taxation of the working population and high import duties, pushing up the prices of homes, consumer goods, services and everything else, leaving most sections of the population mortgaged up to the hilt while financing car purchase and other projects with heavy-interest loans at the same time as living off credit cards and expensive bank overdrafts.

Contemporary political leaders tend to be fully implicated in the ongoing exploitation of the weaker sections of the population and the attendant government corruption. Israel's previous prime ministers as well as countless other ministers and high officials have been subject to police investigations for serious wrongdoing.

Nehemiah, on the other hand, stood up as a true leader of the people, championing the poor and oppressed against the wealthy and powerful. "...And I rebuked the nobles and the rulers..." (v 7). Nehemiah asked them questions to which they could give no answer: "We have redeemed our brothers the Jews who were sold to the heathen; and will you nevertheless sell your brothers, or shall they be sold to us?" (v 8).

Nehemiah initiated a collective remittance of debts, seeing that all the fields, vineyards, olive trees and houses that had been seized as collateral against bad debts were returned (v 11). Nehemiah was not merely acting as the champion of mundane social justice. At every step, he made it clear that helping our brothers and sisters rather than exploiting and oppressing them is an integral part of **fear of God** (vv 9, 13).

The chapter ends with Nehemiah's testimony about his own integrity. We learn from v 14 that the Persian king Darius had appointed Nehemiah as **Governor** of Judah, yet he never used his position for personal gain. He did not even consume the food which the population were obliged to provide for the governor, let alone enjoy the expensive "perks" that previous governors had permitted themselves. On the contrary, Nehemiah supported a sizeable entourage - including many converts - at his own table at his own expense. "Remember me, my God, for good, according to all that I have done for this people" (v 19).

CHAPTER 6

Nehemiah's speedy rebuilding of the walls of Jerusalem caused fury among the adversaries, who now plotted to kill him.

To understand the complexity of Nehemiah's situation, we must read the present narrative in the light of information that is only given towards the end of the chapter.

Nehemiah was the de facto leader in Jerusalem at this time - it was he who took the initiative to get the people to build the wall. The leadership of the nation was vested in the Sanhedrin, which included outstanding prophets and sages who had returned from exile in Babylon. Ezra was still alive and active, as we shall see in Chapter 8, where Nehemiah and Ezra work together as a "team" for the spiritual revival of the nation. But where the two are mentioned together, it is Nehemiah who is given precedence (Nehemiah 8:9). Not only was he an outstanding Tzaddik. He had also been appointed governor of Judea by Darius king of Persia, in whose court he enjoyed a position of the greatest influence. He was also very wealthy (see Nehemiah 7:65,69, 10:2 where Hatirshatah=Nehemiah).

Sanvalat and Tuvia and their associates saw themselves as loyal subjects of Persia, which had taken over the Babylonian empire, and they evidently felt they had the right to dwell in the territories in which they lived in its western provinces maintaining the existing status quo without allowing the Jews - with their history of rebellion against imperial rulers like Babylon - to rebuild the walls of Jerusalem.

It emerges from vv 17-18 that Toviah enjoyed excellent connections with leading figures in Judea, and he and his son were actually married to prominent Judeans. Rashi (on v 17) states that Toviah was a **Yisrael Rasha** ("wicked Israelite"); however, the Talmud in Kiddushin 70a - discussing aspects of the laws of **Yichus** ("lineage") in the light of certain verses in our present chapter and the next - implies that he was a heathen.

To add further subtlety to the scene around Nehemiah, we find that already among the penitent returnees from Babylon there were various false prophets (v 10) and prophetesses (v 14) who were using the language of faith day by day to broadcast gloomy messages of doom to Nehemiah in order to discourage him. Moreover, there were various agents and informers who were spreading disinformation about Toviah and reporting back to him about Nehemiah's every word and movement (v 19).

Keeping all this in mind we can better appreciate the wisdom with which this humble man of action pursued his mission. In vv 2-4 the adversaries try to lure Nehemiah to a location where they could kill him. Nehemiah replies that he is too busy to leave Jerusalem. In vv 5-7 Sanvalat sends an open letter accusing Nehemiah of high treason against the Persian king, planning to have himself declared king of Judah. In vv 8-9 Nehemiah absolutely denies the accusations, but is surrounded by people who are trying to demoralize him. In vv 10-13 Nehemiah comes to a "prophet" in Jerusalem who assures him that he knows prophetically that Nehemiah is in such mortal danger that he must take refuge in the Temple Sanctuary (the only place that had gates - the gates of Jerusalem were still not in place). But Nehemiah recognizes him to be a false prophet and refuses to sin by entering the Sanctuary, which is forbidden to a non-priest.

Amidst all this Nehemiah persisted in building the walls of Jerusalem, which were completed - to the consternation of the adversaries - on the 25th of Elul (v 15), the anniversary of the first day of creation (for man was created on the sixth day, Rosh HaShanah). "For through our God was this labor accomplished" (v 16).

CHAPTER 7

With the completion of the walls of Jerusalem, the last step was to put the doors in position in the city gates, and to charge the gate-keepers of the city and the Temple together with the Temple singers and Levites with their duties. Nehemiah charged his "brother" (=friend) Chanani (see Nehemiah 1:2 and Rashi ad loc.) and Chananiyah, governor of the city - "as a man of truth and a God-fearing man for many days" (present chapter v 2) - to open the gates only briefly at a specified time each day to allow people to pass in and out of the city, in order to prevent a surprise attack from the adversaries.

YICHUS

Having built the physical walls of Jerusalem, Nehemiah (in conjunction with Ezra) set about the work of building the spiritual defenses of the nation through family purity.

Prior to the exile, the people of Israel - as a nation of tribal, clan and family networks - carefully guarded their family records and registries of marriages, relationships and personal status. But ever since they had gone into exile intermarriage, immoral conduct and other factors affecting personal status had left considerable confusion. If all this had happened to Judah after only seventy years of exile, it is no wonder that today, two thousand years since the destruction of the Second Temple and two thousand five hundred years since the exile of the Ten Tribes, untold numbers of Jews and Israelites have completely lost track of their lineage. Only in the last couple of centuries, the mass migrations of Jews from Eastern Europe, attended by chronic persecution and culminating in the holocaust, have caused countless family records and community registers to become lost. It may be that the Mormons - who are assiduous collectors of records of lineage, especially Jewish lineage - know more than many about different people's family backgrounds, but the majority of present-day Jews know little if anything about their great-grandparents and even less about earlier generations and their "bloodlines".

Today it is up to each individual who feels his or her Israelite soul stirring within to make a personal covenant of self-dedication to HaShem the God of Hosts, Who knows all the souls and all their incarnations.

One who appreciates what it is to be from the seed of Israel will find it easier to project himself into the mindset of Nehemiah and the Tzaddikim of his time in seeking to establish clear records of the lineage of all the returnees from Babylon in order to lay the foundations of national purity and spiritual strength for the generations to come.

The records of the families of the Israelites, Levites, Cohanim-priests, Gibeonites and Temple servants who came up from Babylon as given in the present chapter overlap with those given in Ezra ch 2. In both chapters the total number of returnees is given as 42,360 (Ezra 2:64, Nehemiah 7:66) but many of the names in our present chapter are different from those found in Ezra, and the individual population figures given for the various families are also not the same.

Metzudat David (on Nehemiah 7:66) explains that the first wave of returnees had come up to Jerusalem with Zerubavel and Yehoshua the High Priest in the second year of Cyrus of Persia, while Nehemiah came up to Jerusalem **over thirty-five years later** in the twentieth year of Darius of Persia. In giving the names and numbers of the various families in accordance with their different statuses as based on the **Scroll of Lineage** Nehemiah found on the completion of the city walls (Nehemiah 7:5), he adjusted them to take account of people who had died and those who had been born since the time of the compilation of the original scroll. In some cases, entire families had almost become extinct by the time of Nehemiah, with their surviving members attaching themselves to near relations in other families. In other cases, individual branches of certain families had been so prolific that they could be counted as families in their own right (See Metzudat David on Nehemiah 7:66 at length).

"And these are they who came up from Tel Melach, Tel Harsha, Keruv Adon and Eemeir, and they could not tell the house of their fathers and their seed..." (v 61). The Talmud (Kiddushin 70a) darshens: Tel Melach (="the mound of salt") - these are people whose deeds are like the deeds of Sodom that was turned into a mound of salt. Tel Harsha (="the mound of dumbness"): this refers to a child who calls out "father" and his mother hushes him. "And they could not tell the house of their fathers and their seed if they were from Israel" - this refers to the **Asufi** who was gathered in from the street. Keruv Adon and

Eemeir: Rabbi Abahu said, "Said (**Amar**) the Lord (=Adon), I said Israel should be before me like an angel (**Keruv**) but they made themselves like a leopard (that mates indiscriminately). Others said in the name of Rabbi Abahu: "Said the Lord, even though they made themselves like a leopard, they are considered before me like an angel." Rabba bar Chana said: Everyone who marries a woman that is not fit for him is considered as if he plowed the whole world and sowed it with salt.

CHAPTER 8

Now that the returnees from Babylon to Judea had settled again in their ancestral towns and villages, they were ready to return to the Torah path of life that is the purpose of Israel's existence.

With the arrival of the first day of the seventh month - Rosh HaShanah, the Head and beginning of the spiritual year - everyone, including both the men and the women, flocked to the Temple.

The account of this unique national assembly - central to which was the public reading from the Torah scroll - is one of our main sources for the laws and customs of: (1) the public Torah reading in the synagogue (2) Rosh Hashanah (3) the Succah.

THE READING OF THE LAW

The central figure in this section is Ezra the Scribe and High Priest. While Moses had instituted the public reading of the Torah on Shabbat, Mondays and Thursdays (so that three days should never go by without the people hearing the Torah), it was Ezra who instituted other customs relating to the Torah reading that are observed until today. Among them are the reading of the Torah during the Shabbat afternoon Minchah service; the calling of **three** people for **Aliyah** ("going up" to the reader's desk to bless and read from the Torah) at the Shabbat afternoon and weekday readings, and the reading of no less than ten verses from the Torah on those days (Rambam, Hilchot Tefilah 12:1). Ezra either instituted or renewed the custom of reading the Torah week by week from the beginning Genesis to the end of Deuteronomy in an annual cycle that starts and ends on Shemini Atzeret (one-day festival following Succot), reaching the reproof at the end of Leviticus just before Shavuot and the reproof towards the end of Deuteronomy just before Rosh Hashanah (Rambam, ibid. 13:2).

Ezra's Torah reading took place "in front of the wide space that is before the Gate of the Water" (v 2). In Talmud Yoma 69b there are different opinions as to whether this was in the main Temple courtyard in front of the House (the Azarah), the Ezrat Nashim ("Women's Courtyard" before the Azarah) or elsewhere on the Temple Mount. In any event, this assembly is emblematic of the assembly of all the people in the Synagogue, to which everyone must come to hear the Torah.

In the light of the widespread feeling today that women have somehow been excluded from Jewish religious life, it is important to note that our text repeats that Ezra's gathering included men **and** women (vv 2 & 3) and that **everyone** was listening to the Torah and receiving a running translation into the vernacular explaining what it is saying (v 3 and see Rashi on v 7). Everyone had their ears tuned only to the Sefer Torah (v 3) - not to the kinds of frivolous conversations that go on during the Torah reading in certain synagogues that are frequented by irreverent ignoramuses who unfortunately have never been sufficiently inspired by their rabbis and teachers to make them want to wake up from their spiritual sleep and grasp that the words of the Torah are the words of the Living God, and that even if they are not fully understood they should still be treated with the utmost respect.

When Ezra read the Torah, he was flanked by six men to his right and six to his left (v 4: Zechariah=Meshulam "because he was **complete** in his deeds" Megillah 23a). The Talmud finds an allusion in the six men flanking Ezra to the six men who go up to the Torah reading on Yom Kippur (Megillah ibid.)

"And Ezra opened the scroll in the eyes of all the people..." (v 5). This alludes to the custom of **Hagbahah**, raising the scroll so that everyone can see the script, which according to the Sefardi and Chassidic **Nusach** ("style", "custom") is performed prior to the actual reading, while many Ashkenazi communities perform it after the reading. At the moment of the **Hagbahah** it is customary for people to stretch out their right hand pointing towards the Torah (cf. v 6).

"And Ezra blessed..." (v 6). This alludes to the **blessing** made by the reader before he begins to read. (The present-day custom where the person called up to the Torah reading blesses but leaves it to the **Ba'al Korey**, to actually read stems from the fact that the level of education has fallen to the point where the great majority, even if they can read Hebrew, are still unable to read the Torah themselves directly from the scroll with the correct vocalization and cantillation / "trope" because only the letters are written in the scroll but not the vowels or musical notations. In earlier times, and in some Sefardic and Yemenite communities until today, each of the men called to the Torah actually reads his portion himself, as do many Bar-mitzvah boys.) It is the blessing over the reading of the Torah - when recited and listened to with the proper intentions - that transforms the occasion from being a prosaic reading of a text into a collective act of devotion in which both the reader and the listeners are attaching themselves to God through hearing His words.

"And they read in the scroll, in the Torah of God distinctly, and gave the sense, and caused them to understand the reading" (v 8). The Talmud (Megillah 3a) darshens from this verse that Ezra established the **Mikra** (way of **reading** the words), the **Targum** (translation into the Aramaic vernacular of the people=**Meforash**), the divisions of the verses (**p'sukim=ve-soom sechel**), the cantillation/trope (=**va-yaveenu ba-mikra**) and the **Masoret** ("tradition" as to how the words in the Torah are to be spelled, whether **maley**, "in full", or **haseir**, "lacking" certain letters, with enlarged or diminished letters etc.) For all this had apparently been forgotten (by the majority, although presumably an inner circle of sages, prophets and priests always preserved and handed down the sacred tradition) and Ezra formally reinstituted and returned to the authentic tradition.

ROSH HASHANAH

From the response of Nehemiah and Ezra in v 9 we can infer that the Torah reading in the precincts of the Temple brought all the assembled people to a great wave of anguish, weeping and repentance for their deeds. Now these two leaders taught a lesson in the proper celebration of Rosh HaShanah that is expressed succinctly by Rabbi Nachman, who once said that God gave him a unique gift in being able to understand what Rosh HaShanah really is. "On Rosh HaShanah one must act wisely and only think good thoughts. One should only keep in mind that God will be good to us. One must be happy on Rosh HaShanah and yet one must cry..." (Sichot HaRan #21).

The lesson of Ezra and Nehemiah, which is brought as Halachah in Shulchan Aruch, is that together with our tearful repentance on Rosh HaShanah, we must also celebrate the festival joyously with good food and drink in the confidence that God will be merciful with us and stretch out His "arm" to accept our repentance. **"For the joy of HaShem is Your strength"** (v 8).

The penitence aroused in the people on this Rosh Hashanah was greatly elevated through the joyous celebration of Succot, which started on the 15th of the month and continued for seven days followed by the one-day festival of **Shemini Atzeret** immediately afterwards. Dwelling in the Succah for seven days helps us internalize the lesson that God's encompassing presence protects us wherever we are in the wilderness of life. From verse 15 the sages learned that the branches and leaves used for **S'chach**, the "roof" of the temporary Succah dwelling, must grow from the ground and must be in their natural state so as not to be susceptible to the **Tum'ah**, "impurity" that attaches itself to man-crafted vessels (Succah 12a).

"And all the assembly of the returnees from the captivity made Succot and dwelled in Succot, for the Children of Israel had not done so since the days of Joshua bin-Nun" (v 17). It was not that under King David etc. they had not celebrated Succot, but with the return under Ezra they now began counting the Sabbatical and Jubilee Year cycles again and observing the laws of walled cities and tithes etc. just as the people had started to do when they first entered the Land under Joshua (Erchin 32b).

CHAPTER 9

After the jubilant celebration of Succot followed by Shemini Atzeret (which is on the 22nd Tishri), the people gave themselves only one day (="**Isru Chag**", the day after a festival, invested with a festive character) before returning to the Temple fasting, in sackcloth and ashes, separating themselves from foreign wives and children (v 2), and presumably from foreign ways of thinking as well. Verse 3 is one of the sources for the laws of proper procedure on public fast-days (Ta'anit 12b).

The Levites now stood on their platform in the Temple and opened up in a song that was a call to all the people to repent.

The passage running from the last part of verse 5 until the end of verse 11 is familiar from the daily morning prayers, during which they are recited after Psalm 150, before **Shirat Ha-Yam**, the "Song of the Sea".

The entire "song" of the Levites, which continues until the end of the present chapter, praises God the Creator of heaven and earth and goes on to recount the history of Israel from the founding father Abraham, to whom God promised the Land of Canaan, through the redemption from Egypt and His providential care of Israel in the wilderness, leading them with pillars of fire and cloud, feeding them with Manna and water from the rocks, giving them the Torah, the Shabbat and other commandments, followed by Israel's rebellion with the sin of the Golden Calf, God's forgiveness and His giving them the lands of kings and nations filled with great goodness..

As the people stood now at the start of the new era of the Second Temple, the story of how Israel had become fat off God's bounty and rebelled, resulting in their exile, had to be sung to them afresh in order to remind them that their mission was to rectify the sins of the past. For each generation must hear again the saga of the nation and to relearn its forgotten lessons all over again.

CHAPTER 10

Stirred to repentance by the song of reproof sung by the Levites on the Temple platform as recorded in the previous chapter, the entire assembly renewed the ancestral Covenant of dedication to God, with the leaders of the Priests, the Levites and Israelites formally signing their names on a written affirmation of commitment.

It may be difficult to assimilate the long lists of names given in these chapters, but they should be read with reverence as part of the fabric of the sacred text, which is the national archive and treasury of all the souls of Israel. With sensitivity to the allusions contained in the different Hebrew roots on which these names are built, careful study will reveal a wealth of insights into the mindset and outlook of the generations of pining exiles and grateful returnees who gave such names to their children.

It was not only the home-born Israelites who reaffirmed their commitment to the Covenant. Among the many unnamed people who followed their leaders in this collective act of repentance were not only many priests, Levites, gate-keepers, Temple singers and servants, but also "all those who have separated themselves from the peoples of the lands to the Torah of God, their wives, their sons and their daughters, everyone having knowledge and understanding" (v 29). "These are the **converts** who separated themselves from the religions of the nations in order to become attached and joined to the Torah of the Holy One blessed be He and to keep his commandments" (Rashi ad loc.).

This affirmation of commitment to the Covenant took the form of a solemn oath which carried the sanction of severe curses on those who would violate it (v 30). The people undertook to observe the commandments of the Torah, specifying those that most needed strengthening, including the maintenance of family purity and rejection of intermarriage (v 31) and the observance of the Shabbat (v 32). It is noteworthy that the specific aspect of Sabbath observance mentioned in the text is abstention from buying and selling, which are prohibited not because they necessarily and intrinsically involve carrying out any of the 39 **Melachot** ("labors") that are forbidden **Mi-D'oraita** (explicitly in the written Torah). Rather they are forbidden **Mi-De-Rabbanan** (through enactments of the sages), whether as a "fence" to keep people well away from infringing **Melachah** (thus trading often leads to writing, which is a forbidden **Melachah**), or because such activities are inconsistent with the sanctity of the day. We thus see how the Written Torah (TaNaKh) goes hand in hand with the Oral Torah as taught by the sages. Observance of Shabbat is a central theme in Nehemiah 13.

"We also laid ordinances (**Mitzvot**) upon ourselves to charge ourselves yearly with the third part of a shekel..." (v 33). This refers to an annual contribution to the Temple over and above the statutory annual contribution of a Half Shekel by every adult male. The Talmud explains that the extra contribution mentioned here represents **Tzedakah** "charity", and learns out from this verse that the mitzvah of charity is counted as equivalent to all of the other Mitzvot since the verse calls it not **Mitzvah** in the singular but **Mitzvot** in the plural (Bava Batra 9a).

"And we have cast lots among the priests, the Levites and the people for the wood offering..." (v 35). The Talmud explains that the returnees did not find wood in the Temple for use on the Altar to burn the sacrifices, and a number of individuals volunteered to bring wood to the Temple at their own expense. They won this right not only for themselves but also for their descendants, who on specified dates during the year would bring their wood offerings together with sacrifices and festivities (Ta'anit 28a).

A very important part of the Covenant was the reaffirmation of all of the commandments relating to the Land and its produce, including the Sabbatical year of rest from agriculture (see v 32, which specifically refers to the remittance of debts in that year), the first-fruits (v 37), sacrifice of first-born animals (v 37), Challah, the gift of dough to the priests, Terumah, the priestly tithe, and Ma'aser, the 10% of produce given to the Levite out of which he in turn had to give 10% as Terumat Ma'aser to the Cohen-priest (v 38ff). From now on collection of these tithes was to be organized under formal supervision in order to ensure proper support for the priests and Levites who were responsible for all of the Temple activities.

CHAPTER 11

Nehemiah had already remarked that in his time, at the start of the Second Temple era, "The city was large and great, but the people in it were few, and the houses were not yet built" (Nehemiah 7:4). The great majority of the returnees from Babylon had gone back to their ancestral farms and rural settlements in what was primarily an agricultural society, and Jerusalem was far from being the kind of industrial or commercial center that could support a large population.

Besides the tithes on agricultural produce, it was necessary to take a ten per cent "tithe" of the population in the form of volunteers who would reside in Jerusalem and strengthen the city. Our present chapter lists only the most important leaders among these volunteers (see Rashi on v 4), who included members of the tribes of Judah and Benjamin as well as priests and Levites. (By no means all the priests and Levites served in the Temple all the time: they were organized into **Mishmarot** who served according to a rota, while the others spent most of their time living in their various towns and villages outside the city, see v 20.)

Our chapter also lists key officers responsible for the maintenance of the Temple fabric (v 16) the prayer services and singing (v 17) and guarding the Temple gates.

"For it was the king's commandment concerning them..." (v 23). Rashi (ad loc.) explains that this refers to the Persian king Darius, who put his trust in certain officers to supervise the disbursement of funds from the royal treasury to pay for various Temple needs. Not mentioned in the text is that when the Temple was built, the Persian kings gave orders to place a decorative frieze representing the Persian capital city of Shushan above the eastern gate of the Temple in order to put fear of the governing power into the hearts of the people so that they would not rebel (see Bartenura on Middot 1:3).

The chapter concludes with a list of the chief habitations in territories of Judah and Benjamin, many of which are settlements in Israel until today.

CHAPTER 12

Our present chapter continues listing the names of the leading Cohen-priests and Levites who returned to Judea from Babylon with Zerubavel - although the list does not include all of them (Rashi on v 12).

Verses 27ff recount the ceremony of inauguration of the rebuilt city walls of Jerusalem by Ezra and Nehemiah. The purpose of this inauguration was to formally sanctify the area enclosed within the walls with the unique sanctity of Jerusalem. Only within the city walls is it permitted to eat **Kadoshim Kalim** ("light" sacrifices, which did not have to be eaten within the Temple courtyard, such as the meat of peace and thanksgiving offerings, the Pesach lamb, animal tithes and firstborn animals), **Bikurim** (the "first fruits" eaten by the priests), **Ma'aser Sheini** (the Second Tithe eaten in Jerusalem by its owners) etc. A variety of restrictions applied in the Holy City unlike other cities in Israel: among them are the prohibition against leaving a dead body to rest in Jerusalem overnight; no graves were permitted there except for those of the kings of the House of David and Hulda the Prophetess; areas within the city could not be plowed or used for agriculture, fruit orchards etc.; pottery furnaces were not permitted because of the smoke, and garbage tips were proscribed as they would have attracted unclean creatures that could have caused defilement to people and foods that had to be eaten in a state of ritual purity, etc. (see Rambam, Hilchot Beit HaBechirah 7:14).

The Sanhedrin were authorized to expand the city and the Temple courtyards as far as they wanted (Rambam, Hilchot Beit HaBechirah 6:10). "And how would they add to the city? The rabbinic court would offer two Todah (thanksgiving) animal offerings and then take the mandatory leavened loaves included with the animal sacrifice, and the rabbis of the court would go in procession after the thanksgiving offerings. They would stand with harps and cymbals by every single corner and every single stone in Jerusalem chanting 'I will exalt you, HaShem, for You have lifted me up.' (Psalm 30:2) and continue until they reached the end of the area that they were sanctifying, where they stopped. There they would eat the bread of one of the thanksgiving offerings while the other was burned..." (Rambam ibid. 6:12; cf. Talmud Bavli, Shevuot 15b).

Rambam maintains that the ceremony conducted by Ezra as recounted in our present chapter was largely symbolic as the area in question was not now actually sanctified anew since the original sanctification of the Temple precincts and the city of Jerusalem carried out by King Solomon was not only for his own time but for all time to come (ibid. 6:14). However, this opinion is disputed by others (see Raavad ad loc.). Rambam thus holds that it is permitted to offer sacrifices on the Temple Mount even when there is no Temple, but this opinion is not universally accepted.

From the account of the ceremony of inauguration as described in our chapter, we see the great importance of **music** and **song** in the Temple rituals (v 28). The arrangements for the Levite singers and Temple musicians reinstituted by Ezra and Nehemiah dated back to King David, the "sweet singer of Israel" (vv 36 & 46). The restoration of the Temple was thus complete, and Nehemiah took steps to ensure the orderly collection of the Terumah-tithe for the priests and the Ma'aser-tithes for the Levites so that they would be freed from the burden of supporting themselves in order to devote themselves to their duties in the Temple.

CHAPTER 13

The work of separating the returnees from their foreign wives was complex and protracted. One of the sons of the High Priest himself was married into the family of Toviah, one of the leading adversaries, and the High Priest even gave Toviah an office in the Temple, where he was in an excellent position to spy on what was happening there.

The exact chronology of the various events described in our present chapter is somewhat obscure. The walls of Jerusalem were built and dedicated by Nehemiah shortly after his arrival there in the twentieth year of the reign of Darius king of Persia, and Nehemiah stayed in the city for twelve years. Thereafter he returned to Babylon to continue serving the king as his wine butler/advisor. Our text seems to imply that it was during Nehemiah's absence that Toviah gained his foothold in the Temple and that Nehemiah thereafter returned to Jerusalem, but it is not clear how long afterwards this was (v 6, see Rashi and Metzudat David ad loc.).

Whenever it was, Nehemiah used his authority as governor of Judea to eject Toviah from the Temple. He also had to struggle with the Temple officers, who had become negligent about providing the Levite Temple singers with their **Ma'aser** tithe, causing them to abandon their duties in Jerusalem in order to go around the farms of Judea to collect it for themselves (vv 10-13).

Nehemiah saw as one of his greatest achievements the restoration of respect for and proper observance of the Shabbat in the Holy City (vv 14-22). He witnessed flagrant violation of the prohibition against **Melachah** on Shabbat in Judea: the treading of grapes in the winepress involves the **Melachah** of **S'chitah** squeezing and separating the juice from the flesh of the fruit, which is a derivative of the **Melachah** of **Dash**, separating the kernels of produce from the stalks. This is forbidden **Mi-D'oraita** (by the law of the written Torah). Nehemiah also saw the shameless marketing of all kinds of produce on Shabbat by various traders and merchants. Commercial activity is not necessarily forbidden on Shabbat **Mi-D'oraita** but is certainly forbidden **Mi-De-Rabbanan** (through the enactments of the sages, cf. Isaiah 58:13).

In order to restore proper observance of the Shabbat, Nehemiah had to struggle with the leaders of Judea (v 17) - not unlike the **Chareidim** in Israel today, who are locked in struggle with the secularized in an attempt to uphold the sanctity of Shabbat.

"What evil thing is this that you do and profane the Sabbath day? Did not your fathers do this, and did not our God bring all this evil upon us and upon this city? And yet you bring more wrath upon Israel by profaning the Sabbath" (vv 17-18). If only we would imbibe this lesson today.

The closing section of our chapter returns to the issue of intermarriage (vv 23-31). Thus, Nehemiah's book ends with his strengthening of two of the most fundamental pillars of Judaism: family purity and observance of the Shabbat.

With this we reach the end of all the narrative books of the TaNaKh with the exception of the Book of Chronicles, which retells the history of Israel until the destruction of the First Temple, concluding with a brief reference to the return of the exiles from Babylon to Jerusalem under Zerubavel.

Blessed be God for ever and ever. Amen.

דברי הימים

CHRONICLES

Divrey HaYamim - literally, "The Words, or Matters of the Days" - known in English as the Book of Chronicles, may be seen as the royal archive of the records of the House of David, tracing the genealogy of King David and his seed from Adam and the Patriarchs, and following their history until the destruction of Solomon's Temple, the exile to Babylon, and the return of the Jews to Jerusalem under the leadership of Zerubavel, who as grandson of King Yeho-yachin was himself heir to the Davidic kingship.

Divrey HaYamim was written by Ezra the Priest at the time of the return of the exiles in order to establish the pedigree of Zerubavel and the House of David and also that of the Levites and Priests who would minister in the rebuilt Temple, the foundations of which had already been laid. Thus, **Divrey HaYamim** seals the unbreakable bond between the House of David and the Temple Priesthood, embodied in the marriage of Aaron the Priest to Eli-sheva, daughter of Aminadav, Prince of the House of Judah.

In Rashi's opening comment on the Book of Chronicles (I, 1:1) he explains: "Ezra wrote this book of genealogies with the help of the prophets Haggai, Zechariah and Malachi during the eighteen years from when Zerubavel and Yehoshua the Priest came to Jerusalem in the time of Cyrus [the "first aliyah" shortly after the collapse of Babylon, when the first foundations of the Second Temple were laid] until the reign of Darius son of Esther [who authorized the completion of the Second Temple, which had been held up for eighteen years through the machinations of Haman and his sons until after the death of Ahasuerus, Darius' father.] And the entire purpose is to provide the genealogy of King David and that of the Levite Temple gate-keepers, guards and singers and the Cohen-Priests in accordance with the order that David laid down for them."

Rashi continues: "Accordingly he traces their lineage from Adam until Abraham. And because he had to trace the line of Abraham, he also mentions the other peoples - his [other] sons and their sons. And on account of Abraham's sons, he had to trace the other peoples - the children of Canaan - to show how Abraham inherited their land. And since he had to trace the line of Canaan, he also traces that of the other peoples. He mentions them little by little and casts them aside until he reaches the main subject of interest. This can be compared to a king who was traveling from one place to another when he lost a precious jewel. The king stopped and took a sieve to sift the dust. until he found the jewel. Likewise, the Holy One blessed be He said, Why do I need to trace the line of Shem, Arpachshad. Terach? Only in order to find Abraham, of whom it is said '...and You **found** his heart faithful before You' (Nehemiah 9:8). And for the sake of the honor of Isaac, he traces the sons of Esau and Ishmael and the sons of Keturah, casting them aside little by little and leaving them behind..."

For many students, the opening chapters of **Divrey HaYamim**, which consist entirely of detailed genealogies, can often seem a formidable barrier to entry into the study of the book. Those who find it difficult to assimilate long lists of names may find comfort in the fact that the continuous, dense genealogies run only until the end of chapter 9, after which the narrative sections begin with the account of the death of King Saul (ch 10) and the beginning of David's kingship (chs 11-12, which give the names of his warriors). From chapter 13 on, the entire remainder of I Chronicles & the whole of II Chronicles consist of almost continuous narrative tracing the history of David, Solomon and their successors until the destruction of the First Temple. The historical narrative in Chronicles runs parallel to and supplements the narrative in the "historical" books of the NaKh - II Samuel and Kings I & II - but Chronicles is more focused on the kingdom of Judah, while Kings traces the history of Judah paripassu with that of the Ten Tribes.

As we stand at the beginning of nine chapters consisting mainly of names and lineages, let us remember that these records of the names of the primary souls of the progeny of Adam and of the house of the messianic King David are an integral part of the precious treasure-house of the King of kings. The very names and Hebrew letters, with all the Midrashim that arise out of them, possess the same intrinsic holiness as all of the writings of the Prophets, and even their mere recital brings holiness into the soul, even if it seems difficult to assimilate or remember every detail.

ADAM, SETH, ENOSH.

"The text does not mention Cain and Abel because they had no surviving offspring, whereas from Seth came the line that led to Noah and Abraham and from Abraham to David" (Rashi on v 1). The focus is not on history but on genealogy.

Commenting on the genealogy of Noah and his sons, Shem, Ham and Japhet, starting in v 4, Rashi (ad loc.) clarifies the organizational "method" underlying the arrangement of the genealogies in **Divrey HaYamim**, which can be highly confusing to beginning students since they often go back and forth. A line is taken up but then apparently dropped while another line is traced, and then the first is picked up again. Rashi writes: "He should have traced the children of Shem immediately in order to find the jewel, Abraham, and likewise then traced the line immediately down to David. But instead he briefly picks up and quickly throws aside the subsidiary lines and only then takes hold of the main line. This is the way of this entire genealogy in **Divrey HaYamim**. Likewise, when he speaks of the children of Abraham - Isaac and Ishmael - he recounts the children of Ishmael before those of Isaac, and similarly, he traces the generations of Esau - the subsidiary - before focusing on Israel (Jacob), the essence."

Vv 1-4: The generations from Adam down to the children of Noah.

Vv 5-7: The children of Japhet.

Vv 8-12: The children of Ham.

Vv 13-16: The children of Canaan.

Vv 17-27: The names of the descendants of Shem down to Abraham.

Vv 28-33: The children of Abraham - Ishmael, Isaac and the sons of Keturah.

Vv 34: The children of Isaac - Esau and Israel (Jacob).

Vv 35-42: Children of Esau.

Vv 43-50: The Seven Kings of Edom. The names of these seven kings, who "ruled and died", allude to the vessels of the seven lower kabbalistic Sefirot, which "broke" and had to be rectified.

Vv 51-54: The Princes of Edom.

All of the above genealogies parallel and supplement the corresponding genealogies in Genesis chapters 5 (Adam-Noah), 10-11 (Noah-Abraham), 25 (Ishmael and the sons of Keturah) and 36 (Esau and Seir).

CHAPTER 2

Vv 1-2: Names of the sons of Israel (Jacob).

Vv 3-4: Names of the sons of Judah.

V 5: Sons of Peretz.

Vv 6-9: Descendants of Zerach - Karmi, Eitan - and Hetzron, son of Peretz. Rashi on v 6 states that the descendants of Zerach enumerated there were outstanding sages who lived in the generations of David and Solomon (cf. I Kings 5;11). **K'luvoi** listed in verse 9 as one of the three sons of Hetzron is identified by Rashi as Kaleb, founder of the line that led to Naval (I Samuel 25:3). His was the only line that was not "flawed" (because his brother Yerachmiel married Atarah, who was not an Israelite, see our present chapter v 26, while his brother Ram's descendant, Bo'az, married Ruth the Moabitess. This is why Naval spoke so disparagingly about his kinsman David: see I Samuel 25:10; Rashi on our present chapter v 9).

Vv 10-17: The line from Ram, second son of Hetzron down to David and his family.

Vv 18-20: Children of Kaleb son of Hetzron. The Talmud associates this Kaleb with Kaleb son of Yephuneh, who together with his comrade, Joshua son of Nun, rebelled against the other spies sent by Moses to scout out the Promised Land (Numbers 13-14; Temurah 16a). However, this identification is questioned by RaDaK (on v 18). Betzalel (v 20) was the craftsman who made the wilderness Sanctuary and its vessels.

Vv 21-24: Children of Hetzron from the daughter of Makhir of the tribe of Menasheh.

Vv 25-41: Children of Yerachmiel son of Hetzron and his descendents. Yerachmiel's "other wife", Atarah (v 26) was said to be a non-Israelite (Yerushalmi Sanhedrin 2:3). From her son, Onam derived the line that went down to Elishama (v 41), grandfather of Ishmael son of Netanyah, who assassinated Gedaliah son of Achikam, thereby destroying the last vestiges of Judean autonomy after the destruction of the First Temple (see Rashi on I Chronicles 2:35; cf. Jeremiah 41:1 and RaDaK ad loc.).

Vv 42-45: Additional children of Kaleb son of Hetzron.

Vv 46-49: Children of Kaleb from his concubine.

Vv 50-55: Children of Kaleb son of Hur (see Rashi on v 50 noting the ambiguity in the Hebrew text, which makes it uncertain whether this Kaleb is identical with Kaleb son of Hetzron mentioned above in vv 18f or was a different Kaleb, the firstborn of Hur).

Rashi commenting on verse 42 gives another clue to understanding the "method" of these genealogies, which is apt to be somewhat confusing. "…And thus, the way of this entire genealogy is not to trace the lines in order. Rather, he traces part of the line of a certain family and then picks up a different family, and after having traced the line of this second family he starts again tracing the line of the first family, and then goes back again to the second. Thus, this whole book of genealogies is somewhat **me-urav –** **mixed up**!!!"

It is noteworthy that the genealogy of the tribe of Judah not only gives the names of the members of its various clans but also in many cases the names of the towns and settlements in which they lived, some of which are still to be found on the map of present-day Israel.

CHAPTER 3

Having traced some of the principle family lines of the tribe of Judah in the previous chapter, including the line leading to King David (I Chron. 2:10-15), the chronicler now gives us the names of David's wives and children and his royal descendants, looking ahead to Melech HaMashiach, as we shall see on v 24.

As a royal archive, **Divrey HaYamim** contains many secrets, hints and allusions, some of which are explained by our commentators but many of which remain hidden except to the most assiduous students. Every family has its own codes and may call certain members by different names (or nicknames) at different times and for different reasons. Thus, David's son by Avigail, called in our present chapter (v 1) Daniel ("God judges me"), because people suspected he was really the child of Avigail's first husband, Naval, is in II Samuel 3:3 called **Kil-av** ("all like his father") because he looked completely like David so there should be no doubts about his paternity (Rashi). David's wife **Egla** (v 6) is Michal daughter of Saul, who was dear to David like a calf (**Egla**, Rashi on v 6).

Vv 1-4 give the names of the wives of David and the sons they bore him in Hebron.

Vv 5-9 give the names of the sons of David born in Jerusalem. Bat-shoo'a daughter of Ami-el mentioned in verse 5 is Bat-sheva, mother of King Solomon.

Vv 10-14 trace all the kings of the House of David from Solomon to Josiah, who was the last saintly king of Judah one generation prior to the destruction of the First Temple.

Vv 15-16 give the names of the last three kings of Judah – Eliyakim (=Yeho-yakim), Yechoniah (=Yeho-yachin) and Mattanyah (=Tzidkiyahu) - all sons of Josiah. [It was Tzidkiyahu son of Josiah - mentioned in verse 15 - who was the last king of Judah, not Tzidkiyahu son of Yechoniah mentioned in verse 16, for after Nebuchadnezzar exiled Yechoniah, he installed his **uncle** as king.]

Vv 17ff: The miraculous story of how the royal line of King David was saved from extirpation when Yechoniah's wife was allowed to visit him in his narrow prison cell when in exile in Babylon has been told in our commentary on Ezra ch 2. Zerubavel, mentioned here in verse 19, was the leader of the "First Aliyah" of returnees from Babylon to Jerusalem. Our text traces Zerubavel's descendants in vv 19-24. According to tradition, **anani** (="He has answered me") mentioned in verse 24 is Melech HaMashiach who is destined to be revealed in time to come (see Targum Rav Yosef ad loc. and Rashi on our chapter v 11; see also Daniel 7:13 "and behold. with the **clouds - ananei -** of heaven"). Thus, **Divrey HaYamim** encompasses the whole of the history of man from Adam (I Chron. 1:1) all the way to Mashiach (I Chron. 3:24).

CHAPTER 4

In chapter 2 we were given some of the main family lines of the tribe of Judah in order to trace the genealogy of King David, and chapter 3 then went on to trace his royal line until the end of days.

Our present chapter (vv -23) returns to the tribe of Judah in order to complete the genealogy of this tribe and to trace in fuller detail certain lines that were mentioned only in passing in chapter 2. After this our text then goes on to trace the family lines of the tribe of Shimon (vv 24-43), who had no territory of their own but occupied territories from the portion of Judah as specified in our chapter.

Vv 1-8: Names of the sons of Judah and his descendants.

Vv 9-10: The greatness of Ya'abetz and his exploits. This Ya'abetz is identified by the rabbis with Otniel ben Kenaz (see Targum) who is mentioned explicitly in our present chapter v 13, and whose exploits are narrated in Joshua 15:17, Judges 1:13, 3:9ff. "And Ya'abetz was more **honored** than his brothers" - "From the beginning of **Divrey HaYamim** you find no **honor** until you reach Ya'abetz. This is because he engaged in Torah, and 'the sages will inherit honor' (Proverbs 3:35)" (Yalkut Shimoni). "Ya'abetz was a good, pure man of truth and kindness. He sat and darshened the Torah, as it says, 'And Ya'abetz called to the God of Israel saying, Surely, bless me.'" (Avot d'Rabbi Nathan). Darshening the Hebrew letters of his names, the Talmud says: "He was called **Otni-el** because God **answered** him. He was called **Ya'abetz** because he gave **counsel** and **spread** Torah in Israel. In his prayer, he was asking God to bless him with Torah, to expand his boundaries to encompass many students, and that God's hand should be with him so that he should not forget his studies. He prayed for companions like him and that his evil inclination should not swell his heart to the point that he would stop reviewing his studies" (Temurah 16a).

Vv 11-12: Names of the men of Reichah.

Vv 13-14: Sons of Kenaz.

Vv 15-20: Sons of Kaleb and of Yehalel-el and his descendants.

While these lists of names may have little meaning for beginning students, particularly when reading them in translation and without commentary, diligent study of the Hebrew text reveals many overtones and allusions, some of which are discussed in the classical commentaries. At times what may at first seem like a dry text can be fleetingly perceived to have a unique poetry of its own and to signify something quite other than what appears on the surface.

This is true in the case of verse 18, which at first appears to contain a string of seemingly unconnected family names. But according to rabbinic drash, "his wife Yehudiyah" alludes to Batyah daughter of Pharaoh (Exodus 2:5ff) whose name is mentioned explicitly at the end of the verse, and whom Kaleb ben Yephuneh married. She is called **Yehudiyah** because she rejected idolatry. The names of the "children" whom she "bore" - **Yered**, **Avi-gdor**, **Hever**, **Avi-Socho**, **Yekooti-el** and **Avi-zano'ah** - are not the names of her children from Kaleb but all allude to Moses. She was considered to have given birth to Moses because, having drawn him from the river, she raised him as an orphan. He was called **Yered** because he brought down the Manna for Israel; **Avi-gdor** because he healed the breaches in Israel; **Hever** because he joined Israel with their Father in heaven; **Avi-socho** because he was like a protective Succah to them, **Yekooti-el** because Israel hoped in God in his time; **Avi-zano'ah** because he cleansed the sins of Israel (see Megillah 13a).

Vv 21-23: Sons of Shelah, third son of Judah (Gen. 38:5). Although Shelah was born to Judah by his first wife long before his daughter-in-law, Tamar, bore him Peretz and Zerach, the genealogies of the latter were given earlier in Chapter 2 in order to give honor to King David, who came from the line of Peretz.

The rabbis interpreted the Hebrew codes in verse 22 as alluding to the prophets and scribes who issued from the line of Joshua, to the Gibeonites, who lied (**chozeiba**) to the princes of Israel, to Machlon

(=Yo'ash) and Chilyon (=Saraf), the sons of Elimelech and Naomi, who took Moabite wives, and to Boaz, who dwelled in Bethlehem engaging in the Torah of the Ancient of Days (see Targum).

V 23: "These were the potters (**yotzrim**) and those who dwelt among the plantations and hedges; there they dwelt occupied with the king's work" - "These are the students of the Torah for whose sake the world was created, who sit in judgment and bring stability to the world and who rebuild the ruins of the House of Israel with the Indwelling Presence of the King through their labor in the Torah and the intercalation of the months and the fixing of the dates of the New Year and the festivals" (Targum).

Vv 24-33: Sons of Shimon and the names of their habitations. The tribe of Shimon had no real share of their own in the land of Israel, because in his blessings to his sons, Jacob had said of Shimon, "I will **divide** them in Jacob and I will **scatter** them in Israel (Genesis 49:7). Thus, we find in Joshua 19:9 that members of the tribe of Shimon, which was relatively small in numbers, occupied some of the territories of Judah, which were extensive (see Rashi on v 27).

V 31: "...these were their cities until the reign of David." Complaints by members of David's own tribe of Judah about the encroachments on their territories by members of the tribe of Shimon led him to drive the latter out from the cities in which they had been living (see Rashi ad loc.)

Vv 34-38: Names of the princes of the tribe of Shimon.

Vv 39-43: Under pressure to find new territories, members of the tribe of Shimon went to conquer land from the remaining Canaanites and from the Edomites and Amalekites. They dwelled there "until this day" (v 43) "because they returned to dwell there when they returned from the exile in Babylon" (Metzudat David).

CHAPTER 5

Vv 1-10: Lineage of the tribe of Reuven and their habitations.

As mentioned a number of times, the primary purpose of **Divrey HaYamim** was to establish the credentials of the House of David and the royal line that came from him. Accordingly, pride of place was given to the genealogy of the tribe of Judah from which David came. The tribe of Shimon was mentioned next (at the end of the previous chapter) because they initially lived in territories that were part of the tribal inheritance of Judah.

The chronicler now continues with the genealogy of the tribe of Reuven, because Reuven was actually Jacob's firstborn and should thus have taken precedence over all the other tribes. Our text notes that the birthright was taken from Reuven because "he defiled his father's bed" (see Genesis 35:22f). The "double share" of the inheritance that is due to the firstborn (Deut. 21:17) was given instead to Joseph (from whom came **two** tribes, Ephraim and Menasheh), but the "birthright" itself - the kingship - was given to Judah, whose traits of character made him uniquely fit for the kingship (see Rashi on vv 1 & 2 of our present chapter).

As recounted in Numbers ch 32, the tribe of Reuven took their tribal inheritance **east** of the River Jordan in territories that were taken from Sichon king of the Emorites.

It is interesting to note that the war waged by the Reuvenites in the time of King Saul (verse 10 of our present chapter) was against the **Hagri'im**, who were none other than Ishmaelites (descendants of **Hagar**, see Rashi ad loc.) - indicating that the Middle East conflicts of today are an ongoing recycling of a very ancient conflict (see below on vv 18ff). The area of Gil'ad that was occupied by the Reuvenites lies to the east of the River Jordan between the River Yarmouk (which flows into the Jordan a few kilometers south of the Sea of Tiberias/Kinneret) and the River Yabok (which enters the Jordan further south at the Adam Bridge).

Vv 11-17: The tribe of Gad and their place of habitation. In the time of Moses, the tribe of Gad joined with that of Reuven in requesting their tribal inheritance east of the Jordan. The region of Bashan where they took their lands lies to the east of the Kinneret in the hinterlands of the Golan, north of Gilead.

Vv 18-22: Wars of the tribes east of the Jordan with other nations. The tribes of Reuven, Gad and half Menasheh were living on the border and had no option but to practice the martial arts (v 18). These they combined with faith and trust in God, and in the wider war they made in the later First Temple period against the Ishmaelite Hagri'im and other related nations (Yitur and Nafeesh v 19 were tribes founded by sons of Ishmael, Gen. 25:15), they turned to God for salvation, which was granted to them (v 22).

Vv 23-24: The half of the tribe of Menasheh who settled east of the Jordan took their territories in the Bashan, Golan Heights and Mount Hermon.

Vv 25-26: Our text laconically relates that the tribes east of the Jordan fell into idolatry and were exiled by the king of Ashur. Whereas the book of Kings deals at length with the idolatry of the Ten Tribes and the moral that must be learned from their resulting exile, the purpose of **Divrey HaYamim** is different and accordingly the exile is mentioned only in passing.

Vv 27-41: Lineage of the High Priests. This begins a new section devoted to the tribe of Levi. It is introduced here because the previous section dealt with the pedigree of Reuven, who came next in order of precedence after Judah since he was Jacob's biological firstborn. (The tribes of Gad and half Menasheh were mentioned with Reuven only because they took their territories adjacent to those of Reuven east of the Jordan.) After Reuven and Shimon (whose genealogy was given in Chapter 4), Leah's third son was Levi, and the most prestigious of the scions of Levi were the Cohanim-Priests, who were an elite separate from the rest of the tribe of Levi since they alone were authorized to conduct the Temple sacrificial rites and they were bound by unique laws of ritual purity and marital restrictions that did not apply to the other Levites.

The line of the High Priests given in this section traces the priesthood down to S'rayah (v 40) who was the father of Ezra the Scribe, the author of **Divrey HaYamim**, as well as of Yeho-tzadok mentioned in vv 40-41. Yeho-tzadok did not serve as High Priest in the Temple but his son, Yehoshua, led the first return of the exiles from Babylon to Jerusalem, and served there as the High Priest (see Rashi on v 41).

CHAPTER 6

Vv 1-6: The lineage of the sons of Gershon son of Levi. Gershon was Levi's firstborn, but the lineage of his descendants is given only after that of the priestly descendants of his younger brother Kehat (previous chapter vv 27-41) since the latter took precedence, being the ancestor of Moses, Aaron and the priestly line.

Vv 7-13: Lineage of the sons of Kehat, Levi's second son. Kehat had other sons besides Amram father of Moses and Aaron. Among the most famous (or infamous) of Kehat's descendants was Korach, (son of Kehat's second son, Yitzhar) who was swallowed up alive by the earth after fomenting conflict against Moses (Numbers ch 16). Nevertheless, Korach's sons were saved from the depths of hell, and his most illustrious descendant was the prophet Samuel, mentioned in our present text in v 13.

Vv 14-15: Lineage of the sons of Levi's third son, Merari.

Vv 16-17: It was necessary to re-organize the Levites in the time of King David because he had brought the Ark of the Covenant up to Jerusalem, marking the end of the era when the Sanctuary had traveled from place to place prior to reaching its final resting place. As long as the Sanctuary was "portable", it was the task of the Levites to carry its component parts and vessels, but as soon as it came to rest, their role changed, and now they became the Temple singers and gate-keepers. These roles were allocated to specific families and it was not permitted to change from one role to another.

Vv 18-23: The most prestigious of the Levitical roles was that of the Temple singers since music contains the deepest wisdom. The genealogy of Heyman the Temple Singer - mentioned as author of Psalm 86 - is traced back through Korach all the way to Jacob (see Rashi on Genesis 49:6).

Vv 24-28: Lineage of Asaph the Gershonite, author of Psalms 50 and 73-83. Note that Asaph stands to the **right** (Chessed) of Heyman the Kehati, who is in the middle (Tiferet).

Vv 29-32: Lineage of the sons of Merari. They are positioned to the **left** (Gevurah) of the Kehati singers.

Vv 33-34: Functions of the Levites and the Cohanim. Besides their functions as Temple singers and gate-keepers, the Levites also skinned the sacrificial animals (see II Chron. 35:11). None of the Levites were permitted to take part in the actual burning of the sacrifices or other Temple rites that were "holy of holies", as these were restricted entirely to the Cohanim.

Vv 35-38: The abbreviated line of the High Priests in these verses is traced down only to the time of King Solomon.

Vv 39-45: Names of the cities of the Priests in the territories of the tribes of Judah and Benjamin. First among the priestly cities was Hebron (cf Joshua 21:11). The fact that this was in the territory of Judah underlies the close bond between the royal tribe and the priesthood. The priests also received habitations in some of the cities of refuge for unwitting killers - the presence of the priests in these cities was a beneficial influence helping to rehabilitate such people.

Vv 46-66: Names of the cities of the Levites among the other tribes. The cities of the Levites were scattered throughout the inheritances of the Tribes - this was how Jacob's curse of "I will scatter them in Israel" (Genesis 49:7) was fulfilled in the case of Levi. In addition, the presence of the Levites through-out the land was intended to ensure that teachers of Torah were at hand in all the different population centers since the Levites were given their **Ma'aser** tithes in order to be freed from the burden of earning a living so as to be able to devote themselves to the study and teaching of Torah.

CHAPTER 7

In the previous chapters, we have been given the lineages of Judah, Shimon, Levi and Reuven (all sons of Leah) - and with Reuven, who settled east of the Jordan, we were also given the lineages of Gad and half the tribe of Menasheh, who also settled there. Altogether that is a total of six tribes.

In the present chapter, we are given the lineages of most of the remaining tribes of Israel: Issachar, Benjamin, Naphtali, the other half of Menasheh, Ephraim and Asher.

It is noteworthy that the genealogy of Naphtali in our present chapter is brief in the extreme compared with those of the other tribes, while no genealogy at all is given for the tribe of Zevulun (although the territory of Zebulun was mentioned in connection with the Levitical cities in ch 6 vv 48 & 62). Nor does there seem to be any mention in our text of the tribe of Dan (although Danites and Zebulunites are both mentioned among the warriors who came to give the kingship to David in Hebron (I Chron. 12:34 & 36).

Members of the tribes of Naphtali, Dan and Zebulun may have been among the early members of the Ten Tribes who went into exile. Zebulun was a tribe of merchants, who very likely traveled and may have found it easier to adapt to foreign lands. As to Naphtali and Dan, in II Chronicles 2:4 we learn that when King Asa of Judah was under attack from Ba'sha king of Israel, Asa bribed Hadad king of Aram to hit the northern territories of Israel, including Dan and some poor cities of Naphtali.

Commenting on the brevity of the genealogy of Naphtali as given in our present chapter in v 13, Rashi makes a comment that throws some more light on Ezra's methods: "The reason why no further details of the genealogy of Naphtali are given is provided at the end of Yerushalmi Megillah (cf. Sifrei on Ve-Zot HaBrachah 33:27): it says that Ezra discovered three books, each of which contained various genealogies. What he found, he wrote and what he did not find he did not write - and he simply found no further details about the tribe of Naphtali. For this same reason all of the genealogies in Chronicles skip around, because he skipped from one book to the other and joined them together, and what he could not write in this book he wrote in the book of Ezra. The proof is that it says further on in our text, 'And all Israel were reckoned by genealogies and surely they are written in the book of the kings of Israel; and Judah were exiled to Babylon' (I Chron. 9:1). This is saying, 'If you want to know the genealogy of the Ten Tribes, go to Halah and Habor, Nahar, Gozan and the cities of Medea [where they were exiled], for their Book of Chronicles went into exile with them, but as for Judah, I discovered their book in Babylon and what I found I have written."

Rashi in his comment on I Chron. 8:29 mentions more about the books of genealogies that Ezra found in Babylon. They were called **Sepher Me'onim** (the book of "residences"???), **Sepher Zatouti** (the book of "lads", "children" or possibly "slaves" cf. Jastrow s.v. **Za'touti**) and **Sepher He-Achim** (the book of "brothers"). According to Rashi, in cases of discrepancy between them, Ezra would follow the opinion of two of the books against one. Likewise, in cases where they found many genealogical scrolls, wherever there was a majority version and a minority version, he would ignore the minority and follow the majority, while if he found an even division of opinion, he wrote both genealogies - one in Chronicles and one in the book of Ezra - on account of the discrepancies between them.

Vv 1-5 of our present chapter give the lineage of the descendants of Issachar and their numbers in the time of David. The tribe of Issachar were particularly prolific (see v 4), and as we will see later (ch 12 v 33) they attained great heights in the deeper wisdom of the Torah, including knowledge of the "times" (astronomy and astrology).

Vv 6-12: Lineage of the descendants of Benjamin and their numbers. RaDaK (on v 6) mentions an opinion that the Benjamin mentioned here is not the son of Jacob and founder of the tribe of that name, but rather one of the members of Issaschar (because the full genealogy of the tribe of Benjamin is given in the next chapter). However, RaDaK finds it more plausible that here too we are being given part of the lineage of the tribe of Benjamin.

V 13: Lineage of the children of Naphtali. This is brief - perhaps for the reasons discussed above.

Vv 14-19: Lineage of the children of Menasheh.

Vv 20-29: Lineage of the children of Ephraim and their territories.

"And the sons of Ephraim. and the men of Gat who had been born in the land killed them because they came down to take their cattle" (vv 20-21). Targum on v 21 brings the story of how some of the tribe of Ephraim tried to leave Egypt and enter the Promised Land before the foreordained time, only to lose their lives: "And Zavad his son and Shootelah his son and Ezer and Elad were leaders of the House of Ephraim and they calculated the date of the redemption from the time of God's Covenant between the Pieces with Abraham (Gen. 15:9ff), but they were mistaken because they should have counted from the day of the birth of Isaac. Thus, they went out of Egypt thirty years before the end, because the Covenant between the Pieces was thirty years before the birth of Isaac. When they went out of Egypt, 200,000 armed warriors from the tribe of Ephraim went out with them, but the men of Gat, who were born in the land of the Philistines, killed them because they came down to capture their cattle" (Targum Rav Yosef on I Chron. 7:21). The Talmud (Sanhedrin 92b) states that the dead whose bones the prophet Ezekiel brought back to life (Ezekiel ch 37) were these fallen members of the tribe of Ephraim. Indeed, Rabbi Yehuda ben Beseira declared that he himself was descended from the dead whom Ezekiel had revived and that he possessed an ancestral pair of Tefilin handed down from them.

One wonders if they went to take the cattle merely to get rich or in order to use the skins for Tefilin. The reason the home-born Philistines of Gat had the advantage over them was because they were familiar with the terrain, while the Ephraimites did not know the escape routes. This teaches how well we need to learn the geography of our land.

The genealogy of the other members of the tribe of Ephraim, that of Noon (v 27) goes no further than his son Joshua (ibid.) because the latter had no sons. He did, however, have daughters (he was married to Rahab, the convert from Jericho) and among his descendants were Huldah the Prophetess and Jeremiah (Megillah 14).

Vv 30-40: Lineage of the children of Asher and their numbers. The Midrash mentions that because of the abundance of olive oil in the territory of Asher (cf. Deut. 33:24) their daughters were very beautiful and married kings anointed with olive oil (Rashi on v 31; Pirkey d'Rabbi Eliezer).

CHAPTER 8

The whole of Chapter 8 is apparently devoted to the genealogy of the tribe of Benjamin. In the words of Rashi (on ch 8 v 1): "He has already given their lineage, but because he wanted to trace the lines down to King Saul he now goes back and gives the line all the way from Benjamin. Here he calls some of them by different names. This is because Ezra found a variety of genealogical scrolls."

I advisedly wrote that Chapter 8 is **apparently** devoted to the genealogy of Benjamin, because under the surface of the names, other things are happening as well. Verse 6 seems to be telling us of a branch of the tribe of Benjamin who were inhabitants of **Geva** but who were taken into some kind of forced exile - Targum identifies **Manachat** at the end of v 6 with a town of Edom. Verse 7 then tells us who it was that took those Benjaminites into exile. Verse 8 appears to be telling us about a certain **Shacharayim** who was one of the exiles, and who fathered a child in the field of Moab after having been released from exile. However, the Midrash on this verse identifies this **Shacharayim** with Boaz (despite his having been from the tribe of Judah) because he had been **released (shachrer)** from sins. His fathering a child in the field of Moab alludes to his marriage with Ruth the Moabitess. "And he begat of **Chodesh** his wife...." This alludes to the renewal (**chadash**) in his time of the Halachah that the Torah forbids only the Moabite from entering the Assembly of HaShem but not the Moabitess (Yalkut Shimoni).

Vv 1-13: Genealogy of the children of Benjamin.

Vv 14-28: Names of the family heads of the tribe of Benjamin who resided in Jerusalem.

Vv 29-31: The Benjaminites who resided in Giv'on.

Vv 33-40: The line of King Saul and his descendants. Since Saul's kingship and death prepared the way for King David, in whose honor **Divrey HaYamim** was written, Saul's genealogy comes here near the conclusion of the genealogical section of the work, shortly before we launch into the story of the death of Saul and kingship of David (chs 10ff).

The Talmud (Pesachim 62b) comments on the fact that in our present chapter v 38, the name of Atzel appears at the beginning and the end of the verse, which contains the names of her six children. "Between **Atzel** and **Atzel** there are four hundred camel loads of **Drashot!!!**"

CHAPTER 9

V 1: "And all Israel were reckoned by their genealogies...." As explained by the commentators, Ezra is saying: "Even though I have not set forth the genealogies of all Israel, their lineages were all invest-igated and are written in the book of the kings of Israel - and this book went into exile with them and is not in my hands in order to copy all of their lineages from it. But Judah went into exile to Babylon because of their sin and the book of their lineages was with them, and what I found in it I have copied, because I am located with them" (Metzudat David, cf. Rashi and RaDaK ad loc.).

In verse 1 of this chapter, Ezra is summarizing and sealing the contents of the introductory genealogical chapters of **Divrey HaYamim** (ch's 1-8). Having thus completed his overall genealogy of the tribes of Israel, Ezra takes most of the remainder of our present chapter (vv 2-38) to set forth the names of leading returnees from the exile in Babylon, including the Israelites, Priests and Levites, enumerating the duties of the latter in the Temple. This account of the population of Jerusalem on the threshold of the Second Temple era (which parallels Nehemiah ch 11) concludes the genealogical part of **Divrey HaYamim**, the whole of the rest of which is devoted to a detailed narrative of the history of the House of David from the time of the death of King Saul until the destruction of the First Temple.

Vv 2-9: Details of the members of the tribe of Judah and other tribes who returned from the Babylonian exile.

The returning exiles who came to Judea with Zerubavel in the first wave of "Aliyah" prior to the arrival of Ezra and his group settled mostly in their ancestral lands in the cities of Judea rather than in Jerusalem. In addition to members of the tribes of Judah and Benjamin, the returnees also included members of the tribes of Ephraim and Menasheh, as specified in verse 2 of our text. Metzudat David (on v 2) states that even though members of the Ten Tribes were exiled to Ashur, many had remained in their land and went into exile in Babylon with the tribes of Judah and Benjamin and returned with them.

Vv 10-16: Genealogies of the Cohanim and Levites. The text emphasizes the strength and devotion which the priests put into their work in the Temple (v 13).

Vv 17-21: Names of the Temple gate-keepers.

V 18: "...And until now they were in the Gate of the King to the east: they are the gatekeepers for the camp of the children of Levi" - "Just as David and Samuel had instituted the gate-keepers, so it remained throughout all the days that the First Temple stood, and so it was until now in the Second Temple" (Metzudat David, cf. RaDaK ad loc.) Ezra is emphasizing the continuity between the service in the First Temple and that in the Second Temple. This would appear to contradict the view of those who theorize that Ezra made radical changes in the Temple, its music and services.

V 20: "And Pinchas son of Elazar was the ruler over them; in time past HaShem was with him." Taken at face value this verse could be construed as referring to the governor of the Temple Levites in the time of the return (see RaDaK ad loc.). However, the Midrashic explanation (taking off from **avoteichem** in v 19, alluding to the **ancestors** of the functionaries in the Second Temple) is that it refers to Pinchas son of Elazar, the hero of Numbers 25:7ff, who later took over from his father as superintendent over the functioning of the Levites in the Sanctuary. According to tradition, God was with Pinchas initially because he protested against Zimri's flagrant immorality, but the Divine Presence later left him because he did not go to Jephthah to release him from his vow (Kohelet Rabbah 10:17).

Vv 22-34: Numbers of the gate-keepers and their roles. It appears from our text that certain Levitical families traditionally provided the guards at specific gates and entrances to the Temple, and that while the captains resided in Jerusalem near the Temple precincts, other members of these families resided in their ancestral Levitical towns and villages, coming up to serve in the Temple at specified times during the year.

V 22: "…these are they that David and Samuel the Seer instituted in their enduring order." The Talmud states that Moses originally instituted a rota of eight watches of priests and Levites, who took turns in serving in the Temple for a week at a time. Owing to the natural increase in the numbers of priests and Levites over the generations, David and Samuel found it necessary to reorganize these watches, which now became twenty-four in number (Ta'anit 27a).

Vv 27ff: The duties of the Levites in the Temple included taking out and returning the Temple vessels for use in the sacrifices and supervising the provision of managing the necessary supplies of grain, wine, oil and incense ingredients. The actual blending of the incense spices was reserved by the priests to themselves (v 30) because only one family of priests knew the carefully-guarded secret of the **Ma'aleh Ashan** - that minute quantity of a certain ingredient that caused the smoke from the incense to rise in a single column directly upwards. Other duties of the Levites included the baking of the pancake offerings brought daily by the High Priest and of the weekly Show Bread (vv 31-2).

V 33: "And these are the singers... they were **exempt from other duties** for they were employed in that work **day and night**" - Because of the depth and profundity of the Temple music, it was necessary to devote themselves to its study **day and night**!!! This just goes to prove the supreme importance of soul music!!!

Vv 35-38: Names of the Benjaminite inhabitants of Giv'on. This entire section together with that which follows on the genealogy of King Saul (vv 39-44) appeared at the end of the previous chapter (I Chron. 8:29-32 & 33-40), which was devoted to the genealogy of the tribe of Benjamin culminating in the lineage of Saul. Metzudat David (on v 35) explains that the section on the Benjaminite inhabitants of Giv'on was introduced into the previous chapter after the account of the Benjaminites who lived in Jerusalem (at the beginning of the Second Temple period). The chronicler then digressed from the beginning of our present chapter until now, enumerating the priests, Levites and other inhabitants of Jerusalem at that time. But now, since he is coming to tell of the kingship of David, which came after the death of Saul, he goes back again to set forth the lineage of King Saul (vv 39-44).

The commentators explain that Saul's son **Esh-Ba'al** (v 39) is **Ish-Boshet** (II Samuel 2:8) etc.) while Jonathan's son **Mereev Ba'al** (v 40) is **Mephiboshet** (II Samuel 4:4 etc.). Because **Ba'al** was the name of an idol, it was referred to as **Boshet**, "shame", while Saul and his family strove (**mereev**) against such idolatry (cf. Gideon-Yeru-ba'al Judges 7:1).

CHAPTER 10

The sad story of the death of King Saul and his sons and their burial by the men of Yaveish Gil'ad is told in I Samuel ch 31. It is retold here since it is the prelude to the story of the kingship of David, who despite having been anointed by the prophet Samuel much earlier, only actually became king with the death of Saul.

The reason why the men of Yaveish Gil'ad specifically took upon themselves the dangerous task of burying Saul and his sons just after the Philistine victory, which threw Israel into turmoil, was because early in his career, King Saul had come to their rescue from the cruel ultimatum issued against them by Nachash king of Ammon (I Samuel ch 11).

Vv 13f: "So Saul died for his transgression... and He killed him and turned over the kingship to David son of Yishai". The chronicler is intent on telling his story and concisely but surely making the moral import of the story very clear.

CHAPTER 11

"And all Israel gathered themselves to Israel to David...." (v 1). With the setting of the star of King Saul, the star of David now shone forth in all its radiance. The present chapter and the next tell of his following of mighty warriors and how all Israel came together in unity and submitted themselves to his leadership. The people said to him, "...You shall be shepherd over God's people" (v 2). But according to the Midrash, David replied: "How can I be shepherd? It doesn't depend upon me, for 'God is my shepherd.' (Psalm 23:1) and only then '...I shall not want' (ibid.) i.e. I shall not be wanting in what you need!" (see Rashi on v 2).

V 3: "And David struck a covenant with them in Hebron before HaShem": as explained by Rashi (ad loc.), this was a three-way covenant in which the people undertook to be God's servants and also to be servants of the king in accordance with the law of the kingship, while King David undertook to treat his servants in accordance with the law and to fight their wars (see Rashi on v 3). David was not an overbearing autocrat: his monarchy was **constitutional**!

V 4ff: "And David and all Israel went to Jerusalem...." The purpose of this passage is not so much to relate the story of the conquest of Jerusalem from the Jebusites as to highlight the role of Yo'av ben Tzeruyah, who thereby became David's commander-in-chief. This introduces the account of all the other mighty warriors of David in vv 10-47.

The inner essence of David, archetype of the messianic king and redeemer, is deeply hidden, but we can learn more about it through knowing about his followers. In the words of Rabbi Nachman, "It is impossible to understand the Tzaddik himself since his intrinsic essence is beyond our grasp. Only through the followers of the Tzaddik is it possible to understand the Tzaddik's greatness. This is similar to a seal. The writing on the seal is unreadable because the letters are back to front. Only when one takes the seal and stamps it on wax can one understand the letters and designs inscribed on the seal, and one then sees what is written on the seal. Similarly, through the Tzaddik's followers one can come to understand something of the Tzaddik himself" (Likutey Moharan I, 140).

"And these are the chiefs of the mighty men...." (v 10). The account of David's leading captains and warriors in the remainder of the present chapter parallels the account in II Samuel 23:8-39 with certain variations in the names and details.

According to the surface meaning of our text, after Yo'av, his commander-in-chief, David had an inner "panel" of three chiefs (vv 11-14): these were (1) **Yashav-Am ben Chachmoni** (v 11); (2) **Elazar ben Dodo** (v 12) and (3) **Shamah ben Agei** who is not mentioned here in Chronicles but is mentioned in the parallel account in II Samuel 23:11. These three chiefs were considered the most outstanding warriors of all.

After them came another three captains, whose names are not given at all in our texts but who distinguished themselves in the self-sacrifice which they displayed in bringing David water from Philistine-dominated Bethlehem (vv 15-19). After them, certain others are mentioned who came very close to their level yet were still not considered as members of "the three": these were Avishai brother of Yo'av (I Chron. 11 vv 20-21) and Benayah ben Yehoyada (vv 22-25). The account then continues with the names of David's other mighty warriors (vv 26-47).

The fact that David's chief warriors were arranged in trios indicates that they represented a perfect balance of the three Sefirotic columns of Chessed-Kindness, Gevurah-Might and Tiferet-Harmony (cf. Likutey Moharan I, 60:4). This entire chapter and the next - which speak of the unified support that the messianic king had from all Israel - deal with **Olam HaTikkun**, the World of Repair.

The passages in our text that deal with David's most outstanding warriors are highly allusive spawning many midrashim. Thus, Targum on v 11, which ostensibly speaks about "**Yashav-Am**", renders the verse as follows: "And these are the numbers of the mighty warriors that were with the mighty David, head of the camp sitting upon the throne of law with all the prophets and sages surrounding him, anointed with the holy anointing oil. When he would go out to battle he was helped from above, and when he sat to teach Torah the halachah came out according to his opinion. Choice, distinguished, beautiful in appearance and noble in bearing, he was proficient in wisdom and understanding in giving counsel, mighty in strength, the head of the assembly, sweet in voice and multiplying songs, and a leader over all the mighty warriors. He was bedecked in armor and took his spear, on which was hung the sign of the ranks of the camp of Judah, and he went out in accordance with the voice of the holy spirit and conquered in battle, carrying three hundred dead on his spear at one time."

The exploits of **Elazar Ben Dodo** (vv 12-14) and "the three" (vv 15-19) were courageous acts of defiance against the Philistines, who were flushed with their victory over Saul and were making life miserable for the Israelites. According to Rashi (on v 13) the Philistines were intending to burn the Israelites' barley, while in v 16 we learn that they had their own garrison in Bethlehem and were evidently putting severe restrictions on the free movement of the Judean population. The fact that Israel was under the shadow of the Philistines at the beginning of the messianic era marked by King David's reign may be of comfort to us today since the shadow cast over our lives by those who continue to bear their name surely signifies that we too are on the very threshold of Mashiach.

Rashi explains that David's sudden craving to taste the waters of Bethlehem (v 17) was very natural since he had grown up in the place and "the water and air that a person is used to are good for him, while if he is not used to them, they can be harmful". [David craved a taste of the vitalizing waters of Torah he knew from his youth.] The reason why David did not want to drink the water when they brought it to him was that they had risked their very lives to fetch it and he looked on the water as if it was their blood (Metzudat David). Instead he poured it out on the Altar as a libation. (Rashi on v 18 brings the view in Yerushalmi Sanhedrin 2:5 that it was the festival of Succot, when a libation of water is daily poured on the Altar.) In this way David put himself and his personal desires aside, elevating the heroic instincts of his warriors as an offering to God.

The description of the exploits of Benayah ben Yehoyada is also highly allusive. Targum (on v 22) states inter alia that one time he accidentally stepped on a dead lizard, thereby becoming ritually defiled, and despite the fact that it was the coldest snowy day, he broke the ice and immersed in the' mikveh and proceeded to recite the entire halachic Midrash Sifra Devey Rav on Leviticus in the course of one short winter's day in the middle of Tevet. Such were David's warriors!

CHAPTER 12

Vv 1-2: "Now these are those who came to David in Tziklag…. They were armed with bows and could use both the right hand and the left in slinging stones and shooting arrows from the bow…." (vv 1-2). Once again, we see how David's warriors were proficient in both hands - the right hand of Chessed-Kindness and the left hand of Gevurah-Might.

V 2: "…from among the brothers of Saul from the tribe of Benjamin" - "Even King Saul's own brothers came to David during the lifetime of Saul" (Rashi).

David's Benjaminite warriors had the faces of lions and the speed of mountain roes (v 9).

Vv 15ff: After the Benjaminites who came to David, the first of the other tribes mentioned as having come to support him are the mighty warriors of the Gaddites, who lived in the territories east of the River Jordan. Verse 16 suggests that they were so powerful that as they entered the river to wade across to make their way to Hebron, the very waters - swelled from the spring-time melted snow - fled. The commentators explain that it was the surrounding nations who fled.

Vv 17ff: For many of the Benjaminites, David was the rival of their fallen hero Saul. David's noble gesture of reconciliation (v 18) elicited the immortal, divinely-inspired words of Amasai, which are included in the collected Biblical verses of blessings recited on the departure of Shabbat and at other junctures: "Yours are we, David, and on your side, son of Yishai: peace, peace be to you and peace be to your helpers, for your God helps you."

Let us all give our hearts to Melech HaMashiach in peace!!!

CHAPTER 13

At the conclusion of the previous chapter, we learned that with the acceptance of David as king by all the Twelve Tribes, "there was **joy** in Israel" (I Chron 12:41).

The new king lost no time in taking advantage of the favorable national climate in order to try to bring the Ark of the Covenant up to Jerusalem from the house of Avinadav in Kiryat Ye'arim, where it had remained since its return by the Philistines following the disasters that struck them after they captured it from the Sanctuary in Shilo in the days of Eli (I Samuel 4:11-7:1).

The taking of the Ark to Jerusalem to dwell in its eternal resting place - the Holy Temple on Mount Moriah - would be the fulfillment of Jacob's dream as he had slept on that very spot. "...and behold a **ladder** (**soolam**) was established on the earth" (Genesis 28:12). The **soolam** alludes to **Sinai** (the Hebrew letters of the two words have the same Gematria). The Sinaitic Covenant would only be complete when the Torah that Israel received in the wilderness would be brought up to God's House in

Jerusalem (symbolizing the "home" of the Shechinah in the heart of each one of us) - from there to shine out to all the world, "For the Torah shall go forth from Zion and the word of HaShem from Jerusalem" (Isaiah 2:3).

King David showed great humility: "And David **consulted** with the captains..." (v 1). He asked the people what they thought. He wanted them to be wholeheartedly with him. "And David said to all the assembly of Israel. let us **break through** and send to our remaining brothers..." (v 2). David fully knew that he wanted to accomplish nothing less than a **breakthrough** - to reach out to those who were still outside the circle of Mashiach and to involve them too in the holy project of bringing the Ark, symbol of the Torah, to its eternal home. David turned this into a national event that was to be no less significant in its way than Moses' inauguration of the original Sanctuary in the Wilderness.

Our commentary on the parallel narrative of this event in I Samuel ch 6 discussed how David could have erred in having the Ark transported on a wagon when even little schoolchildren know that it was supposed to be carried on poles resting on the shoulders of the Levites (Numbers 7:9). Rashi (on verse 7 of our present text) states that David was impressed by the fact that when the Philistines returned the Ark from its captivity, they had put it on a new wagon (I Sam. 6:11).

When the oxen drawing the wagon caused the Ark to shift, making it seem as if the Ark was in danger of falling, Uzza's stretching out his hand to steady it was considered a deep affront to the holiness of the Ark - as if, despite the miracles with which it had returned safely from the Philistines, the Ark could somehow not take care of itself. The tragic death of Uzza (who was not a Levite, RaDaK on v 10) turned this national event into a day of mourning, just as the consecration of Moses' Sanctuary in the wilderness had been marred by the deaths of Aaron's two sons, Nadav and Avihu, who likewise showed disrespect for the holiness of the Sanctuary (Leviticus 10:1ff).

The revelation of the strict hand of God's Judgment brought David to a state of deep awe and fear (v 12): he repented of his error, and when he finally brought up the Ark from the house of Oveid Edom (who **was** a Levite, see Rashi on v 13) to Jerusalem , as described in I Chron. Ch 15, David publicly confessed that he had been wrong in allowing the Ark to be transported on a wagon rather than on the shoulders of the Levites (see ch 15 v 13).

CHAPTER 14

"And Hiram king of Tyre sent messengers to David... and David **knew** that HaShem had prepared him to be king over Israel..." (vv 1-2). Rashi (on v 1) notes that an ancestral love bound Hiram to the tribe of Judah - we find in Genesis that Judah had a friend called Hirah who came to his aid (Genesis 38 vv 1 and 20). It was when David saw how the kings of the nations were sending him gifts that he **knew** that God had prepared him to be His messianic king (see Rashi on I Chron. 14:2).

As noted in an earlier commentary, when David became king, it was the Philistines who were the major challenge to the people of Israel just as those who have chosen to bear their name in modern times remain the most immediate challenge to Israel today. Rashi (on verse 8) explains why the Philistines were so angry at the news that David had been anointed king over all Israel and went up precisely then to try to catch him. "The Philistines had been dominant for the whole time until the arrival of Saul and David (cf. Judges 15:11, 'and they said to Samson, Don't you know that the Philistines rule over us?'). The Philistines themselves had said, 'Be strong, and be men, O Philistines, lest you serve the Hebrews as they serve you...' (I Sam. 4:9). During the seven years when David ruled only in Hebron, the Philistines did not say a word and they were not concerned over the fact that David was ruling over Hebron because they thought that he had been appointed as nothing but a mere local official. But when he was anointed as king over all Israel, all the Philistines went up to seek David because they did not want there to be a king over Israel but that they should continue ruling over them." In other words, they feared a Messianic king over Israel, which would spell the end of their own rule over them. It was the deepest affront to their national pride to have to serve the Hebrews.

Before making any move of major significance, David "asked God" what he should do (v 10), i.e. he consulted the Urim ve-Tumim - these were the lights that appeared on the jewels of the breastplate of the High Priest, which were engraved with the names of the Tribes of Israel and whose flashing letters spelled out the answer to a question of national importance put by the king.

The striking defeat of the Philistines at Baal Peratzim where God "broke through" David's enemies (v 11ff) was a consolation after the breach with which He "broke through" against Uzza when he put his hand out to steady the Ark (previous chapter v 11). However, the Philistines soon regrouped and were ready for another battle. When David again consulted the Urim ve-Tumim the answer came that this time he was not to confront his enemies but to turn aside, and he was not to engage them in battle until he heard "a sound of marching on the tops of the mulberry trees" (vv 14-15). (This would be the "sound" of the angels, who would be fighting the "real" battle on the spiritual plane.)

In the words of Rashi (on v 14): "The attribute of Judgment spoke before God, 'Why did You remove Saul in favor of David?' He answered, 'Because he did not wait for Samuel seven days as the prophet had instructed him' (I Sam.13:8-14). The Holy One blessed be He then said to the attribute of Judgment, 'I will now test David and instruct him to turn aside from the Philistines....'"

"And David did according to how God had commanded him..." (v 16). Unlike Saul, David followed God's commands to the letter - and was blessed with success. With the decisive rout of the Philistines, all the surrounding nations were filled with fear of David, who was thereby in a position to prepare to achieve his greatest goal, the building of the Temple.

CHAPTER 15

The Ark of the Covenant was not intended to rest in the innermost sanctum of the Temple as a mere ornament. The presence of the Tablets of Stone with the Ten Commandments and Moses' Torah scroll in the Ark on the holiest spot in the Temple came to demonstrate that the ultimate purpose of all of its services was to bind Israel to God's Torah and to the keeping of His commandments.

Before the Temple could be built, it was first necessary to bring the Ark up to Jerusalem. Having prepared a tent where the Ark would rest until the completion of the Temple (v 1), David ordered the Levites to carry the Ark up to Jerusalem in the presence of all Israel. This was an act of supreme holy boldness on the part of David since he had been deeply burned by the death of Uzza when he put forth his hand to steady the Ark the first time David tried to bring it to Jerusalem on a wagon (I Chron 13:10-11). A lesser figure would have been deterred from "tempting fate" again, but David was on the level where he could publicly admit that the mistake had been his in having the Ark transported on a wagon instead of on poles carried on the shoulders of the Levites as ordained by the Torah. David's confession of his error is contained in our present chapter in verse 13.

We can understand more of the nature of the true king of Israel when we consider the narrative in this chapter and the next telling how David himself directed the arrangements for bringing the Ark to Jerusalem and personally organized and led the priests and the Levites in the triumphant procession. For the essential goal of the Messianic kingship is to establish the Temple, with the Ark of the Covenant at its center, as the primary focus of Israel's connection with God (see Rambam, Laws of Kings 11:4).

As the Levites carried the Ark up to Jerusalem on poles on their shoulders in the prescribed manner, David organized the Levite singers into a choir and orchestra to accompany it on its way (verses 16ff). David's organization of the Levite singers on this occasion became the prototype for the organization of the Temple choir and orchestra, and important clues about the Temple music are contained in the present chapter and the next.

The conceptual link between the Ark of the Covenant and the Temple music lies in the fact that through Israel's observance of the Covenant, the outer **Kelipah**-husk (**Orlah**, the "foreskin") is peeled away from the world to reveal that behind every detail of creation, including even the seemingly implacable laws of nature, lies the detailed providence (**Hashgachah Pratit**) of God. When this is revealed, all the separate details are seen to interconnect like the notes and words of a song, which links together separate details and makes them into a single whole. (The Hebrew word for a **link** in a chain is **sher**, connected with the word **shir**, "song".) Thus, the song that was sung when David brought the Ark to Jerusalem - in the next chapter vv 8-36 - is the song of God's providence, alluding to His miracles in bringing the Ark out of its captivity in the hands of the Philistines (see commentary on next chapter).

We can but yearn to hear what the Temple music actually sounded like. We know little about the actual nature of the various musical instruments that are mentioned in the present chapter. These include the **nevel** and **kinor** (v 16), two kinds of string instruments differing mainly in the number of strings they had. Although **kinor** in Modern Hebrew usually refers to a violin, it is not clear if the Temple **kinor** was played with a bow or plucked. The **metziltayim** mentioned in our text (ibid.) was a pair of very loud brass cymbals which were used by the leading singers to direct the music (see v 19).

The **alamot** mentioned in verse 20 was a particular kind of instrument that was specifically used for those Psalms that are prefixed **La-M'natzeach Al Alamot** (Psalms 46:1; see Rashi on v 20. **Alamot** also has deeper allusions to the hidden mysteries of God's providence, see Targum on Psalms 46:1). Similarly, the **sheminit** mentioned in verse 21 was a particular kind of eight-stringed instrument used in singing those Psalms prefixed **Al Ha-Sheminit** (Psalms 6:1, 12:1; Rashi on v 21). An eight-stringed instrument can produce a considerably wider range of octaves and chords than the contemporary six-stringed guitar! The concept of **eight** (**shemini**) is also bound up with that of the Covenant, which joins Malchut (this world) with Binah (the world to come): Binah is the eighth Sefirah up from Malchut, just as the top note of a scale is one octave above the bottom note.

In verse 21, the **sheminit** is described as being **le-natzeach**, "to overcome". Rashi (on Psalms 4:1) explains that Psalms prefixed with **La-M'natzeach** "were instituted by David to be chanted by the Levites who **assertively** sing the melodies of their songs from the Duchan ('platform'). The root **nitzu'ach** applies to the strength and assertiveness one puts into one's work".

V 22: "And Khenanyahu, chief of the Levites, was over the song: he was master in the song, because he was **understanding**." The Hebrew word that is here rendered as "he was master" is **yassor**, which literally means "he chastised". "He would chastise and rebuke them over the way they were carrying the melody to bring out the beauty of the song whether through raising their voices or lowering them" (Rashi ad loc.) In other words, he was the **conductor** of the Temple choir and orchestra, and for this he had to possess understanding, **Binah**, for **Binah** takes things piece by piece and puts them all together.

V 24: "...the priests blowing on the trumpets...." The trumpets had a special place in the Temple services and it was the Torah-given right of the priests to sound them (Numbers 10:8).

V 27: "And David was clothed in a robe of fine linen and all the Levites... And David had on him an ephod of linen." David was singing just as were the Levites and accordingly he wore the same ceremonial garments that they wore (see Rashi on v 27).

V 29: The description of King David's whirling dancing and Michal's contemptuous view of it as contained in our chapter is considerably less detailed than in the parallel account in II Samuel chapter 6. Rashi (on verse 29 in our present chapter) explains that since **Divrey HaYamim** was written in honor of King David, Michal's words to David were not written here since they were disparaging to him.

CHAPTER 16

After the Ark had been successfully brought up to Jerusalem, David concluded the national celebration by distributing a loaf of bread, a good piece of meat (**eshpar**) and a cake (**ashishah**) to every man and woman. The **eshpar** was "one sixth of an ox" (Pesachim 36b; Rashi on our chapter, v 3) while the **ashishah** was "one sixth of a **Hin**-measure" (Rashi ibid.) Perhaps this alludes to the fact that the Sefirah of **Yesod** (=**Brit**, the Covenant) is "one sixth" - i.e. the sixth and last of the "Six Directions" (**Shesh Ketzavot**, Chessed-Gevurah-Tiferet-Netzach-Hod-Yesod) and contains the concentrated power of all six.

The Ark was in Jerusalem, but the Temple was not yet built, and the daily sacrificial rites were still being conducted by the priests at the great Altar (**Bamah**) in Giv'on, as we find in v 39 of our present chapter. (After the sacking of Shilo, the Sanctuary had moved to the city of Nov, but when Saul killed the priests of Nov for supporting David, it moved to Giv'on, where Solomon continued to sacrifice until he built the Temple in Jerusalem.)

For the duration of the time until the Temple would be built, David instituted two separate orders. One consisted mainly of Levites, who were to minister before the Ark of the Covenant in Jerusalem "to invoke and to thank and praise HaShem the God of Israel" (v 4) together with two priests to sound the trumpets there. This order is described in vv 4-7 and 37-38 of our present chapter, while the song of the Levites before the Ark is given in vv 8-36. There was no need for many Cohen-priests before the Ark in Jerusalem since their primary function was to conduct the sacrificial rites. In the absence of the Temple, the place for these was not before the Ark but at the Sanctuary in Giv'on. Accordingly, the second order which David now instituted was that of Cohen-priests to offer all the daily and other Torah-ordained sacrifices in Giv'on together with some Levites to sing there during the sacrificial services (vv 39-42).

V 4: "...to invoke and to thank and praise HaShem". These are different aspects of prayer and song. Rashi explains that the Levites were "to invoke" the name of HaShem by reciting the Psalms that are prefixed "A song of David **Le-hazkeer**, to make mention" - i.e. Psalm 38, which is one of deep introspection in face of God's chastisement. "To thank" means to recite "Give thanks to HaShem, call upon His Name" (Psalm 105:1) while "to praise" (**Le-hallel**) means to recite those Psalms that begin with Halleluiah (see Rashi on v 4).

The text of David's song celebrating the bringing of the Ark to Jerusalem (vv 8-36) is familiar to all regular Daveners since it is recited daily at the start of the **P'sukey D'Zimra** ("verses of song") that constitute the second of the four rungs of the morning service. This follows the first rung, the recital of the 18 Morning Blessings, and is in turn followed by the third rung, Shema with its blessings and the fourth rung, the silent Amidah prayer. David's song, **Hodoo La'Shem, Kir'oo Bi-Shmo.** is recited either **before** the blessing **Baruch She-Amar** introducing P'sukey D'Zimra (Nusach Sefard) or immediately afterwards (Nusach Ashkenaz). Either way, David's song of **Hodoo** facilitates the transition from the world of the Morning Blessings (**Asiyah**) to the world of Song (**Yetzirah**). The transition from one level to another is always accomplished primarily through the yearning of Malchut (the davener) to reach out to and join with **Yesod** (the source of the higher spiritual influence). [**Chochmah-Binah-Da'at**, the highest Sefirot of the lower level, which is **Malchut** in relation to the level above it, seek to "clothe" the lowest Sefirot of the upper level, **Netzach-Hod-Yesod**.] Since David's song of **Hodoo** alludes to the miracles through which God returned the Ark of the Covenant (**Yesod**) from captivity, it is the vehicle through which **Malchut** (David) connects with **Yesod** (the Ark).

V 7: "On that day David put it into the hand of Asaph to be the head in giving thanks to HaShem, and his brothers." Rashi explains that David hereby instituted the Temple custom that the leader of the singers would begin the chant and then all his brother Levites would answer after him.

V 8: "Call on His Name" - "Call out HaShem! Let HaShem help His Ark" (Rashi). "Make known His deeds among the nations" - "these are the acts of might and miracles that He performed for the Ark " (ibid.) Rashi is alluding to the way that God sent the plague of mice and other troubles to the Philistines after they captured the Ark, and to the miraculous way in which they sent it back on a wagon drawn by nursing cows (I Samuel ch's 5-6). These miracles show how God carries out His inscrutable purposes with or against the consent of men. The Ark protects itself!

V 11: "Search out (**Dirshoo**) HaShem and His strength! Seek out His face constantly" His "strength" (**oozo**) is the Torah. We seek out His face by constantly studying and darshening His Torah, thereby enhancing the prayers with which we entreat His inner presence.

V 18: "Saying, 'To you (singular) will I give the Land of Canaan, the lot of your inheritance.'" God promised the land of Israel to each of the patriarchs individually, despite the fact that at the time they were mere nomads and sojourners and the future residence of their descendants there may have then seemed entirely improbable (see Rashi ad loc.).

The history of the people of Israel illustrates the survival of a tiny nation against all the odds, through God's providence alone (vv 19-22).

Verses 8-22 of David's song celebrating the coming of the Ark to Jerusalem are parallel to Psalm 105 vv 1-15. This was sung during the morning Temple service. The ensuing passage in David's song vv 23-33, which is parallel to Psalm 96 vv 1-12, was sung in the afternoon Temple service (see Rashi on v 35). In this second section, David moves from telling of God's **past** miracles on behalf of Israel to telling of His **future** redemption and the ingathering of the exiles (see Rashi and RaDaK on Psalms 96:1), which are also miraculous wonders bespeaking His loving providence. The Midrash (Bereishit Rabbah 54:4) states that these were the two songs that the cows sang as they drew the wagon with the Ark of the Covenant up from the Philistines to Beit Shemesh (I Samuel 6:12).

CHAPTER 17

Verse 1: "And David said to Nathan the prophet, 'Here I sit in a house of cedars but the Ark of the Covenant of HaShem is under curtains!'" As a true lover of HaShem, David was distressed when he compared the opulence of his own royal residence with the makeshift, temporary nature of the tent which he had erected to house the Ark in Jerusalem. David knew that man's task is to give all the glory to God, not to take it for himself.

One of the most important keys to understanding the messianic quality of David's kingship is to note that the initiative to build the Temple was essentially his own: he was not directly commanded to build it. This is brought out in Rashi's comment on verse 6 of our present chapter on God's words to David:

"Did I speak a word to any of the judges of Israel...?" Rashi paraphrases: "This I never did, and nor did the thought of building Me a House occur to any one of them in the way that this thought has arisen in your mind."

It was not just now that the thought entered David's mind. When he first fled from King Saul and went to take counsel with his mentor the prophet Samuel, "they sat **be-Noyot**" (I Samuel 19:18). Taken literally this appears to refer to the location where they sat, but our sages taught that they were actually sitting engaged in the **beauty (noy)** of the world - i.e. investigating the proper place to build (**banah**) the Temple (Zevachim 54b; see **Know Your Bible** commentary on I Samuel ch 19).

What gave David to understand that the time had now come to carry out his long-cherished plan was the fact that now "HaShem had given him rest from all his enemies round about" (II Samuel 7:1). As Rashi explains on verse 1 of our present text, David reasoned: "God has fulfilled what He promised in the Torah, 'and He will give you rest from all your enemies around' (Deut. 12:10). Now the obligation rests on me to carry out what is written immediately afterwards, 'And it shall be that the **place** where HaShem your God will choose to cause His Name to dwell, there shall you bring all [the sacrifices] that I am commanding you' (ibid. v 11). That is to say, I shall make Him a Sanctuary" (Rashi on I Chron. 17:1).

Despite David's longing to build the Temple, he was not destined to do so because he was a man of war, whereas the Temple was to rise out of perfect peace and tranquility "for if you raise your sword upon it you will profane it" (Exodus 20:22). The actual Temple would only be built by Solomon, **Shlomo**, the man of peace. God quickly sent Nathan prophecy that very night to stop David from carrying out his plan. In the words of Rashi, "This man that I am sending you to is wont to take vows - go and stop him before he swears to build it. The man I am sending you to is quick and energetic - go and tell him before he hires builders" (Rashi on v 3).

V 9: "And I will ordain a **place** for my people Israel... And they shall be moved no more, nor shall the children of wickedness waste them anymore." From this verse, the sages learned that "The enemies of everyone who has a fixed place to pray will fall before him" (Berachot 7b).

"And HaShem tells you that He will make for you a house" (v 10) - "You [David] thought that you would build a House to My Name. According to that exact same measure shall be your reward. The Holy One blessed be He is announcing to you that He will make you a house. HaShem will give you a son who will rule after you and sit upon the throne of Israel in your place. Everything that endures in a man's son after him is called a **house**, and thus He says, 'And I shall establish your seed after you' (v 11)" (Rashi on verse 10).

V 13: "I shall be to him as a father and he will be to Me as a son...." The parallel account in II Samuel 7:14 warns that if Solomon would sin, God would chastise him, but this is left out of the account here in **Divrey HaYamim** as this work omits anything that would detract from the honor of the House of David (Rashi on our present chapter v 13).

V 16: "And King David came and **sat** before HaShem...." David came to pray before the Ark of the Covenant. From the fact that he **sat**, we learn that only the kings of the House of David are permitted to sit in the Temple Courtyard (**Azarah**) and no-one else (Yoma 69b). All acts of service in the Temple (sacrifices, singing etc.) are carried out standing.

The eloquence of David's humble prayer of gratitude to God for promising him an eternal house vv 16-27 is unsurpassed. In the words of Rashi (on v 25): "If You Yourself had not promised me to bring all these benefits on my seed, it would not have occurred to me to request them, for who am I that you have brought me as far as this, to become king, but since you have said that for Your sake you will bring all these benefits to me, I therefore pray to you to fulfill Your words."

CHAPTER 18

"After David said he would build the Temple and God said, 'You shall not build it', David said, 'Since it is not for me to build the Temple but for my son, I shall now prepare and order everything for him so that when my son comes to build the Temple, he will have everything ready for him'. The narrative now leaves everything else aside in order to go on to tell how David prepared all the building needs for Solomon through fighting with his enemies and dedicating their booty to the building of the Temple" (Rashi on verse 1).

V 4: "...and David lamed all the chariot horses". David did this because he did not want to infringe the Torah prohibition against the king multiplying horses for himself (Deut. 17:16).

V 13: "And he put garrisons in Edom...." The subjugation of Edom to Israel represents the triumph of the World of **Tikkun** (Repair) over the World of **Tohu** (chaos) because the Seven Kings of Edom (Genesis 36:31-39) are emblematic of the seven lower Sefirot in a state of breakage and destruction. The stationing of Israelite garrisons in Edom indicates the repair of the broken vessels in preparation for the building of the Temple.

V 14: "And David ruled over all Israel and he practiced justice and charity to all his people." This indicates that David now withdrew from active engagement in warfare, devoting himself instead to judging the people fairly and charitably. The text goes on to tell us that Yo'av was commander-in-chief of the army, in order to make it clear that although David himself no longer fought, this does not mean that Israel ceased fighting (Rashi on vv 14 & 15).

CHAPTER 19

When Nachash (="serpent") king of Ammon died, King David felt under an obligation to send emissaries to comfort his son Chanoon (="gracious"!!!) in his mourning "for his father performed a kindness towards me" (v 2). This kindness had been performed when David took his father and mother and brothers out of Israel to his great-grandmother Ruth's native country of Moab in order to escape Saul's persecution (I Samuel 22:3). The king of Moab killed the entire family except for David's brother Elihoo, who is the only one mentioned thereafter (I Chron. 27:18) and who escaped by fleeing to Ammon where he was received by Nachash.

Suspecting that David's emissaries had come to spy on Ammon and foment revolution, the gracious Chanoon shaved them and cut off their garments in the middle, exposing their private parts - just about the most demeaning and humiliating thing it was possible to do to anyone. Realizing the dangers to which this provocation exposed him, Chanoon proceeded to hire Aramean mercenary chariots and riders. The Arameans were a people spread across a huge swathe of the Fertile Crescent stretching from Aram Nahariyim (between the Tigris and Euphrates) all the way across to Damascus and the Golan Heights. Our text refers to three major Aramean centers - Aram Nahariyim, Aram Maachah and Aram Tzovah (v 6) all of which were offspring of the Aramean mother people (see Rashi on v 6). The Arameans had set their evil eye against Jacob and his offspring from the times of Laban and Bilaam.

The town of Meid'va where the Aramean mercenaries encamped was about 50 km south west of present-day Amman, Jordan, which, as its name suggests, was the main Ammonite center. Thus, in campaigning against Ammon, David's commander-in-chief Yo'av had one enemy army ahead of him and another formidable enemy army to his rear (v 10). This was why he took a selected elite army under his command to fight the Arameans, sending his brother Avishai against Ammon. [Rashi on v 11 notes that unlike in the book of Samuel, Yo'av's brother is throughout Chronicles called **Av'shai**, because if he were called by his full name of **Av-Yishai** (=father-Jesse) this would have detracted from the honor of King David, who was Yishai's son, whereas **Av'shai**, son of David's sister Tzeruyah, was merely his grandson.]

The Arameans fled and the Ammonites returned to their city, but the Arameans now called in reinforcements from their kinsmen east of the Euphrates. In II Samuel 10:16 their commander-in-chief was called **Shovach** "because he was as tall as a **shovach**" (=a dovecote, positioned high above the reach of predators), while in our text he is called **Shophach**, "because he used to pour out (**shophech**) blood like water" (Rashi on v 16).

It appears from verse 17 that King David himself led the entire people to battle against the Arameans, and scored a decisive victory which left them subject to him thereafter.

CHAPTER 20

Verses 1-3 of our present chapter give a highly condensed narrative of Yo'av's campaign to subdue Rabbah, the capital of Ammon, compared with the version in II Samuel chs 11-12. This is because it was during this campaign that David took Batsheva, sending her first husband Uriah HaHitti to his death in Yoab's campaign. Since that episode does not reflect credit on King David, it is omitted from our text here in **Divrey HaYamim**, which was written to give honor to David and his house.

V 2: "And David took the crown of their king from upon his head... and it was on the head of David." The sages discussed whether David actually wore this weighty crown on his head or whether it was somehow positioned hovering above his head, held in place, perhaps, by the magnetic force of the "precious stone" it contained (Avodah Zarah 44a). [Lovers of Rabbi Nachman may be interested to consider the connection between this crown and the crown above the king's head in his story of "The Spider and the Fly".]

The judgments executed by David upon the Ammonites with saws, iron harrows and axes may seem somewhat barbaric to those with delicate sensitivities, but apparently David knew better how to address cruel people in the only language they understood than those "enlightened" people today who think that terrorists and violent criminals should be handled with kid gloves.

The account in our text (vv 4-8) of David's later wars against the Philistines and their monstrous champions is also somewhat abbreviated compared to the narrative in II Samuel 21:15-22, since the latter indicates that David was in mortal danger and became exhausted, which does not reflect to his credit (see Rashi on our present text v 4). There is some discussion among the commentators as to whether or not Goliath of Gat (v 5) is identical with Goliath the Philistine whom David killed at the start of his career (see Rashi and RaDaK on v 5). From Rabbi Nachman's discussion of Goliath and his death (Likutey Moharan II, 4) it is evident that he and the other giants and monsters described in our text embody tough spiritual **Kelipot** (husks) covering and concealing the unity of God, and their falling before David and his warriors was a spiritual triumph for Israel.

V 1: "And an adversary angel stood up against Israel and incited David to number Israel." The same Hebrew root used here of the Satan **inciting** David to count the people had been used by David himself when he encountered Saul face to face while the latter was pursuing him, and he said: "...if God has **incited** you against me..." (I Sam. 26:19). In the words of our sages: "The Holy One blessed be He said to David: You call me an **inciter**??? I will surely make you stumble in something that even little school children know, as it is written: 'When you take the sum of the children of Israel after their number, then shall they give every man a ransom for his soul to HaShem when you number them in order that there shall be no plague among them when you number them' (Exodus 30:12)" (Berachot 62b).

The "adversary angel" or Satan "is the evil inclination planted in man's heart from his youth" (Metzudat David, RaDaK on v 1). "And as to the verse in I Samuel 24:1 that says 'and HaShem's anger burned increasingly against Israel and He incited David', from which it appears that HaShem was the inciter: the truth is that He incited him through the intermediary of the Satan because of a sin that was present in Israel on account of which they were fit to be punished, and he too is called an Angel of HaShem. It was he that David saw having the appearance of an Angel of HaShem with his sword drawn in his hand (our chapter v 16), for it is he who deceives and he who kills" (RaDaK ibid.).

It is a mystery how David could have defied the Torah by seeking to take a direct census of the population instead of collecting a token charity coin ("ransom") from each person and counting the coins. It may be that as David prepared for a national event as significant as the building of the Temple, he was in too much of a hurry to find out the size of the population to see if it had reached some kind of "take off" point ready for the new era in the history of the people. But having suggested to the saintly King Saul that he might be the victim of the Yetzer Ra (evil inclination), measure for measure David was constrained to make the painful discovery that he himself could also be subject to the Yetzer Ra.

Rashi (on v 1) comments: "Even though this section does not reflect credit on David, it was written here on account of what it says at the end - that David built an altar and God answered him from heaven, and this was an honor to David." Indeed, David's greatness and nobility of character come out from the fact that he had the courage to admit his mistake publicly in the presence of the elders of the people, and he asked God to punish him personally instead of striking the whole nation (vv 16-17). And on account of David's confession, not only did God relent but He also revealed to David the site of the Altar that was to be the centerpiece of the Temple he so yearned to build.

"The place of the Temple Altar is aligned with the ultimate precision and its place may not ever be changed, as it is written, '...and **this** is the altar of the burned offering for Israel' (I Chron. 22:1). It was on the site of the Temple Altar that our father Isaac was bound, as it says, 'Go take yourself to the land of **Moriah**', and it says in II Chronicles 3:1, 'And Solomon started to build the House of HaShem in Jerusalem on Mount **Moriah** where God appeared to David his father, in the place which David had prepared in the threshing floor of Arnan the Jebusite'" (Rambam, Laws of the Temple 2:1).

It is one of the deep mysteries of God's inscrutable providence that the precise location of the Temple Altar - the place of atonement for all mankind - could be revealed to David only through his sin in counting the people, which led to a plague that was only stalled when the Angel of Death stood at that very spot. With complete self-effacement, the repentant David prayed that he should be substituted for the people and punished personally in order to save them. As his reward, he discovered the place where atonement for individual sinners and for the whole nation is accomplished through the mystery of substituting an animal for the sinner.

David's Yetzer Ra had been so strong that he would not even listen to objections from his own commander-in-chief, Yo'av, who was uneasy in the extreme about departing from the Torah norm in order to count the people. Grasping the attendant dangers, Yo'av did everything he could to wriggle out of making a complete count. He did not include the Levites on the grounds that the rules for counting them had been different from the rules governing Moses' counts of the other tribes (Numbers 3:15), and he did not include the Benjaminites because they had lost so many in the battles following the episode of the Concubine in Giv'ah (Judges 19-21) that they would be in danger of extinction if they lost any more through a plague on account of being numbered (I Chron 21:6, see Rashi ad loc and RaDaK on v 5).

When the hand of God struck and David realized his sin, the prophet Gad was sent to offer him the choice of which punishment would be sent to expiate the sin: famine, military defeat at the hands of the nation's enemies or plague. "And David said to Gad, 'I am in great distress: let me fall rather into the hand of HaShem, for very great are His mercies, but let me not fall into the hand of man'" (v 13). This verse is recited introducing the Tachanun supplications during the daily morning and afternoon services. David was in great pain because even the lightest of the options was harsh. "It can be compared to the case of a man who is told, 'You are going to die - which grave would you like to be buried in? Next to your father or your mother?'" (Rashi on v 13). David rejected the idea of famine because it forces people to depend on one another yet they do not have mercy on each other (Metzudat David) and also because the rich suffer less than the poor (Rashi). He also rejected defeat at the hands of his enemies because he knew they would surpass all bounds of cruelty. He preferred the plague, which is sent directly by God - for God can always relent, as indeed He did:

V 15: "…and as [the angel] was about to destroy, HaShem **saw** and relented of the evil" - "What did He see? He saw the ashes of Isaac, as it is written, 'God will **see** the lamb for Himself' (Gen. 22:8; Berachot 62b) - "for it was in the place of that threshing floor that Abraham had offered Isaac his son" (RaDaK on v 15).

Vv 22-25: Just as Ephron had ostensibly offered to **give** Abraham the Cave of Machpelah as the burial site for Sarah **for no charge** (Genesis 23:11ff), so Arnan offered not only the site of the Altar but even the sacrificial animals and his threshing tools as wood for the offering **for no charge**. But David did not want the favors of flesh and blood, which always carry a price tag. He wanted the Altar to be a national **acquisition (kinyan)** and therefore paid Arnan 600 talents of gold - fifty talents from each of the Twelve Tribes - for the site. Despite the fact that Israel purchased the site of the Altar on Mount Moriah with real **gold**, the present robber occupiers of the site continue to deny Israel's ownership until today, and the same applies in the case of the Cave of Machpelah in Hebron.

Even after David built the Altar on Mount Moriah, the Sanctuary remained in Giv'on (v 29) and the Altar continued to be used for all the sacrificial services until the time of King Solomon, who also sacrificed there until he inaugurated the Temple in Jerusalem, which from that time on became the only place where Israel were permitted to sacrifice.

CHAPTER 22

The revelation of the site of the Temple Altar was a great encouragement to David in his mission to prepare for the building of the House. David employed new converts in the difficult work of quarrying the great stones that would be needed. Rashi (on v 2) explains that his reason for employing the converts was that he did not want to burden the home-born Israelites with this work. (Perhaps he reasoned that the Israelites had already done enough of such work in their earlier incarnation building store cities for Pharaoh in Egypt, and it was now time for the converts to earn their place amidst the chosen people by also having a taste of hard labor.)

Solomon was only twelve years old when he came to the throne, and he was even younger when David began to prime him for the task of building the Temple, as described in the present chapter.

David also gave instructions to all the officers of the nation to help Solomon (vv 17-19). Let us take to heart David's words to the nation's leaders: "And now give your hearts and your souls to search out HaShem your God, and arise and build the Temple of HaShem, God..." (v 19). Just as David stood on the very threshold of the building of the Temple and did everything in his power to make all the necessary preparations for it, so do we stand on the threshold of the building of the Future Temple, and each of us should make his or her own personal reckoning of what we can do to prepare for it.

CHAPTER 23

V 1: "And when David was old and full of days, he made Solomon his son king over Israel." Solomon's candidacy as David's successor was by no means uncontested since his older half-brother Adoniyahu considered himself the obvious successor to the throne and was already maneuvering to take over, as we see from I Kings chapter 1. Nathan the Prophet in coordination with Solomon's mother Batsheva alerted King David to Adoniyahu's activities, causing the king to swear an oath to Batsheva that Solomon would indeed be his successor - for he knew prophetically that Solomon was destined to become king and build the Temple, as we saw in the previous chapter (I Chron. 22:9-10). David's giving over the kingship in his lifetime to the son for whom such a glorious future had been prophesied was surely an event of the utmost joy for himself and for all Israel. [Cf. Rabbi Nachman's story of the Seven Beggars, introductory section.]

Not only did David prepare the materials for the building of the Temple so that everything would be ready for Solomon. In this and the following chapters we learn how David reorganized the Levites and Cohen-priests to be ready to take up their duties in the new Temple.

V 3: "And the Levites were counted from the age of thirty years and upwards...." Initially, David counted the Levites fit for service using the same age criterion as God commanded Moses in the wilderness (Numbers 4:3) - only those above the age of thirty were eligible. Later, however, for reasons that will be explained below, the age for beginning their service was reduced to twenty (see vv 24-27). The tasks of the Levites in the Temple are specified at the end of the present chapter vv 28-32.

V 13: "...and Aaron was separated that he should be sanctified as most holy, he and his sons forever." Although Aaron and his sons were from the tribe of Levi, they alone were entrusted with the actual offering of all the Temple sacrifices and with blessing the people with the priestly blessing. They were therefore set apart from the rest of the tribe. The Cohanim-priests were a caste on their own with numerous mitzvot concerning limitations on their possible marriage partners, ritual purity, the consumption of Terumah-tithe produce etc. that only they were required to keep. As a mark of the unique holiness of the Cohanim, it is customary until today for all the rest of the people to give them special honor. Thus, whenever a Cohen is present in the synagogue he is called first to the Torah reading, followed by a Levi, and only then are Israelites in the congregation called to the reading. The Talmud cites our present verse as the Biblical source of this custom (Gittin 59a).

V 14: Despite Moses' unique status as master of all the prophets and the nation's law-giver, and despite the fact that he himself served as the Cohen when he first inducted Aaron and his sons into their role as priests at the time of the consecration of the Sanctuary in the wilderness (Leviticus 8:5ff), Moses' children were not considered Cohanim but were counted with the other Levites.

V 16: "...and the children of Rechaviah multiplied above" - "Rav Yoseph taught that they multiplied over 600,000" (Berachot 7a). Rabbi Nachman taught: "Know that there are children that are born into this world, but in addition there are very great 'children of ascent' who are born as souls that are above the souls that are clothed in the children born into this world. For all the souls in this world are included in the 600,000 souls of Israel, and even though there are greater numbers of people, this is only because the sparks are divided. But the souls that cannot be clothed in this world are above these 600,000 souls... and even when they enter this world they are not considered part of this world at all. This is the category of the children of Moses, of whom it is written that 'the children of Rechaviah multiplied **above**'. This is why the Rabbis taught that they were 'over 600,000' - because they are not considered to be included in the 600,000, for they are above and beyond them (Likutey Moharan I, 273).

Verses 24ff explain why David eventually counted all the Levites who were over 20 years old rather than only those who were above the age of 30. Now that God had "given rest to His people" and chosen to dwell in Jerusalem forever (v 25), the burden of carrying the Sanctuary and its vessels from place to place would no longer fall upon the Levites, who from now on would only be required to sing in the Temple and perform guard and other duties there. For these they would not require the full strength of a mature man of thirty but could already start to serve at the age of twenty (Metzudat David on v 26).

V 27: "For by the last ordinances of David, the Levites were numbered from twenty years old and above" - "This means that even though in David's own words above (v 3) only those Levites above the age of 30 were counted, in his final ordinances those over 20 were also counted. Initially, however, this did not occur to him and he counted them only as prescribed in the Torah (Numbers 4:3) from the age of 30 and above" (Metzudat David ad loc.).

Verses 28-32 give us many important insights into the varied functions of the Levites in the Temple. It is evident from numerous Talmudic sources that they continued carrying out the same functions allocated to them by David until the end of the Second Temple period. "Because their station was at the side of the sons of Aaron [the Cohanim]" (v 28). The role of the Levites was to do everything necessary in the Temple to enable the Cohanim to conduct the sacrificial services. Thus, the Levites were responsible for the guarding and maintenance of the entire Temple precincts including all the different courtyards and chambers, and they also had to ensure the ritual purity of all the Temple areas, vessels and sacrificial offerings (v 28). They prepared and baked the Show Bread and other grain-based offerings (v 29) as well as providing the singers for the Temple services (v 30). They had to ensure that the requisite sacrificial animals were ready and checked for blemishes prior to all the daily, Sabbath, New Moon and festival offerings (v 31) and provided squadrons of guards in key positions around the Temple (v 32). There were times when the Levites also assisted the Cohanim in flaying the sacrificial animals (Rashi on v 31, cf. II Chron. 29:34).

CHAPTER 24

Having organized the Levites and allocated them their duties, David proceeded to reorganize the Cohanim into twenty-four priestly squadrons that would serve in the Temple on a rota basis week after week.

V 4: "And the males of the chief families of the children of Elazar were found to be more numerous than those of the children of Itamar." Rashi (ad loc.) explains: "Initially in the Sanctuary in Shilo there was a total of only sixteen priestly squadrons, eight from the descendants of Elazar and eight from those of Itamar, as is explained in Tractate Ta'anit 27a. But when David saw that the males in each of the chief families of the descendants of Elazar were twice as many as those of the families of Itamar, he organized the descendants of Elazar into sixteen squadrons while leaving the descendants of Itamar in their eight existing squadrons, and we find proof of this in the Hebrew text of verse 6" (Rashi on v 4; see also Metzudat David on v 6).

V 5: "And they divided them by means of lots, these with those...." The purpose of the lots was to determine in which order the squadrons would serve week by week in rotation. The average Jewish year is 51 weeks. During the three-annual pilgrim festivals all twenty-four squadrons would take part in the festival sacrificial services, leaving about 48 weeks for the regular rota. Thus, each squadron had an average of two weeks of Temple service during the year besides the time they served on the festivals.

V 6: "And Shemayah the son of Netan-el the scribe from the tribe of Levi wrote them in the presence of the king...." The apparent **p'shat** of this verse is that Shemayah the scribe recorded the order in which the priestly squadrons would serve week after week as revealed through the lots. However, the Targum darshens that Shemayah ben Netan-el is another name for Moses, "the great scribe", and that it was he who wrote down the original order, which was later read in the presence of the king (see Targum Rav Yoseph on v 6).

Verses 7-18 give the names of the twenty-four priestly squadrons and their order in the rota.

Verses 20-30 review the names of the principle families of the Levites. While many of the functions performed by the Levites in the Temple appear to have involved continual service throughout the year, the Levitical singers were divided into twenty-four squadrons corresponding to those of the Cohanim, and they took turns week by week in singing in the Temple choir. The twenty-four Levitical squadrons consisted of nine from the descendants of Gershon, eight from those of Kehat and seven from those of Merari (see Metzudat David on v 30).

V 32: "And these also cast lots in the same manner as their brothers the sons of Aaron..." - "The purpose of the lots was to see which squadron would serve first, and their work was to sing with their mouths" (Metzudat David ad loc. He specifies that they sang with their mouths in order to distinguish them from the other Levitical **Meshorerim** who played instruments.]

"...the head of each father's house in the same manner as his younger brother": this means that the order of the various families' seniority in terms of age was of no consequence in determining their order in the rota of service: there everything was determined by the lot - **Goral** - which was determined by the Almighty.

CHAPTER 25

Our present chapter gives us the details of King David's organization of the Levite Temple singers into twenty-four divisions corresponding to the twenty-four divisions of the Cohanim. The organization of the Levite Temple gate-keepers and keepers of the Temple treasures is then set forth in the following chapter.

V 1: "And David and the captains of the army **separated** for the service...." "The service" refers to the sublime service of song that accompanied the performance of the sacrificial offerings by the Cohanim and which was the element of **Gevurah**, "might," that "elevated" the sparks of holiness to the Almighty. [Levi=**Gevurah**.] It takes focused strength and understanding - left column attributes - in order to really sing! David "separated" the Temple choristers from the other Levites. They were a hereditary order drawn exclusively from three Levite lines headed in the time of David by Asaph, Heyman and Yedootoon, as detailed in verse 1.

According to the **ktiv** (the Masoretic Hebrew text as written in the scroll), they are called **HaNevi'im**, "the prophets", but the **kri** (traditional pronunciation) is **hanib'eem**, which is a verbal adjective meaning that "they used to prophesy with harps and lyres and the cymbals" (i.e. the **kri** emphasizes the action and not the person). In the words of Rashi (ad loc.): "When they would play with these instruments they would prophesy, as we find with Elisha, who said 'Bring me a player, and it was when the player played that the hand of HaShem was upon him'" (II Kings 3:15). RaDaK (on our verse here in Chronicles) adds: "The children of Asaph would play the instruments and then holy spirit would rest on Asaph and he would start singing with his mouth to the sound of the harps. Likewise, Heyman and Yedootoon were all prophets with musical instruments. For the book of Psalms was composed with holy spirit and it contains prophecies and visions of the future dealing with the exile and the redemption."

"…and the number of the workmen according to their service was:" (v 1). These closing words of verse 1 introduce the following section (vv 2-7), which enumerate the four sons of Asaph, the six sons of Yedootoon and Heyman's fourteen sons - a total of twenty-four. These became the heads of the twenty-four divisions of Levite singers, each of which consisted of twelve singers in the time of David, making a total of two hundred and eighty-eight, as we find in verse 7.

V 3: "The children of Yedootoon... **six**." - "But in the verse, you only find **five**. This is because at that time [i.e. in David's fortieth year, when all these arrangements were made, see chapter 26 v 31] his wife was pregnant with Shim'i and Yedootoon saw with holy spirit that he too was destined to be a head of a division, and this is why the verse says six" (Rashi ad loc. cf. RaDaK).

V 5: "All these were the sons of Heyman, the king's seer, according to the word of God, who bade to lift up his horn." Heyman's "horn" was the **Shofar** of prophecy that spoke through him to the king (cf. Rashi). "…and God gave to Heyman fourteen sons and three daughters" - "That is to say, if not for the fact that God gave him these children it would not have been possible for him to have fourteen sons and three daughters, with all his sons fit to be divisional heads" (Rashi ad loc.). Heyman and his large family were all descended from Korach, as was the prophet Samuel. Indeed, "It was when Korach saw the illustrious lineage was to come from him that he thought he would be able to stand up against Moses - but while he saw, he did not see well enough, because he did not understand that only on account of his children's repentance would these illustrious descendants arise" (Yalkut Shimoni).

V 7: "And their number with their brothers... was two hundred and eighty-eight." Since there were twenty-four rotating divisions each consisting of twelve choristers, there was a total of 288 Temple singers. The number 288 is of great significance kabbalistically. As a result of the "breaking of the vessels", 288 holy sparks fell into the realm of the unholy. This is alluded to in Genesis 1:2, "and the spirit of God was **hovering (merachephet)** over the face of the depth". The first and last letters of MeRaChePHeT spell out **meit** - "dead", while the sum of the numerical values of the three middle letters Reish (200), Chet (8) and Peh (80) is 288. It is these holy sparks that vitalize the realm of the unholy to perform its assigned task in creation. These sparks are redeemed through the spread of God's **Chessed**, loving kindness. This comes about through its successive revelation in each of the four basic expansions of the name of HaVaYaH - AV, SaG, MaH and BaN - through the expansion of the AVs specific to each one in turn. The gematria of AV is 72. 4 x 72 = 288. Thus, as the succession of twenty-four divisions of the Levites sang in the Temple week by week, their prophetic songs elevated and redeemed all the sparks that had fallen into the realm of unholiness. The order that David instituted for the Temple singers derives from the World of Tikkun (Repair).

V 8: "And they cast lots...." As in the case of the priestly squadrons, the order in which the divisions of the Levite Temple singers sang week after week was determined not on account of seniority or expertise but purely through the will of God as expressed through the lots.

V 9: "And the first lot came out for Asaph to Yoseph; the second to Gedaliah: he with his brothers and sons were **twelve**." From the fact that the original divisions of the Levite Temple singers as organized by King David consisted of twelve choristers each, our sages taught: "There should never be fewer than twelve Levite singers standing on the platform [although there could be more]. Twelve corresponding to what? Rav Papa said, Corresponding to the nine harps, two lyres and one cymbals. As it says, '...he and his brothers and sons were **twelve**'" (Erchin 13b. The cited sugya in Erchin is the most detailed of our Talmudic sources relating to the Temple music.)

CHAPTER 26

The Levite Temple gate-keepers did not serve in rotation. Rather, specified Levitical families were allocated by lot to specific Temple locations, where members of the families in question performed their guard duties constantly throughout the year (see Rashi on v 1).

The leaders of the families of the Levite gate-keepers are enumerated in vv 1-11.

Vv 4-5: "And the children of Oveid-Edom... for God blessed him." Oveid-Edom was blessed in virtue of his having given his home to house the Ark of the Covenant for three months after David's first unsuccessful attempt to bring it up to Jerusalem when Uzza died setting his hand forth to steady it on the wagon (I Chron. 13:14).

V 12: The divisions of the Temple gate-keepers were twenty-four in number corresponding to the divisions of the Temple singers, except that they did not serve in rotation week by week as did the singers. Instead, each division was assigned its own hereditary location in the Temple through the casting of lots, as detailed in vv 14-19. The total of four thousand gatekeepers in the time of David (I Chron. 23:5) were distributed more or less evenly among the twenty-four divisions (see Metzudat David on v 12).

THE TEMPLE TREASURERS

V 20: "And of the Levites, Achiyah was over the treasures..." - "He was in charge of the funds with which sacrificial animals etc. were purchased for the Temple" (Rashi ad loc.).

V 24: "And Shevoo'el the son of Gershom, the son of Moses was ruler over the treasures." According to rabbinic tradition, Shevoo'el is identical with Yehonatan, the Levite who ministered before Michah's idol (Judges ch's 17-18, see the **Know Your Bible** commentary there). He was called **Shevoo-el** because he returned to God with all his heart. King David saw that he had a very great affection for money and appointed him over the Temple treasures (Bava Kama 110a). This shows the greatness that can be attained when one learns to elevate the very thing that caused one to stumble so as to use it in the service of God, and also David's greatness in perceiving clearly how to help and elevate Baaley Teshuvah! It is noteworthy that no less than Moses' own grandson was appointed to the office of chief Temple treasurer, which was one that involved enormous responsibility.

V 29: "Of the family of Yitzchar, Kenanyahu and his sons were for the outward business over Israel, for officers and judges." This "outward business" refers to the work that had to be done outside the city for the sake of the Temple, such as preparing the timber and stones. These Levites provided the officers in charge of supervising this work (Metzudat David).

V 31: "...in the fortieth year of the kingship of David they were sought for...." This verse indicates that all of the organization of the Cohanim and Levites described from chapters 23 until our present chapter was carried out in the very last year of King David's life. This shows his extraordinary vitality and power to the very end!

V 32: "...and King David appointed them over the Reubenites, Gaddites and the half tribe of Menasheh...." These tribes lived in the territories east of the Jordan stretching from those to the east of the Dead Sea all the way up into the Golan Heights. Officers were required to supervise the preparation of materials from these areas for use in the forthcoming Temple building project.

CHAPTER 27

Having completed the account of King David's organization of the divisions of the Cohanim and Levites for the Temple services, our text continues with an account of his organization of the Israelite population into twelve divisions that took it in turns to attend to the king's business month by month. Our commentators explain that, unlike the divisions of the Cohanim and Levites, which were instituted in their final form as described in our text (chs 23-26) only in the last year of David's reign, the divisions of the Israelite population as described in the present chapter were in fact instituted at the beginning of his reign. The account of the latter is placed here because the listing of the names of the officers whom David appointed over the Israelite divisions follows on naturally from the previous sections listing the officers he appointed to supervise the building and administration of the Temple (see Rashi and Metzudat David on I Chron. 27:1).

Rashi (ad loc.) also explains that each of the twelve divisions of Israelites included only 24,000 men even though the overall Israelite population was greater than 12 x 24,000. However, David chose only the stronger, more forceful characters and those who possessed sufficient wealth to be able to put aside their own affairs in order to attend to the king's business, but he did not recruit poorer people who were preoccupied with earning a basic living.

The functions of these twelve divisions were to serve in David's army and to attend to all the king's other business (Rashi on v 1). A later section in our chapter (vv 25-21) enumerates the chief officers appointed over David's grain stores, agricultural work, viniculture and winemaking, olive cultivation and oil production, cattle, camels, donkeys and sheep, giving us a picture of some of the main areas comprised under the heading of the king's business. Under the laws of the kingship, the king was not allowed to confiscate other people's private property for himself unless they were traitors, but he was entitled to requisition people, animals and other requirements in return for compensation, and to impose taxes, customs dues and agricultural tithes in order to provide for his own needs and those of his household, staff and armies etc. (see Rambam, Laws of Kings ch 4).

What emerges from our present chapter is that the royal business was conducted not by an entrenched establishment of permanent salaried administrators and workers, but rather by the most talented, able and financially successful members of all of the tribes taking it in turns month by month to run the royal affairs - from the upper levels of the administration down to the actual plowing of the king's fields and the herding of his cattle.

Conceptually, the king is the embodiment of the Sefirah of Malchut, which channels **parnassah** ("livelihood") by mobilizing all the resources of the twelve tribes of Israel upon which he rides (corresponding to the twelve permutations of HaVaYaH revealed through Malchut), just as the Sea of Solomon (the circular Mikveh in the Temple) rested upon twelve oxen. [See **Know Your Bible** on I Kings ch 4.]

Vv 2-15: Names of the officers appointed over the twelve divisions of the Israelite population and the months in which they served, starting from the first month of the year (=Nissan). The officers themselves were not drawn from all of the twelve tribes but came mainly from the tribes of Judah, Ephraim, Benjamin and the priesthood.

Vv 16-22 give the names of the leaders of the Twelve Tribes in the time of King David.

V 23: "But David did not count the number of those who were twenty years old and below, because HaShem had said he would increase Israel like the stars of the heavens." This and the following verse help throw a little more light on the mysterious episode in which King David sought to number the Children of Israel, only to cause a plague (above, chapter 21). Our present verse is saying that even when David made his fateful count of the population, he did not count those aged only twenty or below in deference to God's promise to increase Israel like the stars of the heavens - "Just as a man cannot count the stars, so he cannot count Israel" (Rashi ad loc.).

The text (v 24) then goes on to say that even when Yo'av tried to count those above that age, he did not succeed in completing the count because of the anger that broke forth against the people, because the very thought of counting the people runs counter to God's promises to Abraham: "I will make your seed as the dust of the earth; so that if a man can number the dust of the earth, then shall your seed also be numbered" (Genesis 13:16) and "Look now toward heaven and count the stars if you can count them. So shall your seed be" (ibid. 15:5).

Vv 25-31: Names of the officers appointed over the king's agriculture and livestock.

Vv 32-34: David's inner circle of advisors. "And Houshai the **Arkhi, friend** of the king" (v 33). The Midrash Rabbah states that after David sinned with Batsheva, he asked Houshai whether, if he repented, God would accept his repentance and grant him healing (**aroukhah**). Houshai replied in the affirmative (see Rashi on v 33). Encouraging others to return to HaShem is an act of true friendship.

CHAPTER 28

At the end of his life, David assembled the entire leadership of the people, -- the leaders of the Twelve Tribes, those of the twelve divisions of the population who served the king, the higher and lower rank officers over the people and all his warriors - in order to impress in their hearts and that of his successor, the tender twelve-year old Solomon, that there was now one item only on the national agenda: building the Temple.

V 2: "And King David rose on his feet..." - "As if to say, despite the fact that his strength was diminished on account of old age, he nevertheless determinedly stood on his feet in honor of the leaders of Israel gathered before him" (Metzudat David). "Hear me, my brothers and my people": in his humility, David puts himself on the same level as the people, addressing them as his brothers.

David impresses on the people that his mission was to build the Temple, and that having been unable to do so because his hands were bloodied with war, this mission must now be carried out by his son Solomon, whom God had chosen for this task out of all of his many sons. The success of the mission would depend upon faithful adherence to the Torah by Solomon and by the entire people (vv 2-10).

Vv 11ff: "And David gave to Solomon his son the plan…." In the parallel account of the end of David's life and the start of the reign of Solomon at the end of II Samuel and beginning of I Kings, there seems to be no reference to David's having given Solomon the exact plan of the Temple that he was to build. It can easily appear from the account of the building of the Temple in the early chapters of I Kings as if the conception and design of the Temple were essentially Solomon's, incomprehensible as this may seem since he was only 12 years old when he reigned. The missing link is filled in here in **Divrey HaYamim**, explaining how David already had the exact blueprint of every hall, chamber and courtyard in the entire Temple complex as well as details of the functioning of the Cohanim and Levites and precise specifications for all the different Temple vessels, including the altar, ark, cherubs, candelabra, tables, bowls etc. etc. (vv 11-18).

"All this, [said David], is put in writing by the hand of HaShem, Who instructed me in all the works of this plan" (v 19). Rashi (ad loc.) states that David had received the Temple plan directly from the prophet Samuel, who darshened all the dimensions of the Temple courtyards, buildings and vessels from the Torah through holy spirit (See **Know Your Bible** commentary on I Samuel 19:18-19).

In the presence of the entire leadership of the people, David gave over the precious plans to his wise young son. David had devoted his entire life to making all the preparations necessary to implement the prophetic vision that had been entrusted to him by Samuel. Now it was up to Solomon to take the gold, silver, bronze, timber and stone that David had prepared and mobilize the national apparatus of officers and functionaries that he had established in order to actually build the Temple.

CHAPTER 29

In the previous chapter (I Chron. 28) we learned about the great assembly of all the leaders of the people whom David called to Jerusalem in order to hand over the kingship to Solomon and to deliver his last will and testament - that all the people and Solomon in particular must follow the commandments of the Torah, and that they must build the Temple according to the plan received by David from the prophet Samuel.

In our present chapter David now turns to the assembly with an eloquent appeal to contribute to the Temple building project. David's call to Israel to donate to the building of the Temple bears comparison with Moses' call to the people in the generation of the wilderness to contribute to the building of the Sanctuary (Exodus 35:4ff).

Vv 1-3: David emphasizes the youth and softness of Solomon, his divinely-chosen successor, and the magnitude of the task lying ahead of him - to build a "house" not for a man of flesh and blood but for the great and awesome One whom even the heavens and the heavens of the heavens cannot contain (Rashi on v 1). Before turning to the people to make their contributions, David - who knew that the best way to teach and inspire is through example - recounts how he had put all his strength into preparing the materials for the Temple. Before the entire assembly David now announces that he still has a special treasury of gold and silver which a lesser king might have kept for his successors, but which David dedicates to the Temple project (vv 3-5). Having led the way with his own exceptional display of generosity, David now asks the assembled leaders of the people to take up the challenge: "And who [among you] is going to volunteer to dedicate himself to HaShem?"

Vv 6-9: The dedications by the heads of the various families in each tribe and by the captains of the people and the king's officers.

V 9: "Then the people rejoiced. because with a perfect heart they offered willingly to HaShem" - "They gave with one heart with the desire of their souls and not with two hearts. For sometimes a person gives because he is constrained to do so, not because he really wants to - he may be ashamed of what others might think if he doesn't. This is called 'with two hearts', but in their case, they gave with the will of their very souls" (Rashi ad loc.).

"AND DAVID BLESSED HASHEM..." (v 10)

When David saw the people's great joy in donating to the Temple, he was overjoyed, because all the souls of Israel were unified in this greatest of all projects - to make a House for His Indwelling Presence in Jerusalem, the eternal city. David's beautiful prayer of thanksgiving for God's blessings of wealth and abundance (vv 10-13) is incorporated into the daily morning Shacharit service at the climax of **P'sukey D'Zimra** (the "verses of song" which precede Shema and its blessings) after the conclusion of the Halleluyahs (Psalms 145-150), before the Song of the Sea (Ex. 14:30-15:19).

V 10: "Blessed are You HaShem the God of Israel our father" - "The reason why he mentions Israel (=Jacob) rather than Abraham and Isaac is because Jacob also vowed to make dedications, as it says: 'And Jacob vowed a vow' (Genesis 28:20)" (Rashi ad loc.).

V 11: "Yours HaShem is the greatness (=Chessed) and the might (=Gevurah) and the glory (=Tiferet) and the victory (Netzach) and the majesty (Hod) for all-that-is-in-the-Heaven (=Yesod) and on the earth (=Malchut) is Yours." This verse unites all of the seven lower Sefirot, affirming that all the plurality of creation is under the rule and control of the One God. David thus used this occasion on which all the leaders of Israel dedicated many different kinds of wealth to the Temple to teach about the underlying unity of God.

Vv 14f: "But who am I and who are my people that we should be able thus to offer willingly...?" Lest the generous donations to the building of the glorious Temple become the cause of a swell of national self-satisfaction and arrogance, David reminds the people that everything belongs to God and we only give Him what is His - for we are nothing but temporary residents on His earth. "'Rabbi Elazar a man from Bartota says, 'Give Him from what is His, for you and what is yours, belongs to Him', and so David says, 'For everything is from You and from Your hand they have given to You'" (Pirkey Avot 3:7). "Our days are as a shadow over the earth" (our chapter v 15) - "And not like the shadow of a tree or even the shadow of a bird as it flies over. but like the shadow of the wings of the bumblebee, which has wings yet does not cast a shadow [because of the great speed at which they move]" (Midrash Kohelet 1:2, see Rashi on v 15).

V 18: "O HaShem God of Abraham, Isaac and Israel our fathers, keep this forever in the imagination of the thoughts of the heart of Your people and direct their hearts to You." This verse containing David's prayer that the generosity exhibited at the time of the dedication to the Temple should be eternally planted in the hearts of Israel is also included in the daily prayer services as part of the section **U-Va LeTzion Go'el** ("And a redeemer shall come to Zion") recited after **Ashrey** following the daily morning **Amidah** and **Tachanun** prayers and also prior to the afternoon **Amidah** prayer on Sabbaths and festivals and at the conclusion of the Sabbath.

Vv 20ff: David now leads the assembly in prayer, followed the next day by sacrifices of burnt offerings and peace offerings. But on the day of the assembly itself the people did not have time to sacrifice because they had to go in search of animals to buy for their offerings - Rashi on v 21.

V 22: "And they appointed Solomon the son of David, king a second time." Solomon had already been publicly anointed as king in succession to David after the thwarting of the conspiracy of Adoniyahu (I Kings 1:39). Now he was reconfirmed as the new king with the mission of building the Temple. Tzaddok was concurrently anointed as High Priest because Eviatar, who had served previously, had rebelled by anointing Adoniyahu (I Kings 1:7; Rashi on our verse).

V 23: "And Solomon sat on the throne of HaShem as king…" - "Here it is appropriate to say that he reigned on the throne of HaShem, because the throne is HaShem's to appoint whoever He wants as king upon it. The Midrash explains that his throne was full just like the moon on the fifteenth of the month. For from Abraham to Solomon there were fifteen generations: Abraham, Isaac, Jacob, Judah, Peretz, Chetzron, Ram, Aminadav, Nachshon, Salmah, Boaz, Oved, Yishai, David, Shlomo. And from Solomon onwards the kings became successively diminished in their greatness, like the moon that steadily wanes, until Tzedekiah, whose eyes were finally blinded" (Rashi ad loc.). "And **all** Israel listened to him [Solomon]" - "Which had not been so in the case of Saul - see I Samuel 10:27 - and David too initially ruled only in Hebron for seven years" (Rashi).

V 24: Whereas David's warriors had not given their hand to Adoniyahu, the entire people and all the rest of David's sons now gave their hand in support of Solomon.

V 29: "And the acts of David the king, the first and the last, are surely written in the book of Samuel the seer and in the book of Nathan the prophet and in the book of Gad the seer." It is a tribute to the greatness of King David, that so many books were written recording the events of his life and times (cf. Rashi ad loc.). Metzudat David (ad loc.) comments that the book of Samuel is that which we have in our hands today, while Nathan and Gad wrote books that we do not have. However, this does not answer the question who wrote the sections of the book of Samuel that describe the events after the death of Samuel (i.e. from I Samuel ch 25 to the end of II Samuel). It seems plausible that these actually consist of a weave of the writings of Nathan and Gad, both of whom prophesied until the last days of David.

II CHRONICLES CHAPTER 1

It is quite obvious that II Chronicles is a direct continuation from I Chronicles. In the parchment scrolls of the prophets and holy writings (NaKh), the Hebrew **Divrey HaYamim** is all one book, but in printed Bibles and for reference purposes it is divided into two books for greater convenience, to avoid an unwieldy work of 65 chapters.

Vv 1-6: The first act of Solomon's reign was to assemble all the leaders of the people who had been present at David's final assembly in Jerusalem to Giv'on. It was here that the Sanctuary had been located since Saul's killing of the priests of the town of Nov, to which it had been taken after the destruction of Shilo by the Philistines in the time of Eli the High Priest. After the Philistines returned the Ark of the Covenant, David eventually brought it up to Jerusalem, but the sacrificial altar still remained in the Sanctuary courtyard in Givon. Solomon's sacrifices in Giv'on were to initiate the Temple building project with which he had been entrusted by his father David.

"With **Wisdom** (Chochmah) shall the house be built..." (Proverbs 24:3). Whereas the Future Temple that we daily await is rooted in the highest Sefirah, **Keter**, the crown, Solomon's Temple was rooted in the first emanation from **Keter**, i.e. **Chochmah**, as explained by Rabbi Moshe Chaim Luzzatto in "Secrets of the Future Temple". This is why the narrative of the building of Solomon's Temple is preceded by the narrative of his dream at Giv'on, in which he asked for the Wisdom he needed in order to rule the people and accomplish his mission.

"The king needs a wise heart in order to know how to judge the people - and I am but a young, soft lad! Even a thousand wise men would find it hard to judge a great people like this. It is impossible without enormous effort because many people are constantly coming for legal decisions and he does not have the time to examine their cases. One person starts complaining and doesn't stop talking, and then immediately someone else arrives and starts screaming. Who can decide a thousand cases in one day unless he is a wise and understanding man who has the spirit of God in him? This is what I ask - that you should give me the wisdom and understanding to judge this great people, for this is what I need You to give me" (Rashi on v 10).

God gave Solomon what he requested "...because a person does not ask for such a thing except one who has fear of Heaven in his heart" (Rashi on v 11). Not only did He give him the wisdom he asked for, but also the wealth and glory that he did not request. "Because upon the wisdom that I am giving you depend also wealth and glory and length of days, as it is written, 'Length of days are in her right hand, and in her left wealth and honor' (Proverbs 3:16)" (Rashi on v 12).

CHAPTER 2

The cooperation given by Hiram king of Tyre to King Solomon in building the Temple in Jerusalem is a shining example of how the rectified Middle East should be. In striking contrast to the ceaseless hatred and hostility shown to Israel by the peoples of the neighboring countries in our era, Hiram, a man of outstanding vision as well as immense practical achievement, showed genuine love for the tender, wise young son of his old friend King David, helping to provide Solomon with the physical means to actualize the Temple dream in this material world.

During Hiram's reign Tyre had grown from being a satellite of Sidon into the most important of the Phoenician cities and the center of a large Mediterranean trading empire. Through his alliance with Solomon, Hiram assured himself access to the major trade routes to Egypt, Arabia and Mesopotamia, and with this trade both kings became very wealthy.

As recounted in our present chapter, Hiram sent Solomon not only the immense cedar timbers and other precious woods etc. required for the Temple building project, but also the master craftsman who executed the work. This craftsman, who was also called Hiram, has become a legendary figure particularly in the lore of Freemasonry, where he is revered as the builder of Solomon's Temple. To distinguish him from Hiram king of Tyre who sent him, Hiram the craftsman is sometimes called Hiram Avi or Hiram Abif (based on possible interpretations of II Chron. 2:12, see Metzudat David ad loc. and of II Chron. 4:16, see Metzudat David and RaDaK ad loc.).

Although Hiram's father, who had himself been a master craftsman, is described as a Tyrian (v 13) this is not to say that he was not an Israelite but only that he resided in Tyre. According to Rashi (on v 13) Hiram's father had been from the tribe of Naphtali (cf. I Kings 7:14) while his widowed mother was from that of Dan. As discussed in **Know Your Bible** commentary on I Kings ch 7, it is significant that Dan and Naphtali were both sons of Bilhah, the handmaiden of Rachel. Just as Moses' Sanctuary in the Wilderness had been built by Betzalel (from the tribe of Judah son of Leah) with the help of Oholiab (from the tribe of Dan, foster son of Rachel), so the Temple of Solomon, who came from the tribe of Judah/Leah, could only be built with the help of Hiram the Naphtalite, who was from the children of Rachel. Like the Sanctuary, the Temple had to be built through cooperation between the descendants of the two Matriarchs, Rachel and Leah, who are the embodiment of the two fundamental modes of government through which God runs the world - the kabbalistic Partzufim of Rachel and Leah.

"And Solomon numbered all the strangers (**Gerim**) who were in the land of Israel" (verse 16). As recounted in I Chron. 22:2 King David had already appointed these **Gerim** in the role of hewers and carriers of the immense stones that would be used in the building of the Temple. According to Rashi (on I Chron. 22:2) these **Gerim** were converts. However, RaDaK on verse 16 in our present chapter suggests that they may have been the residue of the Emorite, Hivvite, Perrizite and Jebusite Canaanites whom Solomon requisitioned for these tasks and who are called **Gerim** because they had ceased practicing idolatry, which was stamped out at the height of Israelite power during the reigns of David and Solomon.

CHAPTER 3

"And Solomon began to build the House of HaShem in Jerusalem on Mount Moriah..." (v 1). The text emphasizes that the Temple was built on the exact spot that had been divinely revealed to King David. This was the place where Abraham had bound Isaac and where Jacob had dreamed of the ladder reaching up to heaven.

In our present chapter and the next (chs 3-4) we are given an account of the details of the Temple building and its vessels which is less than half the length of the parallel account in I Kings chs 6-7 but which supplements it in various ways.

All of the dimensions of the Temple buildings and the design and number of its vessels had been received prophetically by Samuel and given to David, who entrusted them to Solomon. They all involve the deepest secrets of sacred geometry and art, through which combinations of divine names and attributes become embodied, expressed and revealed through the stone walls of physical halls and chambers and through the gold, silver and bronze etc. of the vessels. The kabbalistic meaning of the physical Temple buildings and vessels is the subject of Rabbi Moshe Chaim Luzzatto's "Secrets of the Future Temple", which mainly focuses on the vision of the coming Third Temple as seen by the prophet Ezekiel (chs 40ff) but which also clarifies the principles through which the design of King Solomon's Temple can be understood. The author of this commentary is not familiar with any kabbalistic text that specifically discusses the meaning of the First Temple in detail.

Vv 4-7: The best stone, wood, gold, silver and precious gems were used in the Temple for the sole purpose of glorifying God and providing a fitting "House" for the dwelling of His presence in this world. Wealth is rectified when it is devoted to the service of God.

Vv 8-13 give the dimensions of the innermost sanctum of the Temple, the Holy of Holies, which was to house the Ark of the Covenant. The gold-coated Ark, which had been made by Betzalel in the time of Moses, had a golden cover (**Kaporet**) on which stood two golden cherubs with outstretched wings. These are **not** the same as the cherubs described in our present text vv 10-13, which were made for Solomon according to the specifications given to him by King David and which stood with their wings stretched over the Ark of the Covenant and the two cherubs of the **Kaporet** (see Rashi on v 13). The Hebrew word for "cherub", **K'roov**, is explained by the rabbis as having the connotation of "like a child" (**k** is the comparative "like", **roov** from **ravia**, the Aramaic for a child or lad; Chagigah 13b, Rashi and Metzudat David on v 10). One cherub was male and the other female, alluding respectively to **Kudsha B'rich Hu**, "the Holy One blessed be He", and His **Shechinah**, "Indwelling Presence". They were face to face, signifying the perfect alignment of the Supreme God and His immanent Presence.

According to our text, the span of the four wings of Solomon's cherubs was equivalent to the entire floor space of the Holy of Holies, apparently leaving no space for the bodies of the cherubs. Accordingly, our sages stated that "the cherubs stood through a miracle" (Bava Batra 99a), although Rashi (on verse 11) suggests that in simple terms the cherubs' wings can be envisaged like the outstretched wings of a bird whose body protrudes underneath. Only here in the Temple was it permitted to make golden statues of the cherubs (see Rashi on Exodus 20:20). All other statues in the human form are prohibited by the Second Commandment (Exodus 20:4f).

"And before the house he made two pillars...." These two pillars flanked the entrance to the **Oolam**, the Vestibule of the main Temple building. The names given to these pillars - **Yachin** and **Boaz** - signify respectively the moon and the sun, because the royal house of David is compared to the moon, which receives all its light from the sun (see Rashi on v 17 where proof texts are provided establishing the relationship between the two names and what they signify). According to another interpretation (Rashi ibid.), Hiram called one pillar **Yachin** as an allusion to the heroic judge Samson, who came from his mother's tribe of Dan, while Solomon called the other **Boaz** to allude to his own illustrious ancestor from the tribe of Judah. Kabbalistically, the two pillars allude to the two "legs" of the Sefirot, i.e. the Sefirot of Netzach and Hod.

CHAPTER 4

Following the description of the Temple building in the previous chapter, our text continues with an account of the Temple vessels made by Solomon.

V 1: "And he made an altar of bronze...." Metzudat David (ad loc.) explains that the altar that Solomon made was actually of stone (as prescribed in Exodus 20:22) but it is described as being of bronze because it came to replace the portable bronze altar that had been made by Moses in the wilderness (Exodus 27:1-8).

SOLOMON'S SEA

"And he made a molten sea..." (v 2). Verses 3-5 describe the great molten bronze pool made by Solomon, while verse 6 explains that its purpose was to serve as a purificatory ablution mikveh for the Cohanim before commencing their daily service in the Temple.

On the basis of a careful analysis of the specifications of this pool as given here and in the parallel text in I Kings 7:23-26, the rabbis in Talmud Eiruvin 14b deduced mathematically that in order to contain the measure of 2000 bats of water (as given in I Kings 7:26), the upper two cubits of Solomon's Sea must have been round, as stated explicitly in our text, while the lower three cubits must have been square (see Rashi on our text v 3). In contrast to the text in I Kings, our present text gives the cubic capacity as having been 3000 bats. The rabbis explained that if a pool of the dimensions given in our text were filled with **dry** material that could be **heaped up**, it would indeed contain 3000 bats, while the actual cubic capacity for **liquid** is as given in the text in I Kings. Each bat measure is the equivalent of three **se'ah's**. The minimum measure of water for a valid Mikveh is 40 se'ahs. Thus, Solomon's Sea contained sufficient water for **one hundred and fifty Mikvehs**.

Verses 3 and 4 speak about two different sets of oxen. The two rows in the "likeness of oxen" that circled it under its rim (verse 3) are the knobs (or "colocynths", a lemon-shaped fruit) described in I Kings 7:24. Our text is saying that these knobs were fashioned in the form of ox-heads. Verse four then describes the twelve oxen on which the entire Sea of Solomon stood, three in each direction of the compass. (The square formation of the oxen as described in our text supports the above-cited rabbinic teaching in Eiruvin 14b that the lower part of the pool was square.)

Solomon's "Sea" - the actual pool itself - alludes to the Sefirah of Malchut, "Kingship", for in order to enter the service of God we must first immerse ourselves entirely in the acceptance of the yoke of His kingship. The twelve oxen allude to the twelve angels upon which the Shechinah "rides" in the world above - with four camps of three angels each in each direction of the compass - and to the twelve tribes of Israel upon which she "rides" in this world - with four camps of three tribes each surrounding the Sanctuary in each direction of the compass. The twelve angels and twelve tribes correspond to the twelve permutations of the essential Name of HaShem, each of which rules through Malchut at its appointed time. The twelve oxen of Solomon's Sea correspond to the twelve words in the verses **Shema Yisrael HaShem Elokeinu HaShem Echad** and **Baruch Shem Kevod Malchuto Le-Olam Va-Ed**. When we recite these words with the intention of taking upon ourselves the yoke of the kingship of Heaven, we bind ourselves with all the souls of Israel - the twelve tribes - and we become the chariot of the Shechinah (Zohar Vayechi 241a; Likutey Moharan I, 36:3).

V 6: The ten bronze lavers made by Solomon were in addition to the original bronze laver of Moses (Exodus 30:18), which was now placed in the Temple with five of Solomon's lavers flanking it on each side.

Vv 7-10: In accordance with the same principle as in the case of the lavers, Solomon made ten **Menorahs** (candelabra) and ten **Show-Bread Tables** to stand flanking Moses' Menorah and Show-Bread Tables respectively. Moses' Menorah stood on the south side of the Sanctuary with Solomon's Menorahs flanking it to its south ("right") and north ("left"), while Moses' Show-Bread Table stood on the north side of the Sanctuary with Solomon's tables to its north and south (Shekalim 17b). There is a division of opinion in the Talmud (Menachot 98b) as to whether all of the Menorahs were lit daily or only that of Moses and whether bread was placed on all the tables or only on that of Moses (see RaDaK on II Chron. 4:6). In the case of the Menorahs, our text says that he made them "according to their prescribed form" (**ke-mishpatam**). This indicates that Solomon did not make these additional Menorahs and Tables on his own initiative but on the basis of instructions he received from King David founded on prophecy and midrashim on Biblical verses (see Rashi on II Chron. 4:7 and RaDaK on II Kings 8:6).

Following the account of the sacrificial vessels made for Solomon by Hiram (verse 11) the text in vv 12-18 gives a summary of all the bronze vessels that he made, as described in detail in the previous chapter and the earlier part of the present chapter.

V 17: "The king cast them in the plain of the Jordan... between Succot and Tzereidatah." Rashi points out that Tzereidatah was the hometown of Jeraboam, who in the reign of Solomon's son and successor, Rehaboam, led the rebellion of the Ten Tribes against the authority of the House of David and prevented them from going up to the Temple in Jerusalem. Rashi brings a midrash of his uncle that **Tzereidata** as found in our text indicates that Jeraboam **constricted (tzar)** the **law** of the Torah (**Dat**).

Vv 19-22 give a summary of the Temple vessels that were made of gold. The "perfect gold" mentioned at the end of verse 21 was said by the rabbis to have been the product of casting one thousand talents of gold into the crucible and successively refining them until only a single talent of purest gold remained (Shekalim 18a).

CHAPTER 5

Verse 1: "…And Solomon brought in all the things that David his father had dedicated…." Rashi (ad loc.) explains that on the level of **p'shat** the verse suggests that Solomon brought into the Temple whatever was left of his father's dedications after using the rest for the work. Rashi also brings a midrash of the sages that Solomon brought into the Temple treasury **everything** that David had dedicated from the treasures plundered from the nations he defeated because Solomon did not want to use them in the Temple building. This was because he knew prophetically that it was destined to be destroyed, and he did not want the idolaters to be able to say that this came about through the vengeance of their gods after the plunder from their temples was used for the Temple in Jerusalem.

Vv 2ff describe the great assembly called by Solomon in the eleventh year of his reign at the conclusion of seven years building the Temple in order to bring in all the vessels to their proper places and inaugurate the Temple service.

The account in our text of how the Levites brought the Ark of the Covenant to its place in the Holy of Holies (vv 5ff) supplies the outer facts but does not give any indication of the great drama that took place when Solomon tried to get the Ark through the entrance of the Holy of Holies, only to find that "the gates were firmly stuck together and could not be opened. Solomon recited twenty-four prayers, but he was not answered. He started saying, 'Lift up your heads, O gates…and let the King of Glory enter' (Psalms 24:7) but the gates ran after him to swallow him up. Even when he concluded, 'HaShem of Hosts, He is the King of glory, Selah!' he was still not answered. At last he said, 'O God, do not turn away the face of Your anointed one, remember the kindnesses of David Your servant' (II Chron. 6:42; cf. Psalms 132:10). Only then was he answered - and all the faces of David's enemies turned black as the bottom of a pot because the entire people and all Israel knew that the Holy One blessed be He had forgiven him for that sin [with Batsheva]" (Talmud Shabbat 30a).

Verse 9: "And they drew out the poles of the Ark so that the ends of the poles were visible from the Ark before the Sanctuary, but they were not seen outside." The commentators provide a variety of explanations of this verse. The most plausible seems to be that of RaDaK (ad loc.): that the poles on which the Ark used to be carried were now drawn forward towards the eastern partition of the Holy of Holies to indicate that the Ark was now positioned in its permanent resting place and no longer needed to be carried from place to place as in the days before the Temple was built. However, the poles could not simply be removed, because they were needed to guide the High Priest on Yom Kippur when he had to burn incense and sprinkle the sacrificial blood in front of the Ark and not on either side. According to the Talmudic sages (Yoma 53b) the poles extended to the **Parochet** (screen) dividing the Holy of Holies from the main Sanctuary, protruding just a little so that while the poles themselves could not be seen in the Sanctuary, two protrusions were visible on the Parochet like two nipples, in order to fulfill the verse, '…He dwells between my breasts' (Song of Songs 1:13).

V 14: "And the priests were unable to stand to minister because of the cloud, for the glory of HaShem filled the House of God." With all the vessels in their proper places, the Divine Presence came to dwell in the House and the Temple was complete.

May it be rebuilt quickly in our days! Amen!

CHAPTER 6

"**Then** Solomon said, HaShem has said that He would dwell in the thick darkness" (v 1) - "When Solomon saw the cloud [in the last verse of the previous chapter, II Chron. 5:14] he said, Now I see that the Shechinah rests in the House that I have built, for He indeed promised to come and dwell in it from the midst of a cloud and thick darkness. And where did He say so? 'For in a cloud I shall appear over the cover of the Ark'" (Leviticus 16:2; Midrash Sifri).

The text of King Solomon's prayer on the inauguration of the Temple as given in our present chapter, II Chron. 6:1-39, is almost completely identical with the text as given in I Kings 8:12-52 with minor verbal differences, except that our text here in Chronicles adds the extra detail that the king - who was aged only 23 at this time - positioned himself on a bronze laver where all Israel could see him while he kneeled and spread his hands to heaven in order to offer his prayer (verses 12-13, see Rashi on v 13).

"God has spoken once; twice I have heard this" (Psalms 62:12). It is surely significant that the lengthy text of Solomon's prayer is given twice in our Scriptures in almost identical versions, as if to emphasize the great importance of the lessons it teaches us about the true meaning of the Temple that he built, whose rebuilding we await daily. King Solomon makes no mention of the animal sacrifices that are to be brought in the Temple as ordained in Leviticus and Numbers, but only of the prayers that Israelites and gentiles alike are to direct to God through the House and of the repentance in the heart that is necessary in order to elicit God's forgiveness and favor.

Solomon begins with thanksgiving for God's fulfillment of his promise to King David to establish his son as the king who would build the Temple, because this shows His detailed providence over all the affairs of the world. Nothing is subject to fate or chance, and this is why prayer and repentance "work", because everything is in the hands of God, who is responsive to men's prayers, deeds and efforts.

Vv 22-23: "If a man sins against his neighbor and an oath be laid upon him to make him swear and the oath comes before Your Altar in this House, then hear from heaven and do and judge Your servants by requiting the wicked by recompensing his way upon his own head and by justifying the righteous by rewarding him according to his righteousness." Rashi (ad loc.) explains that these verses refer to an Israelite who is engaged in a lawsuit before the Beit Din (rabbinic court) who forces his opponent to take an oath in God's name swearing that he is telling the truth. [Under the Torah law of court procedure, imposing oaths of various kinds on one or both sides in a case is one of the most important sanctions that can be taken to pressure them to tell the truth or else risk the terrible consequences of the curse included in the oath. Imposing of oaths is rarely if ever practiced today because the great majority of people do not understand the seriousness of lying under oath.] If the side that imposes the oath does so truthfully while the side that swears does so falsely, God will hear in heaven, and so will He hear if the side that imposes the oath does so unnecessarily, in which case he is called wicked.

Another explanation of the oath in verses 22-23 is given in Tosephta of Tractate Sotah cited by Rashi, where the man who "sins against his neighbor" is the adulterer who goes with someone else's wife, and who is liable to the consequences of the oath and curse administered to the wife by the priest in the Temple when she drinks the bitter waters in accordance with the laws of Sotah, the disloyal wife

(Numbers 5:19). In the light of Rashi's explanation and that of Tosephta Sotah we see how Solomon's prayer teaches that God watches providentially over all the deeds and affairs of men in detail and knows the intentions in their hearts, and repays each one according to his ways.

Vv 24-25: "And if Your people Israel are smitten before the enemy because they have sinned against You, and they repent... forgive the sin of Your people Israel and bring them back to the Land which You gave to them and to their fathers." With Israel today being smitten by our enemies virtually every day on the military, strategic and international diplomatic battlefields, we must learn from these verses and from verses 34-39 below that the only sure way to have our territories restored and to live in them in peace is through repentance and prayer.

Vv 26-31 teach that prayer and repentance are also the first remedy for various natural disasters such as drought, famine, crop failure, locusts and other plagues as well as illness and disease.

Vv 32-3: "Likewise concerning the stranger who is not of Your people Israel... and You hear from the heavens... and do according to everything for which the stranger calls out to You" - "In the case of an Israelite I prayed that You should give him **in accordance with his ways**, but in the case of the stranger, that You should give him according to **everything** for which he calls out to You. This is because Israel recognize the Holy One blessed be He and know that He has the power in His hand to carry out what He wants and if the prayer of an Israelite is not answered, he attributes it to his own sins and examines his deeds. However, if the stranger is not answered, he complains of injustice and says, I heard His fame through all the world and I made a great effort and followed many roads until I came and prayed in this place, and I have not found anything of substance here just as in the case of other gods. This is why Solomon prays that 'You should do according to all that the stranger calls out to You'" (Rashi on v 33).

Vv 36-39: Even in exile near or far from their land, Israel must direct their prayers to God specifically through their Land, through the city of Jerusalem and through the Temple - even if it be in ruins. For in their very essence, the Land of Israel, Jerusalem and the Temple all attest to God's watchful providence over all the details of creation and to His responsiveness to prayer and repentance.

V 41: "And now arise, HaShem O God, to Your resting place... "so as not to wander about as until now, from Shilo to Nov and from Nov to Giv'on". "...You and the Ark of Your strength" - "The reason why it is called the Ark of Your **strength** is because through it He executed His wonders and mighty deeds against the Philistines" (Rashi ad loc.). These wonders attest to His protective providence over the Ark and over all Israel.

CHAPTER 7

The parallel account of King Solomon's prayer on the inauguration of the Temple as given in I Kings ch 8 continues in vv 55-61 with his blessing and address to the people, asking God to incline our hearts to Him so as to follow His pathways and keep all his commandments, and urging the people to serve Him with all their hearts (I Kings 8 vv 58 & 61). This blessing and appeal to the people is not recorded in our present text here in Chronicles.

On the other hand, our present text adds a most important detail that is not recorded in the parallel account in I Kings - namely the descent of **fire from Heaven** to consume the sacrificial offerings brought by Solomon and the people (I Kings 7:1 & 3). This was the greatest possible testimony to God's watchful providence over the Temple and the indwelling of the Shechinah as well as being the greatest honor to Solomon, the scion of the House of David in whose honor Chronicles was written.

The account of Solomon's inaugural sacrifices and the conclusion of the celebration of the consecration of the Temple as given in our present text vv 4-10 is parallel to the account in I Kings 8:62-66.

In verse 7 of our present text, we read: "And Solomon sanctified the middle of the courtyard that was before the House of HaShem... for the altar of bronze that Solomon had made was not able to contain the burnt offerings and the meal offerings and the fats" (v 7). There is a difference of opinion in the Talmud (Zevachim 59a) as to whether Solomon literally sanctified the floor of the Temple courtyard (**Azarah**) with the sanctity of the Altar so as to be able to offer sacrifices on it, or whether this verse in fact alludes to the Altar of stone which Solomon built attached to the floor of the courtyard in order to replace the bronze Altar made by Moses for the Sanctuary in the wilderness (see Rashi on II Chron. 7:7 and **Know Your Bible** commentary on II Chronicles 4:1).

Verses 12-22 in our present text recounting God's second appearance to Solomon in a dream (following His first dream-revelation to him at Giv'on, II Chron. 1:7-12) are almost identical to the parallel account in I Kings 9:1-9, except for verses 13-16 in our present text, in which God specifically answers Solomon's prayers that He should heed the people's supplications and repentance if He sends them drought, famine and plague (see II Chron. 6:26-28 and Rashi on II Chron. 7:12-13).

God concludes His revelation to Solomon with a warning that the durability of the House of David, the Temple and Israel's possession of their land is conditional upon our observance of the Torah.

May He turn our hearts to Him, gather in our exiles
and rebuild His Temple quickly in our days. Amen.

CHAPTER 8

With the completion of the Temple the Shechinah came to dwell on earth, and during the reign of Solomon the kingdom on earth fully reflected the heavenly kingdom just as in the middle of the lunar month the moon (**Malchut**) is directly aligned to the sun (**Tiferet**) and reflects its light to perfection. Solomon's reign was thus a time of splendor and glory in which peace reigned throughout the land and kings, queens and princes came to listen to his wisdom.

V 2: "And as for the cities that **Hiram gave to Solomon**, Solomon built them and settled Israelites there." In I Kings 9:12-13 we only hear of twenty cities that **Solomon gave to Hiram** in the Galilee (which in fact did not find favor in Hiram's eyes) while in our present text we only hear of these cities that **Hiram gave to Solomon**. In the words of Metzudat David (ad loc.): "This is the way of the Biblical text: what one verse passes over in silence another reveals." RaDaK (ad loc.) suggests that Hiram gave Solomon cities in his own land in which the latter settled Israelites in order to keep them in his possession, while Solomon gave Hiram cities in the Galilee in order to strengthen the covenant between the two of them.

In sad contrast to the international amity that prevailed in the time of Solomon, in today's Middle East the Arabs demand the right to settle the entire Land of Israel while strictly prohibiting any Israelis from taking up residence in any of their territories. But at a time when the earthly kingdom truly reflects the heavenly kingdom as in the reign of Solomon, it is possible for the kind of "population exchange" that is indicated by our present text in Chronicles and that in Kings, in which Israelites can live at peace in the territories of other nations and vice versa.

V 4: "And he built Tadmor in the wilderness...." Rashi (ad loc.) notes that in I Kings 9:18 its name is written in the parchment scroll as **Tamor** (the "ktiv") although it is traditionally pronounced as

Tadmor (the "kri"). Rashi quotes the Talmud Yevamot (16a) as saying that converts are not accepted from the **Tarmoodim**, citing Bereishit Rabbah on the Akeidah giving the reason as being because they assisted Israel's enemies, thereby **changing** themselves (**heimeero**, from the same root as **Tamor**, cf. **Temurah**). "This is why in Kings the name is written as **Tamor** having the connotation of exchange (**Temurah**) because they should have acted kindly towards Israel just as Israel acted kindly to them. However, in honor of Solomon the text here in Chronicles does not call it **Tamor** but **Tadmor**, a city of importance, as it would not be an honor to Solomon to say here that he built a city that rebelled against him" (Rashi on v 4). [Kabbalistically, the **Heichaley Temurot**, "Palaces of Exchanges", are the source of all the confusion in this world in which evil appears to be good and vice versa; see Rabbi Nachman's comments on his story of The Exchanged Children, Rabbi Nachman's Stories p. 231.]

In fact, even in the reign of Solomon the seeds were planted for the disasters that befell Israel later on, particularly through the degeneration that set in as a result of his marriage to the daughter of Pharaoh (v 11), but in honor of the House of David, Chronicles glozes over the negative aspects, focusing only on the positive.

Thus our text describes how Solomon built, embellished and consolidated his kingdom on all sides (vv 3-6 and 17f). While the Canaanites who still remained in the land despite the Israelite conquest were usually a thorn in their sides, during the reign of Solomon they were fully subjugated and set to work to build the Torah kingdom, while the Israelites directed the work (vv 7-9). The Temple functioned in accordance with all the laws of the Torah and the arrangements of the Cohanim and Levites in their various orders as established by David (vv 12-16).

CHAPTER 9

We cannot call the visit of the Queen of Sheba to Solomon a case of "international cultural **exchange**" because although the two exchanged many kinds of material gifts, the cultural influence was all in one direction, from Solomon to the Queen of Sheba.

The Targum calls her the Queen of **Z'margad** (=Emerald? Turquoise? Cf. Targum on Ex. 28:18). Likewise, the Targum on Job 1:15, "And **Sheva** struck and took [Job's cattle]," renders: "And Lilith the Queen of **Z'margad** attacked", thereby linking the Queen of Sheba with the legendary queen of the demons. As discussed in **Know Your Bible** on I Kings ch 10, there is a Talmudic opinion stating that "whoever says that the Queen of Sheba was a woman is simply mistaken; what is **Malkhat** Sheba? It is the kingdom (**Mamlekhet**) of Sheba!" (Bava Batra 15b). However, Maharsha (ad loc.) explains that all the Talmud means here is that the Queen of Sheba was not merely the wife-consort of a King of Sheba but that she was actually a Queen in her own right, and the classical rabbinic commentators relate to the story of her visit on the level of **p'shat** as a visit paid by one monarch to another.

Sheba is traditionally associated with Ethiopia, although the Arabs venerate a Temple of the Queen of Sheba in Yemen. It is quite plausible that the sea-faring Ethiopian kingdom colonized and held sway over the Arabian coastline, which is quite nearby across the Red Sea. It was doubtless through King Solomon's trading ventures from the Red Sea port of Eilat as described in the previous chapter (II Chron. 8:17) that his fame spread to Sheba.

According to Rashi (on v 4) what impressed the Queen of Sheba about Solomon's table was the geese and other abundant delicacies, while the way his servants sat impressed her because each one knew his proper place according to his rank. Each stood at his post of duty without changing it every day, yet the apparel they wore today they would not wear tomorrow! She was particularly impressed by the special pathways by which he would ascend to the House of HaShem (for Solomon, everything led to HaShem)

- "...and there was no more spirit in her". "She used to think that there was no wisdom in any of the other kingdoms except for hers, because her land was in the east and for this reason they were exceptionally wise because they gazed at the constellations... but 'the wisdom of Solomon was more abundant than all the wisdom of the children of the east' (I Kings 5:10; Rashi on I Chron. 9:4).

V 17: "And the king made a great throne of ivory and he coated it with pure gold." Solomon's throne - which expressed how the earthly kingdom reflects the heavenly kingdom - is the subject of an abundantly rich tapestry of midrashic embellishment collected at very great length in Targum Sheini on Esther verse 2. According to Targum Sheini on Esther, it was made for Solomon by Hiram the craftsman to symbolize Solomon's rule over all aspects of creation, but as a result of our sins it was captured by Nebuchadnezzar and taken to Babylon, after which it finally came to the hands of Ahasuerus. The latter was unable to sit on it and was forced to order his craftsman to make an inferior version in order to make it appear as if he was sitting on the throne of Solomon.

V 29: "And the other acts of Solomon, the first and the last, are written in the words of Nathan the Prophet and in the prophecy of Achiyah the Shilonite and in the visions of Yedo the seer against Jeraboam son of Nevat." According to Rashi, the "words of Nathan" are contained in II Samuel 12:1-25 while the prophecy of Achiyah is in I Kings 11:29-31.

V 30: "And Solomon ruled in Jerusalem over all Israel for forty years." In this respect Solomon was greater than his father David, who ruled in Hebron for seven years over the tribe of Judah and only ruled in Jerusalem over all Israel for thirty-three years (Rashi ad loc.).

CHAPTER 10

"And Rechav'am went to Shechem..." (v 1). The town of Shechem had already been marked out for troubles from the times of Jacob and Joseph (Gen. ch's 34 and 37:13). Shechem (="Nablus") was in the very heartland of the tribe of Ephraim, the tribe of Yerav'am (Jeraboam). Since the book of Chronicles was written to give honor to the House of David, our present text refrains from clarifying why Yerav'am had fled from King Solomon to Egypt. However, what is lacking here is set forth in I Kings 11:26-40, which tells that Yerav'am - who had been handpicked for his diligence by Solomon to serve as his chief collector of taxes from the tribe of Ephraim - had dared to criticize the king for encroaching on the pilgrims' right of way in Jerusalem in order to build accommodations for Pharaoh's daughter and her household. This turned Yerav'am into a traitor, thereby preparing him for his subsequent role as the leading antagonist against the House of David. Thus, it was that Solomon's marriage with Pharaoh's daughter kindled the popular resentment that culminated with the tearing of the kingdom into two at the start of the reign of his successor Rechav'am, as had been prophesied by Achiyah HaShiloni (I Kings 11:29ff).

V 4: "Your father made our yoke hard...." According to the simple meaning of the text (**p'shat**), the people's main grudge against the monarchy was because of the heavy taxes they had to bear. In the words of Rashi (ad loc.): "[Your father] was a man who was preoccupied with the exertion of building, and he put on us the burden of financing his workers and paying taxes."

From Rechav'am's eventual answer to the people's request to lighten their burden, "My little finger will be thicker than my father's loins" (v 10), our commentators infer that the new king had every intention of further enhancing the glory and splendor of the monarchy at the expense of the people. In the words of Metzudat David (on vv 10-11): "I am on a higher level than my father and it is necessary for me to have many horses and to expand my household. And if I am going to have more horses and a bigger household, seeing as my father already put a weighty yoke upon you, I am going to add to the burden because everything will be upon you to finance." From the program of fortifications and military strengthening which Rechav'am later initiated in Judea and Benjamin as described in the following chapter (II Chron. 11:5-12), we can only imagine what he initially had in mind prior to the split in the kingdom in order to fortify the territories of the other tribes and to build Israel into the supreme world power.

One wonders if another dimension of the dispute between Yerav'am and the populace relates to the spiritual "burden" that Solomon had placed upon the people. It is known that certain important rabbinic ordinances were instituted by Solomon and his Beit Din - such as the washing of hands **Netilat Yadayim**) before eating **Chulin** (regular food as opposed to Terumah) and the practice of using an **Eruv** on Shabbat in order to permit carrying in enclosed public areas even though this is not forbidden **Mid'oraita** without an **Eruv**. Were the people asking Rechav'am to adopt a new course of spiritual leadership that would involve fewer stringencies and greater leniency? If this is so, we may discern an interesting parallel between the split in the time of Rechav'am and the split in today's Jewish "kingdom", where various halachic stringencies (**Chumrahs**) pursued in certain sections of the Torah-observant community appear to impel other sectors to seek greater leniency and "freedom" and even to abandon Torah observance altogether.

If there is any validity in this parallel, it may be that the elders who counseled Yerav'am to come towards the people were offering similar counsel to that of Rabbi Nachman, who urged us not to adopt unnecessary stringencies in our practice of the Torah but rather to strive to keep all the commandments according to the simple interpretation of the law without seeking to go beyond it (Rabbi Nachman's Wisdom #235). However, the "children" who had grown up with Rechav'am (who in the age of Solomon would all have been brilliant Torah scholars) advocated what a tough, inflexible front, advising the new king not to loosen up by providing **Koolas** (leniencies) but rather to tighten up and impose even more **Chumrahs** (stringencies, vv 8-11).

In this context, it is highly illuminating to consider comments made by R. Baruch Halevy Epstein, author of the "Torah Temimah", about his father, R. Yechiel Michel Epstein 1829-1907, author of **Aruch HaShulchan**, a brilliant, detailed multi-volume analysis of every law and subject area in the **Shulchan Aruch** by an outstanding **Gaon Olam** (luminary of world stature). The Torah Temimah quotes his father - who was a Rav in Belorussia - as having emphasized that while it is much easier to give a stringent ruling than a lenient one, the latter requires greater Torah wisdom, and wherever possible the Rav should endeavor to give a lenient ruling as long as it is fully in accord with all the principles of the Halachah.

Rechav'am promised to chastise the people with scorpions, and this is indeed what happened, because when Yerav'am led the Ten Tribes in their rebellion against the House of David, he decided to stop people going to Jerusalem for the pilgrim festivals (which would have led to their reconciliation) by establishing an idolatrous festival in Beit El to rival the festival of Succot. Yerav'am's festival was a month after Succoth on the 15th of Marcheshvan, the astrological sign of which is **Scorpio**!!! The month of Marcheshvan has often proved to be a time of chastisement and suffering for the people of Israel.

"...and now, David, look to your house!" (v 16). The people's contemptuous rejoinder to Rechav'am was, in the words of Rashi (ad loc.): "We can bear neither you nor your Temple!" With this began the split between the Ten Tribes and those of Judah and Benjamin under the House of David that has been the defining feature of the history of Israel ever afterwards, and which has ramifications until today. In many ways, the gulf between today's remnant of Torah-observant faithful and the extensive rainbow of other latter-day orientations to being Jewish or Israeli is a manifestation of this same split.

CHAPTER 11

Civil wars among the tribes of Israel had recurred from the times of the Judges until the war between the House of Saul and the House of David, and only the generously conciliatory attitude of King David had brought peace and unity to the nation. Eighty years after the death of Saul, Rechav'am initially wanted to use military might to coerce the Ten Tribes into returning under his tutelage (our present chapter, verse 1) but he had the good sense to heed the words of the prophet Shemayah and to abstain from unleashing an all-out civil war, which could only have led to disaster because the split in the kingdom was divinely ordained.

Instead, Rechav'am had to content himself with a lower-key way of pursuing the expansionist ambitions of his father Solomon by building new and reinforcing existing fortified towns all over Judea and Benjamin (vv 5-12). As we learn from our text, all these towns were well provided with abundant supplies of food and water (see Rashi on v 5) as well as military arms.

With the Ten Tribes under the leadership of Yerav'am deviating ever further into idolatry, they had little use for the Cohanim and Levites, whose entire function and organizational basis were bound up with their service in the Temple in Jerusalem. Ever since the marriage of Aaron the High Priest with Eli-sheva, daughter of Aminadav, Prince of the Tribe of Judah (Ex. 6:23), the priesthood had been closely bound up with the kingship of the royal tribe, and thus it was natural for the priests and Levites to continue their alliance with the House of David and gravitate to Jerusalem (verse 13). Yerav'am established his own religious functionaries to serve in Beth El and other cult centers (v 15), while the remaining Torah-faithful members of the Ten Tribes went to Jerusalem to serve the God of their fathers (v 16).

Rechav'am sensibly used a series of marriage alliances within the tribe of Judah to consolidate his power over his fellow tribesmen (vv18-21).

V 23: "And he **dealt wisely** (**va-yiven**, lit. 'and he **understood**') and dispersed all of his children throughout all the districts of Judah and Benjamin to every fortified city." Metzudat David (ad loc.) explains: "He understood that he was faced with a rebellion and he was afraid of it, and for this reason he consolidated his position by scattering all his sons to all the different territories of Judah and Benjamin and to all the fortress cities in order to guard him from any rebellion. 'And he sought many wives' - to marry them to his sons in order to consolidate his kingship with the help of the fathers of these wives."

CHAPTER 12

Our chapter traces the beginning of Judah's descent into degeneracy, which started in the reign of Rechav'am, and the consequences to which it led.

"And it came to pass that as Rechav'am established the kingdom and strengthened himself, he forsook the Torah of HaShem and all Israel with him" (v 1). The conventional printed Bibles make this verse the first verse of a new chapter, but in the Hebrew text as written in the parchment scroll it is actually the closing verse of the previous section, which runs continuously from II Chron. 11:18 until 12:1, while the new section (**Parshah Petuchah**), which opens at 12:2, relates the consequences of their deviation from the Torah - the attack on Jerusalem by Sheeshak king of Egypt. In concluding the previous section, which explained how Rechav'am consolidated his hold over Judah, by saying that he then forsook the Torah, our text seems to imply that the reason was because he fell into complacency, saying that "My power and the strength of my hand have gotten me this might" (Deut. 8:17).

The parallel account in I Kings 14:22-24 specifies in what way Rechav'am and the people forsook the Torah - by making private altars after the Temple had already been built, establishing Asherah (tree-worship) cults, and permitting the spread of prostitution and immorality, all of which were strictly forbidden under Torah law. We need not assume that the people totally forsook all kinds of Torah practice in the same way that today many have become completely "secularized". The flaw lay in the fact that while they continued following the commandments, particularly those relating to the Temple, they simultaneously opened themselves to other cults and practices, which weakened their loyalty to HaShem, who wants us to serve Him with undivided hearts.

In retribution God sent Sheeshak with a vast army of Egyptians, Libyans and other African peoples to invade Israel. It appears that Sheeshak may have been a Libyan general who had replaced the previous dynasty of Pharaohs with whom Solomon had been allied in marriage. Sheeshak had already showed his hostility to the royal house in Jerusalem by giving hospitality to Yerav'am when he fled from Solomon I Kings 11:40). It appears that Sheeshak now wanted to take advantage of Rechav'am's weakness in order to turn Israel back into being essentially a province under the dominion of Egypt as it had been in former times.

Sheeshak's invasion caused a wave of repentance in Rechav'am and his officers when the prophet Shemayah explained to them that they had brought it upon themselves because of their own backsliding. After two generations of national independence and dominion over others in the reigns of David and Solomon, Israel would once again taste the bitterness of threats from and subjugation to other nations in order to learn the difference between serving God and serving the kingdoms of the various lands (cf. verse 8). As a result of the repentance of Rechav'am and his officers, God did not let Sheeshak realize his imperial ambitions, but the Egyptian king did succeed in looting many of the treasures amassed by David and Solomon. Despite being chastened, Rechav'am did not repent completely and is criticized in our text for failing to set himself wholeheartedly to search out Hashem (v 14).

"Now the acts of Rechav'am. are written in the book of Shemayah the prophet and of Iddo the seer." (v 15). Rashi (ad loc.) writes that each prophet wrote his own book containing his prophecies. In the following chapter (II Chron. 13:22) Iddo's book is called a **Midrash**. It seems possible that the Book of Kings consists of a weave (**Masechet**) of such writings.

CHAPTER 13

Having reigned for seventeen years, Rechav'am was succeeded by his son **Avi-yah**, who in the parallel account in I Kings 15:1 is called **Avi-yam**. There in Kings only the barest outline is given of the brief three-year reign of Avi-yah, who is simply described as having followed all the sins of his father before him and as having not been whole-hearted with HaShem in the way that David had been (I Kings 15:3).

Our present text gives us a closer look at Avi-yah, who apparently sought to bring back the Ten Tribes under the tutelage of the House of David through a combination of military might (or bluff?) and intense psychological pressure. He was bold enough to take an army of four hundred thousand soldiers against an opponent who was able to field double that number (verse 3). In his speech to Yerav'am and the Ten Tribes, Avi-yah asserts the legitimacy of the Davidic monarchy against Yerav'am's rebel regime, whose sham idolatrous priesthood of upstarts he contrasts with the authentic Cohanim and Levites who practiced all the Temple rites in Jerusalem exactly as ordained in the Torah. In the merit of their service Avi-yah was apparently confident that he would be granted an easy victory, but his army was in great danger when Yerav'am sent a detachment to attack them from the rear. They rose to the occasion with a display of trust in God, and Avi-yah was able to deliver a mighty though not decisive blow to the Ten Tribes. According to Midrash Rabbah cited by RaDaK on v 17 of our present text, "the great blow" with which Avi-yah struck them was more than just killing five hundred thousand of them. He intentionally left the bodies of the slain Israelites until their faces were unrecognizable so that they would not be able to be identified, with the result that women whose husbands had gone to the battle would not know definitely if they had been widowed or not and would thus be left as **Agunahs** never able to remarry.

"Nor did Yerav'am recover strength in the days of Avi-yah **and HaShem struck him and he died**" (v 20). The simple meaning appears to be that HaShem struck Yerav'am, who died, but in fact it is clear from our texts that Yerav'am lived for two years after the death of Avi-yah, and the Midrash learns that **and HaShem struck him** refers not to Yerav'am but to Avi-yah, who was punished because after capturing Beit El he failed to uproot the idolatrous cult of the Golden Calf, and also because in his speech to the Ten Tribes he castigated Yerav'am publicly (see Rashi on v 20 and RaDaK at length ibid.).

CHAPTER 14

Asa already began to rule over Judah when his father Avi-yah became sick, and after his death reigned for forty-one years spanning the rule of eight kings of Israel (Yerav'am ben Nevat, Nadav, Ba'sha, Eilah, Zimri, Tivni, Omri and Ahab). Asa is considered to have been a righteous king (although this was somewhat marred towards the end of his life, as we will see in II Chron. 16).

It happened numerous times in the history of the kings of Judah that one or more generations of kings who veered from the Torah were succeeded by a saintly revivalist king who effected a spiritual re-arousal in the people. This was so in the case of Asa, the fourth king after David, following Rechav'am and Avi-yah, both of whom had strayed successively further from the true path of the Torah. Asa's first acts were to remove the various idolatrous cult altars etc. that had infiltrated Judah, and as we read in our text (v 5) God rewarded him with peace and quiet after the warfare that had plagued the people in the reigns of Rechav'am (vs. Sheeshak of Egypt) and Avi-yah (vs. Yerav'am king of Israel).

"And Zerach the Kushite went out with an army of a thousand thousands..." (v 8). According to the rabbis (Pesachim 119a), God saw Asa's righteousness and wanted to return all the treasures that had been plundered from Jerusalem in the time of Rechav'am. He thus arranged for Zerach to carry all these treasures with him as he went out to battle. Zerach is identified by some historians with Pharaoh Assarchan I, who like Sheeshak was the founder of a Libyan dynasty of kings of Egypt and who shared his ambitions to reincorporate Israel as a province under the Egyptian sphere of influence. Zerach advanced with his million-strong army along the coastal plain via Gaza to Ashkelon, from where he turned eastwards to Gat and onwards to Mareshah (which is about midway between Gat and Hebron), threatening the very heartland of Judea.

Asa's prayer as he went out to meet these hordes in battle is in the tradition of bold Davidic faith and trust that God has the power to help even the weak and helpless (vv 10-11). God struck the Zerach and his African armies and Asa and his men chased them back to G'rar (known to us from the days of Abraham, Gen. 20:1ff) southwest of Gaza, returning with enormous plunder.

CHAPTER 15

The prophecy of Azaryahu ben Odeid to Asa and all the people was intended to take advantage of the atmosphere of triumph after the defeat of Zerach and his hordes in order to drive home the essential message of all the prophets: that if Israel will search out HaShem and follow His Torah, their enemies will fall before them and they will have peace in their land.

"Now for a long time Israel has been without the true God and without a teaching priest and without Torah" (v 3). In the Hebrew text, the same words can be read as a comment about the past or a prophecy of what was yet to come. In Midrash Vayikra Rabbah ch 19 they are interpreted as a future prophecy that a time would come when no justice would be visible in the world, when the role of the high priest would become defunct and when there would be no more Sanhedrin. The Midrash says that on hearing this, the people of Asa's generation felt completely helpless, until a prophetic voice said to them, "But as for you, be strong and do not let your hands become weak, for there is a reward for your work" (v 7). We may learn from this that even though in our own times the world seems to be becoming darker and darker in many ways, it is up to us to strengthen ourselves and continue in the path of the Torah, "...for there is a reward for your work!"

Azariahu's prophecy inspired King Asa to redouble his efforts to purify the land of idolatry and to renovate the Temple Altar, after which he called a great assembly of all the people in Jerusalem, including many from the other tribes besides Judah and Benjamin who had come to join him. Being held in the third month (Sivan) this assembly was like a new Receiving of the Torah (which originally took place in the month of Sivan) and Asa renewed the Covenant between God and Israel. Present-day lovers of freedom and tolerance may be interested to note that any man, woman or child who did not join in this national commitment to search out HaShem was to be killed (v 13).

"And even Ma'achah the mother did Asa the king remove from being queen..." (v 16). There is some debate about the exact identity of this Ma'achah (see Rashi and RaDaK ad loc. and Rashi on II Chron. 13:2). According to RaDaK she was Ma'achah daughter of Absalom, who was not Asa's mother but his grandmother - i.e. the mother of King Avi-yah and the widow of Rechav'am. She was thus the dowager Queen Mother and a woman who presumably had formidable prestige and influence in the kingdom. That Asa was able to remove her entrenched idolatry (which according to the rabbis was sculpted with a phallus that she used regularly, see Rashi on v 16) was an enormous achievement, and in reward for his efforts he was spared war for most of the rest of his reign (v 19).

CHAPTER 16

The last verse of the previous chapter said, "And there was no war until the thirty-fifth year of the reign of Asa" (II Chron. 15:19). The first verse of our present chapter then continues: "In the **thirty-sixth year** of the reign of Asa, Ba'sha king of Israel came up against Judah..." (II Chron. 16:1).

As the Midrash Seder Olam points out, it is impossible to take these verses literally, because Ba'sha king of Israel had already died in the twenty-sixth year of the reign of Asa (see I Kings 16:8). As explained by Seder Olam and the commentators (Rashi on II Chron. 15:19, Metzudat David and RaDaK on II Chron. 16:1), Ba'sha's attack on Judah actually took place in the **sixteenth year** of Asa's reign, which was **thirty-six years** after the death of King Solomon (because Rechav'am reigned 17 years and Avi-yah for 3 years. 17 + 3 + 16 = 36).

Solomon had married Pharaoh's daughter in the fourth year of his reign, and since he died after reigning forty years, he was with her for **thirty-six years**. Because of this sin, it was originally decreed that the kingdom would be split into two, Judah and Israel, for **thirty-six years**, ending in the **sixteenth year** of Asa's reign. Had Asa stood up properly to the test when Ba'sha attacked Judah, trusting only in God for deliverance, our rabbis say that He would have given him victory not only over the Ten Tribes but over the Arameans as well, and Asa would have been able to restore the kingdom of the House of David over all the Twelve Tribes of Israel, thereby bringing complete redemption. But instead of relying on prayer and faith alone, Asa employed material means to try to overcome Ba'sha through bribing Ba'sha's Aramean allies to attack him from the rear (vv 2-3). As a result, the opportunity for the reconciliation of Judah-Benjamin and the Ten Tribes was lost, and at the end of this Asa became angry, tyrannical and physically sick.

Ba'sha apparently wanted to recover the areas of Mount Ephraim that King Avi-yah had captured (II Chron. 13:19; 15:8). Ba'sha imposed a blockade on the northern border of Judah by fortifying Ramah to the north of Jerusalem, south of the Ephraimite cult center of Beit El (the present chapter, v 1). Asa's bribe to Ben Hadad king of Aram in Damascus (vv 2-3) persuaded the latter to stage predatory attacks on the tribes Dan and Naftali way up in the north of Israel (v 4), and news of these attacks caused Ba'sha to end his blockade of Judah (v 5).

V 6: "And King Asa took **all Judah** and they carried away the stones and timbers of Ramah that Ba'sha built...." In the parallel account in I Kings 15:22 we learn that not only did Asa take **all Judah** but also that "**no one was exempt**" (**eyn naki**). Our rabbis explain that he considered the work so urgent that he mobilized all the Torah scholars despite the law that Torah scholars are not required to go out in person when the public is mobilized to carry out building and excavation works in the country (Rambam Talmud Torah 6:10), and he even mobilized brides and grooms from their marital canopies, contrary to the Torah law that a groom is exempt from any wartime duties in his first year after marriage in order to be "clean" and free for his house (=his wife, **naki le-veito**, Deut. 24:5).

At exactly this time Hanani the Seer came to reprove Asa for having relied on the stratagems of this world in bribing the king of Aram to attack Ba'sha instead of relying only on God. Had Asa put all his trust in God as he had done when Zerach the Kushi attacked with his million-strong army (II Chron. 14: 9ff), the king of Aram would have been delivered into his hands as well as the king of Israel, "for the eyes of HaShem run to and fro throughout the whole earth to show Himself strong on behalf of those whose heart is perfect towards Him" (v 9). Instead, the Arameans continued as hostile enemies of Judah and Israel until the time of King Ahaz, when they and the Ten Tribes fell into the hands of Pilessar king of Assyria (see Rashi on our present chapter verse 4).

Having failed in his test, King Asa was in no mood to hear the reproof of the prophet, whom he angrily imprisoned, after which he subjected part of his own population to tyrannical oppression, presumably in order to stamp out protests.

V 12: "And Asa was diseased... in his **legs**, **up to above was his illness**...." The saintly Asa, whose early career had been filled with such promise, was one of five who were "created with a semblance of the supernal form" and all of whom were punished accordingly. These were Samson, who suffered with the loss of his **strength**; Saul, whose **neck** was above everyone else's but who eventually fell with it on his own sword; Absalom, who died hanging by his Nazirite **hair**, Tzedekiah, whose **eyes** were gouged out, and Asa who became sick in his **legs** (Sotah 10a).

Asa's "podagra" (=gout), which is said to cause pain like pins in raw flesh (ibid.) was not only a physical illness. It was **up to above**, i.e. it had spiritual ramifications at the highest levels, because Asa had been destined to be the **legs** upon which the House of David would rise and stand again but for his flaw of employing the Torah scholars, who are **Tomchey Oraita**, the **legs** and supporting pillars of the Torah, in demeaning physical labor together with the unlearned common people. This flaw was the spiritual root of his illness, but Asa did not want to go to the prophet in order to seek out what God was teaching him through this illness. Instead he tried to cure it by physical means, turning to the doctors.

Despite this tragic end, Asa was buried with the utmost honor, having in his earlier career succeeded in swinging Judah around from its descent into idolatry and immorality and bringing about a spiritual revival among the people that lasted into the reign of his son Yehoshaphat.

CHAPTER 17

The time of Yehoshaphat, who reigned in Jerusalem for twenty-five years, was a golden age in comparison with the clouded times of Yerav'am, Avi-yah and the later years of Asa. This was because "HaShem was with Yehoshaphat because he walked in the first ways of his father David…." (v 3) - i.e. as David had walked in righteousness before his sin with Batsheva and in conducting a census of the population. Solomon's reign had been marred because his foreign wives led him astray; Rechav'am had abandoned the Torah, and Asa had not depended on HaShem in war, but Yehoshaphat was like his "father" David, who was wholeheartedly devoted to HaShem (see Rashi on verse 3). At a time when the prestigious kingdom of Israel under Ahab was worshipping the Baal, Yehoshaphat remained loyal to the God of his "father" and followed His commandments (vv 3-4).

V 6" "…And his heart was lifted up in the ways of HaShem…" (v 6). Despite the material support that Yehoshaphat enjoyed from all Judah giving him enormous wealth and glory (v 5), he did not become arrogant as a result. For him wealth and glory were of no significance at all compared to the ways of HaShem (Metzudat David ad loc.).

THE OUTREACH KING

The rabbis said of Yehoshaphat that when he would see a Torah scholar, he would rise from his throne and hug and kiss him, calling him "My teacher! My teacher! My master! My master" (Makkot 24a). His father, King Asa, had demeaned the Torah scholars in taking them out of the study halls to work side by side with the common people, carrying, digging and building. But King Yehoshaphat now took the Torah itself out to the ordinary people in order to teach and elevate them. "In the third year of his reign he sent his ministers. to teach in the cities of Judah, and with them the Levites... and with them the Sefer Torah of HaShem, and they went around all the cities of Judah and they taught the people" (vv 7-9).

This mass arousal to the study of the Torah was sufficient to throw all of the surrounding kingdoms into **fear**: "And the fear of HaShem was on all the kingdoms of the lands that were around Judah and they did not fight with Yehoshaphat" (v 10). Here in a nutshell is Israel's true and lasting solution to the entire Middle East problem and the hostility of all the surrounding countries: send outreach rabbis with Sefer Torahs into all the cities and gather the people to teach them the Torah! Simple!!! Even the Philistines (=Palestinians?) and the Arvee-im (=Arabs?) sent gifts of gratitude to Yehoshaphat (v 11) for saving them from having to make war with Israel!!!

"And Yehoshaphat was continuously getting greater (**holech ve-gadel**) up above" (v 12). "Three were described with this same expression (i.e. using the continuous present verbal form **gadel**, instead of the adjective **gadol**, which would suggest that they had attained absolute greatness): Isaac, Samuel and Yehoshaphat. The reason in Yehoshaphat's case is because it says that he was getting greater **up above**, and it would not be appropriate to say that he was 'great' compared to Hashem. Similar reasons necessitate the use of the same phrase in the cases of Samuel and Isaac. But three were described with the adjective **gadol**, 'great' in absolute terms: Moses, David and Mordechai" (see Rashi on v 12).

"And Yehoshaphat… allied himself in marriage with Ahab" (v 1). The book of Chronicles was written in honor of the House of David and therefore, unlike the parallel texts in the book of Kings, gives only those details of the story of the kings of Israel that are strictly relevant to that of the kings of Judah. For better understanding of the narrative in the present chapter about King Yehoshaphat's joint military campaign with Ahab against Aram, which ended up with Ahab's death on the battlefield, it is necessary to keep in mind what we already know of the story of Ahab from the book of Kings

Yehoshaphat's marriage alliance with Ahab - Yehoshaphat married his son Yehoram to Ahab's daughter - was itself an aspect of his policy of "outreach", which was evident in the previous chapter in his sending sages with a Sefer Torah on a circuit of all the cities of Judah in order to teach the people Torah. It appears that in reaching out now to Ahab with this marriage alliance and following it up with strategic cooperation despite the fact that Ahab "did evil in the eyes of HaShem more than all who were before him" (I Kings 16:30), Yehoshaphat was hoping to coax the sinful idolaters of Shomron back into the fold of the Torah. In this case Yehoshaphat's outreach activities very nearly cost him his life when he narrowly escaped being killed in battle (vv 31-32 in our present chapter).

Ahab's campaign against the Arameans in Ramot Gil'ad as described in our present chapter followed his miraculous victories over Ben Hadad of Aram when the latter laid siege to Shomron, after which Ahab allowed himself to be enticed by the wily Arameans into showing entirely misplaced magnanimity in not only forgiving Ben Hadad but even making a covenant with him (I Kings ch 20). Now Ahab found it necessary to go up to the Golan Heights to fight the Arameans again. As we learn from the commentators on our present chapter, he was seduced into entering the battle in which he was to die by the vengeful spirit of Nabot, whom Ahab, at the instigation of his wife Jezebel, had killed on trumped up charges in order to take his vineyard, which the king so coveted (I Kings ch 21).

Ahab asks his in-law Yehoshaphat if he will join him in his forthcoming campaign and Yehoshaphat - anxious to reach out to Ahab - unhesitatingly agrees: "I am as you are, and my people are as your people" (v 3). As if to say with a face wreathed in smiles, "You may be idolaters while we are loyal to the Torah, but aren't we all one people?"

Despite going so far overboard in reaching out to the sinful Baal-worshipper Ahab, Yehoshaphat was anxious to hear what the prophets would say about the prospects for the success of the coming campaign. Rashi (on v 5) deduces that the four hundred prophets that Ahab assembled must have been true prophets of HaShem as opposed to the usual run of Ahab's Baal-worshiping Shomronite false prophets, because Yehoshaphat - disconcerted by their unanimous answer - asks, "Is there not here **yet another** prophet of HaShem?" (v 6). Rashi (on v 5) explains that Yehoshaphat had a tradition that no two prophets ever prophesy in exactly the same style and exactly the same words, and this was why he felt uneasy.

Michayahu ben Yimla, the true prophet whose messages Ahab did not like to hear but whom he nevertheless now summoned, may already have been held in prison at this time, because in verse 25 Ahab orders him to be **returned** into custody (see Rashi on v 26). Tzidkiyahu ben Kenaanah, who made iron horns prophesying that "with these shall you gore Aram" (v 10) and who later struck Michayahu on the jaw, is cited in the Talmud as the archetype of the false prophet who delivers messages he has not received prophetically (Sanhedrin 89a).

In order to hear the prophets, the two kings are seated on their thrones attired in magnificent ceremonial garb in a threshing floor - a large open space - outside the entrance to the city of Shomron. Rashi (on v 9) explains that the reason why our text specifies that they were in this open space is to let us know that the entire spectacle was witnessed by Aramean spies, who would have aroused suspicion had they been found in the city but who could claim that they had stopped by to take a look at the assembly outside the gates because it had caught their attention while they were innocently passing by. These Aramean spies apparently knew better than Ahab which of the prophets was telling the truth and they heard how Michayahu, when pressed, told his vision of all Israel scattered on the mountains like a flock with no shepherd and no master, which clearly indicated that while the people would escape from the battle, it was decreed that Ahab would be killed (v 16 and Rashi ad loc.). This was why the king of Aram gave his troops specific instructions not to fight with any Israelite, small or great, except the king (v 30) - "targeted assassination"!

In Michayahu's vision of the celestial court in judgment against Ahab (vv 18-22), the **Ru'ach** ("spirit") that stands before HaShem offering to entice him into battle was the soul of the murdered Nabot (Rashi on v 20). In order to avenge his killing, this spirit was permitted to inspire even the true prophets with a false message so that Ahab would go into the battle and meet his death.

Sensing the danger he was in, Ahab attempted to disguise himself so that he would not be recognizable to the Arameans, but no human ploys can thwart the will of God and an archer innocently fired an arrow that penetrated the gap between Ahab's helmet and body armor, killing him. Interestingly, Rashi on verse 33 argues that the archer must have been an Israelite because Ahab's identity was not visible while the Arameans had been instructed to attack no-one except the king. Yet on I Kings 22:34, Rashi states that the archer was the Aramean captain Na'aman (whom Elisha cured from leprosy, II Kings ch 5).

CHAPTER 19

King Yehoshaphat was fortunate to escape the battle in Ramot Gil'ad alive and return to Jerusalem, where Yehu ben Chanani castigated him for helping the wicked and showing love to those who hate HaShem (v 2). But as Yehu's prophecy shows, God prefers to look at a person's good side rather than dwelling on the bad, and He would not abandon Yehoshaphat.

The king did not follow the example of his father Asa or that of Ahab, both of whom chafed against prophetic rebuke (II Chron. 16:10 and 18:25ff). On the contrary, it stirred Yehoshaphat to greater heights of spiritual endeavor. Rabbi Nachman of Breslov taught that one of the greatest dangers to those who engage in Torah outreach is that of falling prey to the negative influence of the very people to whom they reach out, whose evil tends to attach itself and cling to them. Their way to "burn out" this evil influence is through **Mishpat**, judgment, scrutinizing themselves with the utmost honesty and truth (Likutey Moharan I, 59). This seems to throw light on why Yehoshaphat, who responded to Yehu's rebuke about his alliance with the wicked by embarking on a massive personal Torah outreach campaign throughout the whole of Judah from the south to the north (v 4), then appointed **judges** in every city in the kingdom (v 5) teaching them eternal lessons about true **Mishpat** (v 6). If the judge feels tempted to twist his judgment against the weak and in favor of the wealthy, he must remember that it is the judgment of heaven that he is twisting, and that everything he does is under the continuous scrutiny of God, who knows the innermost secrets of the heart (Rashi and Metzudat David on v 6). Yet if the judge wants to step aside so as to evade the awesome responsibility of his role, he is not allowed to do so (Sanhedrin 6a).

In Jerusalem too, Yehoshaphat established a strong judiciary "for the judgment of HaShem and for controversies" (v 8). In this verse, the "judgment of HaShem" refers to financial cases while "controversies" are capital cases and suits for damages. In verse 10, "controversies. between blood and blood" are questions about whether a certain killing was carried out intentionally or unwittingly (see Rashi on these verses).

CHAPTER 20

A LESSON IN ISRAELITE WARFARE

The story told in our present chapter appears only here in Chronicles, with merely the faintest reference to it in the parallel account of the reign of Yehoshaphat in I Kings 22:46. This in no way diminishes the great significance of this story as a teaching about the proper way for Israel to react in the face of attacks by their enemies.

The children of Moab and Ammon who now made war on Judah lived in the territories east of the Dead Sea and the River Jordan respectively. The Hebrew text of v 1 gives the third group of attackers as the **Ammonim**, who cannot be identical with the children of Ammon mentioned in the same verse (as it would be redundant to mention them again) and who some commentators suggest might be identified with the **Me'unim** (see Metzudat David ad loc.). However, Rashi, Metzudat David and RaDaK (ad loc.) all bring the Midrash saying that these were actually **Amelekites** from Mount Seir, which is part of the chain of mountains extending from the southern tip of the Dead Sea down to the Gulf of Aqaba, and which was part of the inheritance of the descendants of Esau. The main body of Edomites who lived east of Seir were not directly involved in the present war - it was in the reign of Yehoshaphat's son Yehoram that they rebelled against Judean sovereignty (see next chapter). The Amalekites themselves were a clan of Edomites, and according to Rashi and Metzudat David (ibid.) the reason why they are here called Ammonim is because they disguised themselves in Ammonite costumes and also used the Ammonite language in order to try to conceal their true identity (cf. Num. 21:1 and Rashi thereon).

King Yehoshaphat was informed that this great multitude had "come. From beyond the sea from Aram". The "sea" is the Dead Sea, and Aram in this verse is not to be confused with Aram to the northeast of Israel (whose wars with Ahab and Yehoshaphat were the subject of Chapter 18). Rather, it is identified with **Aran** (Gen. 36:26; I Chron. 1:42), whose name is preserved in that of the town Jibel Aram about forty kilometers to the east of Aqaba. (Targum on our present chapter v 10 renders Seir as **Givla**.) This invading army was intent on striking at the very heart of Judah and Jerusalem. They either marched around the southern end of the Dead Sea or else they crossed its narrow tongue on rafts, after which they advanced to the ancient strategic town of Eyn Gedi in order to make their way inland through the mountain passes along Nachal Arugot to Teko'a in the heart of Judea.

"And Yehoshaphat was **afraid**…" (v 3). What he did was not to summon his military advisors but rather to "set his face to seek out HaShem". He called a national fast, assembling all the people in the Temple in Jerusalem (vv 3-4). The "new court" before which he rose to address the people was not a newly-built addition to the Temple. It was "new" in the sense that - perhaps as part of the campaign to bring everyone to higher levels of repentance and purity - a new decree was made prohibiting the entry of a **Tvul Yom** (one who had only purified himself from impurity by immersion on that same day) even into the "Levitical Camp", the **Ezrat Nashim** or "Women's Courtyard", let alone into the **Azarah** itself, the main Temple Courtyard, the "Camp of the Shechinah", which is prohibited by the written Torah (Numbers 5:2-3; see Pesachim 92a and Rambam Hilchot Beit HaBechirah 4:17).

Yehoshaphat was turning to God in the Temple at this moment of national emergency in exactly the way that Solomon had taught in his prayer on the inauguration of the Temple (II Chron.ch 6). Yehoshaphat began his prayer affirming that it is God who rules over all the kingdoms of the nations and who therefore has the power to defeat Israel's enemies.

"Are you not our God who... gave this land to the seed of Abraham Your friend forever?" (v 7). Rashi (ad loc.) explains Yehoshaphat's argument: "Therefore it is Your obligation to strengthen Israel's possession of the land and to drive these peoples out, because even a king of flesh and blood or indeed any man who has given a gift to his friend only to find someone else coming to rob him of it would surely exert himself in every way to keep the gift in his friend's hand - how much more so should You!!!"

In vv 10-11 Yehoshaphat addresses the present attack of the peoples of Ammon, Moab and Mount Seir (the king was in no way deceived by the Amalekites' disguise), arguing that it exemplified the utmost ingratitude since when the Children of Israel had originally journeyed from Egypt to Israel, they had specifically refrained from attacking the Edomites, Moabites and Ammonites (Deut. 2:4, 9 & 19). Yehoshaphat concludes by asking God Himself to judge the invaders, because Israel had no strength in the face of such a multitude.

In the merit of the king's prayers and the national repentance, Yahazi-el the Levite immediately received prophecy that God would fight for Israel. Yahazi-el was one of the Levitical Temple singers from the family of Asaph, and the spectacular salvation that he prophesied was very much bound up with song and thanksgiving to HaShem. Thus, immediately after he delivered his prophecy (vv 14-17) Yehoshaphat and all the people prostrated in gratitude while the Levite singers rose to sing praises "in a great voice **on high**". Their songs shook the very heavens!!!

The following morning everyone went out of Jerusalem southwards to the wilderness of Teko'a to witness the salvation that they believed with perfect faith would surely come. Yehoshaphat led the way not with weapons but with a call to the people to strengthen their faith in God. Marching before the armed warriors went not an advance contingent of fighters but Levitical **singers** offering praises and thanksgiving. They sang **hodu la-Shem ki le'olam chasdo**, "Give thanks to HaShem for His kindness is forever", although they omitted the words **ki tov** ("...for He is good." Psalms 118:1 etc.) because "the Holy One blessed be He does not rejoice at the downfall of the wicked" (Megillah 10b).

It was precisely when the Levites sang that God sent His salvation by turning the various peoples making up the invading armies against each other. First the people of Ammon and Moab thought that the people of Seir (=the Amalekites) were attacking them from the rear and proceeded to attack them, after which they fought with and slaughtered each other. All that was left for Yehoshaphat and his forces to do was to gather in the spoils of battle. After this great salvation, they did not forget HaShem and His kindness, but went straight back to Jerusalem to the Temple with harps, lyres and trumpets to give more thanks and praises.

[It is interesting that the Biblical commentator **Malbim**, R. Meir Leibush ben Yechiel Meir Weiser 1809-79, writes on Ezekiel 32:17 that in the war of Gog and Magog, Edom and Ishmael will join forces to go up together against Jerusalem but that in the course of this campaign they will become embroiled in conflict with one another since their faiths are different and they will make war against each other, and this is how God will judge them. The salvation of Judah from the combined forces of Ammon, Moab and Amalek in the time of Yehoshaphat as described in our present chapter appears to be the prototype of the future salvation as described by **Malbim**, making the lessons of our present chapter about how Israel goes to war particularly timely.]

The reign of Yehoshaphat was a golden age compared with the reigns of the kings who came before and after him. However, "As yet, the people had not directed their hearts to the God of their fathers" (v 33) - the repair was far from complete, and the people would have to endure harsh times in order to bring it about. The close of Yehoshaphat's reign was marred by his alliance with Ahab's son Ahaziahu, with whom he embarked on a luckless joint trading venture (vv 35-7).

CHAPTER 21

One of the striking features of the story of the kings of Judah is how a saintly king was often succeeded by a very wicked king, and vice versa. The reign of Yehoshaphat's firstborn son and successor Yehoram was marred from the outset when he killed all his brothers in order to eliminate any possible contenders to the throne. Yehoram was obviously following in the ways of the kings of Israel, being married to the wicked Ataliah, who was the daughter of King Ahab (verse 6 in our present chapter, and see next chapter v 3, where Ataliah is called the daughter of Omri, who was Ahab's father, and who in all probability raised her, see Metzudat David there). Yehoram himself led the people astray into idolatry (v 11).

After Isaac gave his blessings to Jacob rather than Esau, he consoled the latter by saying that if Jacob's descendants would veer from the Torah, Esau would break their yoke from upon his neck (see Rashi on Gen. 27:40). Eight kings had ruled over Edom before there was a king in Israel (ibid. 36:31) but from the time when the Children of Israel became united under Saul, Edom lost its independence and was subject to an Israelite garrison in their territory. Edom remained subject to Israelite rule during the reigns of eight kings: Saul, Ish-Boshet, David, Solomon, Rechav'am, Avi-yah, Asa and Yehoshaphat. However, when Yehoram led Judah away from the Torah, this opened the way for the Edomites to rebel, and they have not been subjugated until today (our chapter vv 8-10; see Rashi on Gen. 27:40; cf. I Kings 22:48 and Rashi there).

"And there came to him a letter from Elijah the Prophet..." (v 12). From the fact that Elijah's disciple Elisha was prophesying independently during the reign of Yehoshaphat (II Kings 3:11) we may learn that Elijah had already ascended to heaven prior to the reign of Yehoshaphat's son Yehoram. In the words of RaDaK on our present chapter v 12: "This letter came after Elijah's ascent to heaven. What happened is that Elijah was revealed through prophetic spirit to one of the prophets and he put in his mouth the words of this letter and told him to put them in writing and to bring the letter to Yehoram telling him that this letter was sent to him by Elijah in order that Yehoram would believe that it came to him from heaven in the hope that he would humble his heart and understand that he had done great evil." [The phrase in verse 12, "A letter from Elijah", **Michtav Mi-Eliyahu**, was taken as the title of a major latter-day work on Torah "Hashkafah" - worldview and outlook - by the late saintly Rabbi Eliyahu Dessler, 1892-1953.]

The illness that had taken hold of Judah was because they had failed to eliminate idolatry from their midst, and this spiritual illness was reflected in the terrible physical disease that gripped King Yehoram in his very bowels, the organ of elimination, which became so morbid that they literally burst. Yehoram died just as he had lived – **be-lo chemdah**, without any joy and delight - and the legacy of turmoil he left after him almost brought the House of David to extinction.

CHAPTER 22

The alliance between the House of David and the house of the wicked Ahab king of Israel almost led to the extinction of the royal line of David after the death of King Yehoram of Judah, son of King Yehoshaphat, which we read about at the end of the previous chapter (II Chron. 21:19-20). In retribution for Yehoram's leading Judah into idolatry, an invading army of Philistines and Arabs had captured and apparently killed all his sons and wives, leaving only his smallest son Yeho-achaz (ibid. v 16-17). When Yehoram died at the age of forty, the people of Jerusalem chose Yeho-achaz (also called Ahaziahu and Azariahu) to succeed him.

"Ahaziahu was **forty-two** years old when he reigned..." (verse 2). It is impossible to take this verse at face value since this would mean that Ahaziahu had been born before the birth of his father Yehoram, who died at the age of only **forty** (II Chron. 21:20). In II Kings 8:26 it says that Ahaziahu was **twenty-two** when he reigned. Rashi on verse 2 of our present chapter explains that when Ahaziahu came to the throne, it was **forty-two** years since the decree of destruction that had been made against the House of David two years before the birth of Yehoram, when King Asa had married his son Yehoshaphat to the daughter of Omri, Ahab's father. This tradition is based on Midrash Seder Olam and Tosephta of Sotah, but the written Biblical text itself nowhere states that Yehoshaphat married the daughter of Omri, although it does say that Yehoshaphat "made a marriage alliance with Ahab" (II Chron.18:1). This may refer to his marrying Ahab's sister, although it is usually understood to refer to Yehoshaphat's marrying his son Yehoram to Ataliah, daughter of Ahab, who plays a central role in our present chapter and the next.

From the above-quoted comment by Rashi, we see how the text alludes to something that is not at all explicit: namely, that the association between the House of David and the family of Omri and Ahab had already begun in the latter years of the reign of Asa, when Omri rose to power as king of Israel. Perhaps this was intentionally obscured in our text in order not to impugn the honor of King Asa.

Ataliah, who was the daughter of Ahab (despite her being called daughter of Omri in v 2, see RaDaK ad loc.) and a formidable woman in her own right, was the mother of the new twenty-two year old king Ahaziahu, and it was all but inevitable that he would fall prey to her insidious advice and follow the idolatrous path of Ahab that she and her late husband Yehoram had introduced in Judah.

King Ahaziahu's alliance with Ahab's son and successor, Yehoram King of Israel, in the latter's military campaign against Aram in Ramot Gil'ad, led to the death of both kings at the hands of Yehu ben Nimshi, who had been anointed by the prophet Jonah at the command of the prophet Elisha with the mission of destroying the house of Ahab. The entire story, which is given in brief in our present chapter (II Chron. 22:5-9), is told in greater detail in the parallel account in II Kings 8:28-9:28.

When Ataliah saw that her son King Ahaziahu had been killed, she immediately set out to kill all male members of the Davidic royal line in Judah in order to destroy all possible opposition to the tyranny she now intended to impose there under herself. Rashi based on hints in the written text (II Kings 11:2) states that Ataliah used sorcery and poison to bring a protracted, painful death upon them. "It was of this generation that David said, 'La-M'natzeach upon the Eighth' (Psalms 12:1). He saw with holy spirit that in the eighth generation all his seed would be killed by Ataliah, for from Solomon until now there were eight generations, and he prayed that his seed should be left as a memorial and said: 'Help, HaShem, for the godly man ceases...' (ibid. v 2)".

It was only the courage of another woman - Yehoshav'at, daughter of King Yehoram of Judah and sister of the slain King Ahaziahu - that saved the Davidic line from complete extinction when she took Ahaziahu's one-year old baby son Yo'ash and hid him in the "chamber of the beds" (verse 11). According to rabbinic tradition, this was in the Holy Temple, either in the priests' sleeping quarters in the Temple Courtyard where Yehoshav'at lived with her husband Yeho-yada, who was the High Priest, or in the upper storey over the Holy of Holies (Rashi on v 11). The Holy of Holies is called the "chamber of the beds" because "He lays down between my breasts" (Song of Songs 1:13,) i.e. between the poles of the Ark (see **Know Your Bible** commentary on II Chron. 5:9). Of this moment of dire peril, when the survival of his entire line was in danger, King David had prayed, "For He will conceal me in His tabernacle on the day of evil" (Psalms 27:5).

Evidence of the comprehensive tyranny that Ataliah wielded over Judah lies in the fact that Yo'ash had to be concealed in the Temple for six full years before Yeho-yada the High Priest felt strong enough to reveal him to the people. During those six years Ataliah raided the Temple treasures in order to pay for the construction of the idolatrous temples and altars she was busy building in order to entrench herself in Jerusalem and Judah.

CHAPTER 23

"And in the seventh year Yeho-yada strengthened himself...." Yeho-yada the High Priest had received the prophetic tradition from Elisha and was a key link in the transmission of the Torah tradition from Moses to the later prophets: Yeho-yada's son Zechariah (II Chron. 24:20ff) handed the tradition to the prophet Hosea (see Rambam, Mishneh Torah, Introduction). All the true prophets knew that God had promised never to cut off the seed of King David completely, while Elijah and Elisha had prophesied that the House of Ahab would be cut off. The time now came for Yeho-yada the High Priest, heir to the prophetic tradition, to take the initiative to overthrow Ataliah, who was the last surviving vestige of the House of Ahab after Yehu ben Nimshi had killed all the other members, and to re-establish the House of David through the public coronation of Yo'ash. The Cohanim and Levites, as guardians of the Temple and its services, were also direly threatened by Ataliah and her idolatrous ambitions, and now stood at the side of the royal line of David in an alliance that had begun with the marriage of Aharon the High Priest to Eli-sheva daughter of Aminadav, Prince of the tribe of Judah.

Yeho-yada took what today would be called maximum security measures in the Temple to ensure that the coronation of the seven-year old King Yo'ash would proceed without any danger from Ataliah and her mafia. Only trustworthy Cohanim and Levites were to be admitted into the inner Temple precincts, and flanking the Temple building and the young king were heavily armed guards. Yeho-yada's public display of Yo'ash after six years of concealment must have been a moment of consummate drama.

"And they brought forth the son of the king and put upon him the **crown**..." (v 11). This was the crown that David had taken from the head of the king of Ammon (I Chronicles 20:2). David had it studded with a precious magnetic (charismatic?) stone engraved with the name of HaShem. The crown weighed a centenarium of gold, and was testimony for the House of David, for any king who was not from the seed of David was unable to fit the crown on his head and bear its weight. When the people saw that it fitted Yo'ash and that he was able to bear it, they immediately proclaimed him king (Targum on v 11, cf. Rashi ad loc.).

On hearing the celebrations in the Temple, Ataliah rushed to find out what was happening, discovering to her dismay that a successful coup had already put an end to her regime. Yeho-yada had her killed, after which he struck a Covenant between himself, the people and the king returning the kingship to its true mission of making Israel the people devoted to HaShem (v 16). While the people cleansed Judah of the Baal worship instituted by Ataliah, Yeho-yada re-established the Temple services of the priests and Levites, which had perhaps fallen into partial disuse during her tyranny. The king was escorted to his palace to sit on his throne and the people rejoiced.

CHAPTER 24

"And Yo'ash did what was right in the eyes of HaShem all the days of Yeho-yada the Priest" (v 2). The wonder boy-king Yo'ash remained faithful to the way of the Torah as long as he was under the tutelage of Yeho-yada, who had saved his life and with it the entire royal line of David, as told in the previous chapter. However, after Yeho-yada's death, Yo'ash went astray, as told later in our present chapter vv 17ff.

"And Yo'ash's heart was stirred to renew the House of HaShem" (v 4). From the time of the completion of the Temple by King Solomon until the time of Yo'ash was a period of one hundred and twenty-five years (see Rashi's calculation in his comment on v 7). Solomon had built a mighty structure that was designed to last, and it would not have required refurbishing after only 125 years but for the fact that it had been pillaged and damaged during Ataliah's six-year tyranny by sons she had from another marriage previous to that with King Yehoram (Metzudat David on v 7).

As we have learned in our studies of I Chronicles from chapter 13 onwards, King David had seen his preparations for the building of the Holy Temple in Jerusalem as his main mission in life, and in Rambam's Laws of Kings 11:4 we learn that the main qualification for being accepted for certain as Mashiach is that the candidate rebuilds the Holy Temple. There was thus unquestionably a Messianic quality in King Yo'ash's initiative to refurbish the Temple and to establish a viable system for financing its future maintenance, in which he showed even more zeal than the priests (as we see from v 6 of our present chapter). After the wicked Ataliah's efforts to shift the focus from the Temple to her own idolatrous cults, Yo'ash - who had grown up and been revealed in the Temple itself - set himself to restore it to its true position as the very center of the national endeavor.

The basic means of financing the Temple and its sacrifices was laid down in the Torah, which instituted the collection of one half-shekel annually from every Israelite besides their other donations (Exodus 30:12-16). Yo'ash now reinstituted and reorganized the collection of the Temple funds from the people as described in our present chapter vv 5-14 and also with some additional details in the parallel account in II Kings 12:5-17. The latter is included in the Haftarah read annually on Shabbat Shekalim, first of the four springtime Shabbatot on which special additional Torah selections are read in preparation for the coming festival of Pesach.

Initially, Yo'ash instituted that the Cohanim would collect the moneys for the Temple, but when this proved to be ineffective he established a special chest outside the main Temple gate where the people could deposit their contributions directly, much to their joy (II Kings 12:5-11 and II Chron. 24:5-11). The chest had a small hole that was large enough to insert a coin but not sufficiently large for a would-be thief to insert his fingers. The arrangements instituted by Yo'ash were accompanied by an ethos of financial integrity (II Kings 12:16) that should be a model for all our financial dealings.

"But after the death of Yeho-yada, the princes of Judah came and prostrated themselves before the king" (v 17). This sad sequel to the story of Yo'ash does not appear in the parallel account of his reign in II Kings. According to the rabbis, the princes of Judah made Yo'ash into a god, reasoning that it states in the Torah that "the stranger who draws near [i.e. in the Holy of Holies] shall die" (Numbers 18:7) whereas Yo'ash had spent six years inside the Temple and he was still alive, so that it was only proper to offer him service as a god (Metzudat David on our present chapter verse 18). [Some may find it interesting to note that three of the four Hebrew letters of Yo'ash's name make up the name of another human being whose followers turned into a god.] The new ruler-cult led the people to abandon the Temple in favor of other cults.

When a wave of prophets failed to bring about a change of heart in the people, Yeho-yada's son Zechariah stood up in the Temple to rebuke them. According to the Targum and other Midrashic sources, this took place on Yom Kippur, the Day of Atonement, which that year fell on a Shabbat. The people had set up a graven image in the Temple and were burning incense to it when Zechariah rose to protest, thinking that his prestige as son of the saintly Yeho-yada as well as being the present head of the Sanhedrin would save him from their ire. Displaying total ingratitude to Yeho-yada, who had saved his very life, Yo'ash gave instructions to kill Zechariah.

Midrash Zuta Eichah #1 (cf. Gittin 57b) tells that the blood of Zechariah that was spilled on the Temple floor continued seething and boiling until the time when Nebuchadnezzar's henchman Nevuzaradan came to Jerusalem and slaughtered 2,210,000 outside the city and another 940,000 in Jerusalem itself. Their blood flowed all the way to the blood of Zechariah. When Nevuzaradan enquired whose blood this was, the priests initially tried to conceal the scandal until he threatened that he would comb their flesh with iron combs. After they admitted that it was the blood of a prophet to whom they had refused to listen, Nevuzaradan killed wave after wave of the people to avenge Zechariah until he almost killed everyone. He said, "Zechariah, Zechariah, I have killed all the good ones. If you rest, all the better! If not, I will kill them all!" Only then did the blood cease boiling. Nevuzaradan said, "If Israel killed a single soul and this is what it caused them, what will be of me after killing so many souls?" He fled and converted to become a **Ger Tzedek**.

In the same year in which Zechariah was killed, God's vengeance was already felt in Judah when an invading force of Arameans entered Jerusalem and destroyed the entire ruling class. (This was after an earlier advance by Chaza-el king of Aram against Judah and Jerusalem, in which Yo'ash bought him off using the Temple treasures, II Kings 12:18-19). Yo'ash himself was wounded in this attack and was subsequently killed in his bed by a conspiracy of his own attendants. The mothers of the two leading conspirators are specifically described as having been an Ammonite and a Moabitess respectively, because these two nations, whose father Lot had been saved by Abraham, showed the utmost ingratitude in their later persecutions of Israel just as Yo'ash showed the utmost ingratitude to his savior Yeho-yada in killing his son Zechariah (Rashi on v 26).

CHAPTER 25

King Yo'ash was succeeded by his son Amatziahu, the Hebrew root of whose name, **ematz** means to be strong or courageous. Like his father Yo'ash, Amatziahu showed initial promise, but although a righteous king (as shown by his killing only the murderers of his father but not their children), he was not whole-hearted in his devotion to God (v 2).

Amatziahu wanted to quell the Edomites, who had been in rebellion against Judah since the time of his great-grandfather King Yehoram (II Chron.21:10). Thinking that victory would depend on the deployment of sufficient manpower, Amatziahu supplemented his 300,000-strong army with a hundred thousand Israelite mercenaries that he hired for the colossal price of a hundred talents of silver, but he had the good sense to defer to God's prophet, who told him not to bring the idolatrous Israelites on his campaign against Edom because victory depends upon God's help and not on numbers. It seems that Amatziahu found it easier to defer to the prophet when he told him God would reimburse him for all the silver he had paid out for nothing.

Amatziahu's campaign against the Edomites was highly successful, and he took hold of one of their great fortresses at Sela ("the rock"), which is identified with the site of Sela (=Petra) in the mountains south east of the Dead Sea about 8 km south of the modern Jordanian town of Tafila. His massacre of 10,000 Edomites on this site brings to mind the curse in Psalms 137:9.

Tragically, Amatziahu showed the same kind of fickleness that had brought his father to ruin, because after his great victory over the Edomites, he proceeded to adopt the idolatry of the defeated nation (v 14 of this chapter). This time Amatziahu would not listen at all to the rebuke of God's prophet, who left him to find out for himself where his folly would lead him.

The Israelite mercenaries that Amatziahu had initially hired for his war were furious that they had been sent away before having the opportunity of taking part in the conquest and plunder of the Edomites, and they turned this affront into a casus belli, invading and ravaging Judea (v 13). The dare-devil Amatziahu, swelled with pride at his recent victory, decided to take on the mighty warrior king of Israel, King Yo'ash, challenging him to stop his people's cowardly depredations and fight a fully-fledged battle instead. Yo'ash replied that a "cedar" like himself would find a cooperative alliance ("marriage") with the puny "thistle" Amatziahu demeaning, let alone a fully-fledged battle, and he threatened to trample him underfoot. Amatziahu, puffed up with a self-confidence that was sent by God in order to destroy him because of his idolatry, refused to back down, and Yo'ash invaded Judah and beat him on his own territory in Beit Shemesh, going on to tear down a sizeable section of the fortifications of Jerusalem in order to ensure that Judah would not rebel in the future.

Amatziahu's defeat put him in danger from Judean conspirators, and he was forced to flee Jerusalem and live in the town of Lachish in the maritime plain of Philistia, which had been fortified by King Rechav'am. It appears that Amatziahu reigned as king in Lachish for fifteen years while his wife Yecholiah, guardian of their son Uzziah (=Azariah), ruled in Jerusalem (see Rashi on v 27). But the hand of God's vengeance reached Amatziahu even in Lachish, where he lost his life to assassins.

CHAPTER 26

The sixteen-year old King Uzziah (="God is my strength") became king after Jerusalem had been dealt a harsh blow in the reign of his father Amatziahu with the tearing down of a sizeable section of its fortifications by Yo'ash king of Israel.

Uzziah came to the throne during the reign of Yo'ash of Israel's son Yerav'am II, who "restored the border of Israel from the entrance of Hamat (i.e. northern Syria) to the sea of the Aravah (=the Dead Sea)" (II Kings 14:25). I.e. Yo'ash succeeded in restoring the sovereignty of Israel over all the territories over which David and Solomon had ruled. Likewise, Uzziah restored Judah as a major regional power, beginning his career with the recapture and rebuilding of the Red Sea port of Eilat. Our present account of Uzziah's reign here in Chronicles is considerably more detailed than the parallel account in II Kings 15:1-7.

"And he did what was right in the eyes of HaShem according to all that his father Amatziah had done" (v 4) - "But he did not do according to his wickedness" (Rashi).

"And he set himself to search out God in the days of Zechariahu, who had understanding in the visions of God, and as long as he sought Hashem, God gave him success" (v 5). According to Rashi, Zechariahu was another of the names of Uzziah, who was also called Azariah. He was clearly devout in the extreme - to the point that in later life he thought himself worthy of taking over the role of the Cohen in the Temple (see vv 16ff).

Vv 6-10 describe how Uzziah expanded and strengthened his kingdom, conquering the major Philistine centers in the coastal plain and protecting his southern flank by overcoming the "Arvim" and "Me-unim" (cf. our commentary on II Chron. 20:1), who were Edomite tribes. Thus "his fame reached until the entrance of Egypt" (v 8): he enjoyed international prestige. Uzziah also rebuilt the fortifications of Jerusalem, which had been destroyed in the reign of his father by Yo'ash of Israel (v 9). Not only did Uzziah expand and fortify his kingdom. He also invested heavily in "infrastructure", digging wells for his many cattle and developing agriculture (v 10).

Vv 11-14 describe Uzziah's military command structure and army, while v 15 tells of the ingenious military engines he had positioned on the towers and ramparts of Jerusalem to fight off would-be attackers with showers of arrows and boulders.

273

Tragically, Uzziah's very success led to his downfall when he decided he was on a level to enter the Temple sanctuary to offer incense, "because he said it is fitting for a king to minister to the King of Glory" (Rashi on v 16). No matter how pious his intentions, what he wanted to do was strictly forbidden by the Torah, which says that "no stranger who is not from the seed of Aaron shall draw close to burn incense before HaShem, so that he shall not be like Korach and his assembly as HaShem spoke by the **hand** of Moses" (Numbers 17:5). The wording of this prohibition alludes to the fact that the penalty for its violation is to be struck with leprosy, because Moses' **hand** had become leprous at the Burning Bush (Ex. 4:6; see RaDaK on II Kings 15:5).

As soon as Uzziah tried to offer incense in the Temple, leprosy burst forth on his forehead and spread to his whole body, a cataclysmic event that precipitated an "earthquake". The Midrash Avot d'Rabbi Natan 22a states that "at that hour the Sanctuary was split, and the two halves moved twelve miles in each direction."

This day marked the beginning of the prophetic ministry of Isaiah. The first chapter of the book of Isaiah was not his first prophecy: this is recorded in Isaiah ch 6: "In the year of the **death** of King Uzziah I saw the Lord sitting upon a throne high and exalted." (Is. 6:1; see Rashi ad loc.). Uzziah's "death" alludes to his plague of leprosy.

As a leper for life, Uzziah had to spend the rest of his days isolated from the community (Lev. 13:46) and therefore lived in **Beit Ha-Chophsheet,** literally the "house of **freedom**", i.e. the cemetery (cf. Psalms 88:6, "free, **chophshi**, among the dead"; see Rashi on v 21 of our present chapter).

CHAPTER 27

Uzziah's son Yotam took over the kingship during his father's lifetime, "and he did what was right in the eyes of HaShem according to all that Uzziah his father did except that he did not come into HaShem's sanctuary" (v 2).

Out of all the kings of Judah, Yotam is the only one about whom not a single hint of anything negative appears in any of our texts. (David sinned by taking Batsheva; Solomon's wives turned his heart astray; Rechav'am abandoned the Torah; Avi-yah followed all his father's sins; Asa took money from the Temple treasuries to send to the king of Aram, and he imprisoned a prophet; Yehoshaphat allied himself with the wicked Ahab; Yehoram killed his brothers; Ahaziahu followed his mother's evil advice; Yo'ash killed Zechariah the Priest and allowed himself to be worshiped as a god; Amatziah bowed down to the idols of Seir; Uzziah entered the Sanctuary to burn incense; Ahaz went in the ways of the king of Israel and promoted Baal worship; Hezekiah's heart became swelled and the rabbis challenged three of his rulings; Menasheh did evil in the eyes of Hashem; Josiah did not heed prophecy, and Tzedekiah did evil in God's eyes and did not submit to Jeremiah; see Rashi on 27:2).

King Yotam's exceptional purity helps explain the saying of Rabbi Shimon bar Yochai (Succah 45b): "If only Abraham our father would take on himself to atone for all the sins of the generations until his time, I would take on myself to atone for the sins of all the generations from Abraham until myself. And if **Yotam** son of Uzziah was with me, we would take on ourselves everything from the time of Abraham until the end of all the generations!"

From this we see that merely because our present text devotes only nine verses to Yotam while the parallel text in II Kings 15:32-38 deals with his reign in only eight verses, this in no way detracts from his greatness. From the fact that the king of Ammon - who previously had been under the sway of the kings of Israel - now sent Yotam tribute for three years running (v 5), we may infer that as a result of the latter's diligent efforts to build and consolidate his kingdom, the center of influence was beginning to swing back from the trouble-stricken regime in Shomron to Judah.

CHAPTER 28

The story of the later kings of Judah is one in which, paradoxically, a saintly king fathers a wicked king who then fathers a saintly king and so on. The saintly Yotam's son and successor, Ahaz, went in the idolatrous pathway of the kings of Israel and even practiced Molech-worship at a cult-center in the valley of Ben Hinnom south of Mount Zion, passing his sons through the fire in contravention of the explicit prohibition against Molech worship in Leviticus 18:21. According to Targum on verse 3 in our present chapter, Ahaz also passed his son and successor Hezekiah through the fire, but God saved Hezekiah from being killed in the furnace of the priests of Molech because he saw that three Tzaddikim were destined to come forth from him who would be willing to sacrifice their very lives to sanctify God's name by being thrown into Nebuchadnezzar's furnace: Chananiyah, Misha'el and Azariah (Daniel ch 3).

Just as the devotion to God shown by Ahaz' predecessors, Uzziah and Yotam, had brought them great success in building the kingdom, so Ahaz' backsliding caused him disaster after disaster. His reign fell at a time when Assyria was developing from being merely an aggressive predatory nation into an expanding world empire that was changing the entire balance of power in the region. Ahaz' policy was not to try to challenge Assyria. However, Isaiah's prophecies dating from the reign of Ahaz (Isaiah ch 7) detail the efforts of the kings of Israel and Aram to coerce Ahaz into joining them in campaigns intended to "contain" Assyria. The attacks on Judah by the king of Aram and by Pekach ben Remaliah king of Israel as described in vv 5ff in our present chapter were part of this policy of coercion.

The attack by Pekach in particular was a colossal blow to Judah in which, according to our text, one hundred and twenty thousand men were killed in one day (v 6). The account of the capture of two hundred thousand Judean women and children by the armies of Israel and their subsequent release at the behest of the prophet Oded on "humanitarian" grounds (which does not appear in the parallel account in I Kings ch 16) gives us a fascinating insight into the psychology of the Ten Tribes, who were to be exiled for their sins only one generation later yet still exhibited a basic fear of God as well as the **rachmanut**, "compassion", that is one of the three distinguishing features of true members of the people of Israel, the other two being bashfulness and kindness (Yevamot 79a). Before Israelite armies went out to war, the priest who addressed the troops would remind them that they should fight with all their strength against their enemies from other nations, because if they fell into their hands they could never expect the same kindness that the tribes of Israel would show to each other even when they made war against one another (Sotah 42a).

The Philistines and Edomites were wresting huge swathes of territory from Judah, yet even as his kingdom was being torn to pieces, Ahaz was not chastened. He thought he could save himself from Israel and the Arameans by bribing the kings of Assyria to help him (vv 16ff). They took his bribes but gave him little help, treating Judah as no more than a subject nation. When Tiglat-Pilessar of Assyria did attack and exile the Arameans, Ahaz went to visit Damascus and was so impressed with the idolatrous altar he found there that he sent detailed plans and diagrams to Uriah the priest in Jerusalem with orders to build a copy in the Temple (see II Kings 16:10ff). Ahaz' policies and pathways brought disaster on Judah, which is why Isaiah in the opening prophecy of his book tells the people: Your country is desolate, your cities are burned with fire, as for your land, strangers devour it in your presence, and it is desolate as though overthrown by strangers" (Isaiah 1:7). This was the dire state of Judah when Ahaz died and was succeeded by his son Hezekiah, who was fit to be Mashiach.

We can only speculate what caused the twenty-five year old Hezekiah to go in the diametrically opposite direction to that of his father Ahaz from the moment he succeeded him on the throne. Hezekiah's miraculous delivery from the furnace of the priests of Molech must surely have left a lifelong mark on his very soul. Perhaps this made him particularly open to the preaching of the great prophets of his time - Hosea, Amos and Micah - and particularly that of Isaiah, whose mission had begun on the very the day on which Hezekiah's great-grandfather Uzziah tried to burn incense in the Temple, and who remained the steadfast champion of the true Torah pathway during the reigns of Yotam, Ahaz and that of Hezekiah himself.

Our texts refer to Isaiah's active involvement in the events of Hezekiah's reign only later in the story (II Kings 19:2 and II Chron 32:20 etc.), whereas the purification of Judah and the Temple from the idolatry of Ahaz on which Hezekiah embarked in the very first month of the first year of his reign is described as having been his own initiative (v 3). He showed his boldly independent spirit even before this, when - according to rabbinic tradition - instead of giving his father an honorable funeral, with the approval of the sages of the time he had his bones dragged on a bed of rope in order to bring him atonement (Pesachim 56a).

"**He** in the first year of his reign in the first month **opened** the doors of the House of HaShem…" (v 3) - whereas a few verses earlier, at the end of the previous chapter (II Chron 28:24) we read that "Ahaz... **closed** the doors of the House of HaShem".

We may better appreciate the drama of Hezekiah's address to the Levites and Cohanim whom he immediately assembled in the Temple (vv 4-11, cf. v 36, "suddenly") by referring to some comments of Rashi later in our present chapter and the next. In the course of his comment on v 34 of our present chapter, Rashi writes that "the Cohanim and Levites and all those who feared HaShem had to disguise themselves and make themselves into strangers and even go into hiding all through the days of the wicked kings, and when Hezekiah, who was righteous, came to the throne, they could not immediately sanctify and purify themselves for the Temple service". In further explanation, Rashi writes in his comment on v 15 of the following chapter: "The reason why the Cohanim and Levites delayed coming until now was that they could not prior to that give credibility to the matter [of the reopening of the Temple] because Ahaz had despised and rejected them from serving as priests, and now they said, 'Is it possible that yesterday Ahaz worshipped idols and his son Hezekiah immediately in his first year in the very first month already tells the Cohanim and Levites to serve the One God alone, telling us he needs us?' This was why they were apathetic and delayed coming, and the same was true in the case of the rest of Judah whom Ahaz had despised. However, when they investigated and ascertained that everything was for the sake of Heaven, they all came and sanctified themselves for service" (Rashi on II Chron. 30:15).

Hezekiah's address to the Cohanim and Levites shows the devastation he and Judah faced as a result of Ahaz' idolatry and its disastrous consequences (vv 8-9). To repair the damage, Hezekiah wanted to renew the original Covenant between God and Israel.

Our text relates how representatives of all the Levitical families stood up and volunteered to embark on the work of cleansing the Temple. It was not simply a matter of removing idols. The reason why it took them eight whole days to sanctify the Temple building was because Ahaz had had idolatrous images carved into all the walls (Rashi on v 17). Although a simple reading of verse 19 leaves the impression that they now purified the Temple vessels that in the time of Ahaz had been used for idolatrous rituals, the Talmud (Avodah Zarah 52b) states that those vessels were put in **genizah** ("hiding", never to be used again) and new vessels were brought in their place, because a vessel used for idolatry is unfit to be used for holy service.

"And they brought seven oxen and seven rams and seven sheep and seven goats for a sin offering" (v 21). The sacrifices brought by Hezekiah to atone for the people's idolatry do not correspond exactly to the sacrifices prescribed in the Torah for this sin (Lev. 4:14; Numbers 15:24) - this was **hora'at sha'ah**, a "one-time ruling".

It is significant that for Hezekiah, an integral part of the restoration of the Temple was the restoration of the Temple music as established by King David and the prophets of his time (v 25). It is the Temple music that elevates the entire Temple service, as we see clearly from our narrative (vv 27-30).

CHAPTER 30

When Hezekiah decided to hold a spectacular Passover celebration in the Temple, the like of which had not been seen since the days of Solomon, he did not summon only the people of Judah. In the true Davidic tradition, he took responsibility for all Israel and sent messengers with letters to the members of the other tribes. This was just six years before the Ten Tribes were taken into exile by the Assyrians (see Rashi on verse 1 of our present chapter; cf. II Kings 18:10). The reason for their exile becomes more understandable when we read that many of them simply laughed at and mocked Hezekiah's messengers (v 10).

"For the king took counsel... to hold the Pesach in the second month" (v 2). There were a number of halachic irregularities in the holding of Hezekiah's first Pesach which were forced upon him by the exigencies of the moment. The first is that Pesach is supposed to be held in Nissan, the first month of the Torah year, whereas our verse states that Hezekiah held it in the second month. This was because the work of cleansing the Temple of idolatry lasted until the sixteenth day of the first month whereas the Pesach sacrifice must be brought on the fourteenth, and in any case, the majority of the priests and the people had not yet had time to purify themselves ritually for Pesach because of the suddenness of Hezekiah's initiative. The Torah itself provides that people who are unable to offer the Pesach sacrifice because of being ritually impure at the requisite time may celebrate Pesach Sheini, the "Second Pesach" on the fourteenth day of the second month, i.e. Iyar (Numbers 9:9-11). There is an opinion in the Talmud (Sanhedrin 12a-b) that Hezekiah had the entire people celebrate Pesach Sheini even though according to the halachah, under normal circumstances only if a minority of the people were impure would those particular people celebrate Pesach Sheini, whereas if the majority of the community is impure they are permitted to bring the Pesach sacrifice in a state of ritual impurity on the 14th of Nissan.

However, the more accepted opinion in the Talmud is that Hezekiah did not literally hold his Pesach in the month of Iyar but rather that he decided to declare that year a leap year, turning what should have been the month of Nissan into Adar II, thereby gaining an extra month before "Nissan", which came in what would have been the second month were it not for the insertion of the leap month. In the times of the Great Sanhedrin prior to the introduction of the fixed calendar, it was indeed at the discretion of the leading sages of the Sanhedrin to decide which year should be a leap year. The reason why Hezekiah was criticized by the sages for adding the extra month (Pesachim 56a) was because he waited to do so until the first of Nissan, suddenly declaring that the new month was not Nissan at all, but Adar II and that the following month would be Nissan, whereas he should have made his declaration a day earlier, prior to the consecration of the New Moon (see also RaDaK on verse 2 of our present chapter).

The second irregularity of Hezekiah's Pesach was that "a multitude of the people... had not cleansed themselves, so that they ate of the Passover sacrifice otherwise than was written"(v 18) - i.e. in a state of ritual impurity (Rashi ad loc.). The halachah provides that if the majority of the people are ritually impure on the first Pesach, they still bring the sacrifice on the 14th of Nissan - only if a minority are impure are they pushed off to Pesach Sheini on the 14th of Iyar (Rambam, Hilchot Korban Pesach 7:1). It would appear that on Hezekiah's Pesach more people were ritually pure than impure, yet the ritually impure still joined in the sacrifice. This was what was against the halachah, and this is why Hezekiah had to pray to God to grant them atonement (v 18f). It takes a giant of the stature of Hezekiah to imaginatively transcend the halachah when the circumstances absolutely require it. The fact that he did what he did proves that there are times when this may be done. [However, it is dangerous in the extreme when halachic midgets take Hezekiah's initiative as license to change the halachah any time they want.]

Again. we see that the Temple music was a most important part of the Pesach celebration (vv 21f).

Rashi (on v 26) writes that the unique great joy that accompanied Hezekiah's Pesach was not because there were more people present than in earlier times but rather because throughout the days of Ahaz and the other wicked kings of Judah, the people had simply not come to Jerusalem for the pilgrim festivals, which made this Pesach a tremendous novelty. Having not celebrated the festivals for many years, the seven days of Pesach were too few for them and they therefore added another seven days of celebrations (v 23).

CHAPTER 31

The exuberant joy of Hezekiah's Pesach gave all those assembled in Jerusalem the impetus to go out to the towns of Judah and Benjamin and even further afield into the territories of Ephraim and Menasheh in order to destroy all the idolatrous cult centers and altars. With the kingdom of Israel on the very threshold of its final collapse, the House of David was calling to all the Twelve Tribes to return to the way of the Torah.

Not only did Hezekiah re-establish the orders of the Cohanim and the Levites to serve in the Temple as instituted by King David (v 2), providing the sacrificial animals for the daily, Shabbat and festival services out of his own pocket (v 3). He also grasped that "If there is no flour [food], there is no Torah" (Avot 3:17), and he revived and reorganized the system of collecting the Torah-ordained Terumah gifts for the Cohanim and Ma'aser tithes for the Levites so that, with their livelihood guaranteed, they would be able to devote themselves not only to their Temple duties but even more importantly, to the crucial task of teaching the people Torah. Apparently, the giving of Terumah and Ma'aser had fallen into abeyance in the days of Hezekiah's father King Ahaz.

The sages credited Hezekiah with having made enormous efforts to spread knowledge of the Torah throughout the land, saying that "he stuck a sword over the entrance to the study hall announcing that anyone who did not occupy himself with the Torah would be speared with the sword. They checked from Dan to Beersheba and could not find a single **Am Ha'Aretz** (Torah ignoramus), nor did they find a single young boy or girl who was not expert in the laws of ritual impurity and purification (Sanhedrin 94b).

The general population were not paid to study the Torah - Torah study was the national leisure-time activity before and after work - but in order to bring the people to the highest levels of Torah knowledge, it was necessary for the Cohanim and Levites to be freed from the burden of earning a living in order to devote themselves entirely to this task.

"And as soon as the matter **burst forth**, the children of Israel brought in abundance..." (v 5). The simple meaning of this verse is that as soon as news of Hezekiah's instructions to bring the Terumah and

Ma'aser gifts "broke out" among the people, they responded open-heartedly. However, the rabbis learned from here that while the obligation to bring Terumah and Ma'aser applies only to corn, wine and oil **Mi-D'Oraita** (according to the written Torah, Numbers 18:12), the people "burst forth" beyond the letter of the law and also brought these tithes from other kinds of produce as well even though they were technically exempt (Nedarim 55a). This shows the enthusiastic devotion of the people.

V 9: "Then Hezekiah questioned the Cohanim and the Levites concerning the heaps" (v 9). Rashi (ad loc.) explains that when the king saw such enormous piles of produce, he thought that the Cohanim and Levites must not have touched them or eaten from them so far, but Azariah the High Priest (who had served since the days of Uzziah, II Chron. 26:20) assured him that they had already benefited, and that all this abundance was because of God's blessing to the people in the merit of their renewed devotion to His commandments.

Vv 11-19 describe the administrative apparatus which Hezekiah established in the Temple and in all the towns of the Cohanim and the Levites in order to supervise the orderly collection, storage and distribution of their Terumah and Ma'aser gifts so as to provide them with their livelihood and that of their wives and little children both when they came to fulfill their rota duty in the Temple and when they went about their work - teaching Torah - in and around their towns. From v 16 Metzudat David (ad loc.) learns that the Cohanim and Levites used to bring their small male children with them to the Temple from the age of three - in order to familiarize them with the services. The fact that even the little children and other family members of the Cohanim and Levites received shares of Terumah and Ma'aser testifies to the enormous blessing and abundance in the harvests as soon as the people separated their tithes properly (cf. Rashi on v 19).

CHAPTER 32

At first sight, it is hard to understand why it was that precisely when Hezekiah and his generation repented so whole-heartedly and sought out HaShem, He immediately sent Sennacherib and his hosts to lay siege to Jerusalem (v 1). Our sages addressed this question in their comment on the somewhat unusual phrase in this verse, "After these words and this truth..." - "After what??? Ravina said, After the Holy One blessed-be-He jumped and swore, saying, If I tell Hezekiah I am going to bring Sennacherib and deliver him into your hand, he will say 'I don't want either him or his terror' [i.e. I will forego the whole miracle]. Therefore, the Holy One immediately jumped and swore: 'HaShem of hosts has sworn. I will break Assyria in My land and upon My mountains tread him under foot; then shall his yoke depart from them and his burden depart from off their shoulders' (Isaiah 14:24-25). Rabbi Yochanan said: The Holy One blessed be He said, Let Sennacherib and his supporters come and provide fodder for Hezekiah and his supporters" (Sanhedrin 94b).

In other words, Sennacherib's advance on Jerusalem, terrifying as it was to a kingdom that was tiny in comparison with his world empire, was not a punishment but rather was intended to enrich Judah with the booty they would take after the miraculous overthrow of his army. Indeed, the rabbis taught that Sennacherib and his army had the potential to be Gog and Magog and Hezekiah had the potential to be Melech HaMashiach and to bring about the final repair immediately - except that Hezekiah failed to sing a song of praise to God after all the miracles and thereby lost the opportunity (Sanhedrin 94a).

Sennacherib's advance against Jerusalem and the intense psychological warfare he employed are described in great detail in II Kings 18:13-19:37 as well as in Isaiah 36:1-37:38. Prior to the arrival of the Assyrian armies, Hezekiah took sensible defensive precautions and mobilized the people in preparation for a lengthy siege (vv 3-6 in our present chapter). For the rest, he relied entirely on faith (vv 7-8) and prayer (v 20).

Sennacherib's arrogant boasting about the powerlessness of all the gods of the nations he had conquered to save them and his denigration of Hezekiah's efforts to bring Judah to worship God at only one altar instead of many (which Sennacherib mocked as a slight to His honor, v 12 and Rashi ad loc.) were enough to cause HaShem to overthrow him in order to sanctify His Name. The conclusion of the Talmudic discussion about how He struck his army is that He opened the ears of all the soldiers so that they heard the song of the angelic Chayot, and out of sheer rapture at such beauty, their souls flew out of them and they simply expired (Sanhedrin 95b).

"And in those days Hezekiah fell mortally sick..." (v 24). The story of Hezekiah's sudden illness and the heights of repentance to which it brought him, which secured him another fifteen years' lease of life, is told in detail in II Kings 20:1-11 and Isaiah 38:1-22. What is not directly apparent from our texts is that Hezekiah was struck down by this illness just three days before the overthrow of Sennacherib's army (see Rashi on II Kings 20:1) - i.e. at a time when Jerusalem was under total siege surrounded by hundreds of thousands of enemy soldiers. Bearing this in mind we can better appreciate the magnitude of the crisis and the subsequent miracle.

"But Hezekiah did not pay back according to the benefit done to him, for his heart was proud, therefore wrath came upon him and upon Judah and Jerusalem" (v 25). Hezekiah's pride came to the fore when envoys from the far-off, innocuous-seeming kingdom of Babylon came to congratulate him on his miraculous delivery from mortal illness, and instead of heeding the rabbinic warning that "blessing is found only in something hidden from the eye" (Ta'anit 8b), he wanted to flaunt his wealth and glory, and showed them all his treasure-houses and his most precious possessions. Tragically, Hezekiah, for all his saintliness, was unable to stand up to this subtle test (v 31 of our present chapter), and it was decreed that the Babylonians would capture all the treasures of Judah and take them to Babylon (see II Kings 20:12-19 and Isaiah 39:1-8).

Yet Hezekiah was spared seeing this decree in his days and died peacefully, being buried with the utmost honor side by side with King David and King Solomon (Bava Kama 16b).

CHAPTER 33

It is hard to understand how immediately after the tremendous Torah revival in the time of King Hezekiah, his own son Menasheh could have simply undone all his work and filled Jerusalem and the Holy Temple with every kind of idol and altar.

According to tradition, when Hezekiah was mortally ill, he asked Isaiah why he had said: "You shall die [in this world] and you shall not live [in the world to come]" (II Kings 20:1). The prophet told him it was because Hezekiah had failed to marry and fulfill the commandment to "be fruitful and multiply". Hezekiah told Isaiah that the reason he did not want to have children was because he had seen with holy spirit that his son was destined to be a terrible sinner. The prophet told him that this was not his business, after which Hezekiah asked Isaiah for his daughter's hand in marriage, and out of this union Menasheh was born.

It is unimaginable that Hezekiah taught Torah to all Judah but did not teach his own son. In fact, Menasheh was an outstanding Torah scholar, who was able to expound on the book of Leviticus in 55 completely different ways corresponding to the number of years of his reign (Sanhedrin 103b; compare the story about the lesson Menasheh taught Rav Ashi, redactor of the Babylonian Talmud, when he appeared to him in a dream, **Know Your Bible** II Kings ch 21). Nevertheless, the rabbis (Sanhedrin 90a) listed Menasheh together with Jeraboam son of Nevat and Ahab as among those who have no share in the world to come, although Rabbi Yehudah (ibid.) dissents, arguing that Menasheh did gain a share in the world to come in the merit of his repentance, which is described in our present chapter.

It was not the castigation of the prophets of the time that brought Menasheh to repent. On the contrary, he killed his own grandfather Isaiah, alleging that his prophecies contravened the Torah, as when he said, "And I **saw** the Lord sitting on a high and exalted throne", Isaiah 6:1, whereas the Torah says, "For no man can **see** Me and live" (Ex. 33:20; Yevamot 49b). Menasheh kept on refining his idolatry - starting off by making a one-faced statue in the Temple and ending up by carving four faces on it in order that the Shechinah should see and become enraged (Sanhedrin 103b).

The only thing that brought Menasheh to repent was the suffering he endured when the Assyrians captured him and took him in chains to Babylon, where "they closed him inside a perforated copper pot and lit fires all around it. And when he was in agonizing pain, he begged all the idols he had worshipped but they did not help him. Finally, he prayed to HaShem his God and was very greatly humbled before the God of his fathers. But when he prayed to Him, all the angels appointed over the gates of prayer in heaven immediately closed all the gates and windows in heaven in order that his prayer should not be accepted. But the compassion of the Creator of the World was aroused, because His right arm is outstretched to receive those sinners who return and break the evil inclination in their hearts through repentance, and He created a lattice and a channel in heaven beneath the throne of His glory and heard his prayer and accepted his request, and He shook the world with His mighty word and shattered the pot. A spirit went forth from between the wings of the cherubs and brought him back, and he returned to his kingdom to Jerusalem, and Menasheh knew that HaShem is God" (Targum Yonatan vv 11-13 of our present chapter).

"And he removed the strange gods... and cast them outside the city" (v 15). Rashi comments that Menasheh failed to smash these idols to bits or hide them away out of sight, and this was why his son and successor King Ammon stumbled, as we find later in this chapter (v 22): "And Ammon sacrificed to all the idols that Menasheh his father had made". He simply took them from the place where Menasheh had cast them out (Rashi on v 15). The rabbis said that Ammon burned the Torah scroll and had relations with his own mother. When she asked him what benefit he could possibly have from the place from which he came forth, he retorted: "I am doing it for no other reason than to enrage my Creator" (Sanhedrin 103b).

CHAPTER 34

The same swing from idolatry and degeneracy to repentance and national restoration that had occurred time after time in the earlier history of the House of David - as when Yo'ash was installed instead of Ataliah and when Hezekiah succeeded Ahaz - took place again when the eight-year old Josiah was chosen by the people to succeed his murdered father Ammon.

Unlike Hezekiah, who initiated his radical turnabout from the ways of Ahaz as soon as he ascended to the throne, the young Josiah implemented his change in direction in stages. He was sixteen when he seriously began to "search out the God of David his father" and twenty when he started purifying Judah and Jerusalem of private altars and idolatrous cult-centers and images (v 3). He took responsibility to do the same throughout the Land of Israel, traveling to the territory of Naftali in the far north east of the country in order to supervise the work personally (v 6).

It was at the age of twenty-six that Josiah initiated much-needed repairs to the Temple, which had been damaged during the ravages in the reigns of Menasheh and Ammon. Our chapter lists the Levitical officers who supervised the Temple restoration work, including Levites who were chosen purely because of their deep understanding of music (verse 12), because "everyone who had a masterly understanding of music and song stood by with musical instruments in order to play during the time of the building work" (Metzudat David ad loc.). Once again, we see the central role of music in the Temple, which even had to be built and repaired to the sounds of song.

It was when going to an inner Temple chamber to take money to pay for the work that "Hilkiah the High Priest found a scroll of the Torah of HaShem by the hand of Moses" (v 14). Metzudat David (ad loc.) says: "It is likely that when King Ahaz burned the Torah scroll, the Cohanim feared that he would try to get at the Torah scroll that was placed at the side of the Ark of the Covenant, which had been written by Moses from the mouth of HaShem, and they therefore took it and hid it away. After Ahaz' death they searched for it but could not find it until the High Priest was searching for the money when the Temple was restored." The rabbis had a tradition that the scroll was found rolled in such a way that it fell open at the verse in the curses: "HaShem will lead you and your king that you shall establish over yourself to a nation that you have not known" (Deut. 28:36; Yoma 52b). When this verse was read to King Josiah, he tore his garments, fearing that it applied to him, since he himself had been put on the throne by the people and not by a prophet (Rashi on v 19; cf. II Chron. 33:25).

Our rabbis taught that the reason why Josiah sent to enquire of the prophetess Huldah in preference to Jeremiah, who was also prophesying at that time, was "because a woman is more compassionate than a man" (Megillah 14b; Rashi on v 22). Huldah had her own chamber in the Temple, adjacent to the seat of the Sanhedrin in the Chamber of the Hewn Stones, though it was screened off for reasons of modesty (Masechet Middot; Rashi on v 22).

Huldah's grim message that the fate of Jerusalem was already sealed was softened for Josiah only by the news that the disaster would not strike in his lifetime. He immediately summoned all the elders of Judah to the Temple, where he renewed the Torah Covenant and brought the entire Israelite population to serve HaShem loyally for the rest of his life.

CHAPTER 35

In the eighteenth year of his reign - the same year as the discovery of the Torah scroll in the Temple and the subsequent prophecy of doom by Huldah the Prophetess, as described in the previous chapter - King Josiah held a Pesach celebration in the Temple "the like of which had not been celebrated in Israel since the days of Samuel the Prophet" (verse 18).

Yet even as Josiah celebrated the Pesach, he knew that it was impossible to avert the decree hanging over Jerusalem. "And he said to the Levites who taught all Israel, who were holy to HaShem: Put the holy Ark in the House which Solomon the son of David king of Israel built..." (verse 3). According to the simple meaning of the verse, it would appear that King Menasheh may have taken the Ark out of the Holy of Holies when he placed an idol in the Temple (or if Menasheh returned it after his repentance, his successor King Ammon may have removed it again), and that would be the reason why Josiah now gave instructions to put the Ark back in its place (Rashi, RaDaK ad loc.).

However, the Talmudic rabbis interpreted this verse as hinting that on the advice of the prophet Jeremiah, Josiah had the Ark hidden away in a secret underground chamber that King Solomon had constructed at the time of the building of the Temple, knowing that it was destined to be destroyed. The Foundation Stone at the western end of the Temple in the Holy of Holies covered over the entrance to the narrow, winding passages leading down into this chamber. Josiah had the Ark put away there, together with the Two Tablets of the Ten Commandments, the Flask of the Manna, the Flask of the Anointing Oil, Aaron's Rod and the chest which the Philistines sent as a gift when they returned the

Ark, in order that they should not be taken into exile with the destruction of the Temple (Yoma 52b). For Josiah knew that if they would be taken into exile, they would never be brought back (Shekalim 16a).

Despite the threat of doom hanging over Jerusalem, Josiah and the people celebrated the Pesach wholeheartedly. Josiah himself provided 30,000 paschal lambs and goats for the people - which indicates that many more than that number of people ate of them, because a **chavurah** of up to a hundred people could all be registered to eat an olive-size quantity each of the meat of a single lamb. Leading officers of the people and the Levites provided the Cohanim and Levites with their paschal animals. The oxen mentioned in vv 7, 8 and 9 were for **Shalmey Chagigah**, the festive peace-offerings consumed prior to the Pesach offering so that its meat may be eaten in a state of satisfaction and not out of hunger (Rashi and Metzudat David on v 6; Rambam, Hilchot Korban Pesach 8:3).

All the details of the Pesach celebration - eating the sacrifice roasted, accompanying the offering with the chanting of the Hallel by the Levites, etc. - were observed in strict accordance with all the relevant Torah laws.

Rashi on v 18 offers an explanation as to why "the like of this Passover had not been celebrated in Israel from the days of Samuel the prophet, nor did any of the kings of Israel keep such a Passover as Josiah kept..." - "As long as the people were split into two kingdoms, the tribes of Judah and Benjamin used to celebrate Pesach in Jerusalem in the name of HaShem, while the other tribes celebrated in the name of idols in Beit El and Dan. However, in the days of the judges it had never happened that Israel was split into two families, for in each generation they never had more than one judge, and that judge made them all go in the way of Hashem. Thus, in the times of the judges, all the Ten Tribes used to go to Shilo to celebrate Pesach in the name of HaShem, but throughout the period of the kings of Israel there was never a Pesach in which Israel and Judah were together. However, by the time of Josiah the kingdom of the Ten Tribes was already defunct, and when Jeremiah brought members of the Ten Tribes back from their exile, he did not establish a separate king over them, but Josiah ruled over them and they all celebrated Pesach together in Jerusalem in the name of HaShem.

After this Pesach, Josiah lived on for thirteen more years before his tragic end at the hands of Pharaoh Necho, who was marching his armies through the Land of Israel on his way to Karkemish on the River Euphrates in order to strike a blow against Assyria. The king of Egypt had no hostile intentions against Judah, but Josiah still went out to intercept him because he darshened the verse, "No sword shall pass through your land" (Lev. 26:6) to mean that in times of blessing, even the sword of a nation who is at peace with Israel should not pass through their land, let alone the sword of their enemies (Ta'anit 22b). Josiah thought he was sufficiently worthy to have this blessing fulfilled in his time. What he did not know was that the people still worshiped idols in the privacy of their own homes. He used to have inspectors visit each house to check for idols, but the people craftily had the idols carved on the insides of the two doors that opened up into their homes. When the inspectors threw open the doors in order to enter, the carvings were concealed from them, but as soon as they left, the people in the house would shut the two doors, thereby bringing the two carvings together to make one image, which they then proceeded to worship (Midrash Eichah Rabbah 1:53).

Josiah failed to consult the prophet Jeremiah as to whether he should go out against Pharaoh Necho, and he was shot with three hundred arrows that left his body full of holes like a sieve. As the king lay dying, Jeremiah noticed his lips moving and stooped down to try to hear what he was saying. What he heard was, "HaShem is righteous for I have rebelled against His mouth" (Lamentations 1:18; Ta'anit 22b). With the death of Josiah, the sun went down on the House of David, and Jeremiah instituted the mourning elegy that he composed in honor of the slain king to be recited by all Israel (v 25). This is contained in Chapter 4 of the Book of Lamentations (Eichah), which is recited on the Fast of Tisha b'Av commemorating the destruction of the Temple.

CHAPTER 36

V 1: "And the people of the land took Yeho-ahaz son of Josiah and made him king…." It appears that Yeho-ahaz was two years younger than Yeho-yakim, yet the people preferred him as king (RaDaK on II Kings 23:30). It seems that Yeho-ahaz invaded Egypt and struck a heavy blow there in order to avenge the death of his father at the hands of Pharaoh Necho, but when the latter returned from his campaign against Assyria, he captured and exiled Yeho-ahaz and replaced him with Yeho-yakim (RaDaK on II: Kings 23:33). It was Pharaoh Necho who changed the new king's name from El-yakim to Yeho-yakim, just as Pharaoh had changed Joseph's name to the Egyptian name of Tzaphnat Pa'neach and Nebuchadnezzar gave Babylonian names to Daniel, Chananiyah, Misha'el and Azariah. The purpose was to show the ruler's supremacy over his officers, whose names he changed at will (see Rashi on v 4 of our present chapter).

Yeho-yakim was the object of many rebukes and prophecies by Jeremiah, whom he tried to kill and eventually put in prison, while killing the prophet Uriah son of Shemayah (Jeremiah 26:23). It was in the fourth year of Yeho-yakim's reign that Baruch ben Neriyah wrote the Book of Lamentations at the dictation of Jeremiah. After he read it to the people, it was brought to King Yeho-yakim, who on hearing what was written in it, tore the scroll to shreds with a razor and threw the pieces into the fire (Jeremiah 36:23).

"…and his abominations that he did and **what was found on him**…" (v 8). The rabbis stated that Yeho-yakim had the name of an idol (or, according to another opinion, the Name of HaShem) inscribed on his member (Sanhedrin 103b).

Jeremiah had prophesied that Yeho-yakim would receive the burial of a donkey (Jer. 22:19) - i.e. his flesh would be eaten by the dogs. After the rise of Nebuchadnezzar, Yeho-yakim served him for three years but then rebelled, after which the Babylonian king laid siege to Jerusalem and captured him. Yeho-yakim died as he was being dragged off into exile and his corpse was thrown into an open field where he suffered his prophesied end.

Yeho-yakim's son Yeho-yachin ruled for only three months before Nebuchadnezzar demanded that the Sanhedrin deliver him over to be taken into exile to Babylon. Before leaving Jerusalem, Yeho-yachin took all the keys of the Temple and went up to the roof of the House, saying: "Master of the World: Since we are not worthy to be the guardians of Your treasures, here are Your keys before You." Yeho-yachin threw the keys upwards, and a hand of fire came down to receive them (Midrash Vayikra Rabbah 19:6).

Together with Yeho-yachin, Nebuchadnezzar took all the leading royal officers, warriors, sages and elders of Jerusalem into exile in Babylon, including Ezekiel the prophet, Mordechai, Daniel, Chananiyah, Misha'el and Azariah, so that only the poor and lowly people were left in Jerusalem. Thus, when Nebuchadnezzar installed Yeho-yachin's uncle Tzedekiah as king of Judah (and governor of Edom, Moab, Ammon, Tyre and Sidon as well), the population of Jerusalem over whom he ruled were on a low moral level. Tzedekiah himself was considered by the rabbis to have been exceptionally saintly: he was counted (together with Jesse, Saul, Samuel, Amos, Zephaniah, Elijah and Mashiach) among eight "princes among men" (Succah 52b), and his original name of Shaloom (I Chron. 3:15, see RaDaK ad loc.) indicated that he was perfect (**shalem**) in his deeds (Horayot 11b). The reason why it is written of Tzedekiah that "he did evil in the eyes of Hashem" (II Kings 24:19) was because he failed to protest against the deeds of his contemporaries, as when they freed their slaves only to re-enslave them immediately afterwards.

"And he also rebelled against King Nebuchadnezzar, who had made him swear by God." (v 13 of our present chapter). According to tradition, once Tzedekiah had chanced upon Nebuchadnezzar precisely while the latter was ravenously devouring a rabbit when it was still alive. Nebuchadnezzar made Tzedekiah swear an oath that he would never reveal what he had seen, but eventually Tzedekiah asked the Sanhedrin to annul his oath and told what he had seen (Nedarim 65a). It was in vengeance for this that on capturing Tzedekiah, Nebuchadnezzar had his eyes put out for revealing what he had seen, while the members of the Sanhedrin who annulled his oath were tied to horses' tails and dragged from Jerusalem to Lod (Eichah Rabbah 2:18).

With the destruction of Jerusalem and the Holy Temple and the exile of all the people to Babylon, it might have seemed as if the Royal House of David - in whose honor Ezra the Scribe wrote **Divrey HaYamim**, the Book of Chronicles - would soon become extinct. However, God's watchful eye was on the seed of David, and even as Yechoniah (Yeho-yachin) rotted away in solitary confinement in his narrow cell in Babylon, God opened a way to facilitate a visit to him by his wife. She conceived and gave birth to She'altiel, who was the father of Zerubavel (see **Know Your Bible**, Ezra ch 2). It was Zerubavel, scion of the House of David, who went up to Jerusalem to rebuild the Temple after Cyrus of Persia gave the signal for Judah to return there, as described in the closing verses of Chronicles and as told in detail in the Book of Ezra. The whole of **Divrey HaYamim** was written to explain where Zerubavel came from and why it was his mission to build the Temple.

And just as Zerubavel went up to Jerusalem to build the Second Temple, so may our Righteous Mashiach quickly reveal himself and lead all Israel up to Jerusalem to build the Temple very soon in our times. Amen.

www.ingramcontent.com/pod-product-compliance
Lightning Source LLC
Chambersburg PA
CBHW080456110426
42742CB00017B/2909